Homicide:
Life on the Stree

Homicide:
Life on the Street

The Unofficial Companion

DAVID KALAT

BOOKS

RENAISSANCE BOOKS
Los Angeles

Library of Congress Cataloging-in-Publication Data

Kalat, David
    Homicide—life on the street : the unofficial companion / David Kalat.
        p. cm.
    Includes bibliographical references and index.
    ISBN 1–58063–021–9 (pbk. : alk. paper)
    1. Homicide—life on the street (Television program) I. Title.
PN1992.77.H62K36 1998
791.45'72—dc21   98–12985
                                                                      CIP

10 9 8 7 6 5 4 3 2

Distributed by St. Martin's Press
Manufactured in the United States of America
First Edition

Design by Tanya Maiboroda

Dedicated to my beautiful, perfect daughter Ann,
who arrived just as this manuscript left.

Contents

Acknowledgments

I want to express my deepest gratitude to those whose support and encouragement have made this book a reality: my wife Julie Stapel, my editor James Robert Parish, and my agents Sheree Bykofsky and Janet Rosen. I also wish to thank Jonathan Rosenthal at the Museum of Television and Radio, whose contributions to the research occurred at a critical moment.

Many people on *Homicide*, both in front of and behind the cameras, were very kind to take time out of their busy days to talk with me about their experiences. I have heard horror stories about how studios, agitated at "unauthorized" books like this one, have taken retribution on those who helped the authors. I hate to give in to this unnecessary paranoia, but I would also hate to compromise the relationship any of these people have with Tom Fontana and Barry Levinson. So, to be on the safe side, I will assert my journalistic privilege and decline to name my sources. I only hope these men and women recognize how important their contributions were to this project, and how grateful I am to them.

Finally, I wish to acknowledge the work of *Homicide*'s online fans. From Sandi Lemon's e-mail list to Dave Locke's wonderful collection of articles, as well as Dennis Kytasaari's exhaustive episode guide, I cannot recommend highly enough the work of these dedicated fans. I urge all serious "Homicidal Maniacs" to take advantage of these resources. (Please see Appendix G for Web addresses and additional online resource information.)

Introduction

In the summer of 1992, I moved to Washington, D.C. and started looking for work in the film and video industry. I was unaware at the time that famed movie director Barry Levinson was in Baltimore filming a new series for NBC called *Homicide: Life on the Street*. Being a loyal local boy, Levinson was relying heavily on talent based in the Baltimore-Washington area to staff his series. This meant, among other things, that he was having the film processed and transferred to videotape at the motion picture laboratory Colorlab in Rockville, Maryland. As it happened, I had recently used the services of Colorlab for a short film of my own, and had sent them a resume.

To make a long story short, Barry Levinson never knew it, but he gave me my first break in this business. A sound recording problem on *Homicide*'s set forced the crew to reshoot several episodes, and the added demands placed on Colorlab convinced them to hire me to help out. My contributions were trivial, but I became very loyal to *Homicide* nonetheless.

When the series first aired, the folks at Colorlab were divided in their reactions. Many were turned off by the disorienting camerawork, the almost monochromatic pictures, and the bizarre editing. However, others (like myself) were exhilarated. Before I saw the pilot episode "Gone for Goode," I believed the world had seen enough police dramas for many lifetimes. Afterwards, I couldn't get enough.

I've written this guidebook to tell some of the stories I witnessed from behind the scenes that, until now, have never gotten any press. I also wanted to share with others why I think this is "The Best Damn Show on Television."

The fact that this show is produced so close to my home is one of the reasons it has kept such a low profile. While its refusal to pander to audiences and its unfortunate Friday-night time slot are mainly to blame for its middling ratings, there's more to the story than that. By being filmed in Baltimore,

Homicide has never benefited from the kind of relentless publicity that graces many lesser, lower-rated series.

The vast majority of television shows are produced in Los Angeles, which is where most TV stars live. L.A. also is home to most of the entertainment reporters, critics, and tastemakers. *Homicide* is shot entirely on location in Baltimore, thousands of miles away from the "real" entertainment industry. As a result, its stars and creators don't get to hobnob with other celebrities, don't get photographed and interviewed, don't have their lives dissected in the tabloids. As far as the entertainment industry is concerned, *Homicide* might as well be an import from another country.

This is one of the reasons why *Homicide* has been so grievously over-looked in the Emmy award ceremonies. The voters don't know the makers of *Homicide* personally, and are more inclined to vote for their friends.

As far as the general public is concerned, *Homicide* sports a cast of unknowns. They may be supremely gifted performers, and they may have some major TV critics championing them at every opportunity, but folks like Andre Braugher, Clark Johnson, and Kyle Secor simply don't show up on magazine covers in the grocery-store checkout aisle.

As I write this, *Homicide* has just survived yet another ultimatum by the network: improve its ratings or be canceled. Significantly, NBC has renewed the show despite its failure to improve its ratings in any major way. I really don't think *Homicide* is going to get better ratings, not on Friday nights. With its somber themes and often grisly plot lines, this is a difficult, weird, troubling show for mass viewer consumption. A lot of people are afraid of such fare. The fact that, despite its grim stories, millions of TV watchers love *Homicide*'s unique qualities, and tune in loyally week after week, is a wonderful achievement, of which NBC should be proud. I have written this guidebook as my humble contribution to the cause. I hope that the readers of this book can use it to enhance their understanding and appreciation of this very special television program.

CHAPTER 1

The Best Damn Show on Television

In October of 1996, Carlester Eric Robinson tore out of a Rite-Aid drug store in Baltimore, Maryland, with security guards hot on his heels.

He was just a petty shoplifter, trying to make off with a bag full of stolen Q-Tips and Polaroid film. He figured he should avoid busy Charles Street, and, instead, turned down the less-populated Trenton Street. As Robinson rounded the corner, he found himself surrounded by police cars. Directly ahead of him was the imposing sight of uniformed officers and a pair of plainclothes detectives. Obviously, there was no way out.

Realizing he had no escape, the thief raised his hands and promptly surrendered himself to Detectives Meldrick Lewis and John Munch.

As it happens, Lewis and Munch are fictional characters on a TV show, played by Clark Johnson and Richard Belzer respectively. How was the thief to know that the cops were actors, wielding plastic prop guns?

Poor Mr. Robinson suffered a great deal of embarrassment that day, and his mistake gave local news teams something to chuckle about on-air. But he was not the first, nor the last, to find it hard to tell fact from fiction on the set of *Homicide: Life on the Street*. Even the producers admitted that they sometimes forgot what is real and what is not on this show, a show that takes such intense pride in its mind-bending "art-imitates-life-imitates-art" recursions.

The producers of *Homicide* even incorporated the thief's embarrassing arrest into an episode broadcast a few months later, and topped off this self-reference with a cameo appearance by series producer Barry Levinson, playing himself as the producer of a TV series called *Homicide*. The TV detectives then offer Levinson some words of advice about how to make the show more "realistic."

Homicide: Life on the Street

From its gritty and convincing realism to its cinematic, avant-garde style, this drama from acclaimed feature-film director Barry Levinson announced itself as something special with its very first broadcast in January 1993.

Homicide is an innovation in a medium best known for playing it safe, and it has garnered loyal fans and critical praise while challenging audiences to demand more from television. Fans have responded by nicknaming the series "The Best Damn Show on Television."

Homicide owes much of its realism to the work of Baltimore Sun crime reporter David Simon. In 1988, Simon spent a year shadowing the real-life detectives of Baltimore's Homicide Unit, and published his experiences as the highly acclaimed Homicide: A Year on the Killing Streets (1991, Houghton Mifflin Company).

Barry Levinson and his co-creators adapted the book into a TV series, keeping many of its stories and dialogue intact. In later years, David Simon joined the team as a staff writer, while continuing his nonfiction crime writing.

Mind Over Matter

For all its intensity, Homicide is not known for dramatic action. The brilliant detectives of Baltimore's homicide division capture their perpetrators, or "perps," by wit and will alone. These men and women are prized for their brains, not their bodies, and so it is little surprise that their bodies are not as finely tuned or honed as so many other TV police characters seem to be.

On those rare occasions when action is called for, the detectives will find themselves unprepared for it. The simple act of chasing a suspect a measly block

---

THE CHESS PLAYERS

The cast and crew of Homicide have often noted that their detectives aren't typical action heroes. Actor Richard Belzer (Detective John Munch) calls them "the chess players." As it happens, Richard Belzer and Andre Braugher (Detective Frank Pembleton) keep this motif strongly in mind while shooting the show. Between takes, the two play a running chess game against one another. Braugher, who has maintained an overwhelming winning streak over his costar, plays the black pieces ("I've had four hundred years' practice," he jokes), and uses the same defense ten games in a row.

THE ONE THING THIS COUNTRY'S STILL GOOD AT

The United States leads the industrialized world in homicide rates. It is the tenth leading cause of death, claiming some 24,000 people each year, roughly a murder every twenty minutes.

The news media sensationalize exciting, abnormal murders or homicides involving celebrities. This creates an image in the public mind of who kills and why. That image then fuels popular culture, where fictional psycho killers, hit men, and gangsters roam in disproportionate numbers.

Sociologist Marvin Wolfgang conducted a classic study of homicide in 1958. He found that a third of American murders result from "altercations of a relatively trivial origin." Another twenty percent result as a part of another crime.

President Johnson's 1968 National Commission on the Causes and Prevention of Violence concluded that the "primary motivating forces" for most homicides in the United States were "usually trivial...disagreements."

In the late 1980s, at the same time that David Simon was living among the Baltimore Homicide team, another crime journalist, Edna Buchanan of Miami, concluded that "the little things in life sometimes trigger the urge to kill: a stereo too loud, a game of checkers."

becomes a dangerous and costly act. In Episode 34: "Fire, Part One," Detective Tim Bayliss strains his back as a result of his exertion. Bayliss' real-life counterpart, Detective Tom Pellegrini, chose to join the Homicide Unit because he found the mental stimulation of solving crimes much more appealing than the hazardous duties he performed in Baltimore's Quick Response Team.

In fact, statistics show that real police work has very little in common with the usual shoot-em-up TV clichés. Police officers are more likely to die by suicide than to be killed by bad guys. It is hardly surprising, then, that *Homicide* has addressed suicide on numerous occasions in its stories.

Homicide detectives find that their stimulation is mental: the challenge of finding order in a disorderly world, the challenge of making sense out of senseless acts. As for the latter, however, the detectives on *Homicide* seldom can do such a thing, although they valiantly try. In the end, the senselessness of murder almost always defies them.

The detectives close cases, they do not solve them. "Solve" implies putting the situation right again. However, that's not possible for the lives of those left victimized by murder but still alive, usually the grieving family and friends who will never be the same again. Furthermore, the killers may be as much victims of it all as those they killed. Putting a kid behind bars doesn't make things right again at all.

So the detectives seek sense and order elsewhere.

Who Killed Lincoln?

One of the most memorable examples within this TV series is Detective Steve Crosetti's obsession with the assassination of President Lincoln. He pursues that case, over a hundred years old, at times with more zeal than he does the cases at hand, weaving a complicated but fully-researched conspiracy theory worthy of a JFK buff.

As his partner Meldrick Lewis caustically reminds him, the Lincoln case is not an open case. Instead, Crosetti's drive to solve fully the Lincoln assassination is purely personal. It *means* something to him. He hopes that perhaps he can expose a century-old conspiracy, and thereby truly "solve" the case and set things right.

In the end, he never achieves that goal. Crosetti ultimately kills himself (see Episode 19: "Crosetti"), and his former colleagues must now "solve" that death. Detective Lewis may discover how his partner died, and perhaps he can guess at why, but closing the case on his friend's suicide will never "solve" it.

Loneliness

Homicide is especially frank in depicting the toll the job takes on the detectives' families. Detectives Munch, Bolander, and Kellerman are divorced. Detectives Felton, Pembleton, and Lewis find their families torn apart when their wives realize that their husbands are married first and foremost to the street. Like her male colleagues, Detective Kay Howard is too much of a dedicated detective to have a normal romance. Shift Commanders Al Giardello and Megan Russert are both alone after the death of their spouses. Even the eligible bachelor Detective Tim Bayliss is too tortured to hold down a steady relationship.

The men and women of *Homicide* are a lonely lot.

The Many Colors of Blue

Among its many achievements, *Homicide* has earned a place in television history for its unprecedented portrayal of race.

Although repeatedly denied an Emmy, Andre Braugher has been called the best actor on television. Everett Collection

Even by the end of the twentieth century, black Americans have made fewer inroads of progress in pop culture than they have in the real world. Increasingly, blacks and whites are working together, but it would be hard to discern that fact from the boob tube.

There are shows with predominately black casts which target a black audience, shows which tend to be racy sitcoms aired on marginal networks. Then there are shows, mostly major network dramas, aimed at a "mainstream" audience, with mostly white casts. The rare examples of minority characters in network dramas often carry the burden of being the sole representative of their race in that program. Their characterizations are seen and interpreted by the viewers as being a generalized example of what their race is like as a whole.

By contrast, *Homicide* features numerous black characters: major and minor, cops and crooks, figures of authority and powerlessness, each one a complex and fully realized human being. No single character can be seen as a racial representative. At no point has *Homicide* attempted to trumpet this racial inclusiveness. The series has never marketed itself as a "black" show.

In 1995, the *Atlanta Journal* hailed *Homicide* as a groundbreaking series for its realistic racial composition. The producers demurred, uninterested in taking credit for trailblazing. Instead, executive producers Barry Levinson, Tom Fontana, and Henry Bromell insisted they merely strove to depict the overwhelmingly black-majority city of Baltimore honestly.

Nevertheless, the National Association for the Advancement of Colored People wrote a letter to NBC praising *Homicide*, especially Yaphet Kotto's portrayal of Lieutenant Al Giardello. In 1997, the NAACP nominated *Homicide* for its annual Image Awards, for projects that have made significant contributions towards advancing the image of people of color. The NAACP also singled out Kotto and Andre Braugher for Outstanding Actor nominations.

"The fact that we were lucky enough to get three outstanding actors of African descent [Yaphet Kotto, Andre Braugher, and Clark Johnson], who could play off that or not depending on the stories, has been a great enlightenment to us as writers," says executive producer Tom Fontana.

Some industry analysts have noted that *Homicide*'s famous ratings troubles could be partly blamed on its prominent black cast members. Although Andre Braugher of *Homicide* earned phenomenal critical attention, it was Dennis Franz and David Caruso, the white leads of *NYPD Blue*, who became national stars.

The trend of black casts for black audiences and white casts for white audiences is not simply a reflection of racism on the part of network programmers, but a sad fact of American life that American audiences segregate themselves. In 1995, only three shows rated in the Top 20 among both black and white viewers. By including a rich variety of black characters, *Homicide* turned off white viewers. By including so many white characters, *Homicide* also kept away black viewers.

As a result, while *Homicide* has the unique distinction of realistically depicting an integrated America, low ratings have discouraged other producers from following suit.

Homicide has also addressed the glass ceiling of the police department, taking on gender issues in the workforce as well. Like *Prime Suspect* (1990–)—the superb British crime drama often compared to *Homicide*—the mostly male world of the police department does not take well to the idea of women in positions of authority.

On one end of the spectrum is the series' Kay Howard, a brilliant and hardworking detective who never lets her guard down. Always pushing herself to be better than the best, Howard earns a promotion to sergeant based on her outstanding performance. However, the male detectives under her supervision bristle with resentment. The ingrained notions of women's roles are so powerful that they even surface behind the scenes, where actress Melissa Leo found herself consistently excluded from the impromptu games of football her male costars play on the set (she had to bring her own Hacky-Sack to be allowed to play with the boys).

On the other end of the spectrum is Megan Russert. As the shift commander of *Homicide's* second shift, she meets the same kind of wounded pride from the men under her charge. Unlike Howard, though, Russert is promoted up the ladder to captain, not on the basis of merit, but as an act of pure political tokenism. It's not that she lacks leadership skills. In fact, Russert is an exemplary detective and an uncharacteristically courageous captain. But her sudden success is both too soon and too short, since neither her promotion nor her later demotion have anything to do with merit.

The Killing Streets

In the urban sprawl of a city marked by rising crime rates and increasing fear of crime, the elite members of Baltimore's Homicide Unit continue their daily crusade against the forces of killing. At times, it seems hopeless. They are a mere handful of investigators pitted against some 300 murder cases a year.

Indeed, some of the city's murders are quite odd: one man killed for his pen; another life is snuffed out because the victim didn't think Spiro Agnew should be remembered with a statue; a lover killed in a fit of passion by a woman who then stores the corpse in a deep freezer full of brisket. Others are gut-wrenching: a little girl molested and murdered by a killer who goes free; a boy shot dead by another one for no reason; a political activist assassinated at the order of a drug cartel; three saintly women murdered and left nude in dumpsters.

It's a combat waged with brains, not guns. An average homicide detective may not even draw his gun for any reason other than to pass the departments' firing-range test.

The cops are aided in their task by the fact that the killers they track are so incredibly stupid. Unlike the usual TV crime-show stereotypes, these murderers are not criminal masterminds or serial killer psychopaths. The steady stream of dead bodies flow mainly from a single river: hotheaded folk who settle their grudges with a bang.

These petty grievances, the motives for murder, are either so banal or so personal as to be irrelevant to the detective's job. Most TV detectives use the "why" to find the "who," but the detectives of Baltimore city know the "why" will lead them nowhere. They look simply for the "how." That's what turns red names to black.

The central feature of the Homicide squadroom is "The Board," a massive chart of each detective on the shift. Beneath each detective's name are the names of the murdered people whose cases they must solve. As each new case is opened, the victim's name is written in red. As each case is closed, the name is reinscribed in black. A single glance at the board can reveal the ratio of red to black, and, thus, who is catching killers, and who is not.

Not all of the detectives' cases involve murder. As the city's premiere team of investigators, the Homicide Unit also handles all police-involved shootings, suspicious deaths, and other high-profile cases.

The most-high-profile cases, called "red balls," place the detectives in the media spotlight and the department hot spot. The investigators have the full resources of the police department to draw upon, but they are expected to produce results fast or there will be political hell to pay.

The cases are distributed randomly. The detective who answers the call will be the primary detective on that case. Each cop answers the phone without knowing what it will bring: an easy "dunker" that will help their closure rate or a "stone-cold whodunnit" that will linger in red under their name for all time.

Whydunnit

The detective of *Homicide* pits his or her wits against the physical world: the natural decay of evidence, the limitations of forensic science, the social situations that encourage witnesses to lie. However, the detective does not, in most cases, pit his or her wits against a worthy criminal opponent. There is no Moriarty for these Sherlocks.

Homicide's writers understand that most murders have little to do with the conventions of most detective fiction. Not only is the work itself more mental than physical, but that mental work bears little resemblance to the exploits of Miss Marple or Hercule Poirot. The cornerstone of most traditional crime fiction is *motive*. The first order of business for a Colombo, a Perry Mason, or a Jessica Fletcher is to determine *why* the victim was killed. From that, they deduce *who* "dunnit."

On *Homicide*, however, the "whys" are often absurdly trivial. *Homicide* depicts a world in which the petty squabbles of everyday life provoke violence and mayhem. This is a world where small talk turns into trash talk, where the slightest grievance is cause for killing. These motives are too common to be distinctive, and cease to be useful clues at all. *Homicide*'s detectives won't find their killers by understanding why the victims were killed because no ordinary person can ever really understand how such simple complaints result in such violence.

Contrary to pop culture's depiction, most murders are the trivial kind depicted on *Homicide*, though no less brutal and horrifying for that. Most murders just happen, without a specific motive, because our society is awash with guns and drugs and poor self-control. These are not carefully planned "perfect crimes" executed by calculating villains for specific reasons. These are mundane murders, unsettlingly common and meaningless.

Reel Life

Homicide has often been compared to the famed TV series *Hill Street Blues* (1981–87). Like *Blues* before it, *Homicide* weaves together multiple subplots and story lines as it follows the lives of an ensemble cast of cops. Both shows also share a surprising blend of comedy with gritty drama.

The series has also been likened to the TV series *St. Elsewhere* for many of the same reasons. As it happens, *Homicide*'s executive producer Tom Fontana cut his teeth on *St. Elsewhere* (1982–88), and has relied on many of the same cast and creators to develop *Homicide*.

For all of its critical acclaim, however, *Homicide* has often been overshadowed by more popular TV crime dramas like *NYPD Blue* (1993–) and *Law and Order* (1990–). Ironically, while *Homicide* hails from some of the same producers as *St. Elsewhere*, *NYPD Blue* is by the same folks as *Hill Street Blues*. *NYPD Blue*, however, eschews the ensemble format for a simpler buddy-cop drama.

On the one hand, *Homicide* has its roots in the crime journalism of David Simon, while, on the other, *NYPD Blue* is inspired by the experiences of New York homicide detective Bill Clark. The nudity and adult language of *NYPD Blue* may have stirred up more controversy, but in many ways *Homicide* is the riskier show.

Homicide dares to show the tedium of police investigations and the unsettling role of luck in catching crooks. *Homicide* doesn't always close its cases in one hour, and some are never closed. Sometimes criminals are identified, but

GALLOWS HUMOR

Many of *Homicide*'s guest stars have been comedians: Robin Williams, Lily Tomlin, Chris Rock, Howie Mandel, and Jerry Stiller, to say nothing of star Richard Belzer. Executive producer Henry Bromell told *Entertainment Weekly* that comics naturally fit the tone of the show. "There's a certain danger inherent in comics. They're up there and anything can happen. They're not quite in control."

cannot be brought to justice. Sometimes the notion of justice is so ambiguous as to be useless. In addition, these detectives do not get along all the time. The tension simmering beneath the surface can, at times, be more dangerous than what is waiting for them on Baltimore's streets.

NYPD Blue has lost many of its female cast members over the years because the actresses quickly have grown tired of being sex objects and ciphers. On *Homicide*, the women characters can be seen as true peers to their male colleagues. The men and women of Baltimore's Homicide Unit are too busy being relentless, intense perfectionists to think about interoffice dating. A few love affairs have arisen (Detective Beau Felton and Lieutenant Megan Russert, Detective Mike Kellerman and Chief Medical Examiner Julianna Cox), but these are the exception rather than the rule.

Compared to *NYPD Blue*, *Homicide* is vastly more challenging, more disturbing, less predictable. *Homicide* is not the kind of show that reassures the audience. In the end, this fearless storytelling is more provocative than some mild nudity or swearing will ever be, as well as being much more realistic.

The writers of *Homicide* (including Tom Fontana, Henry Bromell, David Simon, James Yoshimura, Julie Martin, Jorge Zamacona, Bonnie Mark, Anya Epstein, and Darryl LeMont Wharton) not only look to the true crime stories of Simon's book and current news stories for realistic inspiration, but also many of the series' subplots and relationships are based on the real lives of its stars. The actors who play Frank and Mary Pembleton are married in real life; the actors who play Megan Russert and Beau Felton continued their onscreen affair offscreen, as well; the brief affair between Detective John Munch and Medical Examiner Alyssa Dyer failed onscreen whereas the two actors have been in love in real life for over sixteen years. Sometimes the relationships between onscreen events and offscreen reality became so complex that *Homicide* has been called a dramatic version of *Seinfeld* (1990–98).

Producer Tom Fontana once said he thought it would be great, albeit unlikely, if they could get Jerry Seinfeld to guest star on the show. Some other *Seinfeld* performers have made appearances on *Homicide*. Jerry Stiller, better known as the abrasive Frank Costanza on *Seinfeld*, played a perfectionist bartender for *Homicide*. Michelle Forbes joined the cast in the fifth season as Medical Examiner Julianna Cox, having previously appeared on *Seinfeld* as George Costanza's girlfriend.

Homicide's impressive roster of guest stars also includes Robin Williams, James Earl Jones, Chris Rock, Howie Mandel, Julianna Margulies, Gloria Reuben, Al Freeman Jr., Steve Buscemi, Valerie Perrine, Chris Noth, Mandy Patinkin, John Waters, Bruno Kirby, Jay Leno, Tim Russert, Lily Tomlin,

Charles Dutton, Edward Herrmann, Wilford Brimley, Chris Eigeman, Rosanna Arquette, Elijah Wood, Neil Patrick Harris, the Reverend Horton Heat, Melvin Van Peebles, Vincent D'Onofrio, and real-life Baltimore mayor Kurt Schmoke.

Not all of *Homicide*'s notable contributors have done their work in front of the cameras. Thanks to the prestige bestowed upon the show by esteemed producer-director Barry Levinson, numerous feature-film directors and other luminaries have lent their talents to being guest directors: Nick Gomez, Michael Lehmann, Stephen Gyllenhaal, John McNaughton, Ted Demme, Whitney Ransick, Peter Weller, Michael Radford, Kathy Bates, Whit Stillman, Barbara Kopple, etc.

It should be noted that without a regular director, the role of cinematographer on this series has greatly increased in importance. The cinematographer has assumed a role otherwise performed by the director, that of keeping a consistent look and feel for the show. That style has, of course, become exceptionally distinctive.

Cinematographer Jean de Segonzac swirls about the set on a rolling stool, whirling around the cast members with a hand-held camera. While other shows, such as *NYPD Blue*, fake a hand-held look to suggest a documentary realism, *Homicide* does it for real. Shot as if it were a real documentary, de Segonzac's camera becomes a player in the action.

In addition to giddy camerawork, *Homicide*'s editing (often the work of Cindy Mollo's nimble fingers) breaks all the rules TV producers are taught. Continuity goes out the window as Mollo and the other editors focus solely on getting the *emotion* of the scene right. Sometimes, capturing the full emotional punch of a scene demands that they replay a certain shot or line of dialogue several times, as if it is being drilled into the audience's skull.

The Winning Touch

Although it took a few years for its influence to be felt on other shows (see sidebar), *Homicide*'s effect on critics was all but instantaneous. *Homicide: Life on the Street* has won two Emmy awards and two Writers Guild of America awards. It has been named Program of the Year and Drama of the Year by the Television Critics Association, and Electronic Media's semiannual poll of television writers named it "Favorite Series." It was also nominated for the Producers' Guild of America Golden Laurel Award. In addition, Viewers for Quality Television has awarded *Homicide* the "Q" award, the highest honor they can bestow on a series.

EVERYBODY'S DOIN' IT

As *Homicide* entered its sixth year on TV, other shows started to borrow its experimental editing techniques. NBC's *Pretender* (1996–) started using the trick of repeating the same shot in rapid succession in 1997, about the same time the producer of *Babylon 5* (1994–) asked his editor to duplicate "the *Homicide* look." Even *Seinfeld* (1990–98) borrowed the stuttering jump-cut to underscore a highly emotional flashback as George Costanza recalled getting a wedgie in middle school.

After actor Mandy Pantinkin appeared as his *Chicago Hope* (1994–) character Doctor Geiger in an episode of *Homicide, Chicago Hope*'s producers included a detective obviously modeled on Frank Pembleton in one of their episodes. Richard Belzer appeared in a *Homicide* parody in the feature film *A Very Brady Sequel* (1996), and then appeared as Detective John Munch in a 1997 episode of *The X-Files* (1993–).

Finally, *Homicide* won the highly coveted Peabody Award, and it has done so three times (in 1993, 1995, and 1998). Named for philanthropist George Foster Peabody, the Peabody Award is considered the television industry's most prestigious honor. In selecting *Homicide: Life on the Street* from over 1200 entries, the Henry W. Grady College of Journalism and Mass Communication, which administers the Peabody Award, identified the show as "a socially relevant dramatic series that manages continually to improve upon its impressive record of achievement." In the more than fifty-five-year history of the award, only two drama series have ever been so honored: *Homicide*, and *St. Elsewhere*. Notably, both shows were coproduced by Tom Fontana.

Despite such accolades, *Homicide* has never been a ratings hit and has faced the threat of cancellation on several occasions during its history. Fans may have called *Homicide* "The Best Damn Show on TV," but *TV Guide* dubbed it "The Best Show You're Not Watching."

However, there is a meaningful distinction between *successful* and *popular*. In this age of focus groups, test screenings, and market research, movies and TV shows can be fashioned by creators who serve more as manufacturers than storytellers.

Entertainment that is sufficiently inoffensive and predictable, if heavily promoted, can become a major success without ever actually being *liked* by anyone. Major summer-movie blockbusters can be considered hits even before they open, if a sufficient number of people have decided on the basis of the marketing to go see the film. Thus, the actual quality of the content of the film becomes irrelevant to its popularity. Such programming is successful insofar as it doesn't drive away viewers.

Perhaps it is true that *Homicide* does drive away viewers. The show demands a lot from its audience, and its uncomfortable depictions of the dark side of life can be too much for some TV viewers. However, for those who have warmed to its immeasurable charms, *Homicide* is satisfying in a way no other show can be. Its audience may be fewer in number than its immediate competition (like the exceptionally unexceptional *Nash Bridges*, which first went head-to-head against *Homicide* in 1996), but they are committed and loyal fans, whose enjoyment of the show runs very very deep. This is a level of success that only a rarefied number of television shows can ever hope to achieve.

CHAPTER 2

The Cast and Crew

They have been called the best ensemble cast on television. The regular players of *Homicide: Life on the Street* have changed over the years, with characters coming and going as frequently as the turnover in the real-life Baltimore Homicide Unit.

Veteran homicide detective Donald Worden remarked in late 1997 that he was the last one left. That is, of the almost twenty detectives profiled in David Simon's book, *Homicide: A Year on the Killing Streets*, he alone remains with the squad. At the same time, the TV series based on that book was entering its sixth year on NBC, with only five of its original nine cast members intact.

THE REGULAR CAST

Daniel Baldwin

Detective Beauregard ("Beau") Felton (1993–95)

"It's hard to outrun that bullet in your life that's called your past," Daniel Baldwin told *Cosmopolitan* in 1994.

The second oldest of the Baldwin acting clan (younger than Alec and Adam, older than Stephen and William), Daniel is the self-described "black sheep" of the family. He was born in 1961 in Long Island, and from an early age began to exhibit a rebellious, disobedient streak. "We constantly fought each other when we were kids," Daniel admits, "It always pissed Alec off that I was bigger than he was."

That youthful exuberance soon got Daniel into trouble. When their father (a high-school teacher in Long Island) died in 1983, Daniel was unable to attend the funeral. Baldwin explains, "I was jailed for driving without insurance and with switched license plates."

It was a sobering experience. Stricken with guilt for missing his father's passing, Baldwin resolved to straighten out. He graduated from Ball State University in Indiana with a degree in psychology, married, and fathered a daughter. Deciding that acting was too uncertain a career path for a man with a family to support, Daniel chose not to follow in his brothers' footsteps.

Instead, Baldwin became a professional sports handicapper, advising his clients how to bet. When one of his clients lost so much money that she killed herself in despair, Daniel became so disillusioned with the job that he quit, turning gradually towards the acting career that seemed to beckon him from his Baldwin blood.

Daniel Baldwin made his feature film debut in the Tom Cruise drama *Born on the Fourth of July* (1989). Since then, he has taken movie roles in *Nothing But Trouble* (1991), *Harley Davidson and the Marlboro Man* (1991), *Car 54, Where Are You?* (1994), *Twisted Desire* (1996, with *Homicide* costar and real-life love Isabella Hofmann), *Tree's Lounge* (1996), *Mulholland Falls* (1996), *The Invader* (1997), and *John Carpenter's Vampires* (1998).

In 1992, Baldwin essayed the title role in the movie of the week *Ned Blessing: The True Story of My Life*, based on the Larry McMurtry novel. Baldwin also appeared as himself in the critically acclaimed *Larry Sanders Show* on HBO (1993) and costarred with Daryl Hannah in the made-for-TV remake of *Attack of the 50-Foot Woman* (1993).

Along the way, Baldwin reconciled his worries that acting was a poor career path for a husband and a father by choosing to divorce his first wife.

Daniel began courting his second wife, Elizabeth, in 1988, but the two went their separate ways. However, Daniel was in love, and learning of Elizabeth's address in Los Angeles, he paid the landlord a thousand dollars to be bumped to the head of the waiting list for an apartment. He then bullied a tenant into moving out, and moved into the now vacant apartment directly above Elizabeth's. "The next morning I go down with coffee and croissants and say, 'I can't believe this. I live right above you.'" They were married within four months, in April 1990.

This scenario reads like a sitcom, and Baldwin soon joined the cast of a real sitcom. After costarring with Valerie Bertinelli and Matthew Perry in the short-lived series *Sydney* (1990) on CBS, Baldwin described the experience to *Entertainment Weekly* as being "so boring I wanted to pull my fingernails off."

In 1993, Baldwin got a more satisfying role when he won a place on *Homicide*'s ensemble cast in a role based on real-life Baltimore Detective Donald Kincaid. Kincaid's virulent dislike for loner detective Harry Edgerton was translated onto the small screen as the electric tension between Beau Felton (Baldwin) and loner Frank Pembleton (Andre Braugher). In fact,

Daniel Baldwin with his first wife, Elizabeth. *Archive Photos*

through much of the first season, Baldwin's dialogue matched Kincaid's anti-Edgerton rants from Simon's book almost word for word.

Baldwin dyed his naturally blond hair black for his role, and became one of *Homicide*'s most vocal supporters. Daniel boasted that "*Homicide* is the best material I've had the chance to do." During the show's early and beleaguered efforts to stay afloat despite low ratings, the actor personally promoted the program, giving interviews to any reporter who asked.

That he had to fight at all frustrated Baldwin. "I want to say to [NBC President] Warren Littlefield: 'Can you read? Can you read?' I've never seen this kind of critical response to a show before." To Daniel, it was inexplicable that NBC would not be wholeheartedly behind a quality program, despite its initial unspectacular ratings.

When *Homicide* was finally renewed for an almost-complete third season, Baldwin had all but burnt out. "I'd rather do small parts in movies," he sighed, weary of NBC's on-again, off-again games.

Baldwin stayed with *Homicide* for its third season, and delivered some of his best work. However, the third season also saw several changes by NBC that compromised *Homicide*'s original vision. One of those was a new emphasis on sex. Baldwin's character became separated from his wife and kids as a result of an extramarital affair with Lieutenant Megan Russert, played by Isabella Hofmann. Baldwin called the story line "typical TV chicanery."

However, the idea was drawn from Baldwin's own personal life. When he began his *Homicide* gig, Daniel was still married to Elizabeth, the actress he had struggled so tenaciously to woo back in 1990. Together, they had a baby girl in January 1994, as *Homicide*'s second season began.

By the start of the third season, though, the Baldwins were separated, and Daniel had moved in with Isabella Hofmann, who plays Megan Russert on the TV series. They later had a child together in 1996, whose birth removed Hofmann from the cast (in a subplot that had her character running off with a man and having a child).

Although he had found happiness with Isabella, Baldwin was increasingly discouraged with *Homicide*'s evolution. He felt spent. He had used his own time to promote the show, only to face NBC's indifference. He had trumpeted the show's realism and unconventional daring, only to watch what he considered pandering to the viewers with guest stars, gunplay, and soapy, sexy subplots. After three years of his life far from Hollywood, he had appeared in as many episodes as most shows crank out in half that time.

Baldwin departed at the end of the 1994–95 season, returning only to visit cast members offscreen.

In 1998, though, Baldwin resurfaced in seamy headlines. Early in the morning on Monday, February 2, police were called to New York's Plaza Hotel to investigate a disturbance. Reportedly, according to the Associated Press, they found Daniel Baldwin naked and hallucinating from alleged substance abuse, amidst the rubble of his trashed room. The actor put up a struggle with the cops and had to be handcuffed before being rushed to St. Luke's-Roosevelt Hospital for treatment. He was listed in critical condition for a few days before recovering enough to be reportedly charged with two misdemeanor drug offenses. As if the actor had not been humiliated enough, more of his dirty laundry was hung out to view when he faced an outstanding warrant for allegedly failing to make child support payments to ex-wife Elizabeth for their two daughters. While the actor survived this ordeal, it suggested that the mischievous Daniel Baldwin of old had apparently never really grown up.

DANIEL BALDWIN—SELECTED CREDITS

FILMS
Born on the Fourth of July (1989)
Nothing But Trouble (1991)
Harley Davidson and the Marlboro Man (1991)
Knight Moves (1993)
Dead on Sight (1994)
Car 54, Where Are You? (released 1994; made in 1990)
Bodily Harm (1995)
Yesterday's Target (1996)
Twisted Desire (1996)
Trees Lounge (1996)

Mulholland Falls (1996)
The Invader (1997)
John Carpenter's Vampires (1998)

TELEVISION
L.A. Takedown (1989) [telefilm]
Sydney (1990) [TV series]
Ned Blessing: The True Story of My Life (1992) [telefilm]
The Heroes of Desert Storm (1992) [telefilm]
Attack of the 50-Foot Woman (1993) [telefilm]
Homicide: Life on the Street (1993–95) [TV series]
Family of Cops (1995) [telefilm]

Ned Beatty

Detective Stanley ("The Big Man") Bolander (1993-95)

Born July 6, 1937, Ned Beatty, the best-known of *Homicide*'s illustrious ensemble cast, started his show-business career as a youth. The young Beatty went from singing in church to singing in operettas. At the tender age of sixteen, Beatty auditioned for a musical theater company in Louisville, Kentucky, his hometown. Although the directors admired Beatty's vocal talents, they considered him too short.

When his musical theater career did not take off as he had dreamed, Beatty started working at various regional theaters in Virginia, Pennsylvania, and Washington, D.C. He spent eight seasons with Washington's famed Arena Stage, but then decided the time had come to change directions. Discouraged by reaching only the small audience groups that attend live theater, Beatty determined to pursue the wider audience available to motion pictures.

In 1972, Beatty made his feature film debut with a breakthrough role in the fabled *Deliverance*. Just a few years later, the actor took what a fellow actor once called "maybe the one truly great one-day part in cinema history": an Academy Award–nominated cameo role as a TV executive in 1976's *Network*.

Beatty continued to garner attention and recognition for such films as *Silver Streak* (1976), *All the President's Men* (1976), *Superman I* and *II* (1978 and 1980), *The Toy* (1982), and *The Big Easy* (1987). Over time, Beatty racked up an astonishing list of over sixty movie credits. However, he found himself moving away from the poorly written roles in increasingly juvenile Hollywood pictures and taking roles in high-quality but low-budget independent films like 1991's *Hear My Song*. (As it happened, *Hear My Song* offered the actor the chance to finally realize his childhood ambition of performing in a musical.)

Meanwhile, Beatty was also earning Emmy nominations for his work on the small screen on such television movies as *Friendly Fire* (1979) and *Last Train Home* (1990).

In 1993, producers Barry Levinson and Tom Fontana asked Beatty to play Detective Stan "Big Man" Bolander, a character based on Baltimore detective Donald Worden. Although impressed with Levinson and Fontana, Beatty worried that the network would corrupt the show and make it into another generic cops-and-robbers hour. He admits they had to drag him "kicking and screaming" to the role.

The early days of *Homicide* were rough on the cast. On the one hand, Levinson and Fontana pushed them to break the established rules of filmmaking in an effort to create perfect, almost theatrical, performances. On the other hand, this emotional and grueling work was dismissed by NBC executives who could only see the bottom line: *Homicide*'s low ratings, due in part to that very experimental approach. After two years with the show, Beatty and his costars had only appeared in thirteen episodes, and faced two sincere efforts to cancel the series.

As *Homicide* limped and struggled to keep afloat, the producers of Harold Prince's major musical *Showboat* approached Beatty to play the lead, Cap'n Andy. The idea appealed greatly to the actor, who still remembered his musical ambitions as a youth, but his commitment to the TV series forced him to

Ned Beatty, one of the most respected actors in Homicide*'s cast. Everett Collection*

say no. As *Homicide*'s third season drew to a close, NBC started rattling its swords once again about a potential cancellation. Barry Levinson returned to Baltimore to direct Episode 33: "The Gas Man," which threatened to be the show's final episode.

Frustrated with having to turn down other job offers for a role in a show that seemed likely only to stay on the air for another year, Beatty decided to leave. He was also deeply frustrated with the changes NBC had forced upon *Homicide*, changes he had feared from the beginning.

"It wasn't about the money," Beatty confided with the *Los Angeles Times*, "I loved it in the beginning. Some of it was the best thing I'd ever done. But it got to the point where they wanted to see people get shot and car chases and all that. Which is not what homicide detectives really do."

Indeed, *Homicide* had boosted its ratings dramatically by having three of its cast members get shot, one of them the Big Man himself. However, rather than write him out as having died from the bullet to his head, Bolander's departure was explained as being the consequence of his drunken rowdiness at a policeman's convention in New York. The incident in question was taken from real life, and provided an easy way to explain the absence of Bolander and Felton as *Homicide* entered its fourth season. The two detectives were placed on a twenty-two week suspension (which neatly coincided with the length of the season), suggesting that either or both might return one day.

Former Detective Bolander, though, moved on. So too did Ned Beatty, in this case, as a replacement in the role of Cap'n Andy in Hal Prince's production of *Show Boat*.

In preparing for his role as Cap'n Andy, Beatty lost an astonishing fifty pounds in only four months. Slimmed down, Beatty also shed his wife of eighteen years. Tinker Beatty was Ned's third wife, with whom he had fathered a total of eight children.

NED BEATTY—SELECTED CREDITS

FILMS
The Life and Times of Judge Roy Bean (1972)
Deliverance (1972)
White Lightning (1973)
The Thief Who Came to Dinner (1973)
The Last American Hero (1973)
W.W. and the Dixie Dancekings (1975)
Nashville (1975)
Silver Streak (1976)

Network (1976)
Mikey and Nicky (1976)
The Big Bus (1976)
All the President's Men (1976)
The Great Bank Hoax (1977)
Exorcist II: The Heretic (1977)
Alambrista! (1977)
Superman: The Movie (1978)
Gray Lady Down (1978)
Wise Blood (1979)
Promises in the Dark (1979)
The American Success Company (1979)
1941 (1979)
Superman II (1980)
Hopscotch (1980)
The Incredible Shrinking Woman (1981)
The Toy (1982)
Touched (1983)
Stroker Ace (1983)
Restless Natives (1985)
Back to School (1986)
The Trouble with Spies (1987)
Rolling Vengeance (1987)
The Fourth Protocol (1987)
The Big Easy (1987)
The Unholy (1988)
Switching Channels (1988)
Shadows in the Storm (1988)
Purple People Eater (1988)
Midnight Crossing (1988)
Time Trackers (1989)
Tennessee Nights (1989)
Physical Evidence (1989)
Ministry of Vengeance (1989)
Repossessed (1990)
Going Under (1990)
A Cry in the Wild (1990)
Chattahoochee (1990)
Big Bad John (1990)
Hear My Song (1991)

Angel-Square (1991)
Prelude to a Kiss (1992)
Captain America (1992)
Blind Vision (1992)
Warren Oates: Across the Border (1993)
Rudy (1993)
Ed and His Dead Mother (1993)
Earth and the American Dream (1993)
Replikator (1994)
Radioland Murders (1994)
The Legend of O.B. Taggart (1995)
Just Cause (1995)

TELEVISION

Footsteps (1972) [telefilm]
The Marcus-Nelson Murders (1973) [telefilm]
Dying Room Only (1973) [telefilm]
The Execution of Private Slovik (1974) [telefilm]
The Deadly Tower (1975) [telefilm]
Attack on Terror: The FBI versus the Ku Klux Klan (1975) [telefilm]
Hunter (1976) [telefilm]
Tail Gunner Joe (1977) [telefilm]
Lucan (1977) [telefilm]
Szysznyk (1977–78) [TV series]
A Question of Love (1978) [telefilm]
Friendly Fire (1979) [telefilm]
Rumpelstiltskin (1980) [telefilm]
Our Town (1980) [telefilm]
Guyana Tragedy: The Story of Jim Jones (1980) [telefilm]
All God's Children (1980) [telefilm]
The Violation of Sarah McDavid (1981) [telefilm]
Splendor in the Grass (1981) [telefilm]
A Woman Called Golda (1982) [telefilm]
Pray TV (1982) [telefilm]
Kentucky Woman (1983) [telefilm]
The Last Days of Pompeii (1984) [TV miniseries]
Celebrity (1984) [TV miniseries]
Murder, She Wrote (1984) [telefilm/pilot]
Hostage Flight (1985) [telefilm]
Charlotte Forten's Mission: Experiment in Freedom (1985) [telefilm]

Alfred Hitchcock Presents (1985) [telefilm]
Robert Kennedy and His Times (1985) [TV miniseries]
Go to the Light (1988) [telefilm]
Roseanne (1989–96) [TV series]
Spy (1989) [telefilm]
The Tragedy of Flight 103: The Inside Story (1990) [telefilm]
Last Train Home (1990) [telefilm]
Back to Hannibal: The Return of Tom Sawyer and Huckleberry Finn (1990)
    [telefilm]
Trial: The Price of Passion (1992) [telefilm]
T Bone N Weasel (1992) [telefilm]
Lincoln (1992) [telefilm]
Illusions (1992) [telefilm]
Homicide: Life on the Street (1993–95) [TV series]
The Boys (1993) [TV series]
The Affair (1995) [telefilm]
Larry McMurtry's Streets of Laredo (1995) [TV miniseries]
Gulliver's Travels (1996) [TV miniseries]
Crazy Horse (1996) [telefilm]

Richard Belzer

Detective John Munch (1993–)

The role of the acerbic, cynical, ex-hippie John Munch fits Richard Belzer like a glove. The similarities are so close that Belzer has at times been tempted to "borrow" dialogue written for Munch for use in his stand-up comedy act.

Belzer told the press, "It's an actor's dream to have a character written for him saying things I might say anyway."

Ironically, though, the role of Munch had been developed and written long before Belzer was considered for the cast. The part is based on former Baltimore Sergeant Jay Landsman, a practical jokester renowned among the Homicide Division for his morbid wit. "[Landsman] is way out there," Belzer agrees.

Belzer was a frequent guest on Howard Stern's radio show, and Barry Levinson heard the comedian doing a trademark rant on the air and asked him to audition. Many of the parallels between the actor and his character were purely coincidental.

One important difference between the two, however, is that Belzer insists he would never consider being a police officer, because he hates guns and distrusts authority. Nonetheless, Belzer admits that Munch is "exactly as I would be if I were a cop."

Richard Belzer's acerbic comedy comes from a hard, painful life.
Everett Collection

In developing the character of Munch, Belzer created what actors call "backstory"—that is, the life that the character experienced before the story began. Belzer explained on NBC's *Homicide* Web site that Munch's father was a cop, killed in the line of duty, and that that led the onetime hippie to join the force himself.

In real life, Belzer's father committed suicide (after an unsuccessful attempt at overdose, from which twenty-one-year old Richard saved him). Belzer's mother, Frances, was physically abusive to him as a child, and she died when he was twenty. As he told *People* magazine, he still remains bitter toward his mother, as he has yet to forgive her for the way she treated him.

Born in 1944 in Bridgeport, Connecticut, Richard Belzer was an unhappy child. Abused and neglected by his parents, Belzer developed an antisocial streak. "I got kicked outta every school I was ever in," he reveals.

Ultimately, Belzer became a reporter for the *Bridgeport Post* in his Connecticut hometown. To this day, he still reads five papers a day, which provides fodder for his stand-up routines.

Belzer's comedy career only started after a string of unsatisfying jobs: census taker, teacher, dock worker, jewelry salesman. Comedy saved Belzer, as he had started dealing drugs and carrying guns. "I never got arrested, but there were some close calls," Belzer told *People* in 1993, "A friend of mine got shot."

Then in 1971, his first wife, Gail Susan Ross, spotted an ad in the *Village Voice*. Belzer went to an audition, and landed a part in the 1974 cult film *The Groove Tube*, which opened a whole new world to him.

Riding the success of *The Groove Tube*, Belzer began doing stand-up comedy, giving his acid-edged commentary on current events. Soon, he was host of New York's "Catch a Rising Star." He starred with Bill Murray, Gilda

Radner, and John Belushi in the off-Broadway *National Lampoon Show*, and was cohost of the morning radio program *Brink and Belzer*. He was also the regular warm-up act for *Saturday Night Live*.

Belzer began acting, taking both comic and dramatic roles in such films as *Fame* (1980), *Author, Author* (1982), *Nightshift* (1982), *Scarface* (1983), *The Wrong Guys* (1988), *Freeway* (1988), *The Bonfire of the Vanities* (1990), and *The Puppet Masters* (1994, with fellow *Homicide* actor Yaphet Kotto). During breaks in *Homicide*'s production, he worked with director Spike Lee in *Girl 6* (1996) and *Get on the Bus* (1997, with another series costar, Andre Braugher).

On television, Belzer has made repeated visits to *Saturday Night Live* (1975–), *The Tonight Show* (1962–), and *Late Night With David Letterman* (1982–93). He also created comedy specials for Cinemax, Showtime, and HBO.

Belzer wrote the satiric *How to Be a Stand-Up Comic* (1992) for Random House books, and is currently developing a CD-ROM. "You can't just put out a comedy album anymore," he explains.

In fact, Belzer only recently returned to doing stand-up comedy. Once he was cast as Detective John Munch for *Homicide* in 1993, Belzer focused his attention on dramatic acting and rarely ventured onto the stage. In 1997, after five years of near-retirement from stand-up comedy, he started again, filming his act for an HBO special. He found the experience of entertaining live audiences again richly rewarding.

Like his onscreen persona, Belzer has been married three times. Unlike his alter ego, though, Belzer has stayed happily married for fourteen years to actress Harlee McBride, a former *Playboy* model and star of the soft-core *Young Lady Chatterley* films (1977 and 1985). McBride plays medical examiner Dr. Alyssa Dyer on *Homicide*, and her character had a (brief) romance with John Munch. Belzer got a kick out of kissing his wife on TV, even if the perpetually unhappy Munch was unable to keep the relationship alive.

Belzer and McBride have two grown daughters from McBride's former marriage. They lease a condo in Baltimore's Inner Harbor for the eight months that *Homicide* films, but have no permanent address in the United States. Instead, Belzer and McBride own a villa in the south of France.

Richard Belzer shares Detective Munch's dark side. The actor is an ardent conspiracy theorist. He has collected hundreds of articles, almost fifty books, hundreds of hours of recordings, and other documentation in his efforts to investigate the Kennedy assassination. "It won't solve anything, I'm just venting," Belzer admits.

Deeply cynical after the assassinations of his other heroes Martin Luther King Jr. and Bobby Kennedy, Belzer has not voted since 1968. The hopes of the sixties generation are over, he says, "The mean people won."

Nevertheless, he has found great joy in his role as the equally embittered John Munch. Although the departure of actors Ned Beatty and Isabella Hofmann have twice left his character without a partner, and have thereby cost his role some screen time, Belzer shows no resentment. He has said that being part of such a fine ensemble makes him feel like he's "on the all-star team."

"I really am the very happiest I've ever been," Belzer told the *Los Angeles Times* in 1996. "I'm on the best-written show on television."

RICHARD BELZER—SELECTED CREDITS

FILMS
The Groove Tube (1974)
Fame (1980)
Night Shift (1982)
Author! Author! (1982)
Scarface (1983)
Horror House on Highway Five (1985)
America (1986)
Flicks (1987)
The Wrong Guys (1988)
Freeway (1988)
The Big Picture (1989)
Fletch Lives (1989)
The Bonfire of the Vanities (1990)
Off and Running (1991)
Missing Pieces (1991)
Mad Dog and Glory (1993)
The Puppet Masters (1994)
North (1994)
Not of This Earth (1995)
Girl 6 (1996)
A Very Brady Sequel (1996)
Get On the Bus (1996)
Deadly Pursuits (1997)

TELEVISION
Thicke of the Night (1983–84) [TV series]
Homicide: Life on the Street (1993–) [TV series]
Hart to Hart: Crimes of the Hart (1994) [telefilm]
Prince for a Day (1995) [telefilm]
The Invaders (1995) [TV miniseries]

Andre Braugher

Detective Francis Xavier ("Frank") Pembleton (1993–98)

When he was called to audition for the role of Detective Frank Pembleton, Andre Braugher was startled to discover that the character's race was not obvious in the script. In his experience, TV writers tended to write fully developed roles for white actors and two-dimensional stereotypes for black actors.

But Pembleton was different. The creators of *Homicide* had deliberately tried to break out of the conventional racial stereotypes, and Barry Levinson was freely casting actors for roles written with another ethnicity in mind.

The real detective on whom Pembleton was based, Harry Edgerton, is African-American, but *Homicide's* creators added an extra dimension to the role via Pembleton's lapsed Catholicism. Pembleton came to be described as "God's cop" by many reviewers. Religion became such an important feature of the character that the detectives who advise the producers agreed that the only connection between Harry Edgerton and Frank Pembleton is that they are both African-American males.

Braugher was born on July 1, 1962, in Chicago. As an overweight, shy child, Braugher spent his days reading. One day, the young Andre came home to tell his parents his third-grade teacher wasn't calling on him to read in class because he was so far ahead of the other students. Although the family was Baptist, they immediately enrolled Andre in a private Catholic school.

Thanks to his scholarly bent, the young Braugher earned a scholarship to the prestigious St. Ignatius College Preparatory, a four-year Jesuit school. He would later draw from that experience for his role as the Jesuit-trained Pembleton.

Braugher earned his bachelor of arts from Stanford University and a masters of fine arts from The Juilliard School (where he first met future *Homicide* costar Reed Diamond). During his years at Stanford, Braugher considered a medical career, but was persuaded to audition for the role of Claudius in a student production of *Hamlet*. This role would change Braugher's life entirely.

"I discovered doing a play was more exciting than doing math in the library," Braugher says, "Nobody applauds you in the library."

One of Braugher's drama teachers from Juilliard also served as the casting director for the Joseph Papp Public Theater. She remembered the young actor as having been "the shining light" of her Shakespeare class, and began casting him in the Public Theater's acclaimed performances.

Braugher considers Shakespeare one of his great loves. "I find the complexity and the depth and richness of Shakespeare an incredible magnet," says Braugher. He has performed with the New York Shakespeare Festival in *Much*

Andre Braugher shows another side in Spike Lee's **Get On the Bus.** *Everett Collection*

Ado About Nothing, King John, and *Henry V.* He also performed with the Joseph Papp Public Theater in William Congreve's *The Way of the World,* as well as Shakespeare's *Richard II, Measure for Measure, Twelfth Night,* and *Coriolanus.* Braugher played with the Philadelphia Drama Guild in *Macbeth* and with the Folger Shakespeare Festival in *Othello.* Braugher notes with pride, "I plan to carry on this love affair for many, many years."

Critics have praised him as one of the major classical performers of the day, but Braugher insists, "I can't hear about my reviews. They're much too dangerous. They may infect my performance."

In his role as the intense Detective Pembleton, Braugher has also garnered critical raves. *TV Guide* wrote, "If there's anyone doing better dramatic acting on TV these days, we haven't seen it." Surprisingly, the television industry has only granted the highly acclaimed actor a single Emmy nomination. "Having been touted for an Emmy so many times and having nothing materialize, I can't take it too seriously anymore," Braugher told *USA Today.*

Other roles for Braugher have included appearing with Bruce Willis in *Striking Distance* (1993), playing opposite *Homicide* costar Richard Belzer in Spike Lee's *Get On the Bus* (1996); and joining Richard Gere in *Primal Fear* (1996). He played the lead role in the 1990 made-for-television film *The Court-Martial of Jackie Robinson* and starred in 1995's cable movie *The Tuskegee Airmen.* During the hiatus between production of *Homicide*'s fifth and sixth seasons, he teamed with *NYPD Blue*'s Dennis Franz in *City of Angels* (1998), an adaptation of Wim Wenders' 1988 masterpiece, *Wings of Desire*.

Braugher also earned his customary critical acclaim as a free black Bostonian in the 1989 hit film *Glory*, in which he appeared with Denzel Washington and Morgan Freeman. Braugher credits those two stars with teaching him how to act for the camera, as opposed to the stage-bound the-atrical performing to which he was accustomed.

Prior to Detective Pembleton, Braugher played a very different type of TV detective—Winston Blake on the revived 1989–90 run of *Kojak*. Unlike *Homicide*'s treatment of race, Braugher found the experience on *Kojak* frus-trating. The producers wanted Blake to be a sexy bed-hopper, to which Braugher objected. He especially rankled at the stereotype of the sex-mad black male.

Braugher credits *Homicide* with having enough black characters to show a wide range of personality types. Between him, Clark Johnson, Yaphet Kotto, and supporting players like Clayton LeBoeuf, Erik Todd Dellums, and Al Freeman, Jr., the range of black-skinned characters is too broad and diverse to fall into the usual ugly stereotypes.

His role on *Homicide* is different from that on *Kojak* in another important respect. Far from hopping in and out of bed, Pembleton is shown relating closely with his wife and child. Braugher especially likes how the series has allowed his character to evolve, showing the interaction between his intensity on the job and the consequences to his private life.

For his part, Braugher does not take the role of Frank home with him. "I have absolutely no personal investment in my character," he insists. "I'm just a guy who goes home after work and takes out the garbage."

The role of Mary Pembleton, Frank's onscreen wife, is played by Ami Brabson, Braugher's offscreen real wife. Braugher told *Parade* magazine, "We have an instant rapport that we don't have to create." The two first met in 1988, while Braugher was finishing up his studies in Juilliard's drama depart-ment and Brabson was a graduate student at New York University's drama school. It was love at first sight, and they were married in 1991.

While most of his costars on *Homicide* maintain residences in Baltimore only for the eight months of the show's production, Braugher and Brabson fell in love with "Charm City" and moved there. A few months after Braugher began his role as Detective Pembleton, Brabson auditioned for the role of his wife. Shortly thereafter they had their first child, Michael.

They attempted unsuccessfully to have a second child (which was adapt-ed onscreen in Episode 33: "The Gas Man"). In 1997, Braugher and Brabson all but gave up hope and began looking to adopt. Then, Brabson indeed became pregnant with their second child (which was depicted onscreen as Mary Pembleton's second pregnancy, as well).

Braugher is planning to leave *Homicide* after its sixth season. Braugher and Brabson will return to New York with their two children for Brabson to resume her live-theater career. "[*Homicide*] is a wonderful job. But it's time to go."

Braugher says he has no regrets about the experience. "You have to choose very carefully projects that interest you and make you happy. Things you can look back on with pride," Braugher says. "I want to make the kinds of films I can show my son in ten years and he won't be ashamed of me."

ANDRE BRAUGHER—SELECTED CREDITS

FILMS
Glory (1989)
Striking Distance (1993)
Primal Fear (1996)
Get On the Bus (1996)
City of Angels (1998)

TELEVISION
Kojak (1989–90) [TV series]
Somebody Has to Shoot the Picture (1990) [telefilm]
Murder in Mississippi (1990) [telefilm]
Kojak: None So Blind (1990) [telefilm]
The Court-Martial of Jackie Robinson (1990) [telefilm]
Without Warning: Terror in the Towers (1990) [telefilm]
Simple Justice (1993) [telefilm]
Class of '61 (1993) [telefilm]
Homicide: Life on the Street (1993–98) [TV series]
The Tuskegee Airmen (1995) [telefilm]

Reed Diamond

Detective Michael Kellerman (1995–98)

Some *Homicide* fans, trying to find the links between the onscreen characters and the real-life detectives of Simon's book, posited a connection between Mike Kellerman and real-life arson detective Keller, who was only mentioned briefly. With Keller's mere cameo in the book, fans were making the connection on the basis of name alone. Ironically, Kellerman's name was originally different!

Even in this 1992 made-for-TV movie O! Pioneers, *Reed Diamond's simmering intensity can be seen.* Everett Collection

In a press release of July 10, 1995, mere months before the broadcast of Kellerman's debut in Episode 34: "Fire, Part One," NBC announced that actor Reed Diamond was joining the cast as newcomer Mike Driscoll. Diamond even gave interviews to the press describing Driscoll's personality. The producers didn't change the name to Kellerman until just before shooting began.

In joining the cast, Diamond worried about the fans' reaction. He knew that the series had developed a strong cult following, who were very protective of the show. Thus, he was joining an established ensemble already in full stride. Would he fit in?

Diamond realized, though, that just as he was joining an established group of actors that had grown used to working together, his character was also a newcomer to an established unit of detectives. "Any discomfort or conflict I felt coming in would be right for the character," Diamond explained to the *Boston Herald*.

Diamond's good looks and youth singled him out as an addition to the cast chosen more for demographic appeal than anything else. However, the writers found excellent ways to use the new character to enhance existing features of the show. For one thing, by displacing Bayliss as the rookie of the squad, Kellerman allowed the character of Bayliss to mature and move on to a new role in the squad as a wiser, more established detective. Additionally, Kellerman's casual approach made a perfect fit with previously underused Meldrick Lewis, allowing actor Clark Johnson to finally take a prominent role in the show after three years in the shadows.

Fontana described the Kellerman-Lewis pairing as "frat boys with guns," a characterization Diamond resented. "My character is a working-class man, no frat boy, no college boy."

By contrast, Diamond is himself a college boy. He was born in Brooklyn on July 20, 1967, and grew up in New York. He attended the University of North Carolina at Chapel Hill before studying acting at Juilliard. Diamond was a freshman at Juilliard when Braugher was a senior. "The man has got a voice," Diamond marveled to the *Austin American-Statesman*, "I have to do vocal exercises so I can keep up with his tone." Diamond was especially excited to be performing alongside Braugher on *Homicide*. Previously, they had appeared on stage together for a Juilliard production of *Othello*, with Braugher as Iago, and Diamond as a servant.

While at UNC, Diamond began his stage career with his role in *Wait Until Dark*. Other theater credits include Harold Pinter's acclaimed *The Homecoming* at New York's Roundabout Theater and *Peer Gynt* at the Williamstown Festival.

On the big screen, Diamond joined Eric Stoltz and Tate Donovan for the 1990 feature *Memphis Belle*. (The costars were later reunited in *Homicide*'s Episode 71: "Wu's on First?")

When Ned Beatty and Daniel Baldwin chose to leave *Homicide*'s ranks, Tom Fontana and Henry Bromell began looking for a new character to help fill the gap. Diamond eagerly anticipated the chance to play a detective, as he had once seriously considered being a cop himself.

Even after his acting career started to blossom, Diamond seriously entertained the notion of attending the police academy. "I wanted to be a cop when I grew up," says Diamond, "Cops do good. They get the bad guy."

"My cousin is an arson detective in Seattle," Diamond told the *Boston Herald*, "and he was a real hero for me." Inspired by his cousin, Diamond took a tour of the Los Angeles Police Academy and rode along with some cop friends.

However, the cops he met all dreamed of being actors. "I figured the best thing I could do was play a police officer as truthfully as possible and do them proud."

For two years, Diamond waited for a good cop role to come along. While he waited, he found himself "in TV-movie land" as he called it, playing the "bad guy of the week." One such role was a scheming killer on NBC's TV series *Law and Order*, in the 1991 episode "Misconceptions."

Diamond was thrilled to be cast in *Homicide*. Since taking the role of Detective Kellerman, Diamond says that real cops have come up to him and said, "I believe you. You look like a cop." The actor finds such compliments richly rewarding.

Some of that authenticity comes from *Homicide*'s distinctive intermingling of fact and fiction. No cast member's private life is free from being incorporated into the story line, or vice versa. The onscreen Kellerman is a divorced young man, whose one great flame was unfaithful to him and ended their marriage.

When Diamond joined the cast, he was newly married to Frederika Kesten, an apprentice editor on films like *Nobody's Fool* (1986) and *The Seventh Sign* (1988), and an aspiring actress with guest roles on shows like *Melrose Place* (1992–). Together they lived in Los Angeles, home to the vast majority of TV series productions.

However, *Homicide* films in Baltimore. Heading east to take his new job, Diamond marveled at how different the experience was from any other production. Like his costars, Diamond quickly realized the advantages of working so far from NBC's watchful eyes. When the cat's away, Diamond notes, "things can get a little wild."

While the distant location afforded *Homicide*'s cast and crew great freedom, it also put an enormous geographic wedge between Diamond and Kesten. The two had been married in July of 1995, the same month Fontana and Bromell sent Diamond on his press rounds to promote the new character "Mike Driscoll." The couple scarcely had time to settle in together before Diamond disappeared for eight months, a surefire recipe for marital disaster.

"It upsets me personally that we're apart so much, but it's worth the sacrifice," Diamond told the *Houston Chronicle*, "The show couldn't be as innovative and interesting if it were made anywhere else. So we rack up a lot of frequent-flier miles."

Kesten did venture east to Baltimore to join her husband onscreen in Episode 48: "Justice, Part Two," playing police ballistics expert Janine. Otherwise, though, the two were kept apart by thousands of miles. By his starring in a show that received overwhelming critical raves for its writing and acting, Diamond could justify the separation. Kesten, the loser in the arrangement, did not see it that way.

Just nineteen months after tying the knot, Kesten filed for divorce (on the show, Kellerman was married only fourteen months). The couple separated in February 1996, just as *Homicide* began filming the final episodes of its fifth season.

Ironically, after his divorce, Diamond found himself actually falling in love with actress Michelle Forbes, their onscreen characters having been romantically linked for some time.

Although the role of Detective Kellerman cost him his wife, Diamond's work on *Homicide* has been a joy for him: "This is the best project I've ever been involved with. I come to work happy every day." Nevertheless at the end of the 1997–98 season, Diamond chose not to return to the series as a cast regular.

REED DIAMOND—SELECTED CREDITS

FILMS
Two Minute Warning (1976)
Memphis Belle (1990)
Clear and Present Danger (1994)
Awake to Murder (1995)
Assassins (1995)

TELEVISION
Ironclads (1991) [telefilm]
O Pioneers! (1992) [telefilm]
Blind Spot (1993) [telefilm]
Homicide: Life on the Street (1995–) [TV series]
Secrets (1995) [telefilm]
Her Hidden Truth (1995) [telefilm]
919 Fifth Avenue (1995) [telefilm]
Full Circle (1996) [telefilm]

AUDIO
Homicide: A Year on the Killing Streets (1997) [narrator of Book-On-Tape edition of David Simon's book]

Michelle Forbes

Chief Medical Examiner Julianna Cox (1996–98)

When the producers of *Star Trek: The Next Generation* (1987–94) first pitched the spin-off series *Star Trek: Deep Space 9* (1993–), they intended to move over with it two established characters from *The Next Generation*'s ranks: Colm Meany (Engineer O'Brien) and Michelle Forbes (Ensign Ro Laren). Forbes had become a focus of fans' attention for her role as Ro, considered one of the strongest female characters ever on the venerable science-fiction series.

Forbes turned down the offer, saying that she was not interested in regular television work at that point in her career. The producers of *Star Trek* wanted her to commit to a seven-year contract, which the young actress feared would limit her experience at a crucial point in her career.

Forbes was born in Austin, Texas, on February 7, 1967. At age sixteen, she headed to New York to pursue acting. After working Off Off Broadway for a few years, Forbes was cast in the CBS daytime serial *The Guiding Light*, the longest-running soap opera on TV. From 1987 to 1989 Forbes played the dual personality Sonni/Solita Lewis, earning an Emmy nomination for her role.

Following her work on the popular soap, Forbes took guest roles in such shows as *The Father Dowling Mysteries* (1989), *Nasty Boys* (1990), and Showtime's *The Outer Limits* (1995). The latter also featured future *Law and Order* lead Benjamin Bratt and future *Homicide* costar Melissa Leo. In 1994, Michelle appeared on *Seinfeld* as one of George Constanza's girlfriends, notable for unjustly taking credit for buying Elaine Benes "the Big Salad."

After the recurring role from 1991-92 as the Bajoran Ro Laren on *Star Trek*, Forbes hoped to further her feature-film career. She costarred with Brad Pitt, Juliette Lewis, and David Duchovny in 1993's *Kalifornia*. She also appeared with Kevin Spacey in 1995's *Swimming with Sharks*, and with James LeGros in *Just Looking* (1997).

In 1996, Forbes took a role in the made-for-TV film *The Prosecutors*, produced by Tom Fontana. With *Homicide*'s Isabella Hofmann departing due to pregnancy, Fontana was looking for an additional female voice to add to *Homicide*'s ensemble cast. In Michelle, Fontana saw an opportunity to provide the youthful, sexy appeal needed to keep the struggling series afloat in the ratings. Fontana offered Forbes a regular spot on *Homicide*. Her earlier reluctance to take just such a regular television job melted away, and she accepted.

Fontana told Forbes he could picture her as a district attorney or a medical examiner. She liked the idea of a young, female M.E.—to break the conventional stereotype of crusty old coroners.

Fontana described the character of Dr. Julianna Cox as being "a very unsettling spirit on the show." "Julianna has her own way of doing things," he adds.

Forbes drew inspiration for Dr. Cox's hard-living intensity from the Johns Hopkins medical students she observed in Baltimore. Medical examiners and homicide detectives alike spend so much time among the bodies of the dead that they must develop some kind of psychological shielding in order to maintain their composure. Forbes saw passion and excess at work in those students, who compensated for their death-soaked occupation with a fast-living personal life.

The actress also found inspiration in crime novels by Patricia Cornwell, whose recurring heroine is a medical examiner. Additionally, Forbes works with real-life Baltimore medical examiner Aaron Hearne, a consultant to *Homicide*, to keep her characterization accurate.

After having moved from Austin to Los Angeles to pursue her acting career, Forbes found herself moving out of Hollywood in order to take her most visible role to date. Like many of *Homicide*'s cast members, she found it amusing to be working so far from the glitz and power games of L.A. Producer

Michelle Forbes joined the cast of
Homicide in 1996. Everett Collection

Barry Levinson's hometown gave them all the sensation of being in their parents' house while Mom and Dad were away.

Although single, Forbes has formed a tight bond with costar Reed Diamond. Shortly after her character's introduction into the series, the writers had her begin an affair with Diamond's character, Detective Kellerman. It was not long before the two actors found themselves following their characters' leads, and sources close to the show have said that the two are now very deeply in love.

MICHELLE FORBES—SELECTED CREDITS

FILMS
The Nerissa Playboys (1992)
Love Bites (1993)
Kalifornia (1993)
The Road Killers (1994)
Swimming with Sharks (1995)
Black Day, Blue Night (1995)
Escape from L.A. (1996)
Just Looking (1997)

TELEVISION
The Guiding Light (1987-89) [TV series]
Star Trek: The Next Generation (1991-92) [TV series, recurring role]
The Prosecutors (1996) [telefilm]
Homicide: Life on the Street (1996-98) [TV series]

Peter Gerety

Officer/Detective Stuart Gharty (1996; 1997–)

After the departure of Jon Polito and Ned Beatty, the squadroom's average age plummeted. Writer-producer David Simon worried that the series needed an older voice, not just for the sake of realism, but also to balance the characters' interpersonal dynamics. So, the producers looked to actor Peter Gerety to join the cast as Detective Stuart Gharty.

The character had first appeared in the fourth season's Episode 52: "Scene of the Crime" as an experienced beat officer who refuses to respond to an urgent call because he fears for his life. Although Detective Megan Russert brings him up on charges with Internal Affairs for his failure, the show presented the character with a complex blend of sympathy and accusation.

When Gharty returned at the end of the fifth season, viewers were confronted with a nice irony: Gharty was now an Internal Affairs detective himself. At the start of the sixth season, the new departmental policy of rotating detectives throughout different divisions moved Gharty into the Homicide Unit, to join the very detectives who once tried to end his career, and who still distrust his motives.

New York native Peter Gerety brings a wealth of acting experience to the role, although, unlike his costars, little of it has been in front of cameras. Gerety's accomplished career has been on the stage, where he has appeared in over 125 different productions by the award-winning Trinity Repertory Company of Providence, Rhode Island. His work with the company earned him a Best Actor award from the Boston Critics Association in 1983. Not content with merely acting, Gerety has also directed several plays.

On Broadway, Gerety has performed in *Conversations with My Father* and Harold Pinter's *The Hothouse*. Gerety's Off-Broadway experience teamed him with the famed James Earl Jones on two occasions, and they were again reunited in *Homicide*'s sixth season when Jones took a guest role in the three-part "Blood Ties" (Episodes 79–81).

Gerety has taken guest roles himself in various television series over the years, including *Law and Order* (1990–   ) and *Central Park West* (1996-97).

In 1996, producer Steven Bochco, the creator of such famed hits as *Hill Street Blues* (1981–87) and *NYPD Blue* (1993–   ), tried his hand at comedy, with the ill-advised and critically panned *Public Morals* (1996). The short-lived flop was a sitcom(!) about a group of Vice Squad detectives, and featured enough coarse language and cruel humor to alienate critics and audiences alike. Nevertheless, *People* magazine singled out Peter Gerety, playing the squad lieutenant, as being a "standout," whose voice "pops and squeaks like bubble wrap."

Although *Public Morals* wasted Gerety's talents, he was soon snapped up by *Homicide* during the cast shakeups between the fifth and sixth seasons. Gerety had not only already appeared on *Homicide*, he had also worked with producer Barry Levinson on the 1996 feature film *Sleepers*.

In joining the cast of *Homicide*, Gerety proudly noted that "the characters have complexity and depth to them and the writers are always one step ahead of the audience." Indeed, his role is one that is guaranteed to spark interesting confrontations with the other detectives.

PETER GERETY—SELECTED CREDITS

FILMS

Wolf (1994)
Miracle on 34th Street (1994)
Surviving Picasso (1996)
Mrs. Winterbourne (1996)
Sleepers (1996)

TELEVISION

A Case of Deadly Force (1986) [telefilm]
The Kennedys of Massachusetts (1990) [TV miniseries]
Return to Lonesome Dove (1993) [TV miniseries]
Cagney and Lacey: The Return (1994) [telefilm]
Public Morals (1996) [TV series]
Homicide: Life on the Street (1996, 1997–) [TV series]

Isabella Hofmann

Lieutenant/Captain/Detective Megan Russert (1994–96; 1997)

There is a television maxim that women usually decide what gets watched on TV. For the first two seasons, *Homicide* depicted a male-dominated squad with only one major female character. Meanwhile, *NYPD Blue* (1993–) chalked up high ratings with a heady mixture of sex and racy content. Brought into the cast to recalibrate the gender balance, Isabella Hofmann joined the series in the third season and stayed until the end of the fourth. She returned in the two-part finale to the fifth season.

Ironically for an actress hired specifically to attract new viewers, Hofmann calls herself the "queen of anonymity," and told the *Los Angeles Times* that "no one ever recognizes me. I guess for work, at least, I don't get categorized." Indeed, the actress has had a varied career that stretches from the improvisa-

Isabella Hofmann started her TV career on NBC's sitcom Dear John.
Everett Collection

tional comedy of Second City through a long-running TV sitcom to the gritty urban drama of *Homicide*.

Hofmann's role as Megan Russert (promoted from lieutenant to captain and then cruelly demoted all the way down to detective) represented a shift in the series' direction. With the addition of executive producer Henry Bromell in 1994, the show would start to stray farther from the specifics of David Simon's book. Russert would be the first major character not derived from one of Simon's real-life detectives. Hofmann was jealous that her costars had met the real detectives behind their roles, while she only spoke with technical advisers.

In addition, Hofmann felt nervous joining an established ensemble cast. Although future cast changes would indeed provoke the ire of dedicated fans who felt the new characters were stealing screentime from their favorite performers, Hofmann joined early enough in the show's evolution to escape such harsh scrutiny, and was quickly accepted.

Isabella Hofmann was born in Chicago on January 11, 1957. Like several of her *Homicide* costars, Isabella began her showbiz career at a very young age, dancing with the Chicago Park District at age five, even though her German-Lithuanian immigrant parents disliked her chosen path. She recalls her father particularly objected because, he felt, "the American art scene was cheap and seedy!"

She earned her degree in theater and music from Columbia College in her native Chicago in 1981. Along with *Homicide* costar Clark Johnson, she is a veteran of the famed Second City improv comedy troupe, having earned a spot on their main stage. Then followed a successful string of live performances with regional theaters, where she appeared in such shows as *Teibele and Her Demon* and *Uncle Vanya*.

Isabella made her mark on network TV playing Kate McCarron for four years on NBC's *Dear John* (1988–92), as well as guest spots on such shows as *Night Court* (1987) and *Sisters* (1991). Her feature-film credits include *Real Men* (1987), *Tripwire* (1989, with future costar Yaphet Kotto), *I'll Do Anything* (1993), and *Renaissance Man* (1994).

In July 1994, the producers of *Homicide* began looking for a new cast member to add more physical appeal to the show, as part of a set of changes intended to broaden its viewership. Meanwhile, Hofmann was hoping to broaden her range (and credits) with a dramatic role.

She auditioned on a Wednesday with an assistant casting director. On Friday, she was reading for Barry Levinson himself. By Sunday, she left Los Angeles for Baltimore to become Megan Russert.

The character of Megan Russert was devised as a way to add sex appeal and address gender politics in the Police Department at the same time. "[S]he is in a male-dominated arena where she has to show her strength and competence," Hofmann explains, "but she is not trying to be a man."

Above all, Hofmann welcomed the opportunity to dramatize these issues. The actress feels that the women's movement has pushed so hard for gender equity in the workplace that they have driven women to try to act like men in order to be accepted. Hofmann appreciated that her character did not hide from her femininity, and demanded that her male-dominated workplace accept her for who and what she is. Not surprisingly, given their predilection for raiding the lives of the show's performers for story material, the writers of *Homicide* let the character of Russert speak for Hofmann's point of view.

During the 1994–95 season, Megan Russert had a love affair with Detective Beau Felton, played by Daniel Baldwin. As with so many of *Homicide*'s onscreen romances, there is an offscreen connection as well. Hofmann and Baldwin were living together when she joined the show, and they later married.

The couple kept a Baltimore residence for the duration of the shooting schedule, but they officially live in Los Angeles. "Daniel's a great cook," Hofmann enthused to the *Los Angeles Times*, adding that "if Daniel's working on a feature, I'd like to travel with him somewhere."

In October of 1996 she gave birth to their son, Atticus Baldwin (the first grandson for the Baldwin clan). To accommodate her motherhood, Megan Russert was written out at the start of the fifth season as having moved to Paris with a new flame.

During her absence from *Homicide*, Hofmann appeared on NBC's top-rated *ER* (1996) as a doctor attending to Jeanie Boulet, the physician's assistant stricken with AIDS (played by Gloria Reuben, herself a former *Homicide* guest).

Hofmann returned to *Homicide* for an uncredited cameo (by voice only, on a phone call to her former coworkers) in the strangely self-conscious fifth-season Episode 67: "The Documentary." At the end of the season, she briefly returned to the cast, joking that she was "packing us all up and driving to Baltimore, just like the Clampetts." Baldwin returned to Baltimore with his wife, but not to *Homicide*. The season finale that reintroduced Megan Russert involved the death of Baldwin's character Beau Felton.

ISABELLA HOFMANN—SELECTED CREDITS

FILMS
Real Men (1987)
Tripwire (1990)
Renaissance Man (1994)
The Amazing Panda Adventure (1995)
Twisted Desire (1996)

TELEVISION
Independence (1987) [telefilm]
The Town Bully (1988) [telefilm]
Dear John (1988–92) [TV series]
...And Then She Was Gone (1991) [telefilm]
The Boys (1993) [TV series]
Homicide: Life on the Street (1994–96, 1997) [TV series]
She Fought Alone (1995) [telefilm]

Clark Johnson

Detective Meldrick Lewis (1993–)

Born in Philadelphia on September 10, 1954, Clark Johnson began his acting career at the tender age of nine. Johnson started as a child actor in such touring musicals as *Finian's Rainbow*, *Porgy and Bess*, and *South Pacific*.

However, he did not stay with acting as he matured. Johnson had been a wide receiver at Eastern Michigan University (which he attended on a partial football scholarship), and was drafted by the Canadian Football League's Toronto Argonauts in 1979. His stint as a pro football player was in the actor's own words "short and pathetic." Johnson recalls, "The CFL paid me 250 bucks a week one season to stay home."

After attending Montreal's Loyola Film School and the Ontario College of Art as a film major, Clark redirected his energies into special effects. He rigged explosions and other effects on several David Cronenberg features: *The Dead Zone* (1983), *Videodrome* (1983), and *The Fly* (1986). One of the blasts on *The Dead Zone* earned him dozens of stitches in his arm when it misfired. "[David] Cronenberg came over with a pail [to catch the blood]," Johnson told *Entertainment Weekly*. "He has a very strange sense of humor."

Gradually, Johnson found himself migrating back into acting. He trained at the Actors' Lab in New York and joined Toronto's branch of the famed Second City improvisational comedy troupe. In the mid-1980s, he began appearing in made-for-television features, like *Starcrossed* (1985), *Killing 'Em Softly* (1985), *Rockabye* (1986), and *Courage* (1986).

In 1986, he landed a role in the Canadian-produced television series *Hot Shots* (1986–87) as *Crime World* magazine researcher Al Pendelton. At about the same time, from 1986 to 1988, Clark also played the recurring role of Detective Dave Jefferson in the Canadian crime drama *Night Heat* (1985–91).

This experience soon led to roles in major motion pictures such as *Wild Thing* (1987), *Nowhere to Hide* (1987), *Adventures in Babysitting* (1987, with a young Elisabeth Shue), *Iron Eagle II* (1988, with Lou Gossett Jr.), *Colors* (1988, with Robert Duvall and Sean Penn), *Drop Zone* (1994, with *Homicide* costar Kyle Secor), and *Nick of Time* (1995, with Johnny Depp).

His television credits also include a recurring role as Clarke Roberts on the series *E.N.G.* (1990), and Johnson provided the voice of the cartoon version of rapper M.C. Hammer in ABC's Saturday-morning show *Hammerman* (1991–92). In 1996, he appeared with future *Homicide* costar Michelle Forbes in Tom Fontana's made-for-television feature *The Prosecutors*.

In 1993, Barry Levinson and Tom Fontana cast him as Detective Meldrick Lewis in *Homicide: Life on the Street*. The role was very loosely based on Baltimore Homicide Detective Donald Waltemeyer, but Fontana admits he did little to flesh out the character in the first two seasons. "I thought it'd be great to have a character who was totally unwilling to share with the people he worked with," Fontana explained in *Entertainment Weekly*.

After the suicide of his partner Detective Steve Crosetti in season three, more of Detective Lewis's character began to be developed, and he became a much more prominent member of the cast. By the fifth season, with Andre Braugher planning to leave the series, *Homicide* began to shift its focus away from the powerhouse team of Pembleton and Bayliss to the newly partnered duo of Lewis and Kellerman.

Clark Johnson in a made-for-TV movie before his Homicide *days.*
Everett Collection

Although he claims not to be very fond of actors-turned-directors, Johnson has directed several installments of *Homicide*, becoming the first cast member to take the directorial reins. Clark had already proven his skills as a director in live theater, as well as numerous music videos and episodes of *Under African Skies*, a Family Channel series starring Robert Mitchum and Catherine Bach. Recently, Johnson began work on *Chalk Shadow*, a feature film he will both write and direct.

Thus, Johnson is seriously considering leaving acting to pursue directing full-time. "I'm really just enjoying directing. I'm going to slowly ease into the directing side of things and get back to acting when I want to, because that's the perfect career to me."

Clark splits his time between his home in Toronto, and Baltimore where he spends eight months out of the year filming *Homicide*. Around Charm City, the warm and funny actor has earned the respect of locals, who call him "Big Johnson." He is married to documentary producer Heather Salmon, who is close friends with Karen Williams, the actress who plays Johnson's wife on *Homicide*.

Clark has two daughters from a previous marriage. Cassandra and Michaela Johnson have shown an entrepreneurial streak, selling shaved-ice cones to visitors to *Homicide*'s notoriously open set. While their father directed Episode 68: "Betrayal" for season five, Cassandra and Michaela sold impromptu *Homicide* tours to a group of senior citizens.

Johnson enjoys straddling the worlds behind and in front of the cameras. During his time on *Homicide*, the actor has taken side work as a special-effects technician on other projects. He counts his 1965 spring-wound Bolex movie camera as one of his most prized possessions, an affinity which links him with countless independent filmmakers who have likewise discovered the joy of making moving images.

CLARK JOHNSON—SELECTED CREDITS

FILMS
Killing 'Em Softly (1985)
Blindside (1986)
Wild Thing (1987)
Nowhere to Hide (1987)
Adventures in Babysitting (1987)
Iron Eagle II (1988)
Colors (1988)
Renegades (1989)
The Finishing Touch (1992)
Final Round (1993)
Drop Zone (1994)
Soul Survivor (1995)
Rude (1995)
Nick of Time (1995)
Lulu (1996)

TELEVISION
Starcrossed (1985) [telefilm]
Murder: By Reason of Insanity (1985) [telefilm]
Night Heat (1986–88) [TV series]
Rockabye (1986) [telefilm]
Courage (1986) [telefilm]
Hot Shots (1986–87) [TV series]
Hostage (1988) [telefilm]
The Women of Brewster Place (1989) [telefilm]
Psychic (1990) [telefilm]
Personals (1990) [telefilm]
E.N.G (1990) [TV series, recurring role]
Coopersmith (1992) [telefilm]
Homicide: Life on the Street (1993–   ) [TV series]
Silent Witness: What a Child Saw (1994) [telefilm]
Model By Day (1994) [telefilm]

Yaphet Kotto

Lieutenant Al ("Gee") Giardello (1993–)

One of the most accomplished performers in *Homicide*'s ensemble cast, Yaphet Kotto was born November 15, 1944, in Harlem, New York City. His father, also Yaphet Kotto, was a former merchant marine who had immigrated from what was then called the Cameroons. Kotto grew up surrounded by an eclectic mix of cultures. His parents spoke many languages, as did their African-immigrant friends. Additionally, Kotto was born and reared as a black Jew.

As a child in the Bronx, he found his yarmulke marked him as "different" in a community populated by Baptists. "On Fridays I was in some heavy fist-fights," he remembers. "It definitely wasn't too cool being black and Jewish."

Following his parents' divorce, young Yaphet Kotto was raised by his maternal grandparents and was baptized as a Catholic. While he attended Roman Catholic schools, he found himself more and more confused about his religion.

Later in life, Kotto discovered a religious sect called the Self-Realization Fellowship, with tenets derived from many world faiths. As a member of the Self-Realization Fellowship, Kotto became a vegetarian and started meditating three times daily.

After researching his family history for fifteen years, Yaphet discovered his personal background is even richer and more distinctive than previously imagined. He uncovered evidence that he is actually the Crown Prince of the Royal Bell family of Doualla in West Africa's Cameroons.

Furthermore, he claims that he is the great-great-grandson of Queen Victoria! Kotto detailed his lineage in his autobiography *The Royalty*. According to Kotto, he is descended from a liaison between Cameroon's Princess Nakande and Prince Edward Albert VII. Buckingham Palace has denied the claim, to which Kotto responds, "They've been covering up for him for centuries. He was a notorious womanizer."

As a child, Kotto became involved with Harlem street gangs and dropped out of school at age sixteen. While he told his family that he was looking for work, the young man was actually spending time at the movies. Upon seeing a screening of *On the Waterfront* (1954), Yaphet became entranced by Marlon Brando. "I knew from that moment that I wanted to be an actor," Kotto told the *Chicago Tribune*.

Studying acting at the American Conservatory Theater and carefully improving his diction by analyzing recordings of radio personality John Cameron Swayze, Kotto began acting with the Actors' Mobile Theater Studio at the age of sixteen. Within three years, he made his professional debut as Othello in Shakespeare's classic drama.

Moving to California to pursue his dream, the actor began appearing in various television series, and made his feature-film debut in 1964, earning critical acclaim for his supporting performance in director Michael Roemer's underrated *Nothing But a Man*.

This work led to a long and highly acclaimed career on the stage and in film. Kotto's breakthrough role came when he succeeded James Earl Jones as Jack Johnson in the Broadway production of *The Great White Hope*. He was undaunted by taking over the star-making role from Jones, and soon received overwhelming critical praise. Kotto and Jones were later reunited on the set of *Homicide* for the three-part sixth-season opener, "Blood Ties" (Episodes 79–81).

Kotto was also nominated for an Olivier Award for his role as Troy in the London production of August Wilson's *Fences*. The actor took pride in his work in this production, but found it difficult to live up to the classic role of Troy.

His feature film credits now span three decades, from *Four for Texas* (1963) through *Brubaker* (1980), to *Two If by Sea* (1995). He played the villainous Mr. Big in the 1973 James Bond adventure *Live and Let Die*, was killed by the title's star in *Alien* (1979), starred in *Freddy's Dead: The Final*

Yaphet Kotto has played cops so often he has begun to think he is a police officer. *Everett Collection*

Nightmare (1991), and appeared with *Homicide* costar Richard Belzer in *The Puppet Masters* (1994).

In 1972, Kotto stretched his muscles on the other side of the cameras, writing, directing, and starring in *The Limit*. He has also lent his directing talents to a documentary called *The Last Warning*, which he also produced and starred in with Dionne Warwick. Despite his directing skills, Kotto insists he has no interest in directing an episode of *Homicide*, something costars Clark Johnson and Kyle Secor have done. Instead, he penned the script for the fifth-season Episode 76: "Narcissus."

Kotto earned an Emmy nomination for his portrayal of Idi Amin in the 1977 made-for-television feature *Raid on Entebbe*. He also appeared in the acclaimed miniseries *Roots* (1977), and has been a guest star in such television series as *The Big Valley* (1965–69), *Bonanza* (1959–73), *Gunsmoke* (1955–75), *Hawaii Five-O* (1968–80), *Mannix* (1967–75), *Murder, She Wrote* (1984–96), *The A-Team* (1983–87), *Hill Street Blues* (1981–87), *Civil Wars* (1991–93), and *seaQuest DSV* (1993–97).

When Barry Levinson, Tom Fontana, and Paul Attanasio were developing David Simon's book into a series, they based the character of Lieutenant Al Giardello on Shift Commander Gary D'Addario (known to his troops as "Dee"), who joined the series as a consultant and approved scripts for their accuracy. D'Addario maintained his presence on the set, not only as a technical advisor, but also as an actor, playing the Quick Response Team's Lieutenant Jasper.

The creators of *Homicide* chose not to cast an Italian-American actor as Giardello ("Gee"), even though the real-life model was so close at hand. Barry Levinson knew exactly who he wanted for the role, saying that, "Yaphet has great credibility, a simple strength, a quiet passion."

Thus, Levinson's decision added a deeper ethnic nuance to the character. Instead of an Sicilian-American, Kotto's Gee became an Sicilian–African-American. "They had the daring to make the artistic choice without prejudice of any kind," Yaphet marveled. "I don't think there's another network show on the air with this sort of cast composition."

Kotto has drawn from his highly varied experiences with mixed ethnicity to portray the uncommon blend of cultures in his character. As a sort of father figure on *Homicide*, Lieutenant Giardello has earned the trust and respect of his detectives, and of the audience. Kotto even discovered that he had become an unlikely sex symbol, when an enamored female fan French-kissed him on the street.

Although the exposure of the show brought him many starstruck female admirers, Kotto has maintained a celibate life throughout the production of

Homicide's first five seasons. He joked that the celibate life made it easier to concentrate on his lines. Always serious and spiritual, Kotto was saving himself for his beloved.

It was in 1993 that Yaphet met Tessie Sinahon while on vacation in the Philippines. The middle-aged actor stopped to ask a Filipina secretary, twenty years his junior, for directions, and the two immediately fell in love. They were quickly engaged, but also quickly separated (by geography only).

In March 1997, as production ended on season five of *Homicide*, Kotto applied for a visa for Sinahon so that they could marry and enjoy their honeymoon before filming resumed in July. At first, the Immigration and Naturalization Service refused, noting that in five years the couple had not seen each other once. The INS enforces such policies in order to keep phony weddings from being used to win green cards illegitimately.

Kotto protested that he had been unable to visit Sinahon because of the enormous distance involved. The flight between Baltimore and the Philippines is a staggering twenty-two hours, far too long for the kind of weekend breaks the busy actor could afford to take. To demonstrate the seriousness of his love, Kotto showed INS officials his phone bills, which topped $1,000 per month with multiple daily calls to his fiancée.

The INS finally accepted Kotto's "extreme hardship" defense and waived their policy to grant the visa. In May 1997, Sinahon arrived to join Kotto in his Toronto home, where he was completing work on another movie.

Tessie Sinahon is the third Mrs. Kotto. Yaphet also has six children from his previous marriages. One of his daughters, Sarada, has appeared on *Homicide* as a killer, while one of his sons is a San Diego police officer.

Kotto has long been immersed in the world of the police, since his uncle died in the line of duty as a New York City policeman. In his almost fifty movie roles, Yaphet has appeared as a law enforcement officer twenty times. Naturally, he has started to think of himself as a cop.

"Now I believe I am a policeman," he joked as the Frederick, Maryland Police Department named him an honorary captain for his work on *Homicide*, "I suspect everyone I meet of committing a crime. Anyone who talks to me, I think they're lying."

In developing his role as Giardello, Kotto also drew from his experiences on *Live and Let Die* (1973). During that production, he had occasion to meet a British secret-service agent who was advising the producers, and the actor later patterned Gee's speech patterns and persona on this agent.

When he first joined the *Homicide* cast, Kotto became flustered by the loose production style and the wandering camera. "I forgot my lines," Kotto told the *Chicago Tribune*, "I was really embarrassed. That had never happened to me before." Levinson had to take him aside and reassure him that he could handle the role.

Over time, Yaphet found himself becoming more comfortable with the unusual production methods. By the second season, he claimed he sometimes forgot he was acting and would become completely immersed in his character.

Kotto blames *Homicide*'s middling ratings on its lack of gratuitous violence. Although the series has not had the widespread commercial appeal of shows like *Law and Order* (1990–) and *The X-Files* (1993–), both of which Kotto watches regularly, he is proud of his work on it.

When Barry Levinson first offered him the part, Kotto had two competing feature-film offers. He turned those jobs down to appear on *Homicide*, and in the subsequent six years has repeatedly turned away other, much higher paying, offers.

Kotto says that he grew up watching black actors degraded and caricatured. "I swore when I was nineteen I would never do that on the screen. I would always stand up tall and straight. I was not going to leave an image of people to feel ashamed of," and, he adds with pride, "I've upheld that in every single [role] I've done."

For Kotto, working on *Homicide* is a rare opportunity to perform something worthwhile and valuable, and he relishes every minute of it.

YAPHET KOTTO—SELECTED CREDITS

FILMS
Four for Texas (1963)
Nothing But a Man (1964)
Five Card Stud (1968)
The Thomas Crown Affair (1968)
The Liberation of L. B. Jones (1970)
Man and Boy (1972)
Bone (1972)
Across 110th Street (1972)
The Limit (1972) [director]
Live and Let Die (1973)
Truck Turner (1974)
Shark's Treasure (1975)
Report to the Commissioner (1975)
Friday Foster (1975)
Drum (1976)
Monkey Hustle (1977)

Blue Collar (1978)
Alien (1979)
Othello (1980)
Brubaker (1980)
Fighting Back (1982)
The Star Chamber (1983)
Warning Sign (1985)
Terminal Entry (1986)
Eye of the Tiger (1986)
Prettykill (1987)
The Running Man (1987)
The Jigsaw Murders (1988)
Midnight Run (1988)
Ministry of Vengeance (1989)
A Whisper to a Scream (1989)
Tripwire (1990)
Hangfire (1991)
Freddy's Dead: The Final Nightmare (1991)
Intent to Kill (1993)
Extreme Justice (1993)
Almost Blue (1993)
The Puppet Masters (1994)
Dead Badge (1995)
Out-of-Sync (1995)
Two If by Sea (1996)

TELEVISION
Night Chase (1970) [telefilm]
Raid on Entebbe (1977) [telefilm]
Roots (1977) [TV miniseries]
Rage! (1980) [telefilm]
Women of San Quentin (1983) [telefilm]
For Love and Honor (1983) [TV series]
Badge of the Assassin (1985) [telefilm]
Harem (1986) [telefilm]
The Park Is Mine (1986) [telefilm]
Desperado (1987) [telefilm]
In Self-Defense (1987) [telefilm]
Perry Mason: The Case of the Scandalous Scoundrel (1987) [telefilm]
Prime Target (1989) [telefilm]

After the Shock (1990) [telefilm]
Homicide: Life on the Street (1993–) [TV series]
It's Nothing Personal (1993) [telefilm]
The American Clock (1993) [telefilm]
The Corpse Had a Familiar Face (1994) [telefilm]
Deadline for Murder: From the Files of Edna Buchanan (1995) [telefilm]

Melissa Leo

Detective-Sergeant Kay Howard (1993–97)

Despite the trailblazing efforts of TV's *Cagney and Lacey* (1982–88), the majority of roles for women in prime-time dramas amount to little more than window-dressing. Even *Homicide's* better-known rival, *NYPD Blue* (1993–), has relegated its female cast members to love interests and foolish dames (and has been paid back with the almost daily departures of its actresses).

In this environment of televised glass ceilings, Melissa Leo's Kay Howard has stood as a glorious reminder, week after week, that being female doesn't mean you have to be predictable.

With her virtually unbroken streak of closed cases, Kay Howard is one of the Homicide Division's top investigators. David Simon's book *Homicide* describes a female detective named Bert Silver, who matches Kay in some superficial respects, and a male detective, Rich Garvey, whose true-life perfect streak puts the detective closer to Kay in spirit. Garvey's run of luck ran only about a year, however, and had as much to do with luck as skill. In translating the character into Kay Howard, the writers let the streak continue for years, and let the character take personal pride in her obvious professionalism.

Melissa Leo was born in New York on September 14, 1960. Her parents split up when she was young. Melissa sought refuge in the fantasy world of acting, confessing, "I was never very comfortable being myself." When her family split up, her mother moved Melissa and her brother Erik first to Vermont, and then to London.

In London, Melissa Leo enrolled in a theater school. When her mother decided to return to the United States, Melissa chose to stay behind on her own. With her mother's permission, the sixteen-year-old Leo rented her own place and stayed in London. "People say, 'Did you leave home?'" Leo told *People* magazine, "No, home left me."

The decision not only set Leo firmly on her career track, but it taught her an independence and self-reliance that would infuse the characters she would later play.

Melissa Leo in the feature film, **A Time of Destiny.** *Everett Collection*

In 1980, Leo returned to America to study theater at the State University of New York at Purchase, but left before graduating to begin her professional career. Almost immediately, she was cast as Linda Warner on *All My Children* (1970–), a role for which she earned an Emmy nomination in 1985. Other *All My Children* veterans such as Gwen Verdon, Lynne Thigpen, and Anne Meara later appeared on *Homicide* in various guest roles.

Since her breakthrough role on the soap, Melissa has had a career studded with roles in off-beat, independent feature films. The extremely versatile Leo can be seen in *Streetwalkin'* (1984), *Immaculate Conception* (1992), *Code of Ethics* (1997), *Under the Bridge* (1997), and the 1993 feature *The Ballad of Little Jo*, about a female cowboy who pretends to be a man to escape the era's limited choices for women. She costarred with William Hurt and Timothy Hutton in *A Time of Destiny* (1988), and has also appeared in several Henry Jaglom movies: *Always* (1985), *Venice/Venice* (1992, with David Duchovny), and *Last Summer in the Hamptons* (1995).

On the theatrical stage, Leo appeared in the New York Shakespeare Festival's *Don Juan,* The American Jewish Theater's *Today I Am a Fountain Pen,* New York's WPA Theater's *The White Rose* and *Out of Gas on Lover's Leap,* and in *A Touch of the Poet* at the Long Wharf Theater in New Haven, Connecticut. She costarred with Christopher Walken in *Cinders* at the Joseph Papp Public Theater and starred in the world premiere of Tennessee Williams' *Will Mr. Merriwether Return from Memphis?*

Leo also had a recurring role from 1989–92 on *The Young Riders* as the cook Emma Shannon. She has appeared in several TV movies, including *The Carolina Skeletons* (1991) and *Nasty Boys* (1996, which also provided proving grounds for future *Homicide* costar Michelle Forbes and *Law and Order* star Benjamin Bratt). Leo has made guest appearances on *Miami Vice* (1984), *Spenser: For Hire* (1985), *The Equalizer* (1985), and *Law and Order* (1993).

In 1993 she was cast in *Homicide: Life on the Street*. Unlike her costars, Leo declined to shadow the Baltimore detectives as preparation for the role. She explains, "I don't like to look at the horror that's in the world."

The early Kay Howard, with her gently made-up features and occasional sexual dalliances with other cops and district attorneys, belied the character she would become later. Before long, Leo had the clout and the courage to insist that her character would not wear makeup.

Over the years, Melissa Leo and her writers moved Kay away from the confines of the typical female TV role to be her own woman. "She is not the ninth generation of *Charlie's Angels*," said producer Tom Fontana. Leo's fine features and wild red hair displayed a beauty and a femininity that came from within, owing nothing to cosmetics or coiffure. This is not the image TV usually promotes, since cosmetics advertising is more profitable than building female self-esteem.

"Kay has given me all kinds of strength," Leo confided to *TV Guide*, "She doesn't isolate herself. She gets right in there. And that is not only how she has survived but succeeded in this career."

In contrast to the stars of NBC's highly rated sitcom *Friends* (1994–), in which a gaggle of three impossibly thin young ladies spend their days tittering girlishly about clothes, boys, and shopping, Detective Kay Howard is professional, smart, and strong. In the unique group of female performers who are allowed to be such on TV, Kay's character is the only one to escape the usual damsel-in-distress routine or the petty diminutions of becoming a sex object. Even when police videographer J. H. Brodie (Max Perlich) fell head over heels in crush with her, it became an unrequited love affair in which the man longed for the woman.

In 1995, in recognition of her leadership qualities, the writers promoted Howard to sergeant. Unfortunately, these developments moved Kay out of the limelight of the show and into a minor, supporting role. Without a partner and promoted to a desk-sergeant role, Kay no longer went out on cases and therefore had little screentime (although in real life, Baltimore police sergeants do go out on cases).

This fading into the background corresponded with a difficult time in Melissa's private life that interfered with her ability to involve herself as thoroughly in her role as she had done previously. Leo found herself battling an ugly domestic dispute in real-life court when she could have been in front of the cameras.

Melissa splits her time between Baltimore and New York with her young son Matthew. His father is actor John Heard, the dad from the *Home Alone* movies (1990, 1992). Leo and Heard were never married, and Leo currently lives with her boyfriend, ski instructor John Russell. Heard began to harass the two, prompting Leo to take Heard to court, accusing him of assault, harassment, and for reportedly stalking her and Russell in their Fells Point home. Heard claimed the matter was a simple "father's rights" issue.

In court, Leo played tapes of some of Heard's alleged "hundreds" of harassing phone calls. Leo told the court she felt "continually abused," and described the experience "like living in a war zone." Reciting how Heard would watch them through binoculars, violating the terms of the custody agreement, and how he had allegedly physically attacked Russell, Leo said, "I fear for the safety of my son and my safety." Heard countered he was only trying to be a real father for his son.

It was not the first time the two had been in court over the matter. In 1991, Heard was arrested for assaulting Leo in a custody dispute, an incident that had resulted in the restraining order Heard was now accused of violating.

Baltimore District Court Judge Barbara Waxman dismissed some of the charges, but Heard was convicted of trespassing and telephone misuse. Waxman sentenced him to thirteen to eighteen months' probation and ordered him to attend a twenty-two-week program for people who batter their partners. She also ordered Heard to seek psychological counseling and to have no contact with Leo or Russell except to arrange court-approved visitation with his son.

Heard grumbled that the judge was directly to blame for the loss of his theatrical career. However, if the unfortunate public battle hurt anyone's career, Leo lost the most. Already victimized by the incident, Leo found herself fired from *Homicide* to boot. NBC fretted about the effect Leo's prominence in the tabloids would have on the reputation of their prestige drama, and decided not to renew the option on her contract for the sixth season.

NBC's decision, thought to be both unfair and unwise by many fans, depleted the already-dwindling world of prime-time female role models, and cost the network dearly in the public-relations department. Angered fans immediately started a letter campaign against NBC, its affiliates, and its sponsors.

In response to the public outcry, producer Tom Fontana announced that NBC was not responsible for ousting Leo, and claimed he alone had made the decision after losing interest in writing for her character. However, when asked, just a few months earlier, if he anticipated any cast changes after the fifth season, Fontana had insisted he expected the entire cast to return for the sixth season.

"I was saddened and surprised by NBC's decision not to renew my option before my sixth season of *Homicide*," Leo told the press, "I had been looking forward to getting back to work. Detective Kay Howard was a wonderful and unique character, one I took great pride in portraying. There were not enough women like Kay on TV, and now there are none. She will be missed."

Yes, Melissa Leo, you will be sorely missed.

MELISSA LEO—SELECTED CREDITS

FILMS
Streetwalkin' (1984)
Always (1985)
Deadtime Stories (1987)
A Time of Destiny (1988)
Venice/Venice (1992)
Immaculate Conception (1992)
The Ballad of Little Jo (1993)
Last Summer in the Hamptons (1995)
Code of Ethics (1997)
Under the Bridge (1997)
Fear or Fiction (1998)

TELEVISION
Silent Witness (1985) [telefilm]
Nasty Boys (1989) [telefilm]
The Young Riders (1989) [TV series]
The Bride in Black (1990) [telefilm]
Carolina Skeletons (1991) [telefilm]
Homicide: Life on the Street (1993–97) [TV series]
Scarlett (1994) [TV miniseries]
In the Line of Duty: Hunt for Justice (1995) [telefilm]

Max Perlich

Police Videographer J. H. Brodie (1995–97)

Born in Cleveland on March 28, 1969, and raised in Los Angeles, Max Perlich dropped out of high school at age sixteen to pursue acting. Although

**Max Perlich with his
costars from the film
Beautiful Girls.**
Archive Photos

Hollywood usually eats young actors alive, Perlich managed to achieve success at a tender age, demonstrating a flair for character acting that earned him several Independent Spirit Award nominations.

His film credits cover acclaimed and independent features as well as bigger blockbuster productions: *Ferris Bueller's Day Off* (1986), *Gleaming the Cube* (1989), *Drugstore Cowboy* (1989), *Rush* (1991), *The Butcher's Wife* (1991), *Cliffhanger* (1993), *Born Yesterday* (1993), *Maverick* (1994), *Feeling Minnesota* (1996), and *Beautiful Girls* (1996).

In 1995, Perlich joined the cast of *Homicide*, first as a recurring character and later as a regular. "He's a vid kid," said producer Tom Fontana as he introduced police videographer J. H. Brodie in the fourth season. "We live in an age now where everybody wants a video of a crime scene."

Although the character of Brodie has no counterpart in David Simon's book, actor Max Perlich won the unique opportunity to embody the spirit of David Simon himself. In the bizarrely self-referential Episode 67: "The Documentary," Brodie unveils a video he has made of the squad, which provokes the same reactions from the fictional detectives that Simon's book engendered in real life. In defending his journalism, Brodie makes a speech that invokes the same philosophy that guided Simon in his work.

In this regard, though, Perlich shares little of his character's maturity and self-control. In December 1996, Max got into a heated parking dispute with a neighbor at his Baltimore residence. The actor rampaged out of his home, threatening his neighbor with a loaded .45-caliber pistol, and firing two shots into the air.

The police arrested Perlich for alleged weapons violations as well as alleged possession of marijuana. Before going to trial for the claimed felony weapons charges, though, Perlich's lawyer successfully argued that the police had failed to obtain a search warrant before entering the defendant's home and seizing his gun. Ruling the search and seizure illegal, the judge dropped the weapons charges, but initially kept the misdemeanor marijuana charge. Finally, all charges were dropped.

Upset at the unsavory headlines, NBC decided to drop Perlich from the cast at the end of his contract. At the close of the fifth season, NBC announced the character of Brodie would not return in the fall. Perlich's manager Cynthia Campos-Greenberg diplomatically commented, "It was a mutual situation. A lot of people have come and gone from the cast over the years." She added that Perlich was "honored" to have been a part of the excellent series.

MAX PERLICH—SELECTED CREDITS

FILMS
Ferris Bueller's Day Off (1986)
In the Mood (1987)
Can't Buy Me Love (1987)
The Allnighter (1987)
Vibes (1988)
Plain Clothes (1988)
Lost Angels (1989)
Gross Anatomy (1989)
Gleaming the Cube (1989)
Drugstore Cowboy (1989)
The Horseplayer (1990)
Genuine Risk (1990)
Rush (1991)
Liebestraum (1991)
The Butcher's Wife (1991)
Cliffhanger (1993)
Born Yesterday (1993)
Toughguy (1994)
Shake, Rattle and Rock! (1994)
Maverick (1994)
Dead Beat (1994)
Terrified (1995)
Georgia (1995)
Homeward Bound II: Lost in San Francisco (1996)
The Grave (1996)

Feeling Minnesota (1996)
Beautiful Girls (1996)
Truth or Consequences, N.M. (1997)
Men with Guns (1997)
Gummo (1997)
The Brave (1997)

TELEVISION
Home Fires (1987) [telefilm]
TV 101 (1988) [TV series]
Homicide: Life on the Street (1995–97) [TV series]

Jon Polito

Detective Steve Crosetti (1993–94)

When Obie Award–winning character actor Jon Polito auditioned with producer Barry Levinson for a role in the new series *Homicide: Life on the Street*, he read for the role of a Polish cop. Levinson called him back to read for an Irish one (based on real-life detective Terry McLarney). This became the role he landed, but Levinson and Fontana had the part rewritten and renamed to give Polito an Italian background. In casting *Homicide*, the producers took an unusual path in making their selections based upon the actor chosen. Thus, they adapted the genders and ethnicities of the characters to suit the actors. It was a policy that gave *Homicide*'s cast a more eclectic, realistic edge, unlike shows that are carefully crafted to meet some demographic checklist.

Polito found himself in the company of very talented and accomplished costars, under the demanding eyes of perfectionist producers creating an experimental show. "The work itself is so intense. Everybody's working so hard," Jon said, "This is much more of a theater atmosphere."

The actor knew what he was talking about. Polito's twenty-year career included extensive stage work. His Broadway credits go all the way back to 1977's *American Buffalo* and the 1984 revival of *Death of a Salesman*. Polito also starred in the original Hartford Stage Company production of *Other People's Money*.

Polito got his feature film break in *The Killing Hour* (1981), and soon took the role of mobster Tommy Luchese in the 1981 television series *The Gangster Chronicles*. With his raspy voice and distinctive physique, the talented Polito was a natural for crime dramas. Although born in the City of Brotherly Love (Philadelphia, PA) four days after Christmas of 1950, Jon found himself typecast in roles as gangsters and bad guys.

Jon Polito became a favorite actor of the Coen Brothers after his role in Miller's Crossing.
Everett Collection

"That's pretty much all there is for men in movies," the actor said, "Fortunately I've had a few good-guy parts. But I don't see me being cast as a happy father. It just doesn't play."

Not that Polito minded too much. As he explains, "I've always been interested in the Quasimodo type, whose dark side is obvious, but who's also got some redeeming qualities if you just peel back the layers. It's a challenge to make that kind of character accessible."

Despite his many roles, Polito perhaps may be best remembered for his work with the filmmaking team of Joel and Ethan Coen, whom Jon calls "the most gifted nerds I've ever met."

Their association began in 1990, when he was cast in the crime film *Miller's Crossing.* At first, the Coens wanted Polito to play a small role as a bodyguard. He insisted he only wanted to play gangster Johnny Caspar. It would be two months before he heard back, but the Coens ultimately conceded that Polito would be the best choice for the role of the raging, violent mafioso. Critics and audiences loved Polito as Caspar, and the actor returned to work with the Coens in *Barton Fink* (1991) and *The Hudsucker Proxy* (1994).

Although the Coens cast Polito against type in their subsequent collaborations, for the most part the character actor continued to play bad guy after bad guy. In 1993, Polito got another opportunity to escape typecasting. In reviewing the pilot episode of *Homicide: Life on the Street, New York Times* reviewer John O'Connor suggested that Polito's role as Detective Steve Crosetti could be "the kind of career break Joe Pesci found in the *Lethal Weapon* movies."

The role of Steve Crosetti was not only based on Baltimore homicide investigator McLarney, but also shared character traits with series producer

Tom Fontana. Fontana lent the character his own obsession with the assassination of Abraham Lincoln. This quirky and memorable touch gave the first season some of its best comic relief.

If Polito was hoping that *Homicide* would give him a career boost, though, the show would first have to get viewers. *Homicide's* struggles with the ratings in its first years put the show on NBC's chopping block more than once. After two years, Polito had only appeared in thirteen episodes, and NBC was again deliberating whether to kill the show or give it yet a third chance.

Jon was no stranger to this situation. From 1986 to 1988, NBC broadcast what critics called an "ambitious" cop drama, *Crime Story*. Producer Michael Mann (creator of *Miami Vice*) set his new series in Chicago, 1963, and Polito had a guest role as mobster Phil Bartoli. Ratings were poor, but NBC gave the show two seasons in an effort to let that small audience grow. After two years, though, when the ratings continued to languish, NBC dropped the ax.

Polito then played LAPD Captain Ross in the ABC series *Ohara* (1987). ABC built the show around Pat Morita, the elder star of the *Karate Kid* movies. When the first season failed in the ratings, ABC retooled it (without Polito) for a second, and final, season in 1988.

Polito's next experience with network TV was even less encouraging. He played a casino manager in *Hearts Are Wild* (1992) which was canceled in only three months.

Once again, *Homicide* survived cancellation, but without Polito. NBC renewed the series for a third season, but demanded some changes to make it more mainstream. One of the items on their list was to dump Polito, whom NBC executives reportedly considered unappealing.

When informed that he was to be written out of the series, Polito decided that he should be killed off.

"Aside from the fact that real homicide detectives are rarely confronted by violence, I believe it's a real threat in their lives," Jon explained, "The violence aspect should be emphasized, especially since my character has never been good with a gun, obviously. He's been shot several times before."

Polito negotiated with the producers to reprise his character long enough to be shot down in the line of duty. The producers declined, keeping Detective Crosetti's whereabouts unknown until revealing that he had shot himself.

Obviously disappointed, Polito left the show on less than amicable terms, never getting the career boost for which he'd hoped. Ironically, Episode 19: "Crosetti," in which his character's fate is revealed, is one of the series' all-time best, but does not feature Polito himself. While his character left a lasting legacy on the series, the actor himself never reaped the just rewards of all his efforts.

JON POLITO—SELECTED CREDITS

FILMS

The Killing Hour (1981)
C.H.U.D. (1984)
Remo Williams: The Adventure Begins... (1985)
Compromising Positions (1985)
Fire with Fire (1986)
Highlander (1986)
Dream Lover (1986)
Critical Condition (1987)
Homeboy (1988)
Miller's Crossing (1990)
The Freshman (1990)
Delusion (1991)
The Rocketeer (1991)
Barton Fink (1991)
Leather Jackets (1992)
Flodder in Amerika (1992)
Blankman (1994)
The Hudsucker Proxy (1994)
The Crow (1994)
Fluke (1995)
Bushwhacked (1995)
Just Your Luck (1996)
The Corporate Ladder (1996)
Homeward Bound II: Lost in San Francisco (1996)
Whiskey Down (1996)
Inside Out (1997)
The Big Lebowski (1998)
Talos the Mummy (1998)

TELEVISION

The Gangster Chronicles (1981) [TV series]
Death of a Salesman (1985) [telefilm]
A Deadly Business (1986) [telefilm]
Crime Story (1986) [TV series]
Ohara (1987) [TV series]
Alone in the Neon Jungle (1988) [telefilm]
Hearts Are Wild (1992) [TV series]

Fallen Angels (1993) [TV series]
Homicide: Life on the Street (1993–94) [TV series]
Girls in Prison (1994) [telefilm]
The Shaggy Dog (1994) [telefilm]
The Invaders (1995) [TV miniseries]
Robin Cook's Invasion (1997) [TV miniseries]

Kyle Secor

Detective Tim Bayliss (1993–)

The detective stands motionless in the rain, staring down at the body of the child. Wrapped in a red raincoat, the girl lies dead in the alleyway, discarded like so much garbage. Raising his badge to identify himself, the detective gulps his name in anguish at the sight of the body, "Bayliss, Homicide."

It was one of the early tests to establish *Homicide*'s look, and producer Barry Levinson worked with the colorists to bleed out all the colors except the red in the girl's raincoat. Even in its starkest form, the scene's real power lay not in the sight of the child's body but in the horrified reaction on Bayliss's face. No matter how hard Levinson tried to heighten the shock of seeing the girl's corpse, Kyle Secor's understated performance upstaged it.

In his five years as *Homicide*'s most emotionally raw character, Secor has taken his role on a bumpy ride. The series has often plunged its characters into situations where the unpleasant facts of their jobs touch them personally. Almost every character has had to investigate a close friend or be investigated themselves at one point or another. Some characters have even been shot or killed over the years. Yet the writers do not need to put Bayliss on the spot so obviously in order to expose his nerves, almost any incident will suffice to make him squirm.

"Being a detective may be the thing that he chose, but it may not be the thing that he is," Secor told *Television Today*, "He's really more suited to run a halfway house or a homeless shelter."

As the show progressed, the writers began to flesh out the character's background with revelations that sometimes caught the actor by surprise. Secor decided the wisest course was to focus on his role scene by scene, day by day, and not worry too much about character continuity. By letting his instincts guide him, Kyle managed to develop a very consistent, yet complex and fascinating, character.

Over time, Secor found himself making suggestions about how the character should be written. "I now feel I have something to contribute to the overall texture and tone of the show," he told the *New York Daily News* in 1996.

Kyle Secor has rarely been recognized for his quiet, brooding performance as the sensitive Detective Bayliss.
Everett Collection

In the show's fifth season, after sudden and unexpected revelations about Bayliss's past as a political activist, Secor grumbled that sometimes the writers came up with inappropriate character developments. Secor turned to producer Fontana with his own suggestion. The actor invented an element of the character's past that he felt would help link all the bits of backstory already established, and help explain Bayliss's trademark raw nerves: Secor suggested that Bayliss had been sexually abused as a child.

Tom Fontana readily agreed to Kyle's suggestion. Eerily, the notion was so cogent and right that it made sense of moments scattered throughout the earlier episodes which had been written with no advance knowledge of this development. Secor's understanding of his character was so acute that, five years into playing him, he could unveil a piece of the character's history that fit perfectly into what had already been established.

Despite being half of *Homicide*'s most prominent detective team, Kyle Secor has received surprisingly very little press attention or accolades. Instead, he has quietly worked his magic in the shadow of costar Andre Braugher, just as his character has been eclipsed by Braugher's character onscreen. Like a well-oiled comedy team, the easy banter and familiarity between Secor and Braugher seems so natural and so unforced that the audience completely accepts them as the characters they play.

Like several of his *Homicide* colleagues, Kyle Secor cut his acting teeth in the world of daytime drama. Secor was born in Federal Way, Washington, on May 31, 1958. He was fascinated with acting as a child. After graduating from high school, Kyle went to visit his older brother in glamorous Hollywood, where he took a few roles on the stage and managed to catch the eye of talent scouts. In 1987, Secor joined the cast of the cult hit soap *Santa Barbara* in the role of Brian Bradford.

His work on this series led to roles in made-for-television movies such as the 1988 remake of *Inherit the Wind* with Jason Robards and Kirk Douglas. This, in turn let to the greater prestige of feature films such as *Sleeping with the Enemy* (1991), *The Doctor* (1991), and *City Slickers* (1991).

Secor also had a recurring role on *St. Elsewhere* (1982–88) as a gay AIDS patient named Bret Johnson. A bitter man with a shaved head, Secor's role not only moved audiences but caught the attention of *St. Elsewhere* producer Tom Fontana.

When Fontana began looking for an actor to portray the fictionalized version of Baltimore's Detective Tom Pellegrini, he remembered Secor. Soon, the actor had a chance to meet his real-life counterpart. Pellegrini offered advice to Secor on how to play the role, but the actor got his best lessons from things the detective did not say.

In 1997, Secor joined costar Clark Johnson as another *Homicide* cast member to direct an episode. Secor loved the experience of directing Episode 70: "Diener," and looks forward to directing again soon. In between takes, while his colleagues took lunch, Secor huddled over a textbook on film editing. This was a throwback to when his character, rookie detective Bayliss, huddled over a Homicide investigation textbook while working his first case.

Although he read the film guide, Secor enjoyed the freedom to ignore it. Secor especially praised *Homicide*'s defiance of the traditional rules of editing. Instead of concentrating on correct continuity as a way of establishing visual realism, *Homicide*'s directors are encouraged to pursue emotional realism. If the best and most dramatic performance comes at the expense of technically correct continuity, so be it.

Secor knows that *Homicide*'s strength has never been in the breadth of its audience, but in the depth of their commitment. "Maybe the people out there think we're doing something that's good," Secor once reflected, "good for their hearts or their souls."

KYLE SECOR—SELECTED CREDITS

FILMS
Heart of Dixie (1989)
Sleeping with the Enemy (1991)
Late for Dinner (1991)
The Doctor (1991)

Delusion (1991)
City Slickers (1991)
Untamed Heart (1993)
Drop Zone (1994)

TELEVISION
Santa Barbara (1987) [TV series]
Shootdown (1988) [telefilm]
Inherit the Wind (1988) [telefilm]
The Outside Woman (1989) [telefilm]
In the Line of Duty: Siege at Marion (1992) [telefilm]
Middle Ages (1992) [TV series]
Homicide: Life on the Street (1993–) [TV series]
Midnight Runaround (1994) [telefilm]
Beauty's Revenge (1995) [telefilm]
Her Desperate Choice (1996) [telefilm]

Jon Seda

Detective Paul Falsone (1997–)

North Jersey native Jon Seda joined the cast of *Homicide* at the end of its fifth season, playing Detective Paul Falsone. Seda joked that he was doing the reverse of what Nicholas Turturro was doing on the rival cop show *NYPD Blue*. "Nick Turturro is an Italian playing a Puerto Rican," Seda remarked, "and I'm a Puerto Rican playing an Italian."

Born in 1970, Seda quickly distinguished himself as a rising star, with roles in such acclaimed and popular movies as *I Like It Like That* (1994, directed by *Homicide* guest director Darnell Martin), *The Sunchaser* (1996), and *Selena* (1997). With the entertainment industry declaring Seda a hot young actor, the producers of *Homicide* wisely decided to highlight him in the sixth season.

TV critic Michelle Greppi wrote that Seda "has 'breakout' written all over his character." Perhaps the writers were overusing Detective Falsone at first, but they did so in the same way that previous "new guys" Bayliss and Kellerman had been introduced.

TV Guide senior editor Beth Arky proclaimed Seda one of "TV's Top 20 Sexy Stars." When asked about his taste in women, Seda told *TV Guide* that he is "an EOE man: Equal Opportunity Employer," but admits he has a crush on Winona Ryder.

TV Guide *named Jon Seda one of the sexiest men on TV.* Everett Collection

In shaping the role of Falsone, the writers of *Homicide* worked in a few details of actor Seda's personal life. When Falsone reveals that he is the father of a three-year-old, Seda pulled out a photo of his own three-year-old son, Jonathan.

JON SEDA—SELECTED CREDITS

FILMS
Zebrahead (1992)
Gladiator (1992)
Carlito's Way (1993)
I Like It Like That (1994)
Twelve Monkeys (1995)
The Sunchaser (1996)
Primal Fear (1996)
New York Cop (1996)
Dear God (1996)
Selena (1997)
The Price of Kissing (1997)

TELEVISION
Mistrial (1996) [telefilm]
Homicide: Life on the Street (1997–) [TV series]

Calliope "Callie" Thorne

Detective Laura Ballard (1997–)

As the press began to announce details about *Homicide*'s sixth season and the upcoming cast shakeups, even longtime *Homicide* boosters found themselves at a loss to provide details about the latest addition, Callie Thorne as Seattle-transplant Detective Laura Ballard. Not even NBC could provide biographical details about their new star, deferring all questions to Tom Fontana.

Fontana was the only person who could answer them, because he alone was the reason the young unknown actress was brought on board. Fontana so much wanted to cast Thorne on the show that he went on a personal mission to woo her away from the set of an independent feature shooting in Nantucket and down to Baltimore. The *Boston Herald* quoted Thorne's mother saying, "He didn't want anyone else but Callie to play the part of this new female detective. So he went out on a campaign to get her."

Thorne was born in November 1969 in Lincoln, Massachusetts. Her mother, Karen Thorne (an astrologer to the stars) named her daughter after Calliope, the Greek muse of heroic poetry. Callie graduated from Wheaton College and went on to study acting at the famed Lee Strasberg school in New York.

When Fontana tapped her for her role in *Homicide*, the young actress had only a handful of credits to her name, among them the critically acclaimed low-budget feature *Ed's Next Move* (1996) and the action thriller *Turbulence* (1997). Thorne also has had valuable experience with the Naked Angels, an acting troupe in her native Manhattan.

Callie Thorne won Tom Fontana's attention for her role in Ed's Next Move.
Everett Collection

As her debut in the season premiere Episode 79: "Blood Ties" approached, NBC described her character as a sort of female counterpart to Frank Pembleton (which, of course, means that they will not get along) who moved to Baltimore from Seattle because of "the death of grunge."

"They were looking for a certain type of a strong woman," says Thorne, explaining that the writers had incorporated aspects of her personality in her onscreen character. "I definitely follow my instincts, and [Ballard] follows her gut instincts. But the difference is, sometimes, when I come up against people in my real-life confrontations, I'm not up for the fight."

Although she was a self-confessed fan of the show, when the time came to fly to Baltimore and begin filming her first episode, Thorne had butterflies in her stomach. She asked her manager to come with her, but he refused to walk her onto the set. Despite her anxiety, the cast and crew welcomed the latest addition to their ranks with open arms.

"By the third or fourth day, I felt like I'd been there forever," Thorne told the *New York Daily News* "I was hanging out with the boys. And I was really happy they were including me."

CALLIE THORNE—SELECTED CREDITS

FILMS
Ed's Next Move (1996)
Turbulence (1997)
Next Stop Wonderland (1997)
Casanova Falling (1998)
Chocolate for Breakfast (1998)
RopeWalk (1998)

TELEVISION
Homicide: Life on the Street (1997–) [TV series]

THE SUPPORTING CAST

In addition to the seventeen lead players, *Homicide* has also benefited from a very strong supporting cast.

The vast majority of *Homicide*'s players hail from the Washington-Baltimore film and video industry. The series' casting director, Pat Moran, is renowned for her discerning eye and ability to select the precise actor for each role. Moran has a policy that no actor may appear on the show in more than one role. This contrasts with such shows like *Law and Order* (1990–), in which actors routinely play different characters in different episodes.

On a few and rare occasions, Moran's policy has been violated. Walt MacPherson played a beat cop in the first season before appearing as Roger Gaffney, and guest performer John Waters has played both a bartender and a killer.

Otherwise, though, Moran's one-actor, one-role policy meant that performers who landed a recurring role hit the jackpot, while actors who were cast in larger guest roles may have had more screentime but were unlikely to reappear. A handful of actors, such as Dan DePaola and Frederick Strother, found steady employment in nonspeaking roles as detectives, strolling back and forth in the background of each episode. A few, like Beau James (Detective Higby) or Lance Lewman (Detective Castleman) had brief roles that seemed like one-time walk-ons, only to be brought back years later when their characters were reprised.

Even luckier are actors like Richard Pilcher, Julie Lauren, or Peggy Yates, who get to appear week after week in minor, yet speaking, roles as cops, reporters, and so on. These recurring characters create a consistent onscreen community for the series. The following chart outlines these characters by category, and then includes some biographical information on a few of the more prominent faces among them.

CHARACTER

Police

CHARACTER	ACTOR
Deputy Commissioner James Harris	Al Freeman Jr.
Colonel Bert Granger	Gerald F. Gough
Captain/Colonel George Barnfather	Clayton LeBoeuf
Detective/Captain Roger Gaffney	Walt MacPherson
Lieutenant Jasper (Quick Response Team)	Gary D'Addario
Sergeant Mark Deutch	Richard Pilcher
Sergeant Sally Rogers	Kristin Rohde
Officer Chris Thorman	Lee Tergesen
Officer Anne Schanne	Julie (Grossberg) Lauren
Officer Salerno	Jay Spadaro
Detective Higby (Homicide, second shift)	Beau James
Detective Mitch Drummond (Bomb Squad, Stan Bolander's former partner)	Tony LoBianco
Detective Theresa Walker (Sex Crimes)	Gloria Reuben

Naomi (Homicide secretary)   Sharon Ziman
Judy (Homicide secretary)   Judy Thornton

Medical Examiners

Dr. Scheiner   Ralph Tabakin
Dr. Carol Blythe   Wendy Hughes
Dr. Alyssa Dyer   Harlee McBride
Dr. Lausanne   Herb Levinson

The Law

Assistant State's Attorney Ed Danvers   Zeljko Ivanek
Assistant State's Attorney Maggie Conroy   Helen Carey
Darrin Russom (Defense Attorney)   Michael Willis
Monica Murphy (Defense Attorney)   Pat Dade
Gail Ingram (Federal Prosecutor)   Rebecca Boyd
Judge Susan Aandahl   Sagan Lewis

Reporters

Maria Delgado   Peggy Yates
Dawn Daniels (although her character was not
    named for several seasons, and once identified
    herself onscreen as "Rhonda Overby")   Rhonda R. Overby
Grant Besser   Mel Proctor
Matt Rhodes   Tony Todd

Loved Ones

Mrs. Mary Whealan Pembleton   Ami Brabson
Mrs. Beth Felton   Mary B. Ward
George Bayliss (Tim's uncle)   Robert Bornath
Jim Bayliss (Tim's cousin)   David Morse
Wesley Howard (Kay's father)   Michael Currie
Margie Bolander (Stan's ex-wife)   Dana Ivey
Mrs. Barbara Lewis   Karen Williams
Tim Russert (Megan's cousin)   Tim Russert
Linda (Stan's girlfriend)   Julianna Margulies
Mr. Kellerman (Mike's father)   Pat McNamara
Drew Kellerman (Mike's brother)   Eric Stoltz
Greg Kellerman (Mike's brother)   Tate Donovan

Ami Brabson

Mary Whealan Pembleton (1993–98)

Like her real-life husband Andre Braugher, Ami Brabson is a talented theatrical performer. Since receiving her masters of fine arts from New York University's Graduate Acting Program, Brabson has performed in New York in such shows as *The Way of the World* and *Kubuku Rides*. She played Harriet Tubman in *Freedom Train*. Also like Braugher, she is a Shakespearean actor, with roles in *Macbeth*, *Othello*, and *A Midsummer Night's Dream*.

Similar to many of *Homicide*'s cast, she has TV daytime drama (soap) credits to her name as well. In fact, she is arguably best known for her role as Faith Campbell on *One Life to Live*.

Erik Todd Dellums

Luther Mahoney (1996–97)

California representative Ron Dellums has heard it all before—the conspiratorial tone as well-wishers cluck their tongues that his son has turned out so bad....

Of course, his son Erik Todd Dellums has not "turned out bad" at all. He is a rising actor, who merely plays a villainous drug lord on TV. But then, *Homicide* has always confused reality with fiction.

"I knew I had done my job," the younger Dellums told the *Washington Post*, "when a young couple saw me and started packing up their things. We were all standing in front of a restaurant and they immediately reacted as if I was some really bad person."

Like his father, Erik Todd Dellums is officially a California resident who spends the bulk of his time inside the Beltway. He was born in Berkeley but grew up in Washington and studied political science at Brown University. His acting debut was in a feature film about the D.C. "go-go" club scene, called *Good to Go* (1985). A year later, Dellums appeared in Spike Lee's famed independent hit *She's Gotta Have It* (1986). Dellums also appeared in Lee's *School Daze* (1988), and in Oliver Stone's *The Doors* (1991).

Zeljko Ivanek

Assistant State's Attorney Ed Danvers (1993–)

A longtime friend of Tom Fontana's, Zeljko Ivanek (pronounced ZHEL-ko Ee-VAH-nek) has had a remarkably full career for such a young character

Zeljko Ivanek made his motion picture debut in the 1982 film The Sender. *Everett Collection*

actor. In addition to playing Maryland prosecutor Ed Danvers on *Homicide*, Zeljko has had prominent guest roles on *Law and Order* (1993), *The X-Files* (1994), *Frasier* (1997), *Millenium* (1997), and *Chicago Hope* (1997).

Fontana cast Ivanek as Danvers because he felt that the part as written was rather dull and simple, and he knew Ivanek would "make it a real character." Ivanek also makes a natural choice for a prosecutor, since he is often typecast in straitlaced roles of men in suits. "I have this tidy look," Ivanek explained to *Entertainment Weekly*.

In 1997, Ivanek joined a number of *Homicide* alumni on the set of the feature film *Donnie Brasco*. Like *Homicide*, *Donnie Brasco* is a crime drama based on real-life events and characters. Produced by Barry Levinson, Gail Mutrux, and Louis DiGiaimo, *Donnie Brasco* features performances by both Ivanek and Walt MacPherson. Ivanek's other feature films have included *Mass Appeal* (1984), *Rachel River* (1987), *Our Sons* (1991), *School Ties* (1992), *White Squall* (1996), and *Infinity* (1996).

Harlee McBride

Medical Examiner Dr. Alyssa Dyer (1994–97)

Harlee McBride is a former *Playboy* model and the star of the *Young Lady Chatterley* movies from 1977 and 1985. She met Richard Belzer on a blind date in 1981, and the two fell in love. They started living together, and in 1985 they were married. It was Belzer's third marriage and McBride's second, she having two teenage daughters from her first marriage.

"Richard softened me a lot," says McBride, "When I met him, I was cynical about men and life, but he's somebody I've grown to trust and feel comfortable with. Marriage relaxed him too."

In 1994, McBride made her first of many appearances as Medical Examiner Alyssa Dyer on *Homicide*. Her offscreen relationship with Belzer translated into a brief onscreen affair. In a scene during the fifth season finale Episode 78: "Strangers and Other Partners," the character Dyer revealed that after dating Munch she started seeing a stand-up comedian(!!).

Walt MacPherson

Detective/Lieutenant/Captain Roger Gaffney (1993; 1994–)

Baltimore native Walt MacPherson first appeared on *Homicide* as an unnamed responding officer in a handful of first season episodes.

Later, the actor got a bigger recurring role as "the man you love to hate," Roger Gaffney. After butting heads with both Detective Pembleton and Lieutenant Russert on the white-glove murders (Episodes 14: "Nearer My God to Thee"; 15: "Fits Like a Glove"; and 16: "Extreme Unction" of Season Three), Gaffney was transferred out of the Homicide Unit and into Missing Persons. His sloth and arrogance did nothing to hold him back from two swift promotions: first to lieutenant, and then to captain (getting his revenge by taking away Megan Russert's job).

MacPherson has worked with Baltimore's leading directors Barry Levinson and John Waters before: *Tin Men* (1987) and *Donnie Brasco* (1997) for Levinson, and *Serial Mom* (1993) for Waters. He can also be seen in *The Exorcist III* (1990) and *In the Line of Fire* (1993). MacPherson is perennially typecast: aside from his role in *Tin Men* as a car salesman, he has always played law enforcement officers!

Ralph Tabakin

Medical Examiner Dr. Scheiner (1993–)

Grumbly Dr. Scheiner has been a fixture on *Homicide* since the beginning. Character actor Ralph Tabakin has a long history with fellow Baltimorean Barry Levinson. Levinson has cast Tabakin in almost all of his films: *Diner* (1982), *The Natural* (1984), *Young Sherlock Holmes* (1985), *Tin Men* (1987), *Good Morning, Vietnam* (1987), *Rain Man* (1988), *Avalon* (1990), *Bugsy* (1991), *Toys* (1992), *Jimmy Hollywood* (1994), *Disclosure* (1994), and *Sleepers* (1996).

Michael Willis

Darrin Russom (1993–)

As the sleazy defense lawyer Darrin Russom, actor Michael Willis takes pleasure taking on the show's heroes, and defending the bad guys they toil so hard to catch. While the lead actors shadowed real Baltimore detectives to prepare for their roles, Willis admits that, aside from having a low opinion of trial lawyers, he did not engage in any direct research for his recurring part.

Michael began his award-winning career after returning from a tour of duty in Vietnam. He went into acting in search of a social life, and found himself on a track that led him to the floorboards of the Washington-Baltimore area's acclaimed Woolly Mammoth and Roundhouse Theaters. In 1989, he won the prestigious Helen Hayes Award for his work at the Woolly Mammoth.

Willis has also appeared on *Law and Order* (1997), in a guest role that won him a Best Actor award, and in a walk-on part in the smash hit *Men In Black* (1997).

THE PRODUCTION CREW

Barry Levinson

Executive Producer

It comes as no surprise to those who know Charm City's favorite son, that the production company of acclaimed motion-picture director Barry Levinson is named Baltimore Pictures. The executive producer of *Homicide: Life on the Street* admits he wanted to adapt David Simon's book into a television series largely because of its setting.

Levinson has consistently set his productions in Baltimore and drawn from his personal experiences there as a basis for his storytelling. "I don't find it any different from a writer who wrote about his particular region," Levinson explains, citing the works of William Faulkner and Tennessee Williams as examples, "When I would sit down to write these pieces, Baltimore and its characters and its rhythms just made sense to me."

In addition to using Baltimore settings and local color, Levinson's productions have also created a motion-picture community in the Baltimore area that would not have existed otherwise. When he chose to film *Diner* there in

1982, he found production resources and personnel extremely limited. Beginning with *Diner*, Barry developed a production base to support his own creations, and thereby generated the resources for a flourishing film economy in Baltimore.

In producing *Homicide*, Levinson relied on this local talent for a staggering ninety-five percent of his production crew. "We had to come to Baltimore for this series," he explains, "You couldn't shoot it in Los Angeles. You can only fake so much."

In fact, Levinson and his colleague Tom Fontana insist that *Homicide*'s roster of writers live in Baltimore. This demand not only results in only the most dedicated writers staying with the show, but also it keeps the flavor of Baltimore depicted accurately onscreen.

Levinson became one of Hollywood's most highly regarded writer-directors by a rather unusual path. He was born on April 6, 1942, to a family of Eastern European immigrants living in Baltimore. A listless young man, Barry attended the American University in Washington, D.C., studying broadcast journalism because he found it relatively undemanding. Eventually, Levinson dropped out.

"I probably had as little ambition as anyone could possibly have," the producer-to-be told the *New York Times*, "In my own stupidity, I thought that you could go through life and continue to get an allowance."

Levinson started off working in a television station to support himself, but gradually drifted to California. He enrolled in an acting class on a lark and discovered an innate flair for comedy. Writing and performing live comedy sketches led him to London and a stint as a writer for *The Tim Conway Show* in 1970 and for *The Marty Feldman Comedy Machine* in 1971. From 1974 to 1976, he wrote for *The Carol Burnett Show*, where he won three Emmys.

Levinson then graduated to motion pictures, cowriting with Mel Brooks the scripts for *Silent Movie* (1976) and *High Anxiety* (1977), the latter in which Levinson made a brief appearance. Brooks encouraged the young writer to make a film based on the stories he was always telling about "the Ten Boys" with whom he hung out in his childhood.

Inspired by Brooks, Levinson persuaded MGM to allow him to film *Diner* in his hometown Baltimore with a cast of unknowns. The result won him universal critical acclaim and an Oscar nomination for Best Screenplay, as well as becoming a springboard for some of today's best-known actors. David Denby wrote in *New York* magazine that Levinson had written "'overheard' dialogue, so dead-on accurate and funny that one stares at the screen in wonder." Pauline Kael wrote in *The New Yorker* that "Levinson doesn't violate his characters by summing them up—he understands that we never fully understand anybody."

Although MGM had worried at first that *Diner* was nothing more than "a bunch of guys sitting around talking," Levinson confidently explained that a movie is never anything more than "one person talking to another, a series of small moments."

In 1988, Levinson earned Oscars for Best Picture, Best Director, and Best Screenplay for *Rain Man*. He has also been nominated for Best Screenplay for . . . *And Justice for All* (1979), *Diner* (1982), and *Avalon* (1990). In 1991, Barry's *Bugsy* was nominated for ten Oscars, won Best Director and Best Picture from the Los Angeles Film Critics, won a Golden Globe for Best Picture, and was nominated for both Directors' Guild and Writers' Guild awards. Levinson also has directed *Disclosure* (1994) and *Quiz Show* (1994) from screenplays penned by *Homicide's* creator, Paul Attanasio.

Homicide was not Levinson's first foray into television. In 1981, he developed *Diner* as a television series, to star Paul Reiser and James Spader. CBS broadcast the pilot in the summer, but declined to pick up the show as a series. "It was ahead of its time, I think."

Some viewers have said the same of *Homicide*.

Levinson directed *Homicide's* pilot episode, "Gone for Goode," and won the 1993 Emmy for Best Direction. He later directed the third season finale, Episode 33: "The Gas Man," and appeared as himself in Episode 67: "The Documentary."

Part of what has brought Levinson so many awards and so much recognition is his uncompromising belief in taking risks and finding the drama and comedy in places Hollywood typically doesn't look. This is a man who hit the big time with the commercial and critical hit *Rain Man* (1988), who then used his power as an Academy Award winner to make a small, very personal film, *Avalon* (1990). While other producers may have been tempted to disown such a commercial failure as *Toys* (1992), Barry proudly stands by his work and insists if he had to do over again he would not change a thing.

Levinson has consistently chosen to engage in challenging, difficult, experimental projects instead of the play-it-safe approaches of his peers. It is this dedication to quality that has infused every aspect of *Homicide: Life on the Street*.

Levinson is married to Diana Mona (his second wife), whom he met when he cast her daughter in *Diner*. They live with their four children (two of whom are Levinson's stepchildren from Mona's previous marriage) in Bel-Air, California and Annapolis, Maryland.

BARRY LEVINSON—SELECTED CREDITS

FILMS

Silent Movie (1976) [writer, actor]
High Anxiety (1977) [writer, actor]
...And Justice for All (1979) [writer]
Inside Moves (1980) [writer]
History of the World—Part 1 (1981) [actor]
Diner (1982) [director, writer]
Best Friends (1982) [writer]
Unfaithfully Yours (1984) [writer]
The Natural (1984) [director]
The Young Sherlock Holmes (1985) [director]
Tin Men (1987) [director, writer]
Good Morning, Vietnam (1987) [director]
Rain Man (1988) [director, actor]
Avalon (1990) [producer, writer]
Kafka (1991) [executive producer]
Bugsy (1991) [producer, director]
Toys (1992) [producer, director, writer]
Jimmy Hollywood (1994) [producer, director, writer, actor]
Disclosure (1994) [producer, director]
Quiz Show (1994) [actor]
Sleepers (1996) [producer, director, writer]
Donnie Brasco (1997) [producer]
Wag the Dog (1997) [director]
Sphere (1998) [producer, director]

TELEVISION

Homicide: Life on the Street (1993–) [TV series; executive producer, director of Episodes 1: "Gone for Goode" and 33: "The Gas Man"; actor in Episode 67: "The Documentary"]

Tom Fontana

Executive Producer

Barry Levinson's name and prestige may have been the driving force behind *Homicide*'s genesis, but the true creative force behind the show's development has been Tom Fontana. He has been variously described by those who work with him as an "excellent TV writer," a "regular guy," and a "balls to the wall" producer. Throughout his career, Fontana has maintained consistent high standards, placing the quality of a show's writing as his first priority.

In 1993, *Homicide's* first Emmy went to Tom Fontana's daring script, Episode 5: "Three Men and Adena." The award for Outstanding Individual Writing for a Drama Series would not be the last honor for the series, and was not the first for Fontana.

Homicide is one of only two TV drama series ever to be awarded a Peabody. The only other fictional series to have been honored with the broadcast industry's most distinguished award is Fontana's other alumnus, *St. Elsewhere* (1982–88). During his five years with *St. Elsewhere*, Fontana took home not only the Peabody, but also two Emmys (out of fourteen Emmy nominations), the Humanitas Prize, and the Writer's Guild of America Award.

Fontana has often turned to *St. Elsewhere's* pool of talent, both off- and onscreen, to help staff *Homicide*. Veterans of *St. Elsewhere* (Howie Mandel, David Morse, Edward Herrmann, Sagan Lewis, Robert Clohessy, Dan Hedaya, Zeljko Ivanek, Mimi Kennedy, Helen Stenborg, Eric Stoltz, and Jerry Stiller) have taken guest roles in *Homicide*, while *Homicide* regular Kyle Secor once had a recurring guest role on *St. Elsewhere*. Former *St. Elsewhere* crew member Julie Martin is one of *Homicide's* head writers and supervising producers. Onetime *St. Elsewhere* day players, Tim Van Patten and Kathy Bates, have joined *Homicide* as guest directors.

Indeed, *St. Elsewhere's* unusual casting of comedian Howie Mandel in a dramatic role as Wayne Fiscus can be seen as a precursor to *Homicide's* similar tactic with stand-up comedy star Richard Belzer being cast as hard-boiled cop John Munch.

St. Elsewhere producer Bruce Paltrow joined his protégé Fontana to help launch *Homicide*, directing the first season Episode 4: "A Shot in the Dark." Paltrow first hired Tom on *St. Elsewhere* based on the strength of one of Fontana's plays, *The Spectre Bridegroom*, and helped nurture Fontana's talent for scriptwriting. Inspired by Paltrow's mentoring, Tom hopes to use his success to help launch other young careers in turn.

Fontana is very proud of his involvement in the highly acclaimed *St. Elsewhere*, but finds its style dated today. In *Homicide*, Fontana has retooled some of *St. Elsewhere's* narrative and stylistic devices for the 1990s.

St. Elsewhere became noted for its abusive streak toward its main characters, an attitude Fontana has continued on *Homicide*. *New York Daily News* TV critic David Bianculli marveled that "no weekly drama in TV history messed with its main characters more than *St. Elsewhere*...major characters—male and female—were raped. Others became rapists, got their faces slashed, contracted AIDS, committed suicide, had strokes and died." Bianculli goes on to note that week after week, "*Homicide* continues to chip away at [*St. Elsewhere's*] record."

Fontana is also demonstrably fond of settings that place characters in an emotionally charged environment. By situating volatile characters in intense and demanding surroundings, Fontana can spark more naturally the kind of character-based conflict he enjoys writing. For *St. Elsewhere* it was a hospital, for *Homicide* it is a big-city police department, and in his recent venture for HBO, *Oz* (1997–) it is a prison.

Fontana's concern for exceptional writing comes naturally to a trained playwright. He has had his works performed by San Francisco's American Conservatory Theater, the Cincinnati Playhouse in the Park, the Buffalo Studio Arena Theater, the McCarter Theater Company, and the Chelsea Theater Center.

As a playwright-in-residence at New York's famed Writers' Theater, Fontana has had the opportunity to help nurture the theatrical community that he has always prized. Having achieved success as a writer, Tom uses his position at the Writers' Theater to encourage new talent.

Working with the Writers' Theater, Fontana codirected a short film, *Nothing But the Truth*, one of the rare few productions to have been shot on HDTV. However, Fontana admits he has little interest in feature filmmaking, preferring instead to focus his energies on his television career.

Ironically, Tom also confesses he watches very little TV. Yet with *St. Elsewhere* and *Homicide*, he has made significant and lasting contributions to raising the quality of network TV dramas. Before *Homicide*'s premiere, critics were suggesting that the hourlong drama format was dead, killed by cheap sitcoms and "reality TV." Five years later, those same critics are now hailing a new golden age of TV drama, with *Homicide: Life on the Streets* (1993–), *Law and Order* (1990–), *The X-Files* (1993–), *ER* (1994–), and *NYPD Blue* (1993–) as leading examples of the continued power of the medium.

In 1991, Barry Levinson persuaded Fontana not to move to Tuscany and write "epic poetry" as he had planned, but to join Levinson instead as executive producer of *Homicide*. As this show completed its sixth season, Fontana had risen to be one of the five most powerful television producers in the industry. He was born in September 1951 in Buffalo, New York, and calls Manhattan his home.

Henry Bromell

Executive Producer

Henry Bromell joined *Homicide* as an executive producer in 1994 to help the show find a more mainstream viewership.

"When Tom first asked me if I'd be interested in helping out on *Homicide*," Bromell told the Viewers for Quality Television as he accepted an award for *Homicide*, "I said yes for two reasons. One was Friday nights — I figured Warren [Littlefield, President of NBC Entertainment] would be out and he wouldn't know what we were doing; the other reason is it was so good I figured I wouldn't have to work for more than about six months."

Although Bromell was right that *Homicide*'s refusal to play by TV's rules kept it teetering on the brink of cancellation, in fact the show did survive year after year, demanding ever more from its writers.

Bromell came to the show an already experienced novelist and *New Yorker* short-story writer. Furthermore, Henry had television experience as a writer for such acclaimed dramas as *Northern Exposure* (1990–95) and *I'll Fly Away* (1991–93). Through his teaching at the Iowa Writers' Workshop, he has also helped shape future fiction writers as well.

Bromell's goal was to move away from the procedural approach, which had developed from adapting David Simon's journalism, and, instead, focus on the characters. This new approach not only fleshed out the characters in ways that more fully utilized the excellent ensemble cast, but also made the show more accessible to viewers. The approach also blended perfectly with Tom Fontana's desire to put the characters through the kind of mettle-testing personal crises that have been his trademark as a writer.

With his wife Trish Soodik, Bromell developed a kind of spin-off series of *Homicide*, also filmed on location in Baltimore. Ruben Blades starred in Bromell's *Falls Road* (1997), playing a Baltimore police officer married to a paramedic. Unlike *Homicide*, *Falls Road* was a family drama, focusing on the difficult balancing of a demanding career and raising children. Peter Medak, a frequent guest director for *Homicide*, directed the pilot for NBC.

Additionally, Bromell was one of the producers of *413 Hope Street* (1997), along with Damon Wayans (from the 1990–94 comedy series *In Living Color*) and Eric Launeville. Launeville was also a cast member of *St. Elsewhere* (1982–88) for Tom Fontana, and a director on *I'll Fly Away* for Henry Bromell. Launeville also directed episodes of *NYPD Blue* (1993–) one of *Homicide*'s competitors.

413 Hope Street was based on a counseling center Wayans experienced in his younger days. Michelle Greppi of the *New York Post* praised the series in no uncertain terms: "*413 Hope Street* is the kind of drama that sticks to your ribs, stays in your heart and won't let you forget it or not feel it. *Hope* pulls out all the emotional stops and plays mercilessly on our heart strings, but it does so with an authenticity NBC's misbegotten *Crisis Center* never even approached." (*Crisis Center*, as it happened, was the short-lived series NBC tried out during *Homicide*'s 1997 hiatus.)

During his tenure on *Homicide* from 1994–96 for Seasons Three and Four, Bromell made it a point to bring in the best freelance writers, and worked closely with Fontana to develop story arcs, penning several episodes himself (Episodes 20: "The Last of the Watermen"; 21: "All Through the House"; 27: "End Game"; 33: "The Gas Man"; 55: "The Wedding"; and 63: "The Heart of a Saturday Night"). It was thanks to Bromell's efforts that novelist Jane Smiley came to write 1995's Episode 30: "In Search of Crimes Past."

"In some ways, TV writing is better than most novels," says Bromell.

Julie Martin

Supervising Producer

Supervising producer Julie Martin says that she fights more often on *Homicide* than on any of her previous TV shows. The series is so close to her heart, and she cares so deeply about keeping its standards high, that she finds herself being aggressive in order to keep it as good as it possibly can be. Not too surprisingly, she finds that the people with whom she fights are arguing with her for the same reasons, as well.

Even in her prominent role as a writer-producer and one of the people responsible for bringing the show to life, Martin has found that she is not immune to *Homicide*'s mind-bending "art imitates life" twists. She once said that even she sometimes blurs the distinction between the actors and the roles they play onscreen.

Martin began her association with Tom Fontana as a writer's assistant on *St. Elsewhere* (1982–88). She later continued to work with Fontana and *St. Elsewhere* producer Bruce Paltrow when she joined them on the short-lived half-hour drama series *Home Fires* (1992) as a story editor. Additionally, Martin was a story editor on *L.A. Law* (1986–94).

In 1994, she wrote her first *Homicide* script, Episode 18: "Happy to Be Here." Over time, she and fellow writer James Yoshimura worked their way up to becoming story editors and ultimately supervising producers, taking over more and more of the responsibility for the series while Tom Fontana began to pursue other projects.

Although she is disappointed by *Homicide*'s low ratings and lack of Emmy recognition, she also takes pride in making the series unique, with all the attendant risks. "We're doing a smart, dark, difficult show," she says, "I would like to think that the millions of people who do watch our show would be enough."

David Simon

Producer

Baltimore Sun journalist David Simon had no idea what he was setting in motion when he arranged to shadow the Baltimore Homicide Unit in 1988. When he wrote *Homicide: A Year on the Killing Streets* (1991), he admits, "Mostly I was hoping that I'd sell enough copies to do another one."

In fact, the book became an award-winning best-seller and spawned a TV series. Six years after its publication, Simon was still a journalist and an author, but he had also become a producer of one of the most acclaimed series in television history. His book was being reissued as a book on tape, narrated by Reed Diamond, one of the stars of that series. In addition, not only had he written a second book (*The Corner*), but also the biggest television network in the country was putting its muscle behind promoting that book on the *Homicide* Web site.

Not bad for a local boy. But then, Simon's Baltimore home was a tremendous asset as far as Barry Levinson was concerned. When Simon's book was shipped to Levinson in 1991, the producer was in the early stages of developing a TV series for NBC. *Homicide* arrived at a fortuitous time, and Levinson fell in love with the idea of returning to Baltimore for another production.

Levinson even offered Simon the job of developing the book into the pilot script. Simon demurred, and the job fell to screenwriter Paul Attanasio. However, Simon did start penning scripts in 1994, and later joined as a staff writer, gradually working his way up to producer.

As a writer-producer on the show, Simon has been able to help keep it true to the spirit of his book. Although he admits they must make concessions to keep NBC happy, tossing in more action than he knows is realistic, it's a compromise Simon is in the best position to make. In his efforts to keep the series on track, he has been given the nickname "Nonfiction Boy."

James Yoshimura

Supervising Producer

James Yoshimura graduated from the Yale School of Drama with a Master of Fine Arts in Playwriting in 1977. Like many on *Homicide*'s writing staff, he has extensive playwriting experience, and his work has been performed in Baltimore, Dallas, and San Francisco.

A Baltimore native, Yoshimura hooked up with *Homicide* right from the beginning, penning the show's third episode, "Son of a Gun." Yoshimura was a resident playwright at Juilliard when Fontana tapped him to write for Homicide.

James shares a Juilliard connection with two other *Homicide* coworkers, Andre Braugher and Reed Diamond. Also, like Braugher, Yoshimura attended St. Ignatius College Preparatory, and, like Clark Johnson, he attended Loyola University.

Yoshimura's skillful blending of tragic despair and peculiar comedy became a hallmark of this series, and earned him a promotion to producer. Today, he and Julie Martin are the principal supervising producers, attending to the day-to-day operation of the show while Tom Fontana pursues other endeavors.

"I think you have to be clinically certified that you're a little bent to work on this show," he says.

Episode Guides

Note: The following episode guides are divided by season. Each season has an overview chapter that details the important developments behind the scenes, and chronicles the series' struggle for mainstream TV success.

Following the overview chapters are episode capsules that include cast and credit lists, plot synopses, and commentary about the episodes.

These are presented in the order in which NBC originally aired each episode, which is also the order that Lifetime Cable Television has followed for its reruns. However, this order is not always the chronology intended by the producers. Sometimes, in their effort to reshuffle episodes for the best ratings, NBC has done significant damage to the complicated continuity of the overlapping story lines.

In the text of the episode guides, major continuity errors will be noted, as will the most noteworthy instances of airing episodes out of sequence. If the reader is interested in checking the intended order, please consult the episode list in Appendix A. As an additional resource, the "production code" listed after the episode title identifies the order in which the episodes were shot. For example, Episode 64: "The True Test" is coded 508, the eighth episode of the fifth season.

For purposes of clarity, this guide also includes two episodes that are not actually part of *Homicide*. "Charm City" and "Baby It's You, Part One" are in fact episodes of *Law and Order*, but since they include characters from *Homicide* and are the first parts of stories concluded on *Homicide*, they are included here for the sake of completeness.

The episode titles listed in this guide are the ones assigned to each episode by the writers and producers. These titles have never appeared onscreen, but have been made public through press releases, listings in *TV Guide*, and the occasional misplaced script. NBC has often used different titles in their advertising (for example, "Fire, Part One" was promoted as "City of Flames"). As these titles are not official, they are not used here, but are sometimes mentioned in the text.

CHAPTER 3

The First Season:
A Year on the Killing Streets

Nineteen eighty-eight was drawing to a close, and Detectives Terry McLarney and Dave Brown were working a murder case. They spotted a pair of suspects, and prepared to apprehend them. As the unmarked police-issue Cavalier pulled up to the curb, Detective Brown realized he had caught his trenchcoat in the seatbelt. McLarney already had one of the men against a parked car, but Brown couldn't get out of the car. So, Brown asked the young man in the back seat of the Cavalier to help out. Eager to please, the man got out of the car and helped detain and search the other suspect.

Brown and McLarney's assistant that day was not another police officer. It was *Baltimore Sun* reporter David Simon, a "police intern." Just one year earlier, after considerable negotiations with the department's top brass, Simon had won the right to observe the city's most esteemed investigators at work for a full year.

The detectives reluctantly accepted the journalist into their midst, but gradually became accustomed to his being there. Thus, when they finally became comfortable with his presence, they shared with Simon the inner workings of a most gruesome kind of job.

In 1991, Simon published the results of his year with the detectives under the title *Homicide: A Year on the Killing Streets*. Although a work of nonfiction, the book won a distinguished Edgar Award from America's mystery writers. The Associated Press called it a "a true-crime classic." *The Library Journal* highly recommended it, and *Newsday* praised it as "one of the most engrossing police procedural mystery books ever written."

Mr. Baltimore

In addition to winning widespread praise from critics, *Homicide* caught the approving eye of film director Barry Levinson. The crime-drama genre is a

POLISH HILL

In 1991, when Levinson optioned Simon's book for $10,000 to develop it into a series, CBS began work on a pilot for a new cop show of their own called *Polish Hill.* CBS's series featured two female detectives in Chicago.

Levinson turned to his representatives at the Creative Artists Agency for advice on finding a writer to adapt Simon's book. CAA sent a copy of the *Polish Hill* teleplay by John Wells. Levinson was shocked to discover that Wells' script was seemingly a fairly close adaptation of Simon's book already!

For one thing, the first big case is the abduction of a nine-year-old girl, and the prime suspect is the Candy Man. Levinson saw clear parallels to Simon's tale of an eleven-year-old girl and the Fish Man. Furthermore, *Polish Hill* used a central motif of a case board, with open cases listed in red and closed ones in black; something actually used in Baltimore's police department but rarely found anywhere else. After finding lines of dialogue and descriptions borrowed almost word for word, Levinson decided he had read enough.

Backed by Barry Hirsch, one of Hollywood's most powerful lawyers, Levinson threatened suit against Warner Bros. Levinson had paid for the rights to Simon's book, and was appalled at the seeming plagiarism. Furthermore, *Polish Hill* would precede *Homicide* to the airwaves, making the authorized version seem like a knock-off.

Settling out of court, Warner Bros. removed the controversial elements and renamed the show *Angel Street.* CBS canceled the series after only three episodes, and the matter has never been mentioned again.

venerable one, and perennially popular. Levinson thought an adaptation of *Homicide* would have the same appeal, but with a fresh and original edge, in that Simon's stories exploded many of the myths of the genre. These cops did not always get along with each other, they did not always catch the bad guys, and the bad guys they caught were not always punished. Even when they did their best work and closed their cases, these real-life detectives had little use for the killers' motives, unlike fictional counterparts like Sherlock Holmes or Hercule Poirot.

However, instead of adapting *Homicide* into a feature film, Barry Levinson decided to try his hand at television. Levinson believed that Simon's book would be best as a continuing series rather than a onetime movie, because then the interwoven stories of its characters could unfold gradually, and more naturally.

The director was also drawn particularly to *Homicide* because of its setting. As a Baltimore native, Levinson had already made three films in his hometown, and proudly christened his production company Baltimore Pictures. Levinson was even one of the investor-owners of the Baltimore Orioles baseball team.

Thanks to his efforts, Levinson was responsible for having nurtured a Baltimore-based film industry. The TV version of *Homicide* could be shot on location in Baltimore, a city ignored by a business that often saw everything between New York and Los Angeles as "fly-over country." This was a revolutionary decision at a time when all but one network series was filmed in California.

"It was really all Barry Levinson's doing, Mr. Baltimore Barry," *Homicide*'s co-executive producer Tom Fontana told the *News Tribune*, "No television show had ever been shot in Baltimore."

As a former producer of the highly acclaimed *St. Elsewhere*, Fontana brought considerable skill and television expertise to Levinson's new project. Both producers hoped to stretch the boundaries of network television.

Levinson and Fontana agreed that *Homicide* should be grounded in realism. Not a realism just of setting and narrative, either, but the realism of complex personalities as well. The two producers wanted to bring out the drama of real life, with all its banalities, digressions, and warts.

Levinson and Fontana hired esteemed screenwriter Paul Attanasio (the writer behind the later 1994 film, *Quiz Show*, and the 1997 *Donnie Brasco*) to adapt Simon's book into a TV series. Attanasio wrote the pilot episode, "Gone for Goode," and established the writers' guide that would aid future writers for the show. Attanasio based his TV characters on the dozen or so detectives described in Simon's book, and used its many real-life cases as the basis for the show's multiple story lines.

The creators got the real Baltimore detectives (some of whom had retired from the force by that time) to sign waivers. Several detectives joined the production team as technical advisers and consultants.

Gary D'Addario, the shift commander on whom Lieutenant Al Giardello was based, reviewed scripts for accuracy and even appeared onscreen occasionally. Actor Richard Belzer joked D'Addario would be "keeping everyone honest."

Although D'Addario admits the program compresses time and makes other concessions to poetic license, he stresses that Levinson and Fontana have always put authenticity as their highest priority.

For his part, Fontana praises the contributions of the real-life detectives to the series, "They have great stories, and the rhythms of their different personalities are so special that it's great to have them around."

Guerrilla Television

Levinson and Fontana were not content merely to defy the conventions of crime dramas in the show's writing. They also wanted *Homicide* to be visually arresting. Levinson was completing work on *Toys* (1992) at the time, and Baltimore-based cinematographer Wayne Ewing directed the "Electronic Press Kit" for the movie.

To keep costs down on the promotional *Toys* featurette, Ewing used the Super 16mm film format, instead of the more common professional standard of 35mm film. When Levinson hired Ewing as the director of photography for *Homicide*, they decided to use the smaller gauge of Super-16mm for the new series. This decision gave them considerable flexibility in designing a new style of production.

SUPER-16

Super-16mm is a format of choice for low-budget independent filmmakers because it offers a high-quality widescreen image comparable to 35mm while using inexpensive cameras and equipment.

By using 16mm film with sprocket holes striped along only one side instead of both, filmmakers can photograph a widescreen image on low-cost 16mm film with a picture quality virtually indistinguishable from 35mm.

When Levinson and Ewing chose to shoot *Homicide* in Super-16, it not only meant that they could film with a small crew and cheaper cameras, it also meant that *Homicide* would originate in a widescreen format. When (and if) HDTV takes over, *Homicide* will be ready for rebroadcasting as a widescreen program while its competitors languish behind the times.

Furthermore, the equipment needed to shoot in Super-16mm was less expensive and could be operated by a much smaller team of technicians, who would work as if they were shooting a documentary. Each episode would take only seven days to film, compared to the usual eight-day production schedule for other drama series.

This approach kept the show's production costs down, enabling Levinson to produce *Homicide* at a fraction of what such dramas usually cost to make. Levinson's method made life easier on the production team, and it freed the actors to focus their energies on giving their best performances, instead of sitting around waiting for the crew to light the next shot. Many cast members noted that the experience was similar to performing in the theater.

Ewing would shoot *Homicide* using a handheld camera, walking among the actors with ease. Ewing boasted that the camera had a personality of its own, as if it were a cast member in its own right.

Fontana hoped that the peripatetic camera provided enough apparent onscreen action that the show could then focus on characters and dialogue without seeming as slow or stagy as that approach would otherwise appear.

The production methods borrowed from reality-TV shows like *Cops* (1989–) not only created a cinema verité look, but also made for a much looser set. Tony Black, the editor who cut the first episode, remembers, "To [Levinson's] credit, he's created a really good working atmosphere. I mean, there's no doubt who's in charge, but it's an open working atmosphere."

This set atmosphere was so different, it made some people nervous. Yaphet Kotto was so disoriented by the unusual production style that, at the beginning, he forgot many of his lines, and only felt comfortable on the set by the second season.

A Different Kind of TV Set

"The police stations here don't look like police stations," supervising producer Jim Finnerty told *Entertainment Weekly*, "The actual homicide building is just an office building with a logo on it."

Indeed, the real Baltimore Police Department is a simple, nondescript building near a seedy part of Baltimore's busy downtown, a strip of sex shops known as "The Block." Production director Vince Peranio, whose credits include several of John Waters' cult hits (also filmed in Baltimore) opted instead for the much more photogenic Recreation Pier Building in Fells Point. The Rec Pier Building was dedicated in 1914, and once housed the marine police. Since then it has also been home to a tugboat company, a ballroom, and basketball courts. Then, in 1992, Barry Levinson and his team took over the building from the city and converted it into *Homicide*'s principal set.

Inside the Recreation Pier Building, Peranio designed *Homicide*'s squad room, Room 203. Unlike soundstage sets that have a few walls on one side and open out to the cameras and crew on the other, Peranio created the entire environment from the coffee room to The Box (the interrogation room) as if it were the real thing. The camera would wander around the cast as everyone on the set acted their roles, never sure who or what would appear on screen.

The Recreation Pier set was so real, in fact, that Baltimore residents had a tendency to walk in off the street to report crimes.

As a consequence of the realism of the set, the cast began to settle into this fictional workplace. They would post real messages to one another on the bulletin boards, store their personal belongings there, and sip real coffee as they sat at their desks. The desks are adorned with authentic Baltimore Police Department business cards with the characters' names printed on them. On a

---

HOMICIDE NEXT DOOR

In addition to production designer Vince Peranio's main Recreation Pier set, the cast and crew of *Homicide* also filmed around Baltimore, with much of the filming concentrated in the Fells Point neighborhood. The show used real streets, bars, and houses to add authenticity. For a while, the morgue scenes were really filmed in Baltimore's Office of the Medical Examiner. Ned Beatty grumbled, "The one thing you can't get on camera is, oh boy, it smells." In later seasons, Peranio built an identical duplicate of the morgue for use as a more olfactory-friendly set.

---

day off from production, actor Kyle Secor dropped by to say hello on his way to the post office. This casual act of friendship would never have occurred on a soundstage set in Los Angeles.

Black and White and Red All Over

Barry Levinson encouraged Wayne Ewing to concentrate on getting the performances on film but not to worry about the "rules" of television production. Ewing's wandering camera and documentary approach established a distinctive look for the show that Levinson further enhanced in postproduction.

"I don't want it to look like a Doris Day film," Levinson insisted to Colorlab Motion Picture Services, the Maryland lab where *Homicide*'s film is transferred to videotape for editing. Working closely with Levinson and Ewing, Colorlab's Telecine colorist Drexel Williams drained the footage of its color values, leaving an image that was almost black-and-white, except for vivid reds—the only bright color left. (This black-and-white-and-red image reinforces the color scheme of the squadroom's board, and was echoed in the title sequence too.)

Early test scenes for the show were even more severe in this effect than what ultimately appeared on screen. One of the editors recalls seeing test footage of a black-and-white street scene with a glowing red sun. After the first season, Levinson abandoned this "nuked-out" look for a more colorful picture.

Cookies and Cuts

Once the pilot episode "Gone for Goode" was filmed, Levinson began working with editor Stan Warnow. After the two of them disagreed and split up over their "creative differences," Levinson hired Emmy-winning editor Tony Black to finish cutting the pilot. Levinson told Black he explicitly wanted to "break convention." It was at this time that one of *Homicide*'s most famous devices, the jump cut, was created.

By wandering so freely amongst the action, cinematographer Wayne Ewing had captured exciting images and great performances, but he had made no provisions for how the footage would be cut together. Levinson wanted to throw out the rule book and cut the show solely based on the performances. If that meant that the cutting would result in jarring "jumps," so be it. Black cut two shots together that did not match, and he started looking for a shot he could use as a "cutaway" to disguise the edit. Levinson stopped him, saying, "I like that. Keep it."

Over the years, critics have proposed many theories to explain the symbolism of *Homicide*'s technique of repeating some scenes several times in short succession. In reality, Levinson just liked the effect, and asked the program's directors to watch French director Jean-Luc Godard's famed "New Wave" film *Breathless* (1959) as "homework" for working on *Homicide*.

The jump cuts and repeat edits became a house style, later used by the series' regular editor Cindy Mollo. NBC would ultimately decide the house style had become too bizarre and, as the network gained more control, would remove it to a great degree for future seasons.

Cutting the pilot was "really tough," Black remembers, especially due to audio problems that later forced the producers to reshoot several episodes. But it was fun, too. Levinson's mother brought home-baked goodies to the edit suite each day. The atmosphere was so full of excitement that Levinson had to issue a memo asking cast members to stop coming to the edit sessions, as they were slowing the process down. When the cast finally saw the final edit of "Gone for Goode," they hugged each other in triumph.

The Ratings Game

After screening the pilot, NBC was equally ecstatic. The network was desperate for something to lift it out of the doldrums of being in third place. The once-top network had been sidelined by the loss of hits like *The Cosby Show* (1984–92), *The Golden Girls* (1985–92), and *Matlock* (1986–92). With David Letterman's defection to CBS and the impending end of *Cheers* (1982–93), NBC badly needed a hit.

They had recently tried a number of comedies they hoped would appeal to the twenty-something crowd of viewers, but it had not worked. Shifting gears, the NBC programmers decided to work on high-quality dramas.

Other feature film-directors (including Steven Spielberg, George Lucas, Oliver Stone, David Lynch, and Robert De Niro) had already tried their hands at creating television shows, but only with varying degrees of success and no runaway hits. Nevertheless, NBC sought out Levinson and recruited him to develop a drama series.

From the day that Levinson first pitched *Homicide: Life on the Street* to them, NBC couldn't get it on the air fast enough. They planned it as a midseason replacement, and ordered six episodes for its winter 1993 run. Once they saw the pilot, they upped the order to nine episodes, and asked for an additional four scripts, which would ultimately form the show's second season.

At the time, many critics were saying the hourlong drama format was dead, but NBC Entertainment president Warren Littlefield believed *Homicide: Life on the Street* would prove them wrong. Buoyed by the high quality of the pilot, Littlefield called *Homicide* the network's most promising new show, and scheduled "Gone for Goode" in the highly coveted time slot after the Super Bowl.

After the Super Bowl premiere, it would be moved into its regular slot of Wednesdays at 9:00 P.M., between *Unsolved Mysteries* (1988–) at 8:00 P.M. and *Law and Order* (1990–) at 10:00 P.M. to make a block of reality-based shows NBC promoted as "Arresting Television." NBC's vice president for dramatic development Kevin Reilly assumed *Homicide* would link the other two shows nicely, and create a "reality flow" for the evening.

In scheduling *Homicide* on Wednesdays at 9:00 P.M., NBC displaced two comedies that had resided in that slot: *Seinfeld* (1990–98) and *Mad About You* (1992–). What NBC learned the hard way was that the Wednesday-night audience was comprised of comedy fans, who had been torn between the NBC comedies and ABC's *Home Improvement* (1991–). Without that dilemma, the audiences switched channels Wednesday nights to *Home Improvement* in droves, cementing its position as TV's reigning sitcom. Meanwhile, having moved to Thursday nights, away from the competition of Home Improvement, Seinfeld shot up in the ratings overnight, and entered the Top Five.

Scheduled against the powerhouse of Home Improvement, Homicide struggled for viewers. One week it was up against Oprah Winfrey's interview with Michael Jackson, and was preempted twice (for the Grammys and for an address by President Clinton). Not surprisingly, NBC's "most promising new series" never even made it into the top ninety shows. The season's average Nielsen share was a modest fourteen percent.

The Best Show Nobody's Watching

In addition to its scheduling woes, Homicide was an experimental and challenging program. "I imagine anyone who has been drinking a lot at the Super Bowl party might have trouble following the show," Barry Levinson joked.

Even NBC Entertainment president Warren Littlefield acknowledged Homicide was unconventional, and said that NBC needed to "educate viewers that we will be offering something truly different and special here." With the chaos of scheduling, however, NBC scarcely managed to educate viewers that Homicide was even on the air.

Despite low ratings, Homicide: Life on the Street earned some of the most lavish critical praise of any TV series in the nineties. The critical response was overwhelmingly positive, and helped protect the show from the pressures of the network to discard anything that did not earn high ratings immediately.

NBC expected Homicide to rejuvenate its drama format and to give prestige to its primetime lineup. Although not a ratings hit, Homicide lived up to its hype. Warren Littlefield and NBC's West Coast president Don Ohlmeyer insisted they were fans of Homicide, but with NBC in third place they had little room to let a struggling show find its audience.

Critic Marvin Kitman wrote for Newsday, "Homicide is an old-fashioned NBC signature show, recapturing the glory days of NBC under Grant Tinker and Brandon Tartikoff, which will recapture the high ratings of their Hill Street Blues and St. Elsewhere. It's easy to forget the best NBC dramas of the eighties were only succèses d'estime."

Levinson is sure that during NBC's heyday in the 1980s under Grant Tinker, Homicide almost definitely would have been given the room to grow. When asked if he would have renewed Homicide, Tinker replied, "I would guess that I would.... I thought it was stunning."

Without Tinker at the helm, though, the future of Homicide: Life on the Street was in doubt. When it did return a year later, on probation, Homicide would be fighting for its life.

SEASON ONE

January 1993–March 1993
60-minute episodes
Wednesdays 9:00 P.M. EST
(except Episode 1, Sunday January 31, 10:25 P.M. EST)

Production Team:

Barry Levinson (executive producer), Tom Fontana (executive producer), Jim Finnerty (supervising producer), Gail Mutrux (producer), Lori Mozilo (coordinating producer), Paul Attanasio (creator), Bonnie Mark (script coordinator), Vince Peranio (production designer), Dale Davis (art director), Susan Kessel (set decorator), Van Smith (costume designer, "Gone for Goode" only), Rolande Berman (costume designer), Jeff Rona (music), Lynn Kowal (main title theme), Louis Di Giaimo (casting director), Pat Moran (Baltimore casting director), Rick Angelella (sound mixer), Wayne Ewing (director of photography), Dwayne Dell (boom), Charley Armstrong (location manager), Stan Warnow and Tony Black (editors, "Gone for Goode" only), Cindy Mollo (editor), Richard Harkness (editor), Mark Pellington (title sequence), Debbie Sarjeant (postproduction supervisor), Ted Zachary (executive in charge of production).

Regular Cast:

Daniel Baldwin (Detective Beau Felton), Ned Beatty (Detective Stanley Bolander), Richard Belzer (Detective John Munch), Andre Braugher (Detective Frank Pembleton), Clark Johnson (Detective Meldrick Lewis), Yaphet Kotto (Lieutenant Al Giardello), Melissa Leo (Detective Kay Howard), Jon Polito (Detective Steve Crosetti), Kyle Secor (Detective Tim Bayliss).

Episode 1: "Gone for Goode"

[Production Code 101]
Original air date: January 31, 1993.
Written by Paul Attanasio; directed by Barry Levinson.

Additional Cast and Guest Stars:

Wendy Hughes (Dr. Carol Blythe), Ralph Tabakin (Dr. Scheiner), Steve J. Harris (Bernard), Oni Faida Lampley (Dollie Withers), Mary Jefferson (Calpurnia Church), Jim Grollman (Jerry Jempson), Mary Joy (Mrs. Jempson), Joe Hansard (Jimmy Lee Shields), Sandy Gaberman (Johnny), Jason Frazier (Butchie), Carter McNeese (Mr. Goode), Beverly Brigham (Mrs. Goode), Joseph Attanasio (funeral director), Leonard Jackson (cemetery manager), Elizabeth Milnes (girl), Alan Wendl (desk man), Hans Kramm (owner), Lemuel Wills (guard), Keith Johnson and Cliff McMullen (uniforms).

STORY: In this pilot episode, the sprawling narratives and multiple story lines of the series introduce the men and women of the Homicide Unit of the Baltimore Police Department. Steve Crosetti and Meldrick Lewis begin an investigation into a "Black Widow" killer who murders her husbands for their life-insurance money.

Stan Bolander and John Munch look into the hit-and-run death of Jenny Goode, while rookie Tim Bayliss from the mayor's security detail is partnered with the mercurial Frank Pembleton, a brilliant but arrogant detective who prefers to work alone.

HIGHLIGHTS: The first hour of *Homicide* is crammed with personal details, establishing many important character traits, such as Detective Steve Crosetti's obsession with the assassination of President Abraham Lincoln, Detective Beau Felton's antagonism towards loner Frank Pembleton, and Detective Kay Howard's extraordinary winning streak.

COMMENTARY: For its heavily hyped premiere episode, *Homicide: Life on the Street* introduces itself with little fanfare. Unlike the sensational gimmicks of *NYPD Blue*'s premiere the following year, *Homicide* elects to follow the path less traveled: no major cases, nothing obvious, just bizarre morbid humor and the quirky rhythms of people talking.

The naturalism owes much to the influence of David Simon's journalism, on which screenwriter Paul Attanasio relies heavily. The cases, characters, and even the dialogue all come straight off the pages of David Simon's book: from the kid who killed his elderly homosexual lover and drove off in the dead man's car, to the murdered bill collector, to the hit-and-run case that lends the pilot its title.

One of the original ideas Attanasio included in his script but which never made it to the final broadcast was a scene in which Lieutenant Al Giardello and Detective Tim Bayliss talk on the roof. "Gee" compares the difference between their detective work and the challenges faced by Sherlock Holmes. He goes on to remember that Holmes was always up against a master criminal named "Murray." When Bayliss corrects him that the name was "Moriarty," Gee mumbles how hard it is to understand what English people are saying because of their accent.

Ironically, the crew said the same thing of Yaphet Kotto as Lieutenant Giardello. In fact, many of his lines needed to be redubbed later because his deep voice was often indecipherable. Sound recording problems plagued the production in the first season, and several episodes had to be refilmed almost in their entirety.

NOTES: Barry Levinson won the 1993 Emmy for Best Director for his work on this episode. Thanks in large measure to the excellent time slot following the Super Bowl, "Gone for Goode" netted the season's highest rating, with an impressive 18.8 rating. (Each rating point represents 970,000 households. In other words, an 18.8 rating means over 18 million people tuned in to see *Homicide*'s premiere.)

Episode 2: "A Ghost of a Chance"

[Production Code 102]
Original air date: February 3, 1993.
Written by Noel Behn; story by Tom Fontana: directed by Martin Campbell.

Additional Cast and Guest Stars:

Clayton LeBoeuf (Captain George Barnfather), Zeljko Ivanek (Assistant State's Attorney Ed Danvers), Wendy Hughes (Dr. Carol Blythe), Gerald F. Gough (Colonel Bert Granger), Lee Tergesen (Officer Chris Thorman), Taylor Young (Griselda Battel), Gwen Verdon (Jessie Doohen), John Habberton (Thomas Doohen), Matthew Cowles (W.J. Masius), Jeffrey Mandon (Trainee), Michael Sheldon (Ralph Fenwick), Gwendolyn Briley-Strand (Mrs. Watson).

STORY: Rookie detective Tim Bayliss hasn't even been assigned a precinct desk yet when he catches the most traumatic case the city has seen in years: the vicious slaying of a young girl. Not only does the case twist the gut of the sensitive detective, but it thrusts him into the spotlight.

Meanwhile, Detectives Kay Howard and Beau Felton follow a lower-profile case with an odd, otherworldly lead.

HIGHLIGHTS: This episode introduces the concept of a "red ball" case. The etymology of the term is somewhat ambiguous, although most sources agree that it is derived from railroad lingo as a way of identifying a train that takes priority in access to the rail lines. In the Baltimore Police Department, a "red ball" is a case that is so politically important that it takes precedence over all other cases, and deserves the full attention of the squad.

This segment also introduces a number of important supporting characters, from hardworking Assistant State's Attorney Ed Danvers, to the weasely department bosses Colonel Bert Granger and Captain George Barnfather, to patrolman Chris Thorman who will soon be shot in the head by his own service revolver during a failed arrest.

Beau Felton's character starts to come into better focus, as he displays his trademark personality changes from bullying selfishness to kind sweetness.

After exposing his partner Kay Howard to his taunts and the ridicule of the squad for her belief in ghosts, Beau then puts in an extra effort to snare killer Ralph Fenwick and the murder weapon. Kay's superstitious beliefs would be revisited in Season Four's Episode 40: "Heartbeat" with its Edgar Allan Poe–inspired black cat.

COMMENTARY: This episode begins the Adena Watson case, the death of the young girl that becomes the unforgettable backbone of almost the entire season. The story closely parallels the 1988 slaying of Latonya Wallace, described in David Simon's book. Like its TV counterpart, Wallace's case was never solved.

The detective who handled the Latonya Wallace investigation, Tom Pellegrini, consulted the producers of *Homicide* and advised actor Kyle Secor on how to play the character based on him and his experiences. Pellegrini even appears onscreen as the officer who first discovers the body of Adena Watson. Pellegrini asked to be in that scene, and Secor noticed how Detective Pellegrini stayed with the actress who played Adena's corpse. Secor realized the detective was trying somehow to make amends to the real child through the actress playing her. After all these years, the case still haunted him. Secor learned more about how to play Bayliss from watching the detective that night than from anything Pellegrini could have told him.

NOTES: The director of this episode, Martin Campbell, went on to greater fame and success as the director of the 1995 James Bond adventure *GoldenEye* starring Pierce Brosnan.

Guest performer Gwen Verdon received an Emmy nomination for her role as the embittered Mrs. Doohen.

The episode received a 15.3 rating, the second-best for the season. The overall season average was only 12.6.

Episode 3: "Son of a Gun"

[Production Code 104]
Original air date: February 10, 1993.
Written by James Yoshimura; story by Tom Fontana; directed by Nick Gomez.

Additional Cast and Guest Stars:

Wendy Hughes (Dr. Carol Blythe), Gerald F. Gough (Colonel Bert Granger), Lee Tergesen (Officer Chris Thorman), Edie Falco (Eva Thorman), Luis Guzman (Larry, aka Lorenzo), Mary Jefferson (Calpurnia Church), Andre Trevon Browne (James Delahunt), Hillary Danner (Reporter), Larry E. Hull (Charlie Flavin), Mel Proctor (Grant Besser), Jay Spadaro (Officer Salerno).

STORY: Crosetti learns his former partner, Patrolman Chris Thorman, has been shot in the head, and he pursues the case with a vengeance.

Meanwhile, Kay and Beau discover evidence exposing Calpurnia Church, the "Black Widow" killer Meldrick is investigating for killing her many husbands (a plot thread first introduced in Episode 1: "Gone for Goode").

HIGHLIGHTS: Divorced detective Stan Bolander strikes up a relationship with medical examiner Dr. Carol Blythe (and he would not be the last detective to fall for an M.E.).

While out on the town with Blythe, Stan waxes poetic about the soul-deadening effects of working day in and day out with the bodies of the murdered. He wonders if, over time, people like himself and Blythe become so sensitized to black-and-white, they can no longer see the colors of the world. Filmed as it was in *Homicide's* original deliberately bleached-out "look," the almost-monochromatic image powerfully underscores Bolander's bitter comments.

COMMENTARY: Eagle-eyed TV viewers will notice that the Adena Watson case seems suddenly more advanced. In fact, this episode was broadcast third although it was intended to be shown fourth. The official Episode 3: "Night of the Dead Living," was transmitted out of sequence at the end of the season. NBC's programmers worried about the deliberate pace of that episode, feeling it wasn't kinetic enough for a show still trying to woo viewers.

NOTES: This episode was directed by Nick Gomez, a feature-film director who made a critically acclaimed debut with the low-budget independently financed film, *Laws of Gravity* (1993). Incidentally, *Laws of Gravity* was photographed by cinematographer Jean de Segonzac, who would take over as *Homicide's* director of photography in its second season.

This episode also marks the arrival of writer James Yoshimura, a former playwright who would pen many of the series' most memorable episodes. His adroit blending of hard-edged emotion with amusing character comedy is on full display in this very funny segment. Yoshimura would later be promoted to producer for his many contributions.

Speaking of promotions, during a raid conducted by Detectives Bayliss and Pembleton on a houseful of drug addicts, a beat officer discovers a stray earring and offers it to Tim as possible evidence. The actor playing this extremely brief and unremarkable role, Walt MacPherson, would later return to the show in a more prominent part as Roger Gaffney, the piggish detective who steals Megan Russert's promotion. However, there has been no suggestion in the show that this beat cop in the first season is the same man as Gaffney, even though he looks remarkably like him.

Episode 4: "A Shot in the Dark"

[Production Code 105]
Original air date: February 24, 1993.
Written by Jorge Zamacona; story by Tom Fontana; directed by Bruce Paltrow.

Additional Cast and Guest Stars:
Zeljko Ivanek (Assistant State's Attorney Ed Danvers), Clayton LeBoeuf (Captain George Barnfather), Wendy Hughes (Dr. Carol Blythe), Lee Tergesen (Officer Chris Thorman), Edie Falco (Eva Thorman), Jennifer Harmon (Alison Ashley), Sean Whitesell (Doctor), Tim Caggiano (Orville Warren), David DeBoy (Rufus Bond), Mojo Gentry (Alfred Smith), Julie Grossberg (Officer Anne Schanne), Larry E. Hull (Charlie Flavin), Mary West Miller (Lydia Benson), Richard Pelzman (Newton Stuart), Ralph Tabakin (Dr. Scheiner), Sharon Ziman (Naomi).

STORY: Too worn-down by the Watson probe to think clearly, Detective Bayliss doesn't accompany Detective Pembleton on a new lead, which turns out to be a wild-goose chase.

Eager to solve his friend's shooting, Detective Crosetti has narrowed his sights on one suspect, but his partner, Detective Lewis, continues to investigate.

HIGHLIGHTS: Trying to appease the hungry press with good news about the Adena Watson case, Captain Barnfather reveals the one piece of evidence Tim Bayliss had withheld about Watson's murder. In one breath, the captain undercuts the investigation. Furious, Bayliss phones Barnfather at home to call him a "butthead."

Viewers of this series will appreciate the catharsis of watching Bayliss rage at Barnfather. The latter character, played with wonderful smarminess by Clayton LeBoeuf, would earn the name "butthead" many times over during the coming years for his selfish and sometimes craven leadership, but this is the one time anyone had the guts to tell him off directly. (This scene was cut from the syndicated reruns when it was shown on Lifetime Cable Television in 1997.)

In addition, viewers will be surprised by Beau Felton's offhanded joke that "Frank almost bought a dog for his wife and kid." In the fourth season, Mary Pembleton would become pregnant with their first child, so fans of the show have come to see this line as a blooper. Taken by itself, Beau's comment could be interpreted as a mere joke by a man who obviously doesn't know Frank Pembleton very well. However, some fans claim they can spot a picture of a kid on Pembleton's desk in these first season episodes, a detail later dropped.

COMMENTARY: Although the story line of Officer Thorman's shooting is adapted directly from true-life events documented by David Simon, screenwriter Jorge Zamacona adds a notable twist. In the TV version of the tale, the blinded beat cop was a close friend of one of the detectives, who takes the case as a personal mission of revenge.

This approach would become a hallmark of *Homicide*'s writers: time and again, the detectives would be personally touched by the process of criminal investigation. The main characters would find themselves victimized by and accused of wrongdoing more often than would usually be the case in real life, all the better to emphasize the emotional cost of their grisly job.

NOTES: The director of this installment, Bruce Paltrow, told the *Washington Post* that *Homicide* "is to television what abstract expressionism is to art." Paltrow was the producer of *St. Elsewhere*, where he began his long collaboration with *Homicide* producer Tom Fontana. Paltrow went on to direct the made-for-TV version of *Ed McBain's 87th Precinct* in 1995.

Episode 5: "Three Men and Adena"

[Production Code 106]
Original air date: March 3, 1993.
Written by Tom Fontana; directed by Martin Campbell.

Guest Star:
Moses Gunn (Risley Tucker)

STORY: Tim Bayliss's instincts have led him to one conclusion: Risley Tucker aka "the araber" (a nomadic vegetable peddler) was the one who killed eleven-year-old Adena Watson.

But this prime suspect has already withstood multiple interviews, and the detectives have yet to develop a legally meaningful case against him. Unless Bayliss and Pembleton can get a confession within twelve hours this time, whatever they do get will be inadmissible in court.

HIGHLIGHTS: The minimalist setting—three men alone in a room, talking—focuses attention on the dialogue, which becomes a sort of verbal symphony.

At first, Frank Pembleton and Tim Bayliss are almost dissonant voices, attacking "araber" Risley Tucker from different approaches but still modulating the same underlying theme. That is, did he kill Adena Watson? Frank's voice drops out for a while, and Tim's takes over. Then, Bayliss's drops out as Frank's takes over. When they both start speaking in precise rhythm with virtually one voice, it is a powerful moment of emotional satisfaction. At last these two have truly become partners.

But the almost musical satisfaction of that moment is fleeting, and the symphony takes a new twist: the third voice, Tucker's, has lurked in the background all along but now dominates. Tucker attacks his interrogators, using their tactics against them to expose their own weaknesses (he calls Bayliss an "amateur") and leaves them frustrated.

COMMENTARY: Producer Tom Fontana won an Emmy for Outstanding Writing in a Drama Series for this installment, an astonishing tour de force of writing and acting that demonstrates all of *Homicide*'s best qualities.

The situation is a composite of several real interrogations conducted by Tom Pellegrini in the Latonya Wallace probe. Audiences accustomed to typical TV crime fare get their breath knocked out of them, as the good guys lose, and a story line that has dominated the show for weeks ends without resolution. This conclusion is more realistic (literally so, in this case), but is exceptionally provocative for network TV.

NOTES: Veteran character actor Moses Gunn turns in his swan song performance as the suspected child-killer Risley Tucker. Born in 1929, Gunn began his successful theatrical career in 1962 with an Off-Broadway staging of Jean Genet's *The Blacks*. He cofounded the Negro Ensemble Company, and also performed Shakespeare with both the Yale Repertory Theater and the New York Shakespeare Festival.

Gunn's movie roles included the role of gangster Bumpy Jonas in both *Shaft* (1971) and *Shaft's Big Score* (1972). The actor also appeared in *Ragtime* (1981) and *Heartbreak Ridge* (1986). He had a recurring role as Carl Dixon on *Good Times* (1974–79), and earned an Emmy nomination for his role as African chief Kintango in ABC's miniseries *Roots* (1977–78). Nine months after filming "Three Men and Adena," Gunn passed away.

Episode 6: "A Dog and Pony Show"

[Production Code 107]
Original air date: March 10, 1993.
Written by James Yoshimura; story by Tom Fontana; directed by Alan Taylor.

Additional Cast and Guest Stars:

Wendy Hughes (Dr. Carol Blythe), Stivi Paskoski (Danny Blythe), Lee Tergesen (Officer Chris Thorman), Edie Falco (Eva Thorman), Michael Constantine (Jim Scinta), Joy Ehrlich (Penny Babcock), Geoffrey C. Ewing (Pony Johnson), Larry Gillard Jr. (William Lyness), Julie Grossberg (Officer Anne Schanne), Lisa Gay Hamilton (Latoya Kennedy), Lisa Marshall (Clarice Keene), Nick Olcott (John Kuehn), Mel Proctor (Grant Besser), Archie D. Williams (medical examiner).

STORY: Lieutenant Giardello wants Detectives Bayliss and Pembleton to put Adena Watson's unsolved murder behind them but the call they take is anything but ordinary. A police dog has been found dead in the park, and, according to Municipal Code, is to be given the same investigation as any human cop's death.

Detectives Kay Howard and Beau Felton have a grislier case: a woman has been found tortured and killed by weird bullets, which links up with another murder handled by Detective Meldrick Lewis.

HIGHLIGHTS: A outstanding scene in this very humorous episode has Giardello musing about his dual heritage as an Italian-American and as an African-American with a fellow Homicide shift commander who has been forced into retirement. (This retirement would open up a spot on Homicide's second shift, which would be offered to Frank Pembleton in Episode 7: "And the Rockets' Dead Glare" and ultimately given to Megan Russert sometime before Episode 14: "Nearer My God to Thee.")

By casting Yaphet Kotto in the role based on real-life shift commander Gary D'Addario, the producers created this dual ethnicity where it had not been originally planned. However, Kotto's own background as both black and Jewish gives him an unusual insight into portraying such a role.

COMMENTARY: As *Homicide* matured, NBC started complaining about its protracted, interwoven story lines. When the series returned for its second season, its writers were under orders to try harder to keep story lines contained in as few episodes as possible, and have fewer story strands running through any given hour.

NBC considered installments like this one, "A Dog and Pony Show," a prime example of the offending approach. It would be very hard for a new viewer to watch this episode by itself and either understand or appreciate what was happening. Tim Bayliss still is dealing with reverberations from the Adena Watson case (which spanned five full episodes of a nine-episode season); the retirement of the second-shift lieutenant is a subplot not fully resolved until the third season; Stan Bolander's awkward relationship with Medical Examiner Carol Blythe is spread over most of the season; and the case of killers Pony Johnson and Alexander Lyness would carry over to the following episode, "And the Rocket's Dead Glare."

The only self-contained story herein is played for laughs: the investigation of a dog's murder. Viewing this episode by itself is rather like reading the middle chapter or two of a very long novel.

NOTES: Melissa Leo appears more made up in this episode than she would later when she had more influence over how her character, Detective

Kay Howard, should look and act. When Leo began to assert herself, however, NBC brass began complaining to Levinson and Fontana that the actress wasn't wearing enough makeup.

Fontana mocked NBC's complaints: "'What's with her hair?' they want to know. 'Can't you do something about her hair? And how about those baggy clothes? She's such a pretty girl. Why doesn't she dress better? What is she supposed to be, a dyke?'"

The guest director this week is Alan Taylor, the filmmaker behind *Palookaville* (1996). Taylor's debut feature won him critical praise (*Cinemania* wrote, "If *Palookaville*, a class act if there ever was one, doesn't connect strongly enough to put it on the small shelf of classic comedies, then the fault lies with the disreputable state of movie distribution today, not with these filmmakers"), but it was Taylor's student film that won him the directorial gig on *Homicide*.

He shot his half-hour thesis film, called *The Burning Question*, for a seminar taught by movie legend Martin Scorsese. The short appeared on producer Barry Levinson's desk, and prompted him to hire the novice Taylor to join the crew for *Homicide*'s first year. Taylor remembers, "I hadn't even learned the rules of filmmaking, or TV for that matter, and I was being put in a position where I was supposed to break them all."

Episode 7: "And the Rockets' Dead Glare"

[Production Code 108]
Original air date: March 17, 1993.
Written by Jorge Zamacona; story by Tom Fontana; directed by Peter Markle.

Additional Cast and Guest Stars:
Zeljko Ivanek (Assistant State's Attorney Ed Danvers), Ami Brabson (Mary Pembleton), Ed Lauter (Secret Service Agent Gruszynski), Bai Ling (Lin Chang), Alvin Lum (Dengshu), Steven Marcus (Detective DeSilva), Michael Willis (Defense Attorney Darin Russom), Geoffrey C. Ewing (Pony Johnson), Gerald G. Gough (Colonel Bert Granger), Clayton LeBoeuf (Captain George Barnfather), Howard B. Silverman (Judge Madden), Ralph Tabakin (Dr. Scheiner), Irene Ziegler (Mildred Bettis).

STORY: When one of the student leaders of the Tiananmen Square protest in Beijing, China, is murdered in Baltimore, Crosetti and Lewis follow the case all the way to Washington and the Chinese Embassy.

Back in Charm City, the case against Pony Johnson comes to trial, and Kay disagrees with State's Attorney Ed Danvers on how to prosecute it.

HIGHLIGHTS: As Frank considers an offer to take over as shift commander of Homicide's second shift, viewers get their first sight of Mary Pembleton. The role is played by actress Ami Brabson, who is Andre Braugher's wife in real life. Not only would Mary Pembleton become a prominent recurring character in future episodes, but Frank's decision to decline the promotion also returns (see Season Three's Episode 23: "From Cradle to Grave").

This episode features the first appearance of sleazy defense lawyer Darin Russom, played by award-winning character actor Michael Willis.

COMMENTARY: The courtroom scene in this episode owes little to the usual depiction of trials on television. Even a show like *Law and Order* that prides itself on judicial system realism makes concessions for dramatic effect. In this episode, *Homicide* deliberately explodes those dramatic conventions. Instead, we see tedium, waiting, and awkward pauses. Detective Howard misspeaks her testimony, and almost jeopardizes her own case. Ultimately, the defense attorney derails himself with a procedural misstep so oblique that the average viewer is likely to have no clear idea of what just happened.

This is, in fact, exactly how the real trial proceeded, as described in Simon's book.

NOTES: Detective John Munch makes a pro-legalization rant about marijuana that angers a fellow detective in the drug enforcement unit. Actor Richard Belzer's own personal history with drug abuse and drug dealing helped motivate this character development, and will give an especially authentic color to future discussions of Munch's druggie/hippie past.

The opening scene's discovery of a body in the woods features, arguably, the most startling and severe jump cut in the series' history, as the police appear to magically "beam in" to the crime scene.

Episode 8: "Smoke Gets in Your Eyes"

[Production Code 109]
Original air date: March 24, 1993.
Written by Tom Fontana and James Yoshimura; directed by Wayne Ewing.

Additional Cast and Guest Stars:

Gerald F. Gough (Colonel Bert Granger), Clayton LeBoeuf (Captain George Barnfather), John Waters (Bartender), Sean Whitesell (Doctor), Dan Moran (Howell), Steven Marcus (Detective DeSilva), Joe Fersedi (Colin Dietz), Gavin Goren (Evan Hess), Naomi Jacobson (Edith Hamilton), Carter Jahncke (Don Falls), Walt MacPherson (uniform), Rachel Schneebaum (Anna Prager), Sharon Ziman (Naomi).

STORY: Munch and Bolander investigate the beating death of a teenager, who mysteriously waited days after being injured to seek medical help.

Meanwhile, Howard and Pembleton find that their cases share a common suspect, and they plan a joint stakeout. However, since their partners, Kay Howard and Tim Bayliss, are both trying to quit smoking, they switch partners for the stakeout.

HIGHLIGHTS: Beau Howard and Frank Pembleton share the smoking car while discussing the merits of quitting their bad habit. On the other hand, Kay Howard and Tim Bayliss take the clean-air car, but almost talk each other back into smoking.

The "smoke" of the title refers not just to the cigarette-laden conversation of detectives trying to quit, but also to the hazardous asbestos discovered in the police HQ. Lieutenant Giardello heads upstairs for a drink only to wander into a surreal image out of a science-fiction movie: a plastic-filled room patrolled by men in protective respirator suits. In confronting his bosses about the asbestos cleanup, Gee gets to display his tenacious defense of his squad. He even seems to get pleasure out of turning the screws on Colonel Granger and Captain Barnfather (or "the Doublemint Twins" as he later calls them) to win concessions for his team.

The episode features a very memorable and amusing sequence in which Kay Howard describes to Frank Pembleton in exacting detail her attraction to Assistant State's Attorney Ed Danvers.

COMMENTARY: The sight of Stan Bolander singing to himself over a lonely beer was to have been the end of *Homicide*'s first season run, except NBC had delayed broadcasting the slow-paced Episode 3: "Night of the Dead Living," which placed it last in broadcast order. This episode has a somber mood and a sense of story lines being resolved, but the exuberant last scene of the next episode, showing the cast laughing and smiling, is a much less depressing way to sign off than Stan's lonesome woe.

NOTES: Famed cult filmmaker John Waters turns in a cameo appearance as the bartender listening to lonely Bolander's woes. John Waters is the writer-director-producer behind such midnight flicks as *Eat Your Make-Up!* (1967), *Mondo Trasho* (1969), *Pink Flamingos* (1972), *Female Trouble* (1975), *Desperate Living* (1977), *Polyester* (1981), *Hairspray* (1988), *Cry-Baby* (1990), and *Serial Mom* (1994).

Like *Homicide* creator Barry Levinson, Waters is a Baltimore native. The talent pool of craftspeople and technicians that *Homicide* relies on for its production have been developed over the years by Levinson and Waters, who both continue to film features in their hometown. Waters would also return in Episode 28: "Law and Disorder" in a different cameo role.

Baltimore's other homegrown moviemaker, John Waters, has appeared twice on Homicide.
Everett Collection

This episode features a superbly ridiculous stunt in which the detectives convince a suspect that an ordinary photocopier is a radioactive lie detector. As it happens, this hoax was actually pulled off in the real world by Baltimore detectives in 1988, and is among the many events that have leapt off David Simon's pages and onto television. Sometimes truth is indeed stranger than fiction.

Episode 9: "The Night of the Dead Living"

[Production Code 103]
Original air date: March 31, 1993.
Written by Frank Pugliese; story by Tom Fontana and Frank Pugliese; directed by Michael Lehmann.

Additional Cast and Guest Stars:

Lee Tergesen (Chris Thorman), N'bushe Wright (Loretta), Kenny Blank (James Hill), Denise Morgan (Social Services official), Cleve Wall (Santa Claus), Sharon Ziman (Naomi).

STORY: Gee spins the board to start the night shift on the hottest night of the year. Oddly, though, no calls come in, leaving the detectives plenty of time to brood over personal matters.

HIGHLIGHTS: With the pressure of the job turned all the way down to "simmer," we get to look a little deeper into the psychologies of the various characters. Most notably, we get to see the gradual disintegration of Felton's marriage, with just over a year to go before it would spin into disaster.

Also, Crosetti's visible overriding concern for his daughter's well-being led some viewers to think his suicide in Season Three was unrealistic. No matter how depressed he became, how could such a dedicated father abandon his children? Crosetti's daughter Beatrice is only mentioned in this episode, but she would appear onscreen in "Crosetti" to grieve over her father's death.

COMMENTARY: "Imagine a crime show during which no crime occurs," raves *USA Today*'s Matt Roush about *Homicide*'s de facto season finale. Awarding it four stars out of four, Roush writes, "Next to nothing happens. Yet every second counts. . . . Evoking the Mamet of *Glengarry Glen Ross*, but with none of the macho bravado, *Homicide* proves minimalist drama can have maximum impact."

The Writers' Guild of America agreed, awarding Frank Pugliese's script the 1993 prize for Outstanding Achievement in Television Writing for Episodic Drama.

Although the action consists of merely sitting around the sweltering office and talking, the episode takes on some of the show's biggest themes, and displays an unprecedented degree of authenticity. Beau Felton remarks that he solves cases with physical evidence, witnesses, and confessions, not by looking for motives. This accurate insight into real-life detective work is taken directly from Simon, and points up one of the reasons *Homicide* is so revolutionary a TV crime drama.

NOTES: Running this episode out of sequence produced several notable continuity errors. Tim is suddenly back in the Adena Watson case, and Chris Thorman has not yet been blinded. This dark, somberly paced installment is also very similar to the real season-ender that preceded it.

Michael Lehmann, the director of the quirky black comedy *Heathers* (1989), was the guest director for this episode, which, in turn, shares some of the same offbeat humor and bleak outlook as his cult-movie hit.

Mainstream audiences were somewhat turned off by the minimalist approach, and the episode returned the poorest rating of the season, a mere 10.2. In the years to come, however, *Homicide* would long for the good old days when a 10.2 rating counted as "low."

CHAPTER 4

The Second Season: Four Chances

Homicide: *Life on the Street* returned to NBC on January 6, 1994, once again as a mid-season replacement. A year earlier, NBC programmers had come out of a screening of Episode 1: "Gone for Goode" heady with visions of a breakaway hit and commissioned four additional scripts from producer Barry Levinson's team. When the first nine episodes of *Homicide* brought in only middling ratings, though, NBC began to back away.

NBC Entertainment president Warren Littlefield remained committed to the show, but he was in a bind. NBC still trailed in third place after CBS and ABC, and could scarcely afford a fledgling series the time to develop an audience. So, Littlefield made a compromise: *Homicide* would return, but with only those four episodes commissioned in 1993 and nothing more.

At a time when the prevailing wisdom at the network argued that the series should have been canceled outright, Littlefield took a gamble. As executive producer Tom Fontana told *USA Today*, "This is not a casual action on NBC's part. It's a real statement to me that we have a possibility to return."

More importantly, Littlefield scheduled the second mini-season of *Homicide* in a new time slot. The Wednesday, 9:00 P.M. slot had been a significant deterrent to *Homicide*'s success the previous year. For its 1994 run, Littlefield moved the show into "ratings paradise"—Thursdays at 10:00 P.M. In its new slot, *Homicide* would benefit from the strong lead-in of the top rated comedies *Seinfeld* (1990–98) and *Frasier* (1993–). Ironically, *Seinfeld*'s phenomenal ratings had come about only when *Homicide* displaced it out of its Wednesday-night slot, and, thereby, removed it from competition with *Home Improvement*. Now *Seinfeld* could repay the favor.

L.A. Law

The Thursday, 10:00 P.M. spot had long been the cherished home of NBC's grand dramas: *Hill Street Blues* (1981–87) and then, *L.A. Law* (1987–94). In order to make room for *Homicide*'s four-episode run, *L.A. Law* took a month-long break. Consequently, the outcome of *Homicide's* brief run was not only a referendum on the future of that show, but the future of *L.A. Law*, too. *Homicide's* producer Tom Fontana realized the politics of the scheduling decision: "A lot of the people who work at *L.A. Law* are friends of mine, and I know they're very possessive about the time period."

Though in the middle of a creative revival thanks to the return of creator William Finkelstein, *L.A. Law* was arguably on its last legs. Also, NBC was concerned increasingly concerned about the bloated salaries of its stars. Michael Tucker, *L.A. Law's* Stuart Markowitz, could see the writing on the wall: "I'm sure NBC would like to put a cheaper show in the time slot."

Shake-ups

For NBC, the matter of cost had recently become significantly more important. Between the first and second seasons, NBC had bought into *Homicide* to become coproducers with Levinson's Baltimore Pictures. Originally, Baltimore Pictures coproduced *Homicide* with Reeves Entertainment, which had gone out of business after the first season.

The collapse of Reeves coincided with the departure of another of *Homicide's* major players, Director of Photography Wayne Ewing. Even as early as the first episode of the first season, Levinson had started to mistrust the inexperience of his new cinematographer. Ewing had graduated from shooting a glorified movie commercial to being one of the primary creative forces behind a TV series, and Levinson became increasingly convinced Ewing was in over his head.

Homicide's habit of bringing in guest directors on each episode brought prestige to the series and added an extra touch of feature-film panache, but it also placed extra burdens on the director of photography. Without a regular director, the cinematographer necessarily became the person charged with maintaining a consistent look for the show.

Levinson had too little faith in Ewing's abilities to leave him with such a responsibility. Therefore, Levinson replaced Ewing with Jean de Segonzac, an accomplished cinematographer whose credits included *Laws of Gravity* (1992), an independent feature film directed by Nick Gomez, who had been one of the guest directors on *Homicide's* first season.

Lighten Up

In *Homicide's* first year, Tom Fontana had bristled at network suggestions that he thought were ill-advised attempts to reduce *Homicide's* distinctive flavor.

Now that NBC was co-owner of the program, they had earned the right to enact some of their suggested changes.

Some of these changes were cosmetic. As the new director of photography, Jean de Segonzac "reined in" some of Wayne Ewing's more flamboyant camerawork. Levinson praised de Segonzac's more restrained visual style, noting that Ewing had a tendency to "get a little too wild, and someone could complain they got a little dizzy."

Additionally, de Segonzac asked Telecine colorist Drexel Williams at Colorlab to "brighten" the look away from the muted colors of the first season.

Other changes surfaced in the scripts. After being told by a fellow *St. Elsewhere* veteran that for all its style, *Homicide* was not "viewer-friendly," Fontana agreed with NBC to reduce the number of story threads per episode.

Both Fontana and Levinson stated that the changes were not forced on them by NBC. The two producers agreed that the changes were evolutionary developments that the show needed in order to fulfill its promise. Levinson was careful to stress to reporters that NBC was not bullying them into making unwarranted alterations.

Warren Littlefield proudly announced, "It's a refined *Homicide*."

A Show Is a Terrible Thing to Waste

Of the four scripts commissioned by NBC back in 1993, the first three follow the familiar structure of overlapping story lines.

For the fourth episode, however, the producers brought in journalist David Simon, author of the original book *Homicide*. Simon worked with screenwriter David Mills to pen an episode that would stand on its own, and not focus on the show's main cast. Instead, their script follows the grueling ordeal of a tourist whose wife is killed before his eyes while they are vacationing in Baltimore with their young children.

This episode tracks the man's traumatic experiences in the often-indifferent Baltimore judicial system as his case is investigated, and a suspect is arrested, brought to trial, and sentenced. Both Simon and Mills would write further scripts for *Homicide*, and would also lend their writing talents to its chief competitor, *NYPD Blue*.

Although planned and produced as the final installment for this mini-season, NBC elected to run it first. Although the episode shows off *Homicide*'s best qualities, and boasts one of its finest scripts ever, NBC's decision had more to do with the episode's guest star.

Famed actor-comedian Robin Williams turned in a rare dramatic turn as the survivor of his wife's killing. Williams found the role emotionally draining, but rightfully earned an Emmy nomination for his powerful performance.

Although Levinson and Williams have worked together several times in the past, Williams took the role as much out of respect for *Homicide* as for its creator. As he said, "It's the kind of show you wish they would just leave on because it's so good."

Williams joked to *USA Today*'s Matt Roush that *Homicide* needed a "Drama Relief" telethon to save it from low ratings, and proposed the slogan, "A show is a terrible thing to waste."

In fact, Williams' guest appearance brought *Homicide* its highest ratings ever, and NBC got its best rating for the time slot since 1991. "We led with Robin because we've really felt that Robin would get [viewers] in the tent," Warren Littlefield told the press. His strategy proved to be correct.

The Waiting Game

Despite the enormous success of this first episode, NBC was still not ready to renew *Homicide*. Both Warren Littlefield and NBC's West Coast president Don Ohlmeyer reassured critics and fans that they were supporters of the series, but they still needed to see how the remaining three episodes fared before they could commit the network.

For three weeks the cast and crew waited, unsure of their future. Inwardly, producers Levinson and Fontana fumed that their show was being given such a brief window of time to prove itself. Having earned two Emmys and overwhelming critical raves, *Homicide*'s future depended solely on the ratings of four episodes.

As short as that window was, it was a grueling wait for the cast. "Where is limbo?" grumbled actor Jon Polito, "It's in Baltimore."

While NBC waited to see how *Homicide* performed in its new time slot, the cast had to pass up other job offers on the gamble that they would be permitted to return. The wait took the greatest toll on lead actors Daniel Baldwin and Ned Beatty, who expressed the greatest frustrations at the time, and ultimately quit the show a year later to pursue film careers.

"I'm pretty much burnt," admitted Beatty, "I can't think of anything I would less rather do than television at this moment."

Baldwin agreed, "I will never, ever do another series. Ever. Ever. Ever. Ever.... I will never put myself through this again."

NYPD Blue

The cast and creators of *Homicide* took great pride in their work, and the strong critical response reaffirmed that pride. But when *Homicide* returned to the air in its "second season," another program stole its thunder.

"A very good friend of mine said that *NYPD Blue* is the television version of *Homicide*, which is a very good line," joked Tom Fontana.

Steven Bochco's crime drama, based on the real-life experiences of Manhattan homicide detective Bill Clark, debuted in 1993 to considerable controversy. With unprecedented hard language and semi-nudity, *NYPD Blue* pushed out the boundaries of network TV in a more lurid and crowd-pleasing fashion than *Homicide*. Consequently it won high ratings.

NYPD Blue also won the support of TV critics, who defended the series against conservative complaints about its racy content. As ABC saw some twenty percent of its advertisers defect in protest of *NYPD Blue*, critics felt a greater urgency to bolster the program. Both *Homicide* and *NYPD Blue* earned Emmy nominations, but the votes went to the show that had served a full season's worth of episodes and had been under the harshest attack. *NYPD Blue* received a record-setting twenty-six Emmy nominations. *Homicide: Life on the Street* received only one.

> **S O M E T H I N G**
> **B O R R O W E D ,**
> **S O M E T H I N G**
> **N Y P D   B L U E**
>
> In addition to stealing *Homicide*'s thunder, *NYPD Blue* (1993–) also borrowed some of *Homicide*'s talent. Writers David Simon and David Mills lent their hands to both shows, and *NYPD Blue* also featured performances by *Homicide* cast members past and present such as Kyle Secor and Jon Seda.

In its first year, *Homicide* had countered its low ratings with its Emmy-winning critical success. In 1994, that counterargument was taken away by *NYPD Blue*. As fate would have it, though, *Homicide* turned out to be a ratings success!

The Nielsen rating for *Homicide*'s much-touted season premiere with Robin Williams was a startling 18.0. NBC's executives especially noticed that *Homicide* outpaced the numbers for *L.A. Law* in the same time slot. NBC's Don Ohlmeyer raved about *Homicide*'s ratings, and noted that "we certainly have other time slots where *L.A. Law* could be of service." As it happened, May 1994 saw the final broadcast of *L.A. Law*.

Lead actor Richard Belzer relaxed, "I have every confidence, now that the network has seen the numbers, that we can do it in the right time slot, that we will in fact continue."

A Final Hurdle

If *Homicide*'s rocky history finally seemed secure, a new problem loomed on the horizon. Unless *Homicide* planned to regularly feature major movie stars as guests, its future numbers would not be quite so high. If *Homicide* was to return, NBC demanded that Fontana and Levinson agree to more promotable guest stars, more women in the cast, and more "life-affirming" story lines.

Hourlong dramas are network TV's most expensive product. Although *Homicide* cost less per episode than the industry average, each hour still cost in the ballpark of $1 million. In its Thursday, 10:00 P.M. slot, *Homicide* ran against ABC's higher-rated news magazine *Prime Time Live* (1989–).

Consistently in or near the Top Ten shows, *Prime Time Live* did better on half of *Homicide*'s budget. To stay competitive, NBC hoped to bring *Homicide*'s costs down even farther.

Homicide: Life on the Street and *Law and Order* are the only network series not filmed on the West Coast. For years, NBC had maintained pressure on producer Dick Wolf to stop shooting *Law and Order* in New York. Suddenly, Levinson and Fontana found themselves under similar pressure.

Shooting in Baltimore cost the producers of *Homicide* a significant amount in travel expenses for cast and crew, lodging fees, meals, and other costs. The Maryland Film Commission estimated that a full season's worth of *Homicide* would be worth $15.4 million a year to the local economy.

Maryland's then-governor Donald Schaefer sent a telegram encouraging Levinson to stay in Baltimore: "We wish you the best in the discussions and negotiations. I wanted you to know that we are proud of having this exceptional series shot in your native state and stand ready to help toward a positive decision for additional production of the series. Let me know if there's anything we can do to assist you in bringing the series back into production here in Baltimore."

On February 15, 1994, the options on the stars' contracts expired. At midnight, NBC formally renewed the series, but the Baltimore issue remained unresolved. Fontana called the decision "a qualified renewal."

Homicide: Life on the Street had been conceived, developed, and produced as a Baltimore-based series. Relocating production to California would save the network money, but would also compromise the distinctive feel of the show.

However, the issue was complicated by two incidents that conspired to make even Levinson wonder whether *Homicide* should remain in Baltimore anymore. Fontana called it a "reexamination of 'Are we serving Baltimore with the show?'"

Episode 11: "See No Evil," in which Pembleton and Bayliss begin investigating a case of an officer shooting an unarmed suspect in the back and then covering it up, provoked the ire of Baltimore's police. Twenty-two detectives signed a formal letter of protest to Levinson decrying the way the show depicted cops as dishonest. Subsequently, an Associated Press article wondered whether the series' focus on the city's murder rate was bad for the city's image.

Already under pressure from NBC to leave Baltimore, these incidents gave Levinson and Fontana pause. Who were they really serving by filming on location if Baltimore didn't want them?

Finally, an agreement was reached. NBC renewed *Homicide* with a third-season order of thirteen episodes, with the network waiting for the fall ratings to see if they would order an additional nine to make a full season.

The series would continue to be filmed in Baltimore, but it would not return to its Thursday time slot. *Homicide* would return on Friday nights instead, and Thursday, 10:00 P.M. would become the home of NBC's next showpiece drama, *ER*.

S E A S O N   T W O

January 1994
60-minute episodes
Thursdays, 10:00 P.M. EST

Production Team:

Barry Levinson (executive producer), Tom Fontana (executive producer), Jim Finnerty (supervising producer), Debbie Sarjeant (associate producer), Paul Attanasio (creator), James Yoshimura (story editor), Bonnie Mark (staff writer), Chris Friel (script supervisor), Vince Peranio (production designer), Susan Kessel (set decorator), Roland Berman (costume designer), Jeff Rona (music), Chris Tergesen (music coordinator), Lynn Kowal (main title theme), Louis DiGiaimo (casting director), Pat Moran (Baltimore casting director), Bruce Litecky (sound mixer), John Gooch (boom), Jean de Segonzac (director of photography), Debbie Donaldson (location manager), Cindy Mollo (editor), Mark Pellington (title sequence), Ivan Fonseca (postproduction coordinator), Ted Zachary and Allan Chaflin (executives in charge of production).

Regular Cast:
Daniel Baldwin (Detective Beau Felton), Ned Beatty (Detective Stanley Bolander), Richard Belzer (Detective John Munch), Andre Braugher (Detective Frank Pembleton), Clark Johnson (Detective Meldrick Lewis), Yaphet Kotto (Lieutenant Al Giardello), Melissa Leo (Detective Kay Howard), Jon Polito (Detective Steve Crosetti), Kyle Secor (Detective Tim Bayliss).

Episode 10: "Bop Gun"

[Production Code 204]
Original air date: January 6, 1994.
Written by David Simon and David Mills; story by Tom Fontana; directed by Stephen Gyllenhaal.

Additional Cast and Guest Stars:
Robin Williams (Robert Ellison), Julia Devin (Abby Ellison), Jake Gyllenhaal (Matt Ellison), Mel Proctor (Grant Besser), Sharon Ziman (Naomi), Judy Thornton (Judy), Antonio D. Charity (Kid Funkadelic), Lloyd Goodman (Vaughn Perkins), Caron Tate (Renee Perkins), Vincent Miller (Tweedy), Kay W. Lawal (Mrs. Landry), Shawn Woodyard (suspect), Richard Pilcher (Sergeant Mark Deutch), Herb Levinson (Dr. Lausanne), Jay Spadaro (Officer Salerno), Fredella D. Calloway (uniform).

STORY: This grueling episode follows the ordeal of a man widowed in an instant when his wife is shot in the head in front of him and their children during a botched robbery.

The evidence points to a young man with a loving family and everything going for him, who chose to run with the wrong crowd. Trying to understand why, Detective Kay Howard visits the boy in jail, but all she finds is another victim of crime.

HIGHLIGHTS: This episode makes little room for the main cast, preferring instead to follow guest star Robin Williams on his agonizing journey. Williams delivers the goods, turning in probably his finest noncomedic performance ever.

COMMENTARY: Although planned as the fourth episode in the season, NBC chose to lead with this powerful segment because of guest star Williams, who earned a nomination for Outstanding Guest Actor in a Drama Series for his role as Ralph Ellison.

Barry Levinson had worked with Robin before, on *Good Morning, Vietnam* (1986) and *Toys* (1992). Williams, however, insisted he took the *Homicide* role out of respect for the show, not merely as a favor to Levinson.

Thanks to Robin Williams'
showstopping performance,
"Bop Gun" became Homicide's
highest-rated episode.
Everett Collection

"Visually, it was just so different from anything else on television," explains Williams.

Williams found the experience of playing a crime victim draining, "You'd want to go back to the hotel and call home immediately to make sure everyone was all right."

Feature filmmaker Stephen Gyllenhaal directed the episode, having demonstrated his deft ability with actors in the critically acclaimed *Paris Trout* (1991), *Waterland* (1992), and *A Dangerous Woman* (1993).

NBC's decision paid off. "Bop Gun" was seen by 33 million people, and its 18.0 rating was the best for any 10:00 P.M. drama series since 1991.

The stripped-down narrative of the episode hails from the pens of David Simon and David Mills. Simon directs his attention this time away from the detectives and onto the victims of crime. This episode marks a new direction for the series, with *Homicide* reducing the number of story lines, and letting more episodes (like this one) stand on their own. Producer Tom Fontana explained the decision: "I think one of the things we discovered when we were writing the show was that if we told [fewer] stories, we would actually be able to tell the stories better."

NOTES: The title "Bop Gun" is the name of a song by Parliament-Funkadelic. *Entertainment Weekly* found references to P-Funk's music scattered throughout the episode. For example, the name of one of the street thugs is Kid Funkadelic.

Ironically, "Bop Gun" also unveils Chris Tergesen's contributions as music coordinator. Tergesen turns the opening sequence into a mini–music video, set to Seal's appropriately-named song, "Killer." (See Appendix B, "Get the Music Back.")

Episode 11: "See No Evil"

[Production Code 201]
Original air date: January 13, 1994.
Written by Paul Attanasio; directed by Chris Menaul.

Additional Cast and Guest Stars:
Wilford Brimley (Harry Prentice), Michael Chaban (Chuckie Prentice), Clayton LeBoeuf (Captain George Barnfather), Jennifer Mendenhall (Carry Westin), Jeffrey Mandon (Officer Hellriegel), Michael S. Kennedy (Lieutenant Tyron), Stan Brandorff (bartender).

STORY: When Meldrick Lewis and Steve Crosetti investigate an apparent suicide, Meldrick suspects the victim's son did the deed. The suspect, though, is Beau Felton's childhood friend, and Beau knows what actually transpired that night.

Detectives Frank Pembleton and Tim Bayliss have found what they believe to be a cover-up of a police shooting of an unarmed suspect. As the officers close ranks to protect their own, Frank finds resistance even from his own lieutenant.

HIGHLIGHTS: In order to protect his friend, Beau literally has to beg Meldrick to turn a blind eye. A year later, Meldrick would try to cash in the favor, asking Beau's help in stopping Bolander's investigation into Crosetti's death (see Episode 19: "Crosetti").

While Felton and Lewis exercise their discretion in choosing to let a killer go free, Pembleton displays his almost superhuman dedication to his job, relentlessly investigating his fellow officers for a suspicious death. This characteristic would become a hallmark of Frank's persona. For him, every murder must be avenged, every murderer apprehended, no matter what the circumstances. Only after his stroke, in Episode 74: "Double Blind," does his conviction fail him.

COMMENTARY: Series creator Paul Attanasio returns to script this episode, offering only uneasy and provocative questions. Whether "justice" is being served by either of these investigations is a question left up to the audience.

The assisted-suicide plot is surprisingly topical and headline-making for *Homicide*. While shows like *Law and Order* proudly take their plots from newspaper headlines, *Homicide's* brand of realism means their stories are usually taken from the back of the Metro pages, where the tallies of crimes and murders pile up anonymously and unheralded.

NOTES: The plot thread of Frank investigating fellow cops for shooting a suspect in the back also comes from the headlines. Detective Donald Worden, the character on whom Stan Bolander was based, handled the real-life investigation in 1988. This story would continue into the next episode.

Episode 12: "Black and Blue"

[Production Code 202]
Original air date: January 20, 1994.
Written by James Yoshimura; story by Tom Fontana; directed by Chris Menaul.

Additional Cast and Guest Stars:
Julianna Margulies (Linda), Isaiah Washington (Lane Staily), Clayton LeBoeuf (Captain George Barnfather), Jeffrey Mandon (Officer Hellriegel), Michael S. Kennedy (Lieutenant Tyron), Kyf Brewer (Ryan), Mel Proctor (Grant Besser), June Thorne (Dale), Joseph S. Eubanks (Harris).

STORY: As Detective Pembleton becomes convinced that the well-liked Lieutenant Tyron shot suspect C.C. Cox in the back, Lieutenant Giardello fumes at Frank's disloyalty to his fellow officers. To pacify his commander, Pembleton takes a witness into the Box and skillfully elicits a signed confession from him, even though he didn't do it.

Gee may not like it, but he can't accept the tainted confession. Come what may, Pembleton and Bayliss arrest Tyron.

HIGHLIGHTS: In their ongoing policy of making sure as many story lines as possible touch the detectives personally, *Homicide*'s production team adds a touch to the C.C. Cox case not present in the real-life incident on which it was based. Here, it turns out Kay Howard had an affair with the prime suspect, Lieutenant Tyron, and still carries a torch for him. When Frank makes his case against the well-liked policeman, it's not enough that he's ending the career and reputation of a fellow law officer, but he's arresting a man Kay once loved.

In another romantic subplot, Stan Bolander begins falling in love with a waitress named Linda, a woman half his age with whom he shares little aside from a musical hobby. She plays the violin and he plays the cello.

COMMENTARY: This episode features the outstanding writing of James Yoshimura, who considers it his favorite script. Like Andre Braugher, Yoshimura attended St. Ignatius College Prep and The Juilliard School, and like Clark Johnson he attended Loyola University before getting his MFA in drama from Yale. Yoshimura has written some of the series' most memorable installments, but the scene of Pembleton extracting a "confession" from an innocent man is one of his greatest achievements.

NOTES: As the feisty and musical waitress Linda, Julianna Margulies exhibits the same charm and charisma that made her a star on *ER*. Producer Tom Fontana had, in fact, offered Margulies a continuing role on *Homicide*, which she turned down to appear in *ER*.

Episode 13: "A Many Splendored Thing"

[Production Code 203]
Original air date: January 27, 1994.
Written by Noel Behn; story by Tom Fontana; directed by John McNaughton.

Additional Cast and Guest Stars:
Julianna Margulies (Linda), Zeljko Ivanek (Assistant State's Attorney Ed Danvers), Adrienne Shelly (Tanya), Scott Neilson (Jeremy), Cheryl Donaldson (Molly), Julie Lauren (Officer Schanne), Herb Levinson (Dr. Lausanne), Ralph Tabakin (Dr. Scheiner), Sal S. Koussa (Forman), Stan Kelly (Grady), Jane Beard (Newdow), Dan Garrett (Novoselic), Mary L. Watson (Prince).

STORY: Bayliss and Pembleton investigate the murder of a young woman strangled in her apartment, where a note helpfully but inaccurately announces, "Ed did it." The trail leads them to a bondage leather store, a phone sex company, and an S&M club.

Crosetti and Lewis have an even stranger case on their hands, when they discover a man stabbed in a public library by another man who wanted his inkpen.

HIGHLIGHTS: John Munch, on the outs with his (never seen but often mentioned) girlfriend Felicia, is jealous of his partner Stan Bolander's new-found romance. Munch even wants Gee to order Bolander to be miserable again. Stan and Linda double-date with Kay and Ed Danvers (another romantic subplot, an easy way to insert "life-affirming story lines" into a show about murder), only to have Munch crash the party and bring everyone down with his own personal blend of cynicism and bitterness. Munch may not be fun, but he's often right. He accurately predicts the breakup of Danvers and Howard. Interestingly, while the intended finale of Season One, Episode 8: "Smoke Gets In Your Eyes," concluded with Bolander lonely and feeling sorry for himself, the unintended finale of Season Two concludes with Bolander lucky in love.

Before she joined ER, *Julianna Margulies played Detective Bolander's girlfriend on* Homicide.
Everett Collection

COMMENTARY: The title "A Many Splendored Thing" reveals the episode's theme: variations of love. Of course, each instance of love depicted on the show has some kind of kink or twist. This is *Homicide*, after all. Stan and Linda are a mismatched pair of wildly disparate ages. Bayliss and Pembleton investigate the murder of a young woman whose indulgence in phone sex and S & M had more to do with sex than love. In turn, she is killed by a man cheating on his girlfriend with a woman he doesn't even like. John Munch's on-again, off-again affair with Felicia is a destructive relationship, and so he's quick to spot the same signs in the bickering of Kay Howard and Ed Danvers. Ultimately, the most dysfunctional relationship in the show is the man who loves pens so much he'll kill for them.

However, it was not just the fertile imagination of *Homicide*'s writers that was responsible for such a perverse and inexplicable motive for murder. In August 1993, in Maryland's Anne Arundel County, a twenty-three-year-old man shot another man ten times. The murder took place in a doughnut shop when the victim refused to sell the other his pen.

NOTES: The episode is directed by John McNaughton, the filmmaker responsible for the highly regarded and controversial 1990 independent film *Henry: Portrait of a Serial Killer*. McNaughton also directed the much more conventional film *Mad Dog and Glory* (1993), which starred Robert De Niro, Bill Murray, Uma Thurman, and *Homicide*'s Richard Belzer.

CHAPTER 5

The Third Season:
White Gloves and Red Balls

"They're just not promoting us," lamented executive producer Barry Levinson, defeat creeping into his voice.

After two exceptionally truncated seasons, *Homicide* had survived at least two serious discussions of cancellation. Despite overwhelming critical praise, the show had faltered in the ratings in its first year. With the benefit of a more favorable time slot and heavy promotion of guest star Robin Williams, *Homicide*'s second season delivered strong ratings and won the series a reprieve from the network's ax. But as *Homicide* entered its third (and first full-length) season, Barry Levinson fumed that NBC had abandoned them.

In the absence of network publicity, critics who had followed and promoted the series assumed *Homicide* had been canceled.

NBC's Warren Littlefield rejected the accusations, and promised the network would promote the series. "[I]f we didn't believe it could succeed, we wouldn't have gone forward with it the first time, we wouldn't have gone forward the second time and we certainly wouldn't have gone forward with it the third time," the NBC Entertainment president told the *New York Times*.

However, during the nine months between the end of the second season and the start of the third, NBC aired no reruns. "We wanted to make a fresh start and put our best foot forward," explained Littlefield. It would be as if the show was starting over again like new.

Friday Nights

Although *Homicide* had performed excellently in the ratings during its four-episode 1994 run, the new season ushered in a number of important changes. For one thing, NBC moved the series out of the Thursday-night slot that had served it so well. In order to make room for a new showpiece drama, *ER*, *Homicide* moved to Friday nights at 10:00 P.M., a slot that has remained its home ever since.

Traditionally, audiences are much smaller on Friday nights. Thus, ratings are down overall for Friday-night programming, a factor that would contribute to *Homicide's* continued ratings battles. Additionally, the series went head-to-head against the highly acclaimed *20/20* newsmagazine on ABC (1978–) and the Emmy-winning cult hit *Picket Fences* (1992–97) on CBS.

Since *Homicide* and *Picket Fences* appealed to more or less the same audience, the strategy forced viewers to choose between two equally compelling shows. Nielsen's ratings tabulations have no way to calculate how many viewers chose to watch one show while videotaping the other, which meant the head-to-head conflict artificially deflated both shows' numbers. *New York Daily News* critic David Bianculli called the move "the stupidest network showdown since…*Chicago Hope* was pitted against NBC's *ER.*"

"They've shown us exactly how much they care about us by what they do to promote the show and where they place us," lamented actor Andre Braugher about NBC, "It's evident to me what they think of the show."

The 10:00 P.M. slot, however, placed *Homicide* directly after the Fox network's *The X-Files* (1993–), which reached a similar audience. Industry observers would note that the two shows formed a block of dark and quirky programming, with some of *The X-Files'* viewers switching over to *Homicide* at ten. In Episode 24: "Partners," Detective Munch aptly remarks that on Friday nights, most people are home watching *The X-Files* (Yaphet Kotto was, as he admitted, a fan, and Belzer himself appeared as his *Homicide* character Detective Munch in an *X-Files* episode in 1997).

After the first season of only nine episodes, and a second year of only four, executive producer Tom Fontana asked if the third season would be even shorter: "What are we going to be doing? Twelve minutes?"

In fact, NBC started off with an order of thirteen episodes. After the first few installments were broadcast they upped it to twenty, just shy of a full order for a full season. In making this commitment, though, NBC asked that the program lighten its tone.

Red Balls and Other Refinements

"I don't think any purists who have embraced *Homicide* will say, 'Oh my God. What have they done?'" Littlefield told the press, "This isn't ever going to be cookie-cutter TV." Nevertheless, Littlefield admitted NBC asked the show for some more "refinements."

To this end, Levinson and Fontana brought on writer Henry Bromell as co-executive producer. Bromell realized that the best and most popular episodes of the series had been those with high-intensity "red ball" cases.

In Baltimore police lingo, a "red ball" is a high-profile, politically sensitive case that is considered the squad's highest priority. The first season's investigation into the murder of Adena Watson was the first "red ball" for the show, and was closely modeled on a real-life "red ball" described in David Simon's book. The second season saw another "red ball," in Episode 10: "Bop Gun," which was co-written by David Simon. In both instances, the "red ball" cases demanded much of the squad's manpower and resources, but there was still room for detectives to continue other investigations as well.

In the third season, David Simon's influence would lessen and the writers would begin to cater to a more action-hungry audience than before. With an NBC mandate to simplify the stories, "red ball" cases would be shown as being not only the highest priority of the squad, but the only priority.

The third season opened with a three-part tale concerning a serial killer targeting Catholic women. The case consumed the full attention of every detective on both the day and night shifts of the Homicide Unit. Later in the season, another three-parter involved a fugitive sniper who shoots Detectives Bolander, Howard, and Felton. The rest of the Homicide squad naturally had nothing else on their minds but bringing the shooter to justice. These two "red ball" trilogies were the highest-rated episodes of the season. A precedent had been set.

These stories were visceral, violent, and urgent. They brought out the emotions of the characters in times of extreme stress, highlighted the difficult politics of the police department, and enabled the writers to include all the major cast members while still keeping the story line focused and direct. In short, these "red ball" stories were ideal. *Homicide* had its roots in crusty cops talking their way through a dark, bleak world. The new *Homicide* had more sex, more action, and more viewers.

If this new approach took the series farther away from its roots in David Simon's nonfiction reporting, it also led the series into the realm of successful television drama. Arguably, Season Three showed *Homicide* at its best, with a most satisfying blend of the old and new approaches.

Season Three also ushered in a new era of a central set of staff writers: James Yoshimura, Julie Martin, Jorge Zamacona, and Bonnie Mark, who worked with Fontana and Bromell to author most of the season's output. This writing team allowed for a better consistency of characterization, and for subplots and story developments that could evolve over the course of the entire season. Yoshimura and Martin would prove to be so central to the show's development that they would eventually be promoted to producers, taking over as Fontana distanced himself from the day-to-day operations.

As always, *Homicide* strove to bring in guest directors from the world of feature films, giving the show a classy, cinematic touch. However, unlike previous (and subsequent) seasons, the number of guest directors were relatively few. A small pool of directors handled many of the year's installments, which helped to establish the season's consistency of tone.

With the understructure of the show now more consistent, *Homicide* could follow the example set by "Bop Gun" and bring on more guest stars without risking the program's integrity or realism. Steve Buscemi, Howie Mandel, Bruno Kirby, Valerie Perrine, Tim Russert, John Waters, and Chris Noth made notable appearances. Without a doubt, though, the most striking developments in the cast occurred in the main players. Over the course of the year, three cast members left and one was added.

Comings and Goings

Isabella Hofmann joined the show as Lieutenant Megan Russert, the first major character not to have been based, even in part, on one of the figures from David Simon's book. Hoping to compete with *NYPD Blue*'s on-air sexiness, and concerned about the fate of a male-dominated program in an era when women usually decide what TV shows are watched, *Homicide* introduced Russert as a way of delving into the squad's sex lives while also addressing gender issues in the workplace.

Just as Hofmann joined the cast, NBC dropped Jon Polito as Detective Steve Crosetti. In the first few episodes of the season, Crosetti's absence was explained as his being away on vacation. Later in the year, the writers revealed a more permanent explanation: Crosetti had taken his own life.

However, NBC decided that the two-episode story line in which Detective Bayliss becomes sexually involved with the morbid and entrancing Emma Zoole (who consummates her passions in a silk-lined coffin) had a sexy, crowd-pleasing quality necessary for a good "sweeps" week installment. For them, it appeared to be more appropriate than the depressing suicide tale "Crosetti."

At issue were the November ratings sweeps, a period during which the networks' advertising rates are established. The first and last Fridays of November were preempted by NBC for other programming, leaving *Homicide* only two nights out of the entire sweeps period to demonstrate its popularity. Had NBC run "Crosetti" in sequence, only the first part of the Emma Zoole story line would have aired during November, and its follow-up episode would be delayed by a week. NBC's programming executives took one look at the situation and decreed that continuity be damned: Bayliss's "sex in a coffin" story line would be kept intact during the all-important November sweeps.

Although no official word was ever given on the matter, rumor has it that NBC allegedly ousted Polito solely because of his weight. Network executives simply didn't expect TV audiences to warm to a pudgy, middle-aged man. If true, this shows the callousness and pettiness of network thinkers at its worst.

Ned Beatty, whose age and physique placed him in NBC's line of fire as well, held on in large measure due to his fame and remarkable skill. In fact, this season showcased his character Stan Bolander to full advantage, and gave Beatty an excellent send-off. Beatty and Daniel Baldwin both left at the end of the year to pursue their respective feature-film careers.

The decision to leave was theirs, and came as no surprise. Both actors had been very vocal in airing their frustrations with NBC during the 1994 wait-and-see period. Both actors also became discouraged by NBC's so-called refinements, and decided that *Homicide*'s integrity was being compromised while they watched. They turned in some of their best work this season, and left *Homicide* for less frustrating pastures.

By the end of the season, though, none of the cast members knew whether they were returning, or not. Although Beatty and Baldwin decided they'd had enough of wait-and-see games, the rest of the cast hung on, unsure of the future. For the third year in a row, NBC was seriously considering canceling the series. Thinking that it might be their final episode, Barry Levinson returned to direct the season finale himself.

The Third Time's the Charm

Overall, Season Three brought in an unremarkable average rating of 10.6 (each rating point representing 970,000 homes), about half of what Season Two had achieved. It finished in 88th place out of 146 shows. It ranked third in its time slot, while *Picket Fences* finished in 64th place and *20/20* finished in 17th place.

Sometimes programs can survive with unimpressive ratings if they appeal to the key demographic group of eighteen- to forty-nine-year-olds, the audience segment beloved by advertisers. But *Homicide* ranked 95th in this regard, compared to *Picket Fences* at 73rd and *20/20* at 24th.

Although the situation looked bleak, the playing field had changed since 1993. NBC was now in a better position, surging upwards in the ratings. As evidence of this changed outlook, Warren Littlefield announced that "NBC is very encouraged by increasing Nielsen numbers in one of the toughest time periods on the schedule. This season, quality dramas have had a resurgence, and we feel *Homicide* is second to none."

Furthermore, by becoming co-owners of the show, NBC had a financial stake in its survival. Television shows cost more to make than the producers generally get from the networks. After all, the industry is founded on speculation. Producers gamble that their shows will hang on long enough to make it into syndication, where they make back the rest of their investment and start to see a profit. Until a show has generated somewhere around seventy-five episodes, though, there is little chance of selling it to syndicators. With only thirty-three episodes under *Homicide*'s belt, NBC had a good reason to keep it on the air in hopes of making a syndication package to recoup its investment.

Littlefield continued to praise *Homicide*, saying the series was "at the top of its game." NBC's West Coast president Don Ohlmeyer announced that *Homicide* had at least a fifty percent chance of being renewed, a comment that offered the producers little comfort.

Executive producer Levinson cautiously told the press, "I'm never confident. I'm very cynical and very jaded. The ways of the networks have always been strange to me."

Producer Fontana tried to remain optimistic, but noted "there are a lot of things that have to be taken into consideration. The Zen of programming I don't understand."

By the start of May, the network had already renewed half of its existing roster of shows, and was set to publicly announce the next year's schedule in a matter of days. However, there was still no word on the future of one of the most highly praised series in recent memory. Levinson noted, "Nothing comes easy to *Homicide*."

Yet, NBC did renew *Homicide*, finally, for a fourth season. Not only that, but the network also contracted for a full order of twenty-two episodes, which would continue to be run Friday nights at 10:00 p.m. During the summer, NBC ran repeats to keep *Homicide* fresh in the viewers' minds. When it returned, there would be another set of refinements, but Levinson could now say, "I have a sense when I'm out and about that people talk to me about *Homicide* more and more."

The word was finally getting out.

SEASON THREE

October 1994–May 1995
60-minute episodes
Fridays, 10:00 P.M. EST

Production Team:
Barry Levinson (executive producer), Tom Fontana (executive producer), Henry Bromell (co-executive producer), Jim Finnerty (supervising producer), Gail Mutrux (Producer), Debbie

Sarjeant (associate producer), Paul Attanasio (creator), James Yoshimura (executive story editor), Julie Martin (story editor), Jorge Zamacona (story editor), Bonnie Mark (staff writer), Vince Peranio (production designer), Susan Kessel (set decorator), Rolande Berman (costume designer), Douglas J. Cumo (music), Chris Tergesen (music coordinator), Lynn Kowal (main title theme), Louis DiGiaimo (casting director), Pat Moran (Baltimore casting director), John Gooch (boom), Bruce Litecky (sound mixer), Jean de Segonzac (director of photography), Alex Zakrzewski (additional director of photography), Cindy Mollo (editor), Greg Featherman (additional editor), Mark Pellington (title sequence), Dennis A. Brown (executive in charge of production).

Regular Cast:
Daniel Baldwin (Detective Beau Felton), Ned Beatty (Detective Stanley Bolander), Richard Belzer (Detective John Munch), Andre Braugher (Detective Frank Pembleton), Isabella Hofmann (Lieutenant/Captain Megan Russert), Clark Johnson (Detective Meldrick Lewis), Yaphet Kotto (Lieutenant Giardello), Melissa Leo (Detective Kay Howard), Kyle Secor (Detective Tim Bayliss).

Episode 14: "Nearer My God to Thee"

[Production Code 301]
Original air date: October 14, 1994.
Written by Jorge Zamacona; story by Tom Fontana and Jorge Zamacona; directed by Tim Hunter.

Additional Cast and Guest Stars:
Tony Todd (Matt Rhodes), Mary B. Ward (Beth Felton), Walt MacPherson (Detective Roger Gaffney), Beau James (Detective Higby), Ralph Tabakin (Dr. Scheiner), Gerald F. Gough (Colonel Bert Granger), Pamela Payton-Wright (Sister Magdalena Weber), Molly Austin (Dawn), Kristin Rohde (Officer Sally Rogers).

STORY: The new commander of the Homicide Unit's second shift, Lieutenant Megan Russert, is barely a week into her post when a high-profile "red ball" case lands on her desk. The woman named Samaritan of the Year has been murdered and left in a church dumpster, naked save for a pair of white cotton gloves.

The bosses bring in Lieutenant Giardello and his squad of detectives to assist Lieutenant Russert's team. Frank Pembleton immediately butts heads with the case's primary detective, the bigoted Roger Gaffney.

HIGHLIGHTS: This episode unveils the first real use of the "red ball" case. Although the Adena Watson investigation from the first season was officially designated a "red ball," the white-glove murder case that begins in this installment is more typical of the way *Homicide* would depict such high-profile and politically sensitive cases in the future.

In addition to the crisis of this case, the characters have their usual personal crises as well. Detectives Lewis and Munch are preparing to buy the nearby Waterfront Bar, with silent partner Tim Bayliss (in a mostly comic plot line stretched across most of the season).

Meanwhile, Kay Howard is caught in the middle of her partner Beau Felton's deteriorating home life. Thrown out by his wife Beth and cut off from his kids, Beau has begun a secretive affair with Lieutenant Megan Russert.

COMMENTARY: The "white-glove murders" represent an attempt by *Homicide* to recapture the success of the Adena Watson story line. Like Bayliss before her, Russert is inexperienced but well-meaning, saddled with a very public case and thrust into an uncomfortable spotlight. Like the Watson probe, Russert finds her theories of the crime tugged out from under her as more evidence comes to light, and too few good leads to offer much hope.

Although the three-episode-long story establishes a new, more sensational direction for the show, the writers keep *Homicide*'s arch wit intact. The opening sequence has Detectives Bolander, Munch, and Lewis complaining about how network executives force producers to add gratuitous sex to shows. Sure enough, the episode that follows introduces newcomer Megan Russert as a love interest for Beau Felton.

NOTES: One of Lieutenant Russert's detectives, contemptuously described by day-shifters Bolander and Pembleton as "less than our shadows," is one Detective Higby, played by Beau James. Higby has little more than a few brief lines, but he would return in many subsequent episodes. He will reappear memorably in the fifth season Episode 61: "M.E., Myself and I" as the detective who conspires with an M.E. to rule a hooker's murder a drug overdose so he won't have to investigate it.

Tim Hunter, director of "Nearer My God to Thee," previously directed the motion picture *River's Edge* (1987) with Keanu Reeves and Dennis Hopper, as well as episodes of the cult TV series *Twin Peaks* (1990–91).

The Waterfront Bar first seen in this episode really exists, and stands directly opposite the Recreation Pier Building in Baltimore's Fells Point area. When *Homicide* took over the Recreation Pier as its main set, the cast and crew naturally found themselves spending a fair amount of time in the conveniently located Waterfront Bar. The owner joked that they were in there so often, it should be on the show.

Levinson took the idea to heart, and had the writers cook up a script to do just that. Having three of the detectives buy the bar raised the profile of the

Waterfront, and it has became a favorite target for *Homicide* tourists. Since appearing on the show, the Waterfront has experienced a twenty percent increase in business. Asked whether the program has had a bad effect on Baltimore's tourism overall, the Waterfront's owner Mike Working disagreed. "The show is huge here. The murder isn't bad PR. We break murder records every year. Baltimore's as famous for murders as it is for crabs."

Episode 15: "Fits Like a Glove"

[Production Code 302]
Original air date: October 21, 1994
Written by Bonnie Mark; story by Tom Fontana and Julie Martin; directed by Ted Demme.

Additional Cast and Guest Stars:
Tony Todd (Matt Rhodes), Mary B. Ward (Beth Felton), Walt MacPherson (Detective Roger Gaffney), Beau James (Detective Higby), Pamela Payton-Wright (Sister Magdalena Weber), Hugh Hodgin (Fuchs), Traber Burns (Forte), Julie Lauren (Officer Schanne), Herb Levinson (Dr. Lausanne), Peter O'Neal (cameraman), Robert Sommerwerk (Everett), Sharon Ziman (Naomi).

STORY: Shift Commander Russert removes Detective Gaffney from the white-glove case, furious at his carelessness, and assigns the high-profile case instead to Frank Pembleton.

A self-described "entrepreneur of the macabre" offers to buy the gloves from evidence control, telling the detectives that their culprit is a serial killer, with other dead women in church Dumpsters as far away as Montana.

HIGHLIGHTS: In the afterglow of sex, Megan Russert and Beau Felton discuss their dreams and ambitions. Noticing a picture of Megan in Budapest, Beau realizes that he is not only having an illicit affair with a woman of higher rank, but she is of a very different social class than himself. This class difference would be hinted at in future episodes (such as Detective Munch's reactions to seeing Russert's beautiful home in Episode 40: "Heartbeat," and her overdressed appearance in Episode 77: "Partners and Other Strangers"). Russert also talks about having traveled in Europe. (In the fifth season, she would depart the squad to move to France.)

COMMENTARY: Executive producer Barry Levinson eagerly watched the show as it evolved in its first two, truncated years to see what elements clicked; which characters and which situations offered the greatest dramatic potential. Andre Braugher's remarkable performance as the intense Frank Pembleton stood out most conspicuously, especially his interrogation scenes.

As *Homicide* entered its third season, the producers decided to focus more on Braugher in hopes of making the show more "viewer-friendly."

Braugher's scenes in this episode shine with charm, arrogance, and depth. He takes this case personally, and so the viewers are swept into it as well. Although at times this approach would veer toward making *Homicide* into "The Frank Pembleton Show," it also presented some of the most entertaining hours of television.

NOTES: This episode was directed by Ted Demme, nephew of the better-known director Jonathan Demme. Ted's feature films include *Who's the Man* (1993), *The Ref* (1994), and *Beautiful Girls* (1996).

Episode 16: "Extreme Unction"

[Production Code 303]
Original air date: October 28, 1994.
Written by Keith Mano; story by Tom Fontana and James Yoshimura; directed by Keith Gordon.

Additional Cast and Guest Stars:
Lucinda Jenney (Annabella Wilgis), Tony Todd (Matt Rhodes), Mary B. Ward (Beth Felton), Pamela Payton-Wright (Sister Magdalena Weber), Zeljko Ivanek (Assistant State's Attorney Ed Danvers), Gerald F. Gough (Colonel Bert Granger), Wayne Gruen (Monsignor), Sharon Ziman (Naomi), Michael Willis (Darin Russom).

STORY: As the pressure upon the squad to solve the "white-glove murders" increases, Detective Pembleton gets a break with the appearance of a witness he soon realizes is, in fact, the killer herself. Faced with the calculating evil of Pamela/Mary Maude/JMJ/Annabella Wilgis, Pembleton finds himself questioning, and then losing, his faith.

HIGHLIGHTS: After a chance encounter with Beth Felton, Lieutenant Russert's conscience pangs her and she decides to break off her affair with Detective Felton. But Felton cannot really go home again, the fractures are too deep.

Meanwhile, Detectives Lewis, Munch, and Bayliss are faced with an army of bureaucrats in their efforts to buy the Waterfront Bar.

COMMENTARY: Still looking to the first season's Adena Watson case for inspiration, the producers of *Homicide* draw from the well of the Emmy-winning Episode 5: "Three Men and Adena" for this gripping and maddening installment. Detective Pembleton finds himself in the Box once again with a killer of innocents, unable to extract the confession and unable to bring the killer to justice.

NOTES: The guest director this week is not just a feature filmmaker, but also an actor. Keith Gordon has had roles in films ranging from *Jaws 2* (1978), *All That Jazz* (1979), *Dressed to Kill* (1980), *Back to School* (1986), and *I Love Trouble* (1994). Gordon's directorial credits include another prime-time series produced by a prominent movie director: Oliver Stone's *Wild Palms* (1993). Gordon also wrote and directed the acclaimed feature *The Chocolate War* (1988).

Episode 17: "A Model Citizen"

[Production Code 305]
Original air date: November 11, 1994.
Written by Noel Behn; story by Tom Fontana and Jorge Zamacona; directed by John McNaughton.

Additional Cast and Guest Stars:
Joe Morton (Sam Thorne), Laurie Kennedy (Felicity Weaver), Michael Willis (Darin Russom), Lauren Tom (Emma Zoole), Joseph Abramo (Dr. Mantee), Terry Dawson (Lennox Young), Ilona Dulaski (Carla), Andrea Fletcher (Mrs. Young).

STORY: Detectives Howard and Munch investigate a suspicious shooting, hoping to get a deadly weapon out of the hands of some children before it kills anyone.

Meanwhile, the Waterfront Bar partnership is endangered by a rift between Lewis and Bayliss over the lovely yet morbid Emma Zoole. At the same time, Annabella Wilgis, the "white-glove murderer," sues the department, claiming her civil liberties were violated.

HIGHLIGHTS: The disintegration of Detective Felton's home life reaches a tragic peak when Beau returns home from his shift to find that his home is gone. Beth has left him, taking his kids, furniture, everything, and leaving him nothing but hurt (which is underscored, naturally enough, by Nine Inch Nails' mournful song "Hurt").

COMMENTARY: Anxious to get the more sensational Emma Zoole episodes on the air for the sweeps period, NBC swapped several episodes around. As an unfortunate consequence, the audience hears about Detective Crosetti's death before the episode including that (now much less) shocking revelation.

"A Model Citizen" may be sexier than the usual *Homicide* outing, but NBC's demand for "more life-affirming story lines" must have fallen on deaf ears. Bayliss's affair with Emma Zoole is not only morbid, but also an act of betrayal against his colleague, friend, and business partner Meldrick Lewis.

As for the central case of the hour, writer Noel Behn's story makes a nice parallel between activist Sam Thorne's unsuccessful attempts to elicit help from the detectives for his Toys for Guns swap, and the detectives' own unsuccessful efforts to get a gun out of the hands of children. In the following episode, Giardello's friend Sam Thorne (played by Joe Morton) would be murdered.

NOTES: The episode's tale of a young man accidentally shooting his brother, save for the requisite name changes, actually happened. In journalist David Simon's account of the incident, too, the detectives never got the gun out of the house.

Episode 18: "Happy to Be Here"

[Production Code 306]
Original air date: November 18, 1994.
Written by Julie Martin; story by Tom Fontana and Julie Martin; directed by Lee Bonner.

Additional Cast and Guest Stars:
Lauren Tom (Emma Zoole), Joe Morton (Sam Thorne), Darryl LeMont Wharton (Matt Cameron), Bruce Dworkin (liquor store clerk), Herb Levinson (Lausanne), Ruben S. Brown (Dwight), Gerald F. Gough (Colonel Bert Granger), Irving Jacobs (Arthur), Robert Lafferman (Bob), D'Monroe (Jerome), Paul Morella (Andy), Kristin Rohde (Officer Sally Rogers), Ralph Tabakin (Dr. Scheiner), Judy Thornton (Judy).

STORY: Lieutenant Giardello's friend Sam Thorne, editor of *The Black Voice*, is killed in the line of duty, trying to expose the major players in the city's drug trade. Gee confronts the teenage assassin, demanding to know why his friend was killed, only to learn his friend's life was worth nothing more than a new bicycle.

Tim Bayliss's affair with Emma Zoole ends abruptly when the detective learns of her other boyfriend.

HIGHLIGHTS: In one of the series' most memorable moments, the heartbroken Bayliss is driven to robbery. He holds up a liquor store for $10.78 worth of beer and cookies when the clerk refuses to overlook Tim's being eleven cents short.

COMMENTARY: This episode is about the little things in life, and how, for people in desperate situations, those little things can take on exaggerated importance. A pubescent assassin kills a man because the crime (which he does nothing to hide) earns him a new bicycle. In a stunning twist, the killer walks out of the restaurant after executing Sam Thorne only to stop and buy a breath mint. When asked why he paid for the mint after committing a murder, the kid replies that he's not a thief. In his mind, depriving a man of his life is just a job, something he can do in return for money. But a mint, that's an object of value, not to be taken lightly or stolen.

Even a cop on hard times can be pushed over the line, as Bayliss discovers in the liquor store. The detective puts his reputation and his job at stake for nothing more than eleven cents, which he needs to buy beer and cookies. Such are the things and circumstances that can lead anyone to crime.

NOTES: *Homicide* fans on the Internet discussion group alt.tv.homicide adopted the phrase "my eleven cents" in honor of this episode, in place of the phrase "my two cents' worth."

A young man by the name of Darryl LeMont Wharton appears briefly in this episode, playing "Matt Cameron." Wharton later migrated backstage, where he became one of the show's staff writers.

Episode 19: "Crosetti"

[Production Code 304]
Original air date: December 2, 1994.
Written by James Yoshimura; story by Tom Fontana and James Yoshimura; directed by Whitney Ransick.

Additional Cast and Guest Stars:
Lee Tergesen (Officer Chris Thorman), Edie Falco (Eva Thorman), Heather Brown (Beatrice), Gerald F. Gough (Colonel Bert Granger), Clayton LeBoeuf (Captain George Barnfather), Joey Perillo (Bernard Munch), Patsy Brady Adams (secretary), Brilane Bowman (bakery clerk).

STORY: Days after he was supposed to return from his vacation, Detective Steve Crosetti is found dead. Horrified, Detectives Munch and Bolander find themselves at the pier where their former colleague has apparently killed himself.

Unwilling to accept the idea of his partner killing himself, Meldrick Lewis demands a full investigation, and is furious when Bolander finds all evidence pointing to suicide.

HIGHLIGHTS: The closing scene is guaranteed to set your hair on end. Throughout the episode, Frank Pembleton appears as a selfish jerk for refusing to attend Crosetti's funeral, insisting he no longer will set foot in a church (the events of the white-glove murders having soured him on religion forever). Ultimately, he reveals the true depth of his loyalty to his fallen friend by appearing at the funeral in full-dress blues, in direct defiance of orders, a one-man honor guard.

Actor Kyle Secor declared this scene to be his favorite in the series.

COMMENTARY: Although the powerfully emotional scene of Pembleton honoring his fallen comrade in full-dress blues remains one of the most memorable scenes in the series' history, and contributes to making this one of the most popular episodes, "Crosetti" also boasts excellent performances from Clark Johnson and Ned Beatty. Both actors, often overlooked in the past, get to show off the kind of intense soul-searching audiences had come to expect from Andre Braugher and Kyle Secor.

The essence of the drama here, which would be used again and again throughout the series, is the personal consequences of the investigation. Homicide detectives have to remain aloof and cold to keep from being tortured by every fresh corpse, but the producers of *Homicide* found a way to get under their characters' skins. If Episode 10: "Bop Gun" worked its magic by watching a victim's anguish, why not let the main characters experience that pain firsthand?

"Crosetti" is one of the best examples of this approach, in which one of the detectives is connected closely either to the victim or to the suspect of a murder. From its horrifying opening to its tearful ending, this is *Homicide* at its strongest.

NOTES: Joey Perillo plays John Munch's brother, a mortician named Bernard. (John quips that dinner at the Munch household is "one life-affirming story after another.") In real life, Richard Belzer has an older brother, Len. Just as both Munches work with death, the Belzers work with comedy. Len Belzer hosts and produces the syndicated radio show *The Comedy Hour.* Perillo is a character actor who can be seen in John Waters' *Hairspray* (1988), Jonathan Demme's *Philadelphia* (1993), and Terry Gilliam's *Twelve Monkeys* (1995).

The guest director this week is Whitney Ransick, an independent filmmaker whose *Hand Gun* (1993) won rave critical reviews in 1994. Ransick would become one of *Homicide*'s staple of guest directors, responsible for some of its most powerful and memorable hours.

Episode 20: "The Last of the Watermen"

[Production Code 307]
Original air date: December 9, 1994.
Written by Henry Bromell and Tom Fontana; directed by Richard Pearce.

Additional Cast and Guest Stars:

Michael Currie (Wesley Howard), John Dossett (Chick), Gareth Williams (Chris Haskett), John C. Hansen (Josh Howard), David Dossey (Eddie), Jan Austell (Harlan), Vivienne Shub (Millicent), Kristin Rohde (Officer Sally Rogers), Harlee McBride (Dr. Alyssa Dyer).

STORY: Discouraged by the seemingly endless cruelty of the big city, Detective Kay Howard takes some time off and heads for her family's home on Maryland's eastern shore. Not only has her home changed—divorces, retirements, and economic recessions have taken their toll—but her hometown friends also may be involved in a murder.

HIGHLIGHTS: Throughout the series, little hints of Kay's love life have been scattered. She was involved with State's Attorney Ed Danvers for a while, and still has feelings for him. She had an adulterous affair with Lieutenant Tyron, and in future episodes would have an unnamed and very secretive lover. This episode introduces Chick, a former flame she still loves, deep inside, even if she knows they will never be together.

COMMENTARY: "The Last of the Watermen" is an odd episode, more along the line of those of the Angela Lansbury TV series *Murder, She Wrote* (1984–96). Nevertheless, it is played with *Homicide*'s trademark naturalism, which means no twist to the plot at the end as happened frequently on *Murder, She Wrote*. The person you suspect first is the one who did it, and for reasons no more arcane than what was plainly obvious at the time. There is no grand motive, no clever trick to trap the killer, nothing underneath it all.

Kay Howard returns to work apparently refreshed by the experience of seeing a childhood friend arrested for a brutal slaying. She's not happy with the outcome, but it teaches her that her unpleasant occupation isn't merely a result of the evils of the big city. Everywhere, people who should know better do things they shouldn't.

Medical examiner Dr. Alyssa Dyer appears for the first time in this episode. Played by Mrs. Richard Belzer, Harlee McBride, the character appeared throughout the third and fourth seasons, and resurfaced in the season finale of the fifth.

Episode 21: "All Through the House"

[Production Code 308]
Original air date: December 16, 1994.
Written by Henry Bromell; directed by Peter Medak.

Additional Cast and Guest Stars:
Zeljko Ivanek (Assistant State's Attorney Ed Danvers), Harlee McBride (Dr. Alyssa Dyer), Ralph Tabakin (Dr. Scheiner), Nancy Marchand (Lorraine Freeman), Ryan Todd (Fidel MacGaffin), Kevin Cameron (Desmond), Vernon DeVinney (Sam), Beau James (Detective Higby).

STORY: Saddled with the graveyard shift on Christmas Eve, the detectives of Baltimore's Homicide Squad try to find some holiday cheer even in their grim work. Beau Felton has a real problem dredging up holiday spirit, as he is cut off from his children.

Even those who immerse themselves in their work find the special night depressing. John Munch and Stan Bolander discover the corpse of a Salvation Army Santa Claus, and his apparently orphaned son. Lieutenant Russert joins Detective Lewis in tracking a killer, only to ruin another family's Christmas.

HIGHLIGHTS: When Lieutenant Russert goes out on the street with Meldrick Lewis, it gives us a preview of what she will be like when she joins the squad as a demoted detective in the following season. At first, she explains her desire to go out on the call as giving in to "the addiction" of being a homicide detective. Later, she confesses she's also trying to avoid painful memories of her late husband Mike, a former tax lawyer killed by cancer. She loved him, but also admits he was "boring."

Interestingly, both shift commanders Megan Russert and Al Giardello have been left single by the death of their spouses.

COMMENTARY: What an odd Christmas episode this is! There is none of the sappy treacle networks usually trot out at this time of year. Instead, *Homicide* celebrates the holiday season with a quirky, unsettling, and sad tale of lonely people and broken lives. (Not that much uplifting sentiment could be expected from a show about the folks who track murderers.)

The episode is full of downbeat characters and situations: a junkie set on fire, a mother who kills in cold blood to keep her drug-dealing husband out of jail, a child of an alcoholic single parent, and various and sundry crimes for motives as venal and small as can be imagined.

There is a fair bit of comedy, though, much of it to do with Tim Bayliss's ill-advised hustle of Gee in a game of hearts.

This segment proves not to be one of the better episodes, but it is still audacious and daring.

NOTES: Director Peter Medak, the director of *Romeo is Bleeding* (1993) and *Species II* (1998), offers a welcome focus on Munch and Bolander, turning the spotlight on characters often overshadowed by "The Frank Pembleton Show."

Episode 22: "Every Mother's Son"

[Production Code 310]
Original air date: January 6, 1995.
Written by Eugene Lee; story by James Yoshimura and Tom Fontana; directed by Ken Fink.

Additional Cast and Guest Stars:

Baltimore Mayor Kurt Schmoke (himself), Howie Mandel (interior decorator), Sean Nelson (Ronnie Sayers), Harlee McBride (Dr. Alyssa Dyer), Helen Carey (Assistant State's Attorney Maggie Conroy), Gay Thomas (Mary Nawls), Bobby McAdams (Jason Nawls), Rhonda Stubbins-White (Patrice Sayers), Kevin Nelson (David Sayers), Nanna Ingvarsson (Theresa Cousart).

STORY: While Detective Felton searches for his youngsters, Detectives Pembleton and Bayliss find themselves pursuing kids, too: a thirteen-year-old has been shot in the head by a fourteen-year-old.

When the detectives finally catch the callous young killer, they discover he intended to murder a different boy but shot the wrong kid by mistake.

HIGHLIGHTS: The case affects Frank Pembleton enormously, as he is considering having a child of his own. It is the first mention that Frank is considering becoming a father. This plot thread would be revisited in Episode 33: "The Gas Man," and would become a central subplot of future seasons.

COMMENTARY: Considered by fans to be one of *Homicide*'s best episodes, this grueling hour deftly alternates between the horror of kids killing kids to comic relief as Bayliss, Lewis, and Munch face one absurd hurdle after another in opening the Waterfront Bar. Writer James Yoshimura proved himself wonderfully adept at writing these painful juxtapositions of tragedy and comedy.

NOTES: The opening sequence features the first of several cameo appearances by real-life Baltimore Mayor Kurt Schmoke, as the detectives are honored at a football game. The scene was filmed at a real game between the Baltimore Canadian Football League team and the Las Vegas Posse. At

Baltimore's Memorial Stadium, actor Clark Johnson found himself awash in memories. "If they said suit up, I would," Johnson quipped, recalling his brief and unremarkable career in the CFL in 1979.

This episode also includes a cameo appearance by former *St. Elsewhere* star Howie Mandel as an interior decorator hired to revamp the Waterfront. This episode also features the first appearance of Helen Carey as Assistant State's Attorney Maggie Conroy. Beyond her acting (she also appears in 1993's *Pelican Brief* and 1997's *Shadow Conspiracy*), she also is well known in the Washington, D.C. area as a prominent real-estate agent.

Episode 23: "From Cradle to Grave"

[Production Code 311]
Original air date: January 13, 1995.
Written by David Mills; story by Tom Fontana and Jorge Zamacona; directed by Myles Connell.

Additional Cast and Guest Stars:
Al Freeman Jr. (Deputy Commissioner James Harris), Clayton LeBoeuf (Captain George Barnfather), Dick Stilwell (Congressman Jeremy Wade), Christopher Glenn Wilson (Timothy Draper), Kristin Rohde (Officer Sally Rogers), Timothy Wheeler (preacher), Eddie Daniels (Bree Whetherly), Herb Levinson (Dr. Lausanne), Meg Kelly (admitting clerk), Edgar Allan Poe IV (Detective Harvey Easton), Peggy Yates (Maria Delgado).

STORY: Detectives Munch and Lewis find themselves descending into the world of a biker gang called the Deacons, investigating the murder of one of their members.

Meanwhile, Deputy Commissioner Harris asks Frank to look into a kidnapping claim by a political ally, Congressman Wade. When Pembleton learns Wade made up the story to conceal his homosexuality, Harris asks Pembleton to drop the case, and then sets up Pembleton as a fall guy after reporters accuse the department of a cover-up.

HIGHLIGHTS: Writer David Mills refers back to Episode 7: "And the Rockets' Dead Glare," when the bosses once offered Frank a promotion to shift commander. This recollection sets into a motion a chain of events that would lead to Frank's bitter resignation, which proves to be an act intended mostly for show.

COMMENTARY: This episode returns the series to the tone of its early days, with a script that draws heavily from David Simon's book for inspiration.

Acclaimed character actor Al Freeman Jr. in his younger years.
Everett Collection

Although the biker story is original, writer David Mills adapts the other two cases from real events.

Bizarrely, the comic subplot in which a rookie officer allows paramedics to rush a dead body to the hospital, return it, and then tries to restage the crime scene, actually happened.

In another real-life incident, Detective Donald Worden was sent by his superiors to look into a politician's bogus kidnapping story only to uncover a politically damaging domestic quarrel. When Worden cut the deal his superiors wanted and the news got out, they deserted him, letting him take the heat alone.

As dramatized on TV, this story takes on an unexpected, though not unwelcome, added dimension. Pembleton is called into Lieutenant Giardello's office to explain his actions, while Deputy Commissioner Harris and Captain Barnfather watch him twist in the wind. During filming, Andre Braugher suddenly realized that all the actors in the scene were black. It took awhile for the realization to dawn because the scene wasn't about race. After all, few television shows afford black actors much screentime except to dramatize racial issues.

"I realized it was the first time I'd ever been in a room with three other African-American actors and the scene wasn't about us," said Braugher, "It's a long time coming."

"I had the same reaction watching that scene," recalled executive producer Tom Fontana, "It was one of those happy accidents that occurred naturally because of the way the show has evolved . . . . What they were doing was acting the same way Caucasians are allowed to act."

NOTES: This marks the first appearance by acclaimed character actor Al Freeman Jr. as the extremely manipulative Deputy Commissioner James Harris. Freeman's extraordinary career stretches from classic films like *Finian's Rainbow* (1968) to recent ones like *Once Upon a Time...When We Were Colored* (1995). Freeman played Malcolm X in the television miniseries *Roots: The Next Generations* (1979) and later played Elijah Muhammad in Spike Lee's biography of *Malcolm X* (1992). He even had a role in the popular soap opera *One Life to Live*, back in 1968!

Episode 24: "Partners"

[Production Code 312]
Original air date: January 20, 1995.
Written by David Rupel; story by Tom Fontana and Julie Martin; directed by John McNaughton.

Additional Cast and Guest Stars:

Al Freeman Jr. (Deputy Commissioner James Harris), Ami Brabson (Mary Pembleton), Harlee McBride (Dr. Alyssa Dyer), Helen Carey (Assistant State's Attorney Maggie Conroy), Ralph Tabakin (Dr. Scheiner), Robert Clohessy (Douglas Jones), Sean Whitesell (Doctor), David Kevin Michael Bowles (Lenny), Pat Dade (Monica Murphy), Beau James (Higby), Randy Jurgensen (Colucci), Kevin Murray (Malcolm), Craig Wallace (Pauley), Peggy Yates (Maria Delgado).

STORY: Maggie Conroy reluctantly proceeds with her prosecution of Congressman Wade. Her key witness is Detective Pembleton, who could ruin Harris's career. However, on the stand Frank swallows his wounded pride, takes the blame for the poor judgment of his superiors, and returns, chastened, to the Homicide department.

Lieutenant Russert fears her former partner, Doug Jones, may be a wife-beater, and urges him to get therapy, while she begs his wife Natalie to leave him. That night, Russert is called to the Jones' house, where Natalie has shot Doug to avoid yet another beating.

HIGHLIGHTS: Pembleton's return to duty reunites him with Bayliss, with whom he continues to have an on-again, off-again partnership. After their reluctant pairing in the first place and Pembleton's brief resignation, Frank and Tim would later clash in Episode 32: "Colors"; be separated by Frank's stroke in Episode 56: "Work Related"; and then separated yet again by Tim's angry assertion of his independence in Episode 68: "Betrayal."

This episode also features, at long last, the grand opening of the Waterfront Bar.

COMMENTARY: Although the character of Lieutenant Russert gave *Homicide* an additional female presence and a sexy boost, it became difficult to include her in the story line week after week. As the commander of the second shift, her character didn't have much natural interaction with the established cast. "Red ball" cases like the white-glove murders brought the two shifts together, but on normal days Russert wouldn't arrive at the squad house until the other main characters were headed home. In this episode in particular, Russert gets much screentime but has precious few scenes with the other cast members.

NOTES: Appearing as Russert's former partner Doug Jones is actor Robert Clohessy. Clohessy had worked with producer Tom Fontana several years before as a guest performer on *St. Elsewhere*, in a 1987 installment.

Episode 25: "The City That Bleeds"

[Production Code 313]
Original air date: January 27, 1995.
Written by Julie Martin and Jorge Zamacona; story by James Yoshimura and Bonnie Mark; directed by Tim Hunter.

Additional Cast and Guest Stars:
Tony Lo Bianco (Detective Mitch Drummond), Gloria Reuben (Detective Theresa Walker), Mary B. Ward (Beth Felton), Michael Currie (Wesley Howard), Clayton LeBoeuf (Captain George Barnfather), Carlos Campbell (school officer), G. Lee Fleming (porn shop owner), John C. Hansen (Josh), Jay Hilmer (Dr. Biller), Ava Lenet (Shannon), John Ritz Miller (Sergeant Rallo), Rhonda R. Overby (reporter), James Potter (Dr. Carrolton), Nancy G. Robinette (Mary), Peggy Yates (Maria Delgado), Irv Ziff (Mr. Libowitz).

STORY: On their way to serve a routine warrant on a pedophile and child murderer, Detectives Bolander, Howard, and Felton are ambushed and shot. Barnfather places the case on the highest "red ball" priority. Lieutenant Russert's shift is brought on, Bolander's former partner, Mitch Drummond, takes time off from the bomb squad to assist, and Sex Crimes detective Theresa Walker joins them to help track the pedophile.

As primary officer on the case, Frank shows his usual relentlessness, methodicalness, and objectivity, which rankles his fellow detectives as they grieve for their wounded friends.

Gloria Reuben helped Homicide's cops chase pedophile Glenn Holton before she joined the cast of ER. Everett Collection

HIGHLIGHTS: Stan Bolander's former partner, Mitch Drummond, appears in the flesh after being the stuff of legend for years. Since the premiere episode in the first season, "Gone for Goode," Bolander has berated and abused John Munch for not living up to the standards set by Drummond. Indeed, Drummond proves himself a tenacious and hardworking detective, much less prone to distraction than Munch.

Munch is understandably inattentive now, haunted by the sight of seeing his friends and colleagues shot down around him. This sight would continue to haunt him forever. Bolander, shot in the head, and Howard, shot in the heart, don't return to work until Episode 29: "The Old and the Dead." Beau Felton receives relatively minor wounds, shot in the thigh and neck, and returns to work before the others (and before he should) in Episode 28: "Law and Disorder."

COMMENTARY: NBC's ads for this episode boasted "one of the season's most powerful hours of television" and quoted *New York* magazine's praise, "As good as it gets." Broadcast right after the World Professional Figure Skating Championships, "The City That Bleeds" had a strong lead-in audience and heavy hype. In the end, the three-episode story line resulted in some of the show's best-ever ratings. This episode netted a 14.6 rating, the second best for the entire year's run.

"This is something that honestly bothers me," fretted producer Tom Fontana later. "It was the first time in the show's history that a gun had been fired, so for us, it was a very traumatic thing. But people seem to love guns and people running around doing all that normal cop stuff."

The pre-credits sequence opened with the shootings, getting the episode off to an intense dramatic start. This beginning contrasts greatly with the other Season Three opening scenes, which tended to be filled with more jokes than was usual in the show's history. In fact, this emotionally-charged episode features little of *Homicide*'s trademark absurd humor.

Not only did the episode boost the show's ratings, but it also did so without losing *Homicide*'s critical support. *USA Today*'s Matt Roush wrote, "Death is their livelihood, but never has it confronted them with such force. This gripping episode is the first of three parts. A guarantee: If you watch tonight, you'll cancel all plans for next Friday."

NOTES: This segment features a guest appearance by Gloria Reuben, also known to NBC viewers as Jeannie from *ER*. With *Homicide* having already discovered Julianna Margulies, producer Henry Bromell joked, "We have an agreement with *ER*: We discover them, they use them."

Episode 26: "Dead End"

[Production Code 314]
Original air date: February 3, 1995.
Written by Jorge Zamacona and Julie Martin; story by James Yoshimura; directed by Whitney Ransick.

Additional Cast and Guest Stars:

Tony Lo Bianco (Detective Mitch Drummond), Gloria Reuben (Detective Theresa Walker), Mary B. Ward (Beth Felton), Clayton LeBoeuf (Captain George Barnfather), Gerald F. Gough (Colonel Bert Granger), Gary D'Addario (Lieutenant Jasper), Dana Ivey (Margie Bolander), Michael Currie (Wesley Howard), Beau James (Detective Higby), Steve Hofvendahl (Glenn Holton), Robert Lafferman (Bob Reardon), Teresa Payne-Rohan (Alice), Judy Thornton (Judy), John Ventimiglia (Manuel), Gary Wheeler (doctor).

STORY: Working together, if tensely, with the Quick Response Team (QRT), Pembleton and his detectives apprehend suspected sniper Glenn Holton and haul him into the Box. Although they have him dead to rights for a child-killing, Detective Pembleton realizes the creep didn't have anything to do with shooting Howard, Felton, or Bolander. The case is suddenly back to square one.

HIGHLIGHTS: With child-killer Holton cornered and surrounded by dozens of heavily armed officers, Detective Bayliss punches the suspect while arresting him. Bayliss's anger toward people like Holton (or the araber) takes on an extra significance with the later revelation that Bayliss is himself a victim of childhood sexual abuse (see Episode 68: "Betrayal").

COMMENTARY: *Homicide*'s writers put another feather in their cap for their humanizing portrayal of Captain Barnfather in this episode and the one before it. He may play manipulative politics, but underneath it he's a human being. The role offers too great an opportunity for caricature, and, indeed, most episodes paint the department bosses as selfish and petty. However, Clayton LeBoeuf is too good an actor to let his character become a cartoon, and his quiet humility after Lieutenant Russert's rebuke comes as a welcome surprise.

NOTES: The episode sports a wonderfully twisted mix of fact and fiction in the character of QRT Lieutenant Jasper. This recurring character is played by Gary D'Addario, who is the real-life Homicide shift commander on whom Al Giardello ("Gee") was based. Known as "Dee" to his detectives, D'Addario displayed the same fierce loyalty and diplomatic poise that became Gee's characteristics. In addition to playing Jasper in this and subsequent episodes, D'Addario serves as a technical advisor to the producers and occasionally offers his thoughts to fans on *Homicide*'s various Internet sites. At present, "Dee" is considering retiring from the force to return to his former occupation as a rock musician.

Episode 27: "End Game"

[Production Code 315]
Original air date: February 10, 1995.
Written by Rogers Turrentine; story by James Yoshimura and Henry Bromell; directed by Lee Bonner.

Additional Cast and Guest Stars:
Steve Buscemi (Gordon Pratt), Tony Lo Bianco (Detective Mitch Drummond), Gloria Reuben (Detective Theresa Walker), Dana Ivey (Margie Bolander), Clayton LeBoeuf (Captain George Barnfather), Irv Ziff (Mr. Libowitz), Sharon Ziman (Naomi), Dave Droge (truck driver), Gerard Ender (Latino), Kathryn Klvana (April), Rhonda R. Overby (reporter), James Potter (Dr. Carrolton), Jean Schertler (Rachael), William Shriver (Walter), Tony Yarbrough (Laborer).

STORY: With Holton no longer the prime suspect, Detective Pembleton turns his attention to the sinister occupant of Room 201, the room the detectives mistakenly approached in search of Glenn Holton (who lives in Room 210). The inhabitant of Room 201, Gordon Pratt, is a gun-loving racist with multiple arrests in his past.

Guest star Steve Buscemi is no stranger to playing disturbed characters.
Everett Collection

HIGHLIGHTS: Throughout the story line of his colleagues being shot, Frank Pembleton remained the only one not to show the effects of the trauma. Not showing even the slightest shred of emotion, he presses ahead as if he were on any case, with any victims. However, when faced with virulent racist Gordon Pratt, Pembleton, at last, lets his emotions begin to swell up, and they all but overwhelm him.

COMMENTARY: After the grim drama of the previous two installments, "End Game" provides a welcome return of *Homicide's* quirky comic touches. As the psycho Pratt, Steve Buscemi gives an especially amusing and disturbing performance. Poor Buscemi plays such wackos so well he has become rather stereotyped in these kinds of roles. He can be seen in such films as *Kiss Daddy Goodnight* (1987), *Miller's Crossing* (1990), *Barton Fink* (1991), *Reservoir Dogs* (1992), *The Hudsucker Proxy* (1994), *Pulp Fiction* (1994), *Fargo* (1996), *Escape from L.A.* (1996), *Trees Lounge* (1996), and *Con Air* (1997). He also has taken a turn at directing and writing films.

Frank Pembleton fails to crack Pratt, though, and the killer walks out free. Detective Munch accuses Pembleton of letting his emotions compromise his interrogation, which is ironic in that Pembleton has been so cold towards the process up until this point. In response, Frank shoves John angrily. In filming the scene, Andre Braugher got carried away and really shoved Richard Belzer hard. "I went flying. I got a cut on my arm, a cut on my face," Belzer told *TV Guide,* "And he was so sweet. He felt so bad. I thought, 'Thank God I like him.' Because if I didn't, I would've flipped out."

NOTES: As Pembleton tries to wear Pratt down and expose him for the weak, small bastard that he is, the other detectives watch through the one-way glass. Munch makes a comment about Jim Thompson's novel *Getaway*, noting that the Steve McQueen movie version was vastly superior to the forgettable remake. Ironically, the remake starred Alec Baldwin, brother of costar Daniel.

This reference is especially ironic in light of the fact that the producers had repeatedly told the press that Alec Baldwin was going to make a guest appearance during the course of this four-episode story thread. This plan ultimately fell through, and all that remains is this odd, offhanded remark by Munch.

Episode 28: "Law and Disorder"

[Production Code 316]
Original air date: February 24, 1995.
Written by Bonnie Mark and Julie Martin; story by Henry Bromell and James Yoshimura; directed by John McNaughton.

Additional Cast and Guest Stars:

Chris Noth (Detective Mike Logan), John Waters (R. Vincent Smith), Valerie Perrine (Brigitta), Harlee McBride (Dr. Alyssa Dyer), Dana Ivey (Margie Bolander), Sarada Kotto (Angela Brewer), Julie Lauren (Officer Anne Schanne), Scott Wesley Morgan (Westmoreland), Kristin Rohde (Officer Sally Rogers), Ralph Tabakin (Dr. Scheiner), Judy Thornton (Judy), Sharon Ziman (Naomi).

STORY: When Gordon Pratt, the man accused of shooting Detectives Felton, Howard, and Bolander, is found murdered, Detective Bayliss is forced to investigate his friends and colleagues, who now have become the most obvious suspects.

Bayliss's partner, Frank Pembleton, temporarily pairs with Meldrick Lewis on a shooting that pits them as much against each other as against the killer. At the same time Beau Felton, having recovered from his wounds, returns to duty only to end up on a call on his first day back.

HIGHLIGHTS: In a memorable comic subplot, Detective Munch's hippie past starts to catch up with him, with the display of a nude photograph taken during his flower-child days.

COMMENTARY: Although not officially part of the "detectives shot" plot line, this installment does carry that story forward in a meaningful way. Despite some prominent comic elements, the underlying drama ripples with dark and troubling implications. Kyle Secor gets to strut his stuff as the tortured, sensitive Bayliss once again.

Tim's investigation into his coworkers makes for an interesting contrast to the similar case on which Frank worked back in Season Two's Episode 12: "Black and Blue." There, Gee could not stomach Pembleton investigating cops as if they were ordinary suspects. After all, men in uniform are family. However, this time around, Gee does not display any emotion one way or the other about Tim's suspicions, and makes no effort to dissuade Tim from pursuing the case. In fact, when Tim begs to be let off the case, Gee refuses. Similarly, Frank is cold to Tim and shows none of the relentless pursuit of the truth that inflamed him when he was investigating Lieutenant Tyron.

Season Four's Episode 48: "Justice, Part Two" provides another interesting comparison. In that episode, the Homicide squad investigates a fellow cop, one of Meldrick Lewis's friends, for allegedly killing his father's murderer.

However, here the detectives show none of the self-righteous code of ethics that inform these other stories. The Homicide Squad is willing to let Pratt's killer go unpunished.

For Gee and Frank, as well as for the other detectives, Pratt has transcended being just the usual Bad Guy. In their minds, whoever shot him meted out justice, even if it was vigilante justice. There are no pat answers, no sugar-coated homilies here, just a complex set of characterizations that allows Pembleton and Giardello to show different personality traits when presented with different circumstances.

NOTES: The title "Law and Disorder" has an ironic touch to it, since this episode features the first crossover between *Homicide* and NBC's other acclaimed crime drama. Actor Chris Noth appears in the opening sequence as *Law and Order*'s Detective Mike Logan. Logan has come to Baltimore to hand over to Pembleton an extradited suspect, played by John Waters. This scene marks famed cult movie director Waters' second appearance on the show, although as a different character than in Episode 8: "Smoke Gets In Your Eyes." This time, Waters' character is a killer named R. Vincent Smith, which just happens to be the real name of *Homicide*'s props supervisor.

This scene opens an episode crammed with noteworthy cameos and guest appearances. Yaphet Kotto's daughter Sarada appears as a murderess that Frank and Meldrick accidentally stumble across while pursuing a completely different case.

Valerie Perrine (who costarred with Ned Beatty in 1978's *Superman*) turns in a guest performance as one of Munch's former flames. It is she who has put a giant nude photograph of Munch on display in her "Hippie Daze" exhibition at a gallery directly across from the squad house.

Episode 29: "The Old and the Dead"

Production Code 317]
Original air date: March 3, 1995.
Written by Randall Anderson; story by Henry Bromell and Jorge Zamacona; directed by
Michael Fields.

Additional Cast and Guest Stars:

Tim Russert (himself), Shawn Wayne Hatosy (Lyle Warner), Lyle Kanouse (Bret Blakely),
Pete Philopolous (Carl Blakely), Clayton LeBoeuf (Captain George Barnfather), Ralph
Tabakin (Doctor Scheiner), Sharon Ziman (Naomi), Gerald F. Gough (Colonel Bert
Granger), Joe Lane (Colleary), Seamus McLaughlin (Howerchuck), Jill Redding (Mrs.
Krebs), Henry Strozier (Elden Warner).

STORY: Returning to work at last, Detective Kay Howard is frustrated at
being desk-bound, and jealous of Felton and Bolander being back on the
streets since they were shot at the same time she was.

In other office shakeups, Lieutenant Giardello discovers corruption in city
contracts, resulting in the ouster of Colonel Granger. Barnfather moves up the
ladder to colonel, but Gee is passed over for the promotion to captain, in favor
of Megan Russert.

HIGHLIGHTS: Returning to work after her recovery, Kay is irritated to
discover her desk has been moved. Deferring to his partner's wishes, Beau
Felton tries to put the desk back where it was, but, by then, she has developed

*Newsman Tim Russert, a
guest in "The Old and the
Dead," went to high school
with producer Tom Fontana.*
Everett Collection

a superstitious attachment to its new home. Her old winning streak was felled by one of Crosetti's old cases (see Episode 31: "Nothing Personal," aired out of sequence) but even working behind a desk on her first day back, Kay starts a new streak of luck at her new desk.

COMMENTARY: Ned Beatty turns in another top-notch performance in one of the all-too-rare Bolander episodes. He can use a snappy new fedora to hide the horrifying scar of his having been shot, but the mind inside is brilliantly intact. Bolander's struggle to reassert his skills as a detective after his injury reveal a detective too professional to be felled by anything so slight as a bullet in the head.

NOTES: Lieutenant Russert's promotion to captain comes as a surprise to Giardello, but not to viewers who were paying attention to a continuity error in the opening sequence. Tim Russert of *Meet the Press* appears as himself, purportedly as Megan's cousin. In a humorous sequence, he and Megan argue like little kids. However, during the scene, Megan appears in her captain's uniform, although her promotion is not unveiled until the end of the episode.

Tim Russert's cameo would be his only onscreen appearance in *Homicide*, but he would be repeatedly mentioned in dialogue in future episodes. The famed news commentator may not really be cousin to the fictional Megan Russert, but the real-life Tim Russert was a high-school friend of *Homicide* producer Tom Fontana.

Episode 30: "In Search of Crimes Past"

[Production Code 318]
Original air date: April 14, 1995.
Written by Jane Smiley; story by Henry Bromell and Julie Martin; directed by Ken Fink.

Additional Cast and Guest Stars:
Barnard Hughes (Sam O'Donnell), Helen Stenborg (Isabella), Felicia Shankman (Lee Bigelow), Harlee McBride (Dr. Alyssa Dyer), Clayton LeBoeuf (Colonel George Barnfather), Jerry Stiller (Bartender), Judy Thornton (Judy), Martha Caveny (Lisa), Barney Cohen (Horton), Steven Dawn (Keith), Phil de Carlo (homeless man), Kathleen Grennon (Lois), Tim Houston (Matt), Terry Wills (Jeffrey Zwick), Christine Moore (secretary), Ralph Tabakin (Dr. Scheiner), Peggy Yates (Maria Delgado), Sharon Ziman (Naomi).

STORY: As the last hours tick away for a death-row inmate, the convict's daughter takes Colonel Barnfather hostage and demands that Detective Bolander reopen the case to discover her father's innocence.

The trail now sixteen years cold, and his notes long since filed away into storage, Bolander struggles to reacquaint himself with the case.

HIGHLIGHTS: In another great Bolander episode, Stan tortures himself with the realization he overlooked something important. Stan never learned that his victim was sleeping with another man's wife, and therefore never discovered the key to a case that put an innocent man on death row. What works so well is that Bolander obviously cares, and is clearly a thorough and dedicated detective. His error is not the oversight of a sloppy man or the deliberate corruption of a crooked cop. Sometimes, good people with good intentions make mistakes.

COMMENTARY: Eager to raise the prestige of *Homicide*'s writing in the same way that producer Barry Levinson had brought in acclaimed feature filmmakers as guest directors, producer Henry Bromell invited Pulitzer Prize–winning novelist Jane Smiley (*Moo, A Thousand Acres, Separate Keys*) to pen this episode.

Smiley's thoughtful and touching script gives Ned Beatty one of his best chances to display his ample acting skills. In between Bolander's grumbly soul-searching, Smiley also makes a worthy and frightening point that innocent people do get convicted, sent to death row—and, sometimes, executed too.

NOTES: Another notable guest contributor this week is actor Jerry Stiller (the irascible Frank Costanza on *Seinfeld*) who plays a new bartender for the Waterfront. His perfectionist standards don't sit well with his extreme incompetence, and his brief tenure at the bar costs the detectives a lot of money. In the end, Meldrick decides the key to success can be as simple as cheese twists. In addition to his recurring role on *Seinfeld* (1990–98), Stiller was a former player on *St. Elsewhere* (1982–88).

Episode 31: "Nothing Personal"

[Production Code 309]
Original air date: April 21, 1995.
Written by Bonnie Mark; story by Tom Fontana and James Yoshimura; directed by Tim Van Patten.

Additional Cast and Guest Stars:

Walt MacPherson (Detective Roger Gaffney), Dean Winters (Tom Marans), Pamela Isaacs (Amanda Dubreaux), Stan King (Bobby), Rosemary Knower (Laureen Hanrahan), Siv Svendson (Inger), Sharon Ziman (Naomi).

STORY: At last, Lieutenant Giardello decides the time has come to parcel out Crosetti's old cases and remove the deceased detective's name from the board.

The toughest of these cases goes to Kay Howard, who becomes obsessed with being the only cop who could solve Erica Chilton's murder. She is hampered further by the continuing downward spiral of her partner Beau Felton, who loses critical evidence during a drunken binge.

HIGHLIGHTS: This episode depicts the absolute nadir of Beau Felton's deterioration following the breakup of his family. His descent into alcoholism and self-pity not only render him pitiful to watch, but also cause him to lose what may be invaluable evidence. When the Chilton investigation is reopened in Episode 38: "Hate Crimes," the relative importance of Beau's misplaced evidence is finally put in context.

COMMENTARY: Director Tim Van Patten (formerly a bit player on *St. Elsewhere*) presents a tale of raw nerves, not least of which is Kay's burning need to prove herself the lone female supercop on the squad.

A more unsettling subplot, though, involves Lieutenant Giardello's date with one of Megan Russert's friends. The woman rejects Gee for reasons never made explicit, but Gee concludes the light-skinned woman didn't want to be seen with a darker-skinned black man.

Actor Yaphet Kotto proposed the subplot to the writers based on his own life experience, and Kotto's personal anguish at the hurt of black-on-black racism is palpable throughout the episode. "I was not able to attract a lighter-skinned black woman," Kotto told *TV Guide*, "They perceived me to be too ethnic-looking and not Caucasian-looking enough."

Kotto also told *TV Guide* of a saying he thinks held him back in relationships with black women: "'If you're light, you're all right; if you're brown, hang around; if you're black, stay back.' Obviously, I did a lot of staying back."

NOTES: This segment was written and filmed as the ninth episode for Season Three, but was held back by NBC until five months after it was to have appeared. By running this episode months out of sequence, NBC's programming executives caused a number of continuity problems. For one thing, the Chilton case's lack of conclusion has already interrupted Kay's perfect closure rate (see Episode 29: "The Old and the Dead"). Also, this episode occurs before the detectives are shot (Episode 25: "The City That Bleeds") and well before Megan's promotion to Captain (also Episode 29: "The Old and the Dead").

Unfortunately, in addition to the continuity errors, the delayed broadcast also places it directly after Episode 30: "In Search of Crimes Past," which also deals with the reopening of an old case.

Episode 32: "Colors"

[Production Code 319]
Original air date: April 28, 1995.
Written by Tom Fontana; directed by Peter Medak.

Additional Cast and Guest Stars:
David Morse (Jim Bayliss), Zeljko Ivanek (Assistant State's Attorney Ed Danvers), Ami Brabson (Mary Pembleton), Peggy Yates (Maria Delgado), Harlee McBride (Dr. Alyssa Dyer), Mel Proctor (Grant Besser), Johnny Alonso (David Scholtz), Scott Wesley Morgan (Westmoreland), Rhonda R. Overby (reporter), Holly Rudkin (Shannon Bayliss), Makan Shirafkin (Hikmet Gersel).

STORY: A Turkish exchange student in full KISS makeup, on his way to a heavy-metal rock party, accidentally goes to the wrong address and is shot to death by the frightened homeowner. Not only is the case a potentially explosive international incident and disastrous publicity for Baltimore, but the homeowner is Tim's cousin Jim Bayliss.

By being the primary detective on the case, Frank Pembleton opens a fissure between himself and Tim Bayliss, which may never fully heal.

HIGHLIGHTS: Meeting Tim's cousin Jim gives considerable insight into Tim's character (though not nearly as much as watching Tim spar with Frank throughout the episode). Tim and Jim are as close as if they were brothers, and Jim's nickname for Tim is "Teej."

COMMENTARY: "Colors" is an astonishingly provocative episode that doesn't let the viewer off easily. Just when Frank's conviction that Jim is a bigot seems far-fetched, Jim says something outrageously prejudiced. Then, just when Frank's crusade seems most justified, Jim shows a sensitive conscience worthy of his cousin. Along the way, the viewer is kept guessing about what really happened that night.

Tom Fontana's script turns, for once, not to David Simon's book for its inspiration, but to more recognizable headlines. On October 17, 1992, a Louisiana homeowner shot and killed a Japanese exchange student. Sixteen-year-old Yoshihiro Hattori was on his way to a Halloween party, but went to the wrong house. The shooting inflamed international tensions. Japan denounced the United States as a society so frightened of its own shadow and so well-armed that such a tragedy could happen so easily.

The already disturbing implications are only heightened by Tom Fontana's decision to make this another "personal" episode. The audience is not allowed to make pat judgments about the rightness or wrongness of Jim's actions, because the show's two most popular characters sit on opposite sides on the case.

New York Daily News reviewer Eric Mink writes, "Never before—and I stress, never—have I seen a television series render reality into a drama with as much raw power as [this] episode of *Homicide: Life on the Street* does." Mink emphasizes that the tension between Pembleton and Bayliss is so intense "that it literally leaves you grateful for the relief of commercial breaks."

The result is a remarkable television event, and very, very hard to watch.

NOTES: The many different, mutually-exclusive flashbacks, each being twisted by the teller's self-interest, is a technique borrowed from Akira Kurosawa's famed film *Rashomon* (1954). Writing alone for once, Tom Fontana keeps his theme alive with various discussions of color, be it racial color, the color of coffee, or the color of green on the TV screen.

Early in the episode, Meldrick Lewis utters an unrelated anti-foreigner tirade that seems so much less innocent once the details of the shooting start to come to light. His remarks are provoked by a discussion of the newly fired waterfront chef, "Henri de Segonzac," a subtle in-joke reference to the show's director of photography.

David Morse, the actor playing Jim Bayliss, played Dr. Jack Morrison throughout the lifespan of *St. Elsewhere* (1982–88), and has played devious villains in *Twelve Monkeys* (1995), *Extreme Measures* (1996), and *The Long Kiss Goodnight* (1996).

Episode 33: "The Gas Man"

[Production Code 320]
Original air date: May 5, 1995.
Written by Henry Bromell; story by Tom Fontana and Henry Bromell; directed by Barry Levinson.

Additional Cast and Guest Stars:
Bruno Kirby (Victor Helms), Richard Edson (Danny), Ami Brabson (Mary Pembleton), Tyler Buckalew (Victor Helms Jr.), Carlos Juan Gonzales (proprietor), Herb Levinson (Dr. Lausanne), Ralph Tabakin (Dr. Scheiner), Sharon Ziman (Naomi).

STORY: After six years behind bars for installing a defective gas heater that killed an entire family, Victor Helms is released from prison. However, Helms still is seething with rage at Frank Pembleton for putting him away, and refuses to acknowledge any complicity in the death of that family.

Before hunting Detective Pembleton in "The Gas Man," guest star Bruno Kirby appeared with actor Kyle Secor in City Slickers.
Everett Collection

Determined to humiliate and then kill Pembleton, Victor and his cohort Danny follow the detective, tampering with evidence and terrorizing him at home.

HIGHLIGHTS: Frank and Mary's desire to have a child is a central element of the episode, with Frank visiting a fertility specialist only to be diagnosed with a low sperm count. As will become clear in Season Four, the Pembletons overcome this setback.

COMMENTARY: For a time, it seemed this would be the final episode of *Homicide: Life on the Street*. To send off his brainchild with appropriate style, producer Barry Levinson took the directorial reins with a script penned by fellow producer Henry Bromell. Levinson proclaimed the tale "a shaggy dog of a suspense piece."

Not only is the result one of the series' best episodes, but it also achieves this while being completely and utterly unlike any other one. The growing focus on Frank Pembleton at the expense of the other cast members continues, with Victor Helms' obsession forcing the other characters out of view altogether. Yet actor Andre Braugher scarcely appears in the episode himself, and very few scenes take place in the familiar sets.

Instead, Levinson takes us around Baltimore with a pair of reprobates who spend their time endlessly conversing with each other just like the series' detectives do. In this case, their digressions range from the merits of disco lyrics to meaningful insights into what it means to be responsible.

Bruno Kirby may be the headliner guest star, but Richard Edson enacts Danny with memorable, barely articulate gusto. The two are so mesmerizing that when the action switches back to the regular cast members it is jarring for the viewer.

The central case, involving a beheaded fortune-teller, comes from a real crime. The brutal slaughter and decapitation of Sister Myra in 1994 was one of the bloodiest in Baltimore's history. In adapting it for TV, Bromell emphasized the grisly details by having Victor and Danny steal the head and keep it in a refrigerator, mailing Polaroids of it to Frank.

Such quirky, bizarre comic touches downplay the real menace of a murderous stalker pursuing Frank and his wife. The audience is almost too busy laughing out loud to be scared, and the sense of danger gets washed away in the happy sounds of the never-ending disco soundtrack. (Many of the same tunes accompany the Levinson-produced *Donnie Brasco* in 1997.)

Homicide fans can rejoice that this was not the end, after all. Had it been, though, there would have been nothing more apt than for this groundbreaking series to wave good-bye with an episode that broke all the series' own rules.

Critic Matt Roush wrote, "Tonight's season ender would be an event no matter when it aired...you don't want to miss it."

Many viewers did miss it, though, as "The Gas Man" received the lowest Nielsen numbers of the season. A meager 8.2 rating meant that fewer than 8 million people tuned in, much less than half the numbers for the season opener Episode 14: "Nearer My God to Thee."

NOTES: Barry Levinson had previously worked with both Bruno Kirby and Richard Edson on *Good Morning, Vietnam* (1987). Kirby has appeared in such popular Hollywood fare as *The Godfather Part II* (1974), *This Is Spinal Tap* (1984), *When Harry Met Sally...* (1989), *The Freshman* (1990), and *City Slickers* (1991). Edson can be seen in such highly regarded features as Jim Jarmusch's *Strangers in Paradise* (1984), Oliver Stone's *Platoon* (1986), John Sayles' *Eight Men Out* (1988), and Spike Lee's *Do the Right Thing* (1989). Kirby returned to *Homicide* the following season, not as a guest star but as a guest director (Episode 40: "Heartbeat").

CHAPTER 6

The Fourth Season: Law and Order

In May of 1995, Warren Littlefield rented out a Soho bistro in New York City called Match. The president of NBC Entertainment was hosting a party for the actors, writers, and producers of the programs he had just that day announced for the 1995–96 season.

As he made his rounds, Littlefield found Tom Fontana (the owner of Match) at a table in the back, sharing some drinks and cigars with three of his old friends: Barry Levinson, and *Law and Order* (1990–) producers Ed Sherin and Dick Wolf. Littlefield beamed, "Look at this group: great things should come out of this."

A Match Made in Match

The four producers gradually came around to the idea of fusing *Homicide* with *Law and Order*. They planned to link their shows as more than a mere gimmicky stunt. They hoped to stay true to the distinctive spirit of each show while uniting them in a meaningful way.

Littlefield loved the idea, and wanted to unveil it for the November sweeps. Unfortunately, what seemed brilliant in the cozy confines of the Match restaurant turned out to be a logistical challenge that would take until the February sweeps to resolve.

Primary among the concerns was that different corporate entities owned each show: Universal Television produces *Law and Order*, while NBC Productions produces *Homicide*. The two studios worried that the crossover hybrids would not fit neatly into their respective syndication packages. Fontana and Wolf realized they could end up spending millions to create programs that would have no future as reruns.

However, Littlefield loved the crossover concept so much that he encouraged the producers to proceed, and to let the syndication issue sort itself out.

THE TWO SIDES OF JUSTICE

Law and Order premiered on NBC on September 13, 1990. Created by Dick Wolf, the series revived a format originally seen in the short-lived 1960s program *Arrest and Trial* (1963–64). Splitting the story into two halves, *Law and Order* first depicts the police as they investigate a crime and arrest the suspect, then the second half follows the case as it wends it way through the courts. Although *Arrest and Trial* followed the ensuing trial from the point of view of the defendant, *Law and Order* observes from the vantage point of the district attorney.

Dividing the show into two half-hour subprograms meant that the series cannot rely heavily on the cast to carry the drama. *Law and Order*'s stars rarely appear in more than half of any given episode.

Instead of focusing on character, the writers of *Law and Order* emphasize plot—specifically, the drama inherent in the complicated wranglings of the legal justice system. Since its premiere in 1990, *Law and Order* underwent numerous cast changes, and by 1995 only one character from the original cast roster is left: Manhattan District Attorney Adam Schiff, played by Steven Hill. Despite such turmoil, *Law and Order*'s popularity has not diminished. Never reliant on its cast for its principal appeal, *Law and Order*'s ratings even went up with each change.

In the end, the scripts seamlessly wove the two shows together in a way that made watching the episodes together an enhanced experience, but still allowed each installment to stand alone and function dramatically on its own. According to Wolf, the first episode is "classic *Law and Order*," while the second delves into the psychological territory that is *Homicide*'s home turf.

Other concerns were of a more pragmatic. With *Law and Order* on a traditional eight-day schedule in New York City and *Homicide* on a trim seven-day shoot in Baltimore, arranging the actor's schedules was a difficult matter. *Homicide* solved the problem by loaning out only Andre Braugher, Kyle Secor, and Richard Belzer to the *Law and Order* installment, while their home show focused on other members of the ensemble team in their absence. Accommodations had to be made in order to allow actress Jill Hennessey time to film her scenes as assistant district attorney Claire Kincaid in Baltimore while *Law and Order* continued work on other episodes.

Another logistical hurdle was that *Homicide*'s shorter shooting schedule meant that they finished filming a season's worth of episodes nearly a month before *Law and Order* did. While *Homicide*'s half of the tale would be broadcast second, it was the first in the can. When the producers of *Law and Order* began work on what would be part one of the joint story, they began tinkering with the script in ways that threatened to upset the continuity with the already completed Part Two!

The Casts of Two Great Shows—Together!

NBC was no stranger to the gimmick of cast crossovers. The technique was most frequently employed in comedies, aided tremendously by NBC's habit of setting its sitcoms in Manhattan. During the winter of the 1995–96 TV season, three of NBC's Thursday-night comedies shared casts and subplots (*Seinfeld*, ever the iconoclast, remained self-contained).

Although the technique was a ratings-grabbing gimmick, it rarely found its way into drama series because it so easily could disrupt the sense of realism that NBC's dramas carefully cultivated. *Homicide*, however, had already started playing with the technique, at no cost to its unrelenting realism. Early in the fourth season, Mandy Patinkin appeared as his *Chicago Hope* character Dr. Jeffrey Geiger, in an especially daring cross-network character migration. In the previous year, *Homicide* had hosted a cameo by *Law and Order*'s Chris Noth as Detective Logan, in an episode ironically titled "Law and Disorder."

Having already laid the groundwork for a crossover between *Homicide* and *Law and Order*, the producers of both shows pulled off the double trick in the heart of *Homicide*'s Season Four, delivering some of the best ratings of the year for both shows. Nevertheless, combining the two shows demanded a delicate balancing act to preserve the distinctive characteristics of each. The writers had to find a way to stay true to *Law and Order*'s procedural approach, while also accommodating *Homicide*'s character-driven, dialogue-intensive approach.

ON THE SET

Even the production styles of *Law and Order* (1990–) and *Homicide* differ. *Law and Order* seems stagebound and sedate next to the gritty, frenetic pace of *Homicide*. *Law and Order*'s production adheres to strict union rules, which dictate how many crew members are even allowed to speak on the set. *Law and Order* films on New York soundstages, while *Homicide* wanders around Baltimore locations.

When the cast of *Law and Order* arrived in Baltimore to film their scenes, they were shocked to discover that *Homicide*'s producers allowed a school group to visit the set during the shoot, and one child was even allowed to handle the camera!

Ripped from the Headlines

The crossover with *Law and Order* delivered excellent ratings for *Homicide* during a year that saw some of its best audience ratings ever. The crossover story line was surprisingly topical for *Homicide*, but very much in keeping with *Law and Order*'s approach.

The writers and producers of *Homicide* rarely tapped current headlines for story material. "With our kind of writing, it doesn't get you anywhere," says *Homicide*'s executive producer Henry Bromell, "Two scenes into it, you've already told your story. Our writing has to be coming from the characters."

Law and Order's Dick Wolf and his team of writers relied on such recent terrorist incidents as the gas attacks in the Tokyo subway, a fire bombing in the New York subway, and the World Trade Center bombing for inspiration for the tale. The story is typical of *Law and Order*'s "ripped from today's headlines" style.

In turn, *Homicide* had certainly raided real events for inspiration in the past, but the kind of stories told by journalist David Simon were never nationally recognizable incidents. Instead, they were local concerns of the city of Baltimore. Where *Law and Order* dramatized big crimes of national stature, *Homicide* reveled in the seemingly trivial details of ordinary murders. *Law and Order* ripped its stories from the headlines; *Homicide* ripped theirs from the back pages of the Metro section.

Nonetheless, *Homicide* managed to fuse seamlessly with *Law and Order* because in the 1995–96 season its writers began to abandon their previous small-scale approach for a more sensationalized and topical style of writing. In some ways, in its fourth season *Homicide* went about selling its soul.

There's a saying around NBC that in order to save *Hill Street Blues* (1981–87) they had to kill it. As *Homicide* entered its fourth year, the same network pressures loomed large over Fontana's head: make *Homicide* more accessible, more mainstream, or else be canceled. At the same time, neither NBC nor Fontana wanted to lose the special qualities that made *Homicide* distinctive in the first place. The natural conclusion to these seeming disparate needs was to look back at *Homicide*'s more successful episodes of the past and write more in their style.

Arguably, much of *Homicide*'s breathtaking originality comes from its willingness to find the horror in the banal. The triviality of the motives that push *Homicide*'s malefactors to murderous extremes give the show a quirky "News of the Weird" touch. Other crime dramas look for the lurid and the sensational to inflame viewers' fears and drive up the ratings. Unsurprisingly, *Homicide*'s most popular outings had been those that tapped into the lurid and the sensational.

In the third season, *Homicide* re-created some of the appeal of the first season's Adena Watson "red ball" case with two highly rated story lines: the white-glove murders and the shooting of three of the detectives. These stories brought in the highest ratings for the season and established a pattern the show could follow.

This "red ball" pattern, though, owed little to the reality of "red ball" cases. Real-life Baltimore lived through one of the most traumatic and publicized "red ball" cases in 1988 with the slaying of an eleven-year-old girl. As dramatized in *Homicide*'s first season, even during the peak of this case's importance to the squad, the detectives continued to pursue other crimes as well. Catching the killer was vital to the city's sense of justice, but the perpetrator (the araber) had never killed before and never killed again. The new "red ball" pattern developed in *Homicide*'s later years involved serial killers, who had to be caught before they claimed their next victims.

The fact is that there are very few serial killers in the world. The United States may be a blood-soaked country with a murder rate that outstrips the rest of the industrialized world, but most of our murders are drug-related or involve parties who know each other. A psycho roaming the streets lashing out randomly in violence may be terrifying, but it is a notion more fitting for a horror story than a realistic crime drama.

The Baltimore of *Homicide*'s earliest seasons closely resembles the Baltimore in real life. Viewers could sit with a stack of *Baltimore Sun* newspapers and find the correlations to most of the incidents seen onscreen. The Baltimore of *Homicide*'s fourth season exists in a parallel dimension, where serial killers not only roam in enormous numbers but all gravitate toward Maryland's Charm City. The "Sniper" story line involves twelve people killed in a single day, nine by a single killer. There is even talk of calling in the National Guard.

Back in the summer of 1992, as producer Barry Levinson first began developing the series, he boasted to the press that *Homicide* would not show the kind of gunplay typical of TV crime shows. Richard Falteich, one of the real-life detectives from David Simon's book and one of the show's technical advisers, promised that *Homicide* would never depict car chases or shootings. He and the other detective-advisers would see to that.

However, by 1995 Falteich's dedication to realism took second place to the demands of the TV marketplace. As *Homicide* entered its fourth season, it had barely thirty-three episodes in the can and had survived three attempts at cancellation. Money, careers, and reputations were at stake, and the show was still struggling to find an audience. Having three detectives shot in the third season was a ratings coup, and it taught Fontana a sobering lesson about the bloodthirsty nature of the American viewer.

While realism suffered, Season Four opened the floodgates to gunplay, chase scenes, onscreen killings, nudity, and, of course, serial killers galore.

By pursuing the sensational, *Homicide* compromised its authenticity but it gained popularity. Its growing audience could get caught up in its fear of a thrill killer shooting down victims every time he stops for gas. In other words, the show was now creating plot lines that brought a kind of visceral reaction from its audience that the earlier seasons never tried to arouse. These stories have become more frightening, and, therefore, more emotionally engaging. Now, when the detectives catch serial killers, they're doing more than merely their jobs, they're rescuing innocent people from monsters.

They have become heroes.

Homicide as Movie of the Week

For their part, NBC decided that they needed to take the whole enterprise more seriously. Barry Levinson could never again complain that NBC was not advertising the show. Instead, the promotions department put their muscle behind the show and ran ads in high-profile slots during *ER* and *Law and Order*. With an eye toward grabbing the largest possible number of viewers, NBC's promotional experts emphasized the most sensationalistic aspects of the episodes (whether they were really there or not) and hyped each installment as a sort of made-for-TV movie.

The season opener Episode 34: "Fire" became "City of Flames," and Episode 36: "Autofocus" became "Thrill of the Kill." These new titles took prominence in the promotional TV-spot ads, while the *Homicide* logo got smaller, which meant that the show itself got second billing! John Miller, NBC's executive in charge of promotions and marketing, admitted, "*Homicide* basically says 'murder,' and this is one way of making it more accessible." Fontana quipped, "I really don't care what people call it, as long as they watch."

The promotional sequences sometimes revealed plot twists before the episode aired, and sometimes (in a strange reversal) would promise plot twists the shows never tried to deliver.

Ecstatic over the number of high-profile cases to turn into juicy promotional bits, NBC jumbled the episodes for broadcast more than they had ever done before, or would do ever again. As a result, the bulk of the "red ball" cases ended up being pushed early in the season while the more typical installments ran later in the year.

Frat Boys with Guns

Tom Fontana had once joked that *Homicide* had the ugliest cast in television. Although he never really meant that to be taken literally, the line had less and less relevance as the series evolved.

What Fontana meant was that he took pride in the original cast's authentic look. These nine men and women were supposed to look like a real homicide unit, without any regard for the demographic tokenism that usually drives TV casting.

As the show entered its fourth year, however, it shed many of those original cast members. Following Jon Polito's departure, Ned Beatty and Daniel Baldwin left to pursue other projects. Fontana admitted, "They'll be missed." However, he also noted that reducing the number of characters would let the writers explore the remaining characters better.

Nonetheless, *Homicide* added two characters to the cast to replace the outgoing two, and, in addition, let the underused characters of Kay Howard and John Munch fade even farther into the background. In announcing the arrival of Reed Diamond as Detective Mike Kellerman, producer Henry Bromell said that the character would supply "another kind of sound in the orchestra, another rhythm so we're not always playing the same scene."

Fontana has insisted always that he would resist pressure to add cast members solely on the basis of their youthful looks, and would only bring in new performers if he felt a need for their voices in *Homicide*'s verbal orchestra. TV critic Howard Rosenberg caustically noted, "Is it a coincidence, given the network's emphasis on young demographics this season, that [Diamond] looks like he's on loan from *Friends*?" In response, Diamond remarked that he had never been considered good-looking before he was cast on *Homicide*.

As a counterpoint to the increasingly prominent roles of Detectives Pembleton and Bayliss, Tom Fontana paired the newcomer with Detective Meldrick Lewis and began to groom them as *Homicide*'s alternate leads. Calling Lewis and Kellerman "frat boys with guns," Fontana explicitly sought a younger pair of detectives who would be less tortured or soul-searching than Frank and Tim.

Also introduced in the fourth season as a recurring character was Max Perlich as cameraman J. H. Brodie. Perlich's role as an outsider, allowed to observe quietly the Homicide Unit in action, paralleled the true-life experience of David Simon himself. The following year, Perlich joined the cast as a regular.

A Vote of Confidence

Much to the pleasant surprise of the production team, after three years of battling, NBC brought *Homicide* back for its fourth season with a full order of twenty-two episodes. Thus, its fourth season became the first full season in the show's history.

NBC had finally clawed its way to becoming the top network, thus affording NBC's Warren Littlefield the freedom to indulge *Homicide's* slow audience growth. Therefore, under network pressure to make the show more mainstream, Fontana changed the cast composition, increased the sensationalism of the storytelling, and helped devise an effective and publicity-rich crossover with *Law and Order*, a highly rated show.

The tinkering worked. Only halfway into its fourth season, *Homicide* had increased its ratings by a full twenty-five percent. The numbers of viewers in the most desirable demographic of adults from the ages of eighteen to forty-nine were up thirty-five percent. The numbers of men in that age bracket increased by forty-eight percent.

In the network's recent history only *ER* had attracted as many new viewers.

By the end of the fourth season, though, the situation had changed. CBS unveiled a new drama in its Friday, 10:00 P.M. slot, *Nash Bridges* (1996–) starring the well-known and well-liked Don Johnson. NBC's vice president for planning and scheduling, Preston Breckman, worried that *Homicide*, a notoriously idiosyncratic show, was going head-to-head with "a show that's more meat-and-potatoes and by-the-numbers, and there is an audience for that."

In its first three weeks, *Nash Bridges* won a solid 9.6 rating and an 18.0 share (each rating point representing 970,000 households, and the share reflecting the percentage of the overall viewing audience). At the same time, *Homicide's* ratings dropped to new lows.

Breckman insisted that NBC would continue to back *Homicide*. "There are no excuses," Breckman remarked, "There has to be a place for shows like this in network television."

After all, when all was said and done, *Homicide* had increased its viewer base by three million in just one year, and sold its rerun package (including the *Law and Order* crossover double episode) to the Lifetime cable channel for $450,000 per episode. *Homicide's* success in its time slot was so strong that it had squeezed out the previously formidable competition of *Picket Fences* (1992–96). Bolstered by these developments, Littlefield renewed *Homicide* with a staggering order of forty-four episodes, guaranteeing not just one, but two more full seasons.

The vote of confidence both flattered the producers of *Homicide*, and gave them temporary insulation from the rough-and-tumble of the ratings game. Whatever happened over the course of the next season, *Homicide* would not be threatened with cancellation again, at least for a while.

The competition with *Nash Bridges*, however, was far from over.

SEASON FOUR

September 1996–May 1997
60-minute episodes
Fridays, 10:00 P.M.EST

Production Team:

Barry Levinson (executive producer), Tom Fontana (executive producer), Henry Bromell (executive producer), Jim Finnerty (co-executive producer), Gail Mutrux (consulting producer), Debbie Sarjeant (coproducer), James Yoshimura (producer), Jorge Zamacona (producer), Julie Martin (producer), Paul Attanasio (creator), Bonnie Mark (story editor), Anya Epstein (staff writer), Vince Peranio (production designer), Susan Kessel (set decorator), Rolande Berman (costume designer), Douglas J. Cuomo (music), Lynn Kowal (title theme), Louis DiGiaimo and Brett Goldstein (casting directors), Pat Moran (Baltimore casting director), Chris Kellett (boom), Bruce Litecky (sound mixer), Jean de Segonzac (director of photography), Phil Oetiker (additional director of photography), Charley Armstrong (location manager), Cindy Mollo (editor), Jay Rabinowitz (editor), Jay Pires (editor), Sylvia Waliga (editor), Mark Pellington (title sequence), Gary D'Addario (technical adviser), Johanna Persons (executive in charge of production).

Regular Cast:

Richard Belzer (Detective John Munch), Andre Braugher (Detective Frank Pembleton), Reed Diamond (Detective Mike Kellerman), Isabella Hofmann (Captain/Detective Megan Russert), Clark Johnson (Detective Meldrick Lewis), Yaphet Kotto (Lieutenant Al Giardello), Melissa Leo (Detective Kay Howard), Kyle Secor (Detective Tim Bayliss).

Episode 34: "Fire, Part One"

[Production Code 401]
Original air date: October 20, 1995.
Written by Julie Martin; story by Tom Fontana and Henry Bromell; directed by Don Scardino.

Additional Cast and Guest Stars:

Stephanie Romanov (Anne Kennedy), Clayton LeBoeuf (Colonel George Barnfather), Frank John Hughes (Mazursky), Walt MacPherson (Detective Roger Gaffney), Margaret Trigg (Veronica Velez), Dell Grooms (caller), Tara Henson (Lisa DeNardi), Chuck Jeffreys (Calvin Jones), Ralph Tabakin (Dr. Scheiner), Sharon Ziman (Naomi).

STORY: An arson-homicide brings together Detectives Pembleton and Bayliss with Arson Detective Mike Kellerman. They clash over the handling of the investigation, and disagree whether the burned body was an intentional homicide or an accidental death resulting from a planned arson. When a virtually identical fire consumes a second warehouse, the detectives are afraid they may be up against a serial arsonist.

HIGHLIGHTS: The season premiere of *Homicide* has a lot to tell, and little time to tell it. This episode has to usher out old characters, introduce new ones, and unveil not one but three major subplots.

Not least of the new developments is the introduction of newcomer Reed Diamond as Mike Kellerman, helping to fill out the squad's ranks after the departure of Bolander and Felton. Those two detectives were suspended because they had run naked through a New York hotel during a police convention, a real event that had ended the careers of several of New York's finest. In other news, Kay Howard has made the decision to take the sergeant's exam, Frank Pembleton is expecting a child and anxious about his impending fatherhood, and Tim Bayliss has thrown out his back in a bad way.

One subplot would not fully develop for over a year. In this episode, Detective Kellerman accuses businessman Matthew Roland of being responsible for the fire. Kellerman reveals that he has long suspected Roland of involvement in various arsons, but could never make the accusation stick. In season five's Episode 60: "Bad Medicine," Matthew and his son Mitch Roland accuse Kellerman of accepting bribes from them, and effectively derail the detective's career.

This episode also finds time for *Homicide*'s second instance of onscreen nudity, when witness Veronica Velez tries to seduce Kellerman. Since *Homicide* does not get as much attention as *NYPD Blue*, such glimpses of bare flesh seem to pass by without controversy or warning labels.

COMMENTARY: Weighed down by excessive exposition, "Fire, Part One" never lives up to the breathless hype of NBC's promotional push. The ads described a "City of Flames" held in a thrall of fear by a serial arsonist. The story itself unfolds slowly, and involves only two fires and only two deaths. Furthermore, the episode ends with the "shocking" discovery of a second fire, a plot discovery spoiled by all the promotional bits.

With this episode, *Homicide* begins an evolution that takes it into sensationalism at the expense of its soul. *Homicide* enters its fourth year with a more TV-friendly cast composition, simpler, more self-contained plots (seemingly, to make it easier to summarize the episodes in *TV Guide*), and a near-obsession with unlikely "red ball" cases. Cinematographer Jean de Segonzac greets the new tone of the series with the most brightly colored pictures seen yet. That "Doris Day look" Barry Levinson once said he wanted to avoid cannot be that far behind.

NOTES: Informed that colleagues Felton and Bolander have been suspended for twenty-two weeks following their shameful behavior at the police convention in New York, Detective Munch wonders aloud who comes up with such a number. Kay Howard answers that the bosses do. Indeed, *Homicide*'s bosses (NBC executives, that is) had just awarded the series with its first complete season order, twenty-two weeks of episodes.

Episode 35: "Fire, Part Two"

[Production Code 402]
Original air date: October 27, 1995.
Written by Jack Behr; story by Henry Bromell and Tom Fontana; directed by Nick Gomez.

Additional Cast and Guest Stars:
Stephanie Romanov (Anne Kennedy), Adam Trese (Gavin Robb), Harlee McBride (Dr. Alyssa Dyer), Pat McNamara (Mr. Kellerman), Frank John Hughes (Mazursky), Rod Daniels (himself), Dell Grooms (caller), Lois Kelso Hunt (Mrs. Rosen), Kristin Rohde (Sally Rogers), Sharon Ziman (Naomi).

STORY: With a second arson fire and a second burned body on their hands, Detectives Pembleton, Bayliss, and Kellerman begin to wonder whether the crimes are really related after all, and if so, by what? After pursuing a number of dead ends, Kellerman manages to break the case with a deftly handled interrogation. Impressed, Lieutenant Giardello offers the young detective a job on the prestigious Homicide Unit.

HIGHLIGHTS: John Munch challenges Kay Howard to a bet, with the entire squad placing their money on Kay to ace the sergeant's exam. Kay thinks the odds are unfairly one-sided, especially when John doesn't even manage to *show up* at the exam.

COMMENTARY: Despite the sensational promotion, the conclusion of the so-called "City of Flames" story is a quiet, talky, ruminative episode. Far from getting into the mind of a serial arsonist (as the ads promised), "Fire, Part

Two" restates *Homicide*'s anti-motive philosophy. Frustrated by being unable to get into the mind of his serial arsonist, Kellerman turns to Gee for advice. The lieutenant wisely notes that the young detective would be better off *not* knowing why bad people do bad things.

NOTES: Actor Reed Diamond proclaimed the closing scene of this episode to be his favorite from the series. As Mike Kellerman visits his blue-collar father in a beer-bottling plant, he reconsiders Giardello's offer to join the Homicide Unit. "You see there's something he wants to get away from," Diamond explains, "something other than punching the clock."

Episode 36: "Autofocus"

[Production Code 403]
Original air date: November 3, 1995.
Written by Bonnie Mark; story by Tom Fontana and Henry Bromell; directed by Alan Taylor.

Additional Cast and Guest Stars:
Max Perlich (J. H. Brodie), John Epps (Trevor Douglas), Tim McAdams (James Douglas), Sagan Lewis (Judge Susan Aandahl), Ileana Douglas (Jeana Doolen), Fisher Stevens (Jonathan Heine), Frank Buckley (Nick), Sabine Herts (Rita), George E. M. Kelley (Richie), Julie Lauren (Officer Schanne), Judy Thornton (Judy).

STORY: A gas leak in the police HQ forces the Homicide unit to set up shop in a nearby bank.

New guy Mike Kellerman partners with Detective Meldrick Lewis to investigate the slaying of an elderly woman. J. H. Brodie, a cameraman for a local news station, has caught the killers on video and sacrifices his job to share the footage with the cops. The evidence helps Lewis and Kellerman nab a pair of street thugs who videotaped their own crimes.

HIGHLIGHTS: Notoriously difficult to work with, Meldrick Lewis at last finds a match in his new partner Mike Kellerman. The producers rightly saw the team as a possible counterpart to the overused Pembleton and Bayliss, what with their lighter tone and more bantering behavior.

Meanwhile, Kay Howard's exam results come back, and the detective is promoted to sergeant. Although her detective instincts served her excellently on the street, she will find management a tougher challenge, especially as she realizes that many of the male detectives under her harbor some sexist resentment.

COMMENTARY: Of all of NBC's overheated hype, the promotions for "Autofocus" (or, as NBC advertised it, "View of a Kill") were by far the most mystifying. The booming voice of the announcer gravely describes "a band of criminals" and a "unique case with an ending so wild, you'll have to rewind it to believe it!"

For one thing, the "band" of criminals is just a pair of cousins. As to the "wild" ending, the fact that these two have been documenting their crimes on tape is discovered forty-three minutes into the hour, and was revealed by the previews anyway. Although the episode ends with a nice touch of Brodie and one of the killers videotaping each other at the arrest, both of them having taped the crime itself and the arrest from different vantage points, the only twist here is that NBC promised a twist and there isn't one.

NOTES: This episode features the first appearance of actress Sagan Lewis in a recurring role as Judge Susan Aandahl. She would become quite important later, in the fifth season in Episode 64: "The True Test." Like so many of *Homicide*'s guest cast members, the actress has a connection to Tom Fontana through *St. Elsewhere* (1982–88). Lewis played Dr. Jacqueline Wade from 1983 through the end of that acclaimed hospital drama.

This segment also introduces videographer J. H. Brodie. Perlich would move from a recurring role to a regular performer as the year progressed.

In other noteworthy guest appearances, Ileana Douglas and Fisher Stevens appear as a reluctant pair on a blind date. Douglas can also be seen in *Cape Fear* (1991), *Alive* (1993), *Household Saints* (1993), *Grief* (1994), *Search and Destroy* (1994), and *To Die For* (1995). Stevens has credits in *My Science Project* (1985), *Short Circuit* (1986), *Reversal of Fortune* (1990), *The Marrying Man* (1991), *Super Mario Brothers* (1993), and *Hackers* (1995), as well as being a regular cast member of the TV comedy series *Early Edition* (1997–).

Episode 37: "Thrill of the Kill"

[Production Code 407]
Original air date: November 10, 1995.
Written by Jorge Zamacona; story by Tom Fontana and Henry Bromell; directed by Tim Hunter.

Additional Cast and Guest Stars:
Jeffrey Donovan (Newton Dell), Marty Lodge (Steve Van Brandt), Theara J. Ward (Charisse Giardello), Rhonda Overby (Dawn Daniels), Carlos Antonio (gas attendant), Brown Cardwell (rich woman), Jack Mayo (boy's father), Bob Muldonian (candy vendor), Zadalauna Watson (Wendy Simpkins).

STORY: The detectives are handed a "red ball" case by the FBI when they get word of a serial killer headed toward Baltimore, slaughtering bystanders every time he stops for gas. The madman evades the squad's roadblock and nearly escapes them altogether. In a tense showdown at a gas station, Detective Tim Bayliss arrests the man he thinks is the killer, only to learn his identical twin brother, still at large, is the real perpetrator.

HIGHLIGHTS: In a fantastic moment of tension, we are led to believe that serial killer Newton Dell has killed Gee's daughter Charisse. This impression is created solely through careful editing, as nobody says outright that she has been killed. However, the audience's relief when she appears safe and well is every bit as powerful as Gee's, which is conveyed silently, but eloquently by Yaphet Kotto's excellent command of body language.

COMMENTARY: Possibly *Homicide*'s lowest moment, "Thrill of the Kill" is implausible and schlocky from start to finish. Yet another serial killer, and yet another case where the detectives capture a suspect only to discover the "red ball" case continues. For a show that once prided itself on never showing violence onscreen, it is the second onscreen killing in two weeks.

The promotional ads, renaming this episode "Vengeance on the Highway," announced "Just when you think it's over, think again." Unlike Episode 36: "Autofocus," this time we do get a twist, but the twist is that Bayliss has the wrong man, as the killer is this man's *evil twin!*

Furthermore, the story has geographical problems. Bayliss and Pembleton are warned that Dell the killer is on his way north and that he is on a drug-addled speed trip (in both senses of the word). Dell continues northward at a relentless pace, yet the detectives manage to go south to the scene of one crime, investigate there for a several hours, and still return north to Baltimore *ahead* of Dell. What shortcut did they take to be able to set up a roadblock in front of him? Unless Dell stopped to take a nap along the way, he would have blazed through Baltimore while they were still returning from crime scene number one. To help explain his lack of speed, the script has Dell stop for gas at an alarmingly frequent rate. No reasons are given for his stops. Perhaps he has a hole in his tank?

While the segment is undeniably a powerful and dramatic hour, the lack of *Homicide*'s usual quirky, unconventional writing, and its dogged adherence to realism, leads to a major feeling of disappointment over this episode.

Episode 38: "Hate Crimes"

[Production Code 406]
Original air date: November 17, 1995.
Written by James Yoshimura and Tom Fontana; directed by Peter Weller.

Additional Cast and Guest Stars:

Max Perlich (J. H. Brodie), Terry O'Quinn (Bailey Lafeld), Allison Smith (Debbie Haskell), Dean Winters (Tom Marans), James Whalen (Jimmy Kruger), Jeff Bankert (Lambert), Bret Hamilton (Zeke), Susann McCormack-Pike (Ziegler), David Neff (Pinnock), Joan Stueber (Shields).

STORY: As Thanksgiving approaches, Detectives Kellerman and Lewis uncover a new lead in the Erica Chilton case, once an unsolved albatross around Kay's neck (see Episode 31: "Nothing Personal"). However, Kay resents Meldrick's taking over her assignment.

Meanwhile, Detectives Pembleton and Bayliss investigate an apparent hate crime committed outside a gay bar. As they search for the skinhead perpetrator, new evidence suggests that the victim was not homosexual, after all.

HIGHLIGHTS: In this episode Max Perlich's J. H. Brodie officially joins the Homicide Unit as a videographer of crime scenes.

This segment also features the first mention of Kay's sister Carrie Howard, living in Florence, Italy. Carrie will make an appearance at the end of the season in Episode 56: "Work Related."

COMMENTARY: After a heavy concentration of "red ball" cases, it's refreshing to return to *Homicide*'s roots: simple killings, and the difficult process of solving them. The Erica Chilton murder is spread across several seasons, as it was introduced in the third season as an already cold case, revived here, and then revived again in Season Five's Episode 59: "Prison Riot." This is a demanding kind of writing that expects the audience to be paying attention over several years as stories develop at a glacial pace.

The *Law and Order* TV series tackled a gay-bashing murder in this same season, but the difference between the two shows' approaches is noteworthy. Although the subject matter provides an excellent opportunity for characters to discuss topical issues, *Homicide*'s characters avoid talking with the preachiness that can mar other shows. Tim and Frank talk a lot about homosexuality over the course of the hour, but never with any sense of spouting the "author's message." These guys are not wise enough to offer answers to such difficult and divisive social concerns. All they have is the natural wisdom of intelligent people forced by their jobs to spend a lot of time soul-searching.

NOTES: Peter Weller directed this episode, although he is better known for his work in front of the camera as the star of such films as *RoboCop* (1987), *Naked Lunch* (1991), and *Screamers* (1995).

Episode 39: "A Doll's Eyes"

[Production Code 404]
Original air date: December 1, 1995.
Written by James Yoshimura; story by Tom Fontana and Henry Bromell; directed by Ken Fink.

Additional Cast and Guest Stars:

Marcia Gay Harden (Joan Garabek), Gary Basaraba (Paul Garabek), Sean Whitesell (Doctor), Bari Biern (Nurse), Simon Bennett (Donny), Terry Hinz (Loftus), Andreas Kraemer (Tommy), Sharon Ziman (Naomi), Mandy Patinkin (Dr. Jeffery Geiger).

STORY: When a conflict rages out of control between two teens over a girl, they take their grudge to the streets with guns, and end up accidentally shooting a ten-year-old boy in the head. The child is still alive but left brain dead (a condition the doctor describes as having "doll's eyes"), and his parents struggle with the anguishing decision to take their boy off life support and donate his organs to others.

HIGHLIGHTS: Writer James Yoshimura knows how to blend the most harrowing agony with offbeat comedy, but the most memorable jokes in this disturbing hour are in-jokes. At one point, Detective Pembleton talks with the victim's father, and neither of them can recall the name of the doctor attend-

In a daring internetwork crossover, Mandy Patinkin appears as Chicago Hope's *Dr. Geiger in "A Doll's Eyes".*
Everett Collection

ing the boy. This is because the doctor had not been given a name! Actor Sean Whitesell makes his fourth appearance as the doctor, who was only later given the rather striking name of Dr. Eli Devilbliss.

A better known doctor also appears in this episode, with a crossover even more daring (though much less publicized) than the *Law and Order* stunt. Mandy Patinkin appears as Dr. Geiger from the CBS series *Chicago Hope*, in a cameo scene showing him receiving one of the boy's donated organs. Although Patinkin's role is uncredited and he has no dialogue, the scene emphasizes the name *Chicago Hope* to make sure viewers catch the significance. Executive producer Tom Fontana arranged the crossover with his former *St. Elsewhere* colleague John Tinker, who was now a producer of *Chicago Hope*.

COMMENTARY: This episode proves to be another journey into emotional hell, courtesy of James Yoshimura. Although the story shares a lot with Yoshimura's equally discomfiting Episode 22: "Every Mother's Son," the emphasis here is on the parents' heartache. Easily one of the series' all-time best, this episode forces the viewer, vicariously, through the death of a child.

NOTES: Because NBC wanted to run Episode 37: "Thrill of the Kill" earlier, this depressing episode was delayed, resulting in a relatively minor continuity error. This episode takes place in the makeshift bank HQ, while the squad appeared to have returned to the official police squadroom in Episode 37.

Episode 40: "Heartbeat"

[Production Code 405]
Original air date: January 8, 1995.
Written by Kevin Arkadie; story by Henry Bromell and Tom Fontana; directed by Bruno Kirby.

Additional Cast and Guest Stars:

Kevin Conway (Joseph Cardero), Jon Korkes (Boomer Mason), Harlee McBride (Dr. Alyssa Dyer), Duane Chandler Rawlings (Leon), Kristin Rohde (Sally Rogers), Lynn Sellers (Sharon), Kristen Valerio (Serena Boch), Maria Winters (Alexandria).

STORY: Detectives Lewis and Kellerman discover a ten-year-old case that Lieutenant Giardello now assigns to John Munch and Kay Howard. They have little to go on, only a body walled up in a cellar. Nevertheless, John's naturally dark nature helps him understand the psychology of their killer. Munch realizes that the drug-dealer-turned-poet, Joseph Cardero, is an obsessive admirer of Edgar Allan Poe, and committed his Poe-inspired murder against a rival drug dealer.

HIGHLIGHTS: Kay Howard's superstitious nature may seem out of place for someone so levelheaded and professional, but even at the very beginning her character was shown as being a believer of the supernatural. In the first season's Episode 2: "Ghost of a Chance," Detective Howard believed she was getting assistance from a ghost informant in her sleep.

Kay also displays an interest in soap operas. In fact, she and Bayliss both appear transfixed by a daytime drama in the squad's coffee room. This is a subtle in-joke, since both performers Melissa Leo and Kyle Secor had gotten their acting breaks on soap operas.

COMMENTARY: This episode is a highly literary outing that uses its Poe motif well, even if it is a little too prolonged. However, underused characters John and Kay get an episode entirely to themselves for once, with a heavy emphasis on Munch.

Richard Belzer bragged to the press how much fun he had developing a romance with Medical Examiner Alyssa Dyer, played by his real-life wife Harlee McBride. Longtime viewers of *Homicide* may be forgiven for finding the subplot less exciting. The Bolander-Blythe romance in Season One and the Kellerman-Cox romance yet to come in Season Five makes this setup seem a little stale.

Regardless, the episode wins originality points, for the sublime joke of having Munch swoon endlessly over his true love for Alyssa Dyer only, then, to have sex with her roommate within seconds of meeting her and mere minutes before Alyssa is due for their date!

NOTES: *Homicide* fans are familiar with the red-and-black color coding of the Board: red for open cases, black for closed. This episode introduces a new color: blue, for cases reopened from previous years. (Naturally, the color coding is a fairly accurate, if somewhat simplified, depiction of how the real Baltimore police operate.)

Bruno Kirby, the guest star from last year's Episode 33: "Gas Man," returns to *Homicide* to direct this episode.

Episode 41: "Sniper, Part One"

[Production Code 408]
Original air date: January 5, 1996.
Written by Jean Ginnis and Phyllis Murphy; story by Henry Bromell and Tom Fontana; directed by Jean de Segonzac.

Additional Cast and Guest Stars:

Jay Leno (himself), Max Perlich (J. H. Brodie), Carolyn McCormick (Linda Mariner), Andrew Parks (William Mariner), Clayton LeBoeuf (Colonel George Barnfather), Gary

D'Addario (Lieutenant Jasper), Harry A. Winter (handwriting expert Andy Orloff), Cherie W. Brackett (head nurse), Damian Briscoe (Pike Capers), Bill Grimmett (Carl Farrell), Herb Levinson (Dr. Lausanne), Sharon Ziman (Naomi), Granville Adams (officer), Jay Spadaro (officer), Anthony "Chip" Brienza (reporter), Rhonda Overby (Dawn Daniels), Peggy Yates (Maria Delgado), Beau James (Detective Higby).

STORY: The start of a new year brings with it a fresh "red ball" case: a sniper shooting at passersby from rooftops while playing some demented version of hangman. Captain Megan Russert brings on both shifts to work with Primary Detective Tim Bayliss to track the killer. With the sniper shooting at precise time increments, the detectives can feel their time running out.

HIGHLIGHTS: The first signs of Brodie's crush on Kay Howard are revealed, and Colonel Barnfather double-demotes Megan Russert all the way from captain down to detective for her handling of the sniper case. Not that she did anything wrong, of course, other than exercise independent thinking and display a compassion for the victims of the crime. Throughout her brief tenure as captain, Russert showed a loyalty to her troops that did not fit in with the bosses' trademark self-interest. Since she refuses to play his political games, Barnfather gives Russert the boot.

COMMENTARY: This episode's "red ball" case is typical of what has become the hallmark of the series' predictable crisis stories. A serial killer is murdering innocent people, the victims having no connection to one another or to the killer, and the killer follows a regular pattern of striking again and again. Eventually, the detectives have to reevaluate their original theory of the crime, as new victims are discovered.

What sets this one apart from the others is the sheer absurdity of the crime in question. William Mariner is gunning down innocent bystanders as part of a game of hangman he's playing with himself over the name "Baltimore" spelled backward. While this deadly game may be the explanation for the events, it's not an answer that makes any sense at all to any members of the squad. Which is, of course, the point. The mind of someone who goes that far over the edge into psychopathic madness is not going to make sense to anyone else.

NOTES: Directed by Jean de Segonzac with an astonishingly cinematic visual flair, this episode is one of the most beautiful in the series.

Jay Leno appears in a cameo role as himself in a hilarious opening sequence. NBC's promotions department described the scene: "Bayliss and Munch go a bit overboard as they try to be nonchalant about the celebrity patronizing their establishment." The incident is something of an in-joke about how Baltimore has treated local celebrities from *Homicide*'s cast. Producer Tom Fontana has jokingly said that Baltimore goes out of its way to

He may be the most popular talk-show host in America, but Jay Leno gets the cold shoulder from the detectives on Homicide.
Everett Collection

ignore them. Cast members have reported similar experiences, where the locals make a point of refusing to be starstruck.

The episode also features guest star Carolyn McCormick (better known as Dr. Olivet on *Law and Order*) as the sniper's wife.

Episode 42: "Sniper, Part Two"

[Production Code 409]
Original air date: January 12, 1996.
Written by Edward Gold; story by Henry Bromell and Tom Fontana; directed by Darnell Martin.

Additional Cast and Guest Stars:
David Eigenberg (Alex Robey), J. Smith-Cameron (Ms. Griffin), Max Perlich (J. H. Brodie), Ami Brabson (Mary Pembleton), Carolyn McCormick (Linda Mariner), Robert Linver (Billie Mariner), Shawn Michelle Cosby (Helena Aegis), Gary D'Addario (Lieutenant Jasper), Bruce Elliott (newspaper correspondent), Baltimore Mayor Kurt Schmoke (himself), Clayton LeBoeuf (Colonel George Barnfather), Scott Wesley Morgan (Maxwell).

STORY: While the police department reels from the public-relations disaster of the sniper's suicide, the shootings continue on the eight-hour schedule as before. The detectives scramble to find any connections between the new shootings and those by Mariner. They do uncover an odd connection between the most recent incidents: an eyewitness named Alex Robey.

HIGHLIGHTS: Kurt Schmoke makes his second guest spot (his first was in Episode 22: "Every Mother's Son") playing himself as the mayor of Baltimore. The real-life version of Gee, Gary D'Addario, returns in his role as QRT lieutenant Jasper. D'Addario has remarkable skill for an untrained actor, and his scenes butting heads with the *Homicide* guys are always enjoyable.

Even more enjoyable is the almost musical dialogue in the Box as Pembleton, Bayliss, and Russert try to break down Alex Robey. Writing like this is rare outside the Theater of the Absurd, but luckily *Homicide* has enough playwrights on staff to keep the standards high.

COMMENTARY: After solving a copycat crime, Detective Pembleton grumbles at the lack of originality in modern society. He might as well be complaining about the increasingly formulaic plots of *Homicide*. This unrealistic symmetry is blatantly displayed as the first days of 1996 bring sixteen murders, every single one of which is part of a single case (if you include Mariner and his copycat together), all of them solved by the show's most popular detective team, with an on-the-money interrogation by Megan Russert on her first day on the job as a detective.

NOTES: This week's guest director is Darnell Martin, an independent filmmaker who snagged headlines for her unprecedented deal with Columbia Pictures for artistic freedom on the film *I Like It Like That* (1994), which costarred future *Homicide* cast member Jon Seda. Martin got her start as an assistant director for Spike Lee, and became the first African-American woman ever to direct a Hollywood feature.

Episode 43: "The Hat"

[Production Code 412]
Original air date: January 19, 1996.
Written by Anya Epstein; story by Henry Bromell, Tom Fontana, and Trish Soodik; directed by Peter Medak.

Additional Cast and Guest Stars:
Lily Tomlin (Rose Halligan), Zeljko Ivanek (Assistant State's Attorney Ed Danvers), Max Perlich (J. H. Brodie), Walt MacPherson (Detective/Captain Roger Gaffney), Clayton LeBoeuf (Colonel George Barnfather), Madeline L. Austin (Officer Parla), Mary Carole Curran (Elyse), Caroline Jones (waitress), Will Monahan (King Neptune), Alenah Dean Taylor (Mermaid).

STORY: Lewis and Kellerman take a road trip to Pennsylvania to retrieve the ever-prim yet nonetheless deadly killer, Rose Halligan. Returning to

Baltimore with their tails between their legs, the detectives are forced to admit to Sergeant Howard that they let their suspect escape. By the time they track her down, Rose Halligan has killed again.

HIGHLIGHTS: With Megan Russert demoted to detective, the captainship is open. The squad becomes convinced that Gee has finally won the promotion his leadership and seniority have earned. Instead the job goes to the petty, small-minded bully Roger Gaffney. Ironically, Russert had demoted Gaffney out of Homicide for his handling of the white-glove murder case (see Episode 15: "Fits Like a Glove"). While Gaffney is an unlikable fellow, he follows orders and respects the chain of command. It is a testament to *Homicide*'s realistic depictions of office politics that the hardworking but iconoclastic characters are rarely rewarded by the system. In *Homicide*, as in real life, the promotions are usually handed out to those who don't rock the boat.

COMMENTARY: Younger and less tortured than Pembleton and Bayliss, the excellent team of Lewis and Kellerman make lighter frontmen for the show. Their style also allows for a quirkier kind of comedy, which is on full display here.

Many of the show's bigwigs participated in the development of this new approach. Staff writer Anya Epstein wrote the teleplay from a story outline by Tom Fontana and the husband-and-wife team of Henry Bromell and Trish Soodik.

Lily Tomlin was nominated for an Emmy for her guest spot in "The Hat."
Everett Collection

While this episode is not quite a classic, it still marks a change in the direction of the show and features some sublimely silly scenes. Meldrick and Mike get reprimanded when they admit Rose escaped when they stopped for tuna melts and pie, but they never get around to telling Kay that Rose almost escaped earlier when they stopped at the Enchanted Forest to see the world's largest swordfish.

Adding to the festivities is a top-notch guest turn by Lily Tomlin, for which she received an Emmy nomination. Tomlin is well-known for her comedic talents, as displayed on stage and in such films as *The Late Show* (1977), *9 to 5* (1980), *All of Me* (1984), *Big Business* (1988), *The Search for Signs of Intelligent Life in the Universe* (1991), *The Player* (1992), *Flirting with Disaster* (1996), and later in a recurring role on the TV series *Murphy Brown* (1988–98).

Episode 44: "I've Got a Secret"

[Production Code 413]
Original air date: February 2, 1996.
Written by Maria Legaspi; story by Tom Fontana and Henry Bromell; directed by Gwen Arner.

Additional Cast and Guest Stars:
Mimi Kennedy (Dr. Wystan), Gabriel Casseus (Nurse Sherman), Joseph Durika (Peter Wolsky), Joe Palka (Landlord), Bill McLaughlin (Mr. Wystan), Nguyen-Tu Tucker (hospital administrator), Robert Tyree (MC), Robert Carlson (Denys), Shannon Mattaro (nurse), Suzanne Snyder (nurse), Bob Supan (Dr. Battey), Ralph Tabakin (Dr. Scheiner).

STORY: Detectives Lewis and Kellerman try to capture Peter Wolsky, a paranoid schizophrenic. The experience prompts Meldrick to visit the institution where his own crazy brother, Anthony Lewis, has lived for over twenty years.

Meanwhile, Pembleton and Bayliss struggle with the case of a hardened criminal, apparently killed not so much by his reckless lifestyle as by shoddy care from emergency-room physician Dr. Wystan.

HIGHLIGHTS: The "secret" in the title is a stunning revelation, that Meldrick Lewis has an insane brother, Anthony. Although this development is rarely touched on again, Lewis reveals his brother ended up in the institution after a suicide attempt. This development helps shed some light onto Meldrick's pained reactions to Crosetti's suicide (Episode 19: "Crosetti");

Kellerman's later suicide attempt (Episode 69: "Have a Conscience"); and the apparent suicide of Beau Felton (Episode 78: "Strangers and Other Partners").

Kay Howard has a secret of her own, which she jealously guards from John. Detective Munch tries desperately and aggressively to discover the identity of Howard's new lover, but to no avail. This mystery man reappears in next year's Episode 67: "The Documentary," but is never identified.

COMMENTARY: In a wonderfully self-conscious moment, Frank barks at Tim, "You want glory? Go work at *ER*. *Homicide*'s fine by me."

After Tim's starry-eyed idolization of lifesaving doctors, Frank's rebuke reminds the audience that *Homicide* is different, not necessarily better or worse, than *ER*. The scene unfolds in a nonchronological overlapping of past and present that is altogether too arty and disorienting to fit into a more conventional drama like *ER*.

As usual, *Homicide* does not let its viewers off easily. After a fairly funny hour in which the detectives square off against "King Kong" and "Mr. Clean," the end of the hour raises uncomfortable issues. As always, Frank Pembleton insists that every life has value and every murder demands vengeance. In this case, Dr. Wyston did not have the right to decide street-thug Angel's fate for him. Bayliss is torn. While agreeing with Frank in principle, he is driven emotionally to overlook Dr. Wystan's negligence. The show fades out without a clear resolution, but the implication is that Tim lets this murderer go free.

NOTES: *Homicide*'s writers have a trick of giving minor characters pun names, like this week's Dr. Battey, head of a mental-health institution. Fans can keep their ears open for future pun names, such as Agent Borders, the customs agent in Episode 75: "Deception." Notably, these pun names seem always to involve Detective Lewis.

Gabriel Casseus appears as Nurse Sherman, the arrogant young man with a fevered dislike of the street thugs from his neighborhood. Casseus may be a familiar face for viewers of Spike Lee's film *Get On the Bus* (1996).

Appearing as Dr. Wystan is actress Mimi Kennedy, whose previous TV hospital experience includes a 1984 episode of *St. Elsewhere*.

Episode 45
(*Law and Order* Episode 124): "Charm City"

Original air date: February 7, 1996.
NOTE: This episode is a part of the *Law and Order* TV series and is the first part of a two-part joint production with *Homicide*.
Written by Michael S. Chernuchin and Jorge Zamacona; directed by Ed Sherin.

*Jerry Orbach as Detective
Briscoe on* Law and Order.
Everett Collection

Regular Cast:

Jerry Orbach (Detective Lennie Briscoe), Benjamin Bratt (Detective Reynaldo Curtis), S. Epatha Merkerson (Lieutenant Anita Van Buren), Sam Waterston (Assistant District Attorney Jack McCoy), Jill Hennessey (Assistant District Attorney Claire Kincaid), Steven Hill (District Attorney Adam Schiff).

Additional Cast and Guest Stars:

Leo Burmester (Le Clair), Kevin Geer (Brian Egan), Ray Anthony Thomas (George Bell), Richard Belzer (Detective John Munch), Andre Braugher (Detective Frank Pembleton), Kyle Secor (Detective Tim Bayliss), Justin Kennedy (Belcher), Catrina Ganey (Mrs. Chapman), W. T. Martin (Judge Fred Naughton), Ted Kazanof (Judge Daniel Scarletti), Florence Anglin (Marcy), Ntare Mwine (Mark Davies), Robert Turano (Bavarro), Phillip Geoffrey Hough (Kendall Egan), Stephanie Lane (Susan Landsman), Kirk Taylor (Graham), Marcus Naylor (Henry), Robinson Frank Adu (Mr. Johnson), Michael DeVries (Arson Detective Krane), Christopher Prizzi (Adler), John DiMaggio (bartender), David Rainey (Richard Howard), Leila Dannette (Mrs. Donner), Jordan Lage (jury foreman), Karen Ullman (secretary), Gregory Holtz Sr. (man).

STORY: A poison-gas attack on the New York subway sends Manhattan detectives Lennie Briscoe and Rey Curtis searching for the terrorist. Suspecting a connection to a similar bombing in Baltimore years earlier, Detectives Frank Pembleton and Tim Bayliss (of *Homicide*) head to New York.

The four detectives barely cooperate with each other. Frank's barnstorming methods extract a confession, but they violate the suspect's constitutional rights. With the confession excluded from evidence, District Attorney Jack McCoy must use all his skill as prosecutor to win a conviction.

HIGHLIGHTS: *Law and Order*'s formula demands that most of the prosecution's evidence will be thrown out, thereby providing dramatic grist for the second half. In fusing with *Homicide*, this episode of *Law and Order* deftly uses Pembleton's famed interrogations, always a sore point for their questionable legality, as the reason to exclude racist Brian Egan's confession.

In protesting the decision, Detective Pembleton makes much of the difference between Maryland and New York law. He insists that his approach would have been just fine down in Baltimore, and he was merely ignorant of New York's distinctive laws. In fact, this is all a smokescreen. The constitutional issue at stake is the *federally* guaranteed right to a lawyer. When Frank continues badgering the suspect after he has asked for a lawyer, the detective violates the federal constitution, not a regional law of the state of New York.

Legal analysts Roger Cossack and Greta Van Susteren noted in their syndicated Q and A column that "fictional cops like Andre Braugher of *Homicide* make for good drama; real-life officers need to be more careful." They also wrote, "There is a major difference between TV cops and real-life cops. Real police officers must always observe the rights of citizens, or suspects, as guaranteed by our Constitution."

Some legal observers had already criticized *Homicide* for its cavalier portrayal of police methods. Even with the input of technical advisers like Baltimore policemen D'Addario and Falteich, the demands of TV drama often push the writers to depict unrealistic interrogations. Time after time, Pembleton lucks into suspects who waive their right to counsel, and then raise nary a fuss when he tramples all over their rights. Occasionally, as in Episodes 1: "Gone for Goode" and 16: "Extreme Unction," *Homicide* challenges Pembleton's ethics, but it took the new environment of *Law and Order*'s procedural storytelling to bring the issue to the foreground.

COMMENTARY: Much publicized and much lauded, the crossover boosted ratings for both shows. *USA Today*'s Matt Roush enthused, "Either way or either night you look at it, this is state-of-the-art storytelling." Erik Mink of the *New York Daily News* wrote, "From where I sit, this week's TV cross-connection between *Law and Order* and *Homicide* is unbelievably cool."

NOTES: Director Ed Sherin, a longtime director of *Law and Order*, wanted to film an opening sequence depicting the gas attack in New York's Transit Museum, to lend an air of authenticity. Still reeling from a recent firebombing in the subway that all-too-closely paralleled the onscreen events, the

New York City Transit Authority politely declined Sherin's request. The opening scene, therefore, shows only the aftermath of the bomb, as bodies stream out of the gassy entrance onto the street.

Episode 46: "For God and Country"

[Production Code 411]
Original air date: February 9, 1996.
NOTE: This episode of *Homicide* is the second part of the two-part joint production with the *Law and Order* TV series, which began with Episode 45: "Charm City."
Written by Jorge Zamacona and Michael S. Chernuchin; directed by Ed Sherin.

Additional Cast and Guest Stars:
Benjamin Bratt (Detective Rey Curtis), Jerry Orbach (Detective Lennie Briscoe), Jill Hennessy (Assistant States Attorney Claire Kincaid), Zeljko Ivanek (Assistant State's Attorney Ed Danvers), Sagan Lewis (Judge Susan Aandahl), J. K. Simmons (Alexander Rausch), Kevin Geer (Brian Egan), Phillip Geoffrey Hough (Kendall Egan), Valerie Karasek (Roxanna Carlin), Max Perlich (J. H. Brodie), Darla J. Robinson (Stephanie), Ralph Tabakin (Dr. Scheiner).

STORY: Although Brian Egan has been convicted of the Manhattan gas attack, the Baltimore church-bombing from five years ago remains open, and Detective Frank Pembleton intends to uncover the conspiracy behind it, aided by New York detectives Briscoe and Curtis.

Manhattan's Assistant District Attorney Claire Kincaid succeeds in getting their suspect, white supremacist Alexander Rousch, extradited to New York to stand trial, which makes Pembleton fume at losing the chance to bring this monster to justice himself. Ultimately fate deprives them all of that privilege when Rousch dies of a heart attack.

HIGHLIGHTS: On *Law and Order*, watching the series' characters wolf down some carry-out Chinese is what usually passes for character development. Transplanted to *Homicide*'s territory, however, Bayliss is seen trying to woo Claire Kincaid, and it is learned that grumpy Lennie Briscoe once had an affair with John Munch's ex-wife.

COMMENTARY: The *New York Times*' Caryn James wrote that watching these two episodes did not so much tell a single epic story as present "a game that moves from one team's home court to another." *Homicide* has the home-court advantage in this second part, and uses it to full effect. Watching Pembleton's anguish at losing his nemesis to something so mundane as a heart attack is a powerful scene, not easily forgotten.

NOTES: While actress Jill Hennessy filmed her scenes in Baltimore for this episode, *Law and Order* continued shooting its regular episodes in New York. To accommodate her absence, the producers brought in Hennessy's identical twin sister to substitute for her on the set of *Law and Order*.

Episode 47: "Justice, Part One"

[Production Code 414]
Original air date: February 16, 1996.
Written by David Rupel; story by Tom Fontana and Henry Bromell; directed by Michael Radford.

Additional Cast and Guest Stars:
Bruce Campbell (Detective Jake Rodzinski), Zeljko Ivanek (Assistant State's Attorney Ed Danvers), Donald Neal (Augie Distel), John Haynes Walker (Detective Pez McCadden), Jack Dougherty (cemetery manager), Wendell Jordan (Kenny Damon), Michael Willis (Darin Russom), Brian T. O'Connor (Alan Schwenk), Kristin Rohde (Sally Rogers), Ralph Tabakin (Dr. Scheiner), Martha Thimmesch (Carol Rodzinski), Sharon Ziman (Naomi), Lynn Schrichte (Judge Andrews).

STORY: Newly partnered Detectives Munch and Russert head to a cemetery where the body of a retired cop has been found strangled. The slain officer is Edgar Rodzinski, a thirty-year veteran of the Vice Squad and father of Meldrick Lewis's friend, Detective Jake Rodzinski.

Russert, recently demoted twice, and Munch, never a distinguished investigator, find themselves under intense scrutiny from Gee, who is concerned about his "police family," as well as Meldrick Lewis and Jake Rodzinski.

HIGHLIGHTS: After the made-in-TV-heaven pairing of Lewis and Kellerman, Russert and Munch have been joined as partners in name only, not in nature. Munch's cynical ramblings and frequent digressions drive Russert crazy, while she struggles to be a straight arrow and prove herself all over again merely a month after her demotion. This odd couple spends as much time bickering with each other as doing anything else.

For his part, Kellerman doesn't appear in this episode at all. According to the story, he is away at a cousin's wedding in Wisconsin. Temporarily without a partner, Lewis still has a sizable role in the episode, though, which helps give an even better insight into his past. It was in Episode 44: "I've Got a Secret" that it was learned that he had an institutionalized brother, and now a longtime friend and former police academy classmate, Jake Rodzinski, is introduced. Little by little, the long underused Meldrick is coming out of the shadows.

COMMENTARY: The first part of this mini-movie (hyped by NBC as *Badge of Honor*) doesn't display the sensationalism of the earlier "red ball" cases of the season, which gives this story a greater air of authenticity.

However, there are melodramatic flourishes: chase scenes, courtroom drama, and the trial of a cop killer. This episode also shows (twice) Munch and Russert chasing down a suspect with their guns drawn, scenes which argue against *Homicide*'s stated aversion to cop-show clichés.

Also, the case comes to trial remarkably fast. While Kellerman is away in Wisconsin for, supposedly, a short stay to attend a wedding, Edgar Rodzinski's body is found, the investigation stalls, a suspect is found and arrested and put on trial and acquitted.

Although unrealistically swift, the trial scene has emotional verisimilitude. The frustration and torment of Jake and the others anxiously awaiting the verdict adds an edginess to the script. When at last the verdict comes back as "not guilty," Jake corners a juror in the hall. The look of devastation on Jake's face is profound as he realizes his father's killer, Kenny Damon, wasn't acquitted on a technicality, but on juror indifference.

NOTES: The guest star playing Jake Rodzinski is actor Bruce Campbell, well-known to horror-movie buffs as the chainsaw-armed hero of the *Evil Dead* movies (1983, 1987), and the similarly goofy TV series *The Adventures of Brisco County Jr.* (1993–94). Although there is a profound difference between the arch slapstick of *Army of Darkness* (aka, *Evil Dead 3*) (1992) and the brooding psychological drama of *Homicide*, Campbell makes the transition seamlessly.

The other celebrity guest of the week, Michael Radford, puts in his contribution behind the camera as the episode's director. Radford is the Oscar-winning filmmaker responsible for the acclaimed *Il Postino* (1994), one of the most popular and successful foreign films of all time.

Episode 48: "Justice, Part Two"

[Production Code 415]
Original air date: February 23, 1996.
Written by David Simon; story by Tom Fontana and Henry Bromell; directed by Peter Medak.

Additional Cast and Guest Stars:

Bruce Campbell (Detective Jake Rodzinski), Max Perlich (J. H. Brodie), Donald Neal (Augie Distel), John Haynes Walker (Detective Pez McCadden), Martha Thimmesch (Carol Rodzinski), Harlee McBride (Dr. Alyssa Dyer), Frederika Kesten (Janine), Tracy Flint (Crackhead).

STORY: Kellerman returns from Wisconsin in time to join Lewis on the case of the murder of Kenny Damon, the cop killer recently acquitted of slaying Edgar Rodzinski.

Partners Mike and Meldrick are separated by Sergeant Howard, who sends Lewis after other suspects, while telling Kellerman to look into Jake Rodzinski (the most obvious suspect). Kellerman does not know Rodzinski, but he hardly relishes the task of going after a fellow cop.

HIGHLIGHTS: "Justice, Part Two" offers little that is new, only a solid restatement of the difficult choices faced by cops. On the one hand, Lieutenant Giardello, always fiercely loyal to the men and women in blue, wonders aloud whether it was better back in the old days when fear of retribution deterred cop killers, or now when the police are expected to obey the laws they are paid to enforce. Then, there is Detective Meldrick Lewis, a man not above using his discretion to let a killer go free (see Episode 11: "See No Evil"), but also worried about doing the right thing and not giving in to vigilantism. Finally, there is Detective Frank Pembleton, a very minor player in this particular story, but an obsessive and zealous detective who pursues every investigation with the same gusto, no matter who the victim or the suspect.

Pembleton and Bayliss may not have anything to do with any of the cases at hand, but they carry on a pointless war with one another over Frank's failure to bring Tim a grilled-cheese sandwich. Tim bristles at being forgotten by his partner, while Frank condescends to Tim and his "white-boy" tastes. Their battle, in which Tim theatrically brings pastries to everyone (even Brodie) except Frank, culminates in a peace offering by Frank: dozens of grilled-cheese sandwiches scattered liberally throughout Tim's workspace.

COMMENTARY: David Simon returns to *Homicide* to pen this episode and join the crew as a staff writer. Not surprisingly, Simon's story turns on little details other writers would rarely consider. For example, one major plot point is the general lack of ballistics knowledge on the part of most cops.

The soul of the story is the contrast between the old-school police force (represented by Jake, his dead father Edgar, Jake's partner Pez, and Edgar's partner Augie) and the new order (represented primarily by Mike Kellerman). Gee recalls with ambivalence the old days when the police meted out mob-style vigilante justice to defend themselves. It was not a particularly pretty sight, but was it worse than today when the police force is burdened by rules that favor cop killers like Kenny?

Notably, Kellerman is angered by Pez's decision to testify against his partner Jake. Although this is exactly what the detective hoped for when he took Pez into the Box, the thought that the man would give up his partner so easily upsets Mike. In the next season, accusations of bribe-taking against the Arson Unit would prompt Mike's former colleagues to testify against him (although he didn't do it) for the same selfish reasons.

NOTES: Ballistics expert Janine is played by guest star Frederika Kesten, who was, at the time, the real-life Mrs. Reed Diamond.

Episode 49: "Stakeout"

[Production Code 416]
Original air date: March 15, 1996.
Written by Noel Behn; story by Tom Fontana and Noel Behn; directed by John McNaughton.

Additional Cast and Guest Stars:
Max Perlich (J. H. Brodie), Jim True (George Buxton), Kate Walsh (Cathy Buxton), Helen Carey (Maggie Conroy), Tyler Miller (Paul Hassett), Harlee McBride (Dr. Alyssa Dyer).

STORY: The Homicide Unit sets up a surveillance on a man who has slaughtered numerous teenagers. The detectives take turns waiting in the Buxtons' home next door. Eager to close this gruesome case, Lieutenant Giardello even delays leaving for his daughter Charisse's wedding. The stakeout lasts exactly twenty-four hours, when Detectives Pembleton and Bayliss finally arrest the killer in his driveway without incident.

HIGHLIGHTS: Tim reveals that he has been seriously considering leaving the Homicide Unit to run a Los Angeles security company. The experience of catching the serial killer apparently changes his mind, and he agrees to stay in Baltimore until he closes the Lambert case. This subplot would resurface, albeit in a very subtle way, in the fifth season's Episode 62: "White Lies." Bayliss finally gets a suspect for the Lambert case in the Box in that episode, only to ruin his own interrogation with a digression about leaving Baltimore for sunny Southern California. Attentive viewers who recognized and remembered the connection could theorize that Bayliss may have been subconsciously sabotaging his own case in order to stay in the Baltimore Homicide Squad and save face with Frank. In any event, the notion of Bayliss leaving for Los Angeles was never mentioned directly again after this episode.

COMMENTARY: During the course of the twenty-four-hour stakeout, the Buxtons quarrel, break up, get together again, make love, and go back to normal. As they go about their lives, they find that each time one of them ventures into the living room there is a change in the detective watching the house, presenting them with a new person they haven't yet met. Thus, the Buxtons try to bridge the gap by reciting the highlights of recent events to the newly arrived detectives to fill them in about what they've missed.

The setup is a metaphor for watching TV. As *Homicide* grew from a cult show with barely a handful of episodes to its newest incarnation with a rapidly growing audience base, there were suddenly hoards of new viewers who had missed out on past events. While the "Previously on *Homicide: Life on the Street*" opening sequences can recap important plot points, the many overlapping tales and gradual character development over four years had many details that were impossible to fit into such a short moment. Just as the Buxtons take it upon themselves to fill in their guests on the highlights of their lives, the cast of *Homicide* take the opportunity to remind the viewers at home the important moments of *their* lives.

While waiting and watching for the killer to return, the detectives manage to recount that Bayliss is still haunted by the unsolved Adena Watson case, and the fact that the araber went free. Megan Russert reminds us that her cousin is newsman Tim Russert, that her husband, Mike, died of cancer, and that she was promoted to captain and demoted to detective by Colonel Barnfather. Meldrick Lewis talks about his former partner Crosetti's suicide. Detectives Munch and Kellerman are divorced, and Kellerman is still "the new guy," having displaced Tim of that honor. Stan Bolander and Beau Felton were suspended from the force; Lewis, Munch, and Bayliss own the Waterfront Bar; and Kay and Tim are former smokers. Frank is edgy about his impending fatherhood, and, by the way, he used to live in New York City but moved to Baltimore ten years before. Finally Giardello "Gee," is hurt by his estrangement from his daughter Charisse.

In fact, in addition to the self-conscious metaphor for *Homicide*'s new, uninitiated viewers, "Stakeout" also makes sly references to the show's location in Baltimore, far from the West Coast home of the rest of the TV industry. Tim spends the hour considering whether or not to move to Los Angeles, only to be persuaded that Baltimore is just as good if not better. Gee spends the hour preparing to go to San Francisco, only to be held back by fate, fog, and fear. Thus, the characters of this series can dream of California, but Baltimore is where they belong and where they stay.

After reviewing the major character developments and plot points of the last four years, "Stakeout" concludes with a direct and bold restatement of its principles. Tim grumbles that Homicide isn't enough of a family. Frank rebukes him, pointing out that Homicide is like a real family, in that it is full of opinionated people and troubled relationships. Frank idealized the job. They speak for those who can no longer speak for themselves.

It's a great line, and a perfect end to a great episode. As a potential introduction of a new viewer to *Homicide*'s many charms, this episode may be the very best place to start.

NOTES: Writer Noel Behn and director John McNaughton are both veterans of old-school *Homicide*, and thus in an excellent position to guide this retrospective of the show's history.

Episode 50: "Requiem for Adena"

[Production Code 418]
Original air date: March 29, 1996.
Written by Julie Martin; directed by Lee Bonner.

Additional Cast and Guest Stars:
Chris Rock (Carver Dooley), Max Perlich (J. H. Brodie), Nurit Koppel (Susannah Chase), Ami Brabson (Mary Pembleton), Clayton LeBoeuf (Colonel George Barnfather), Walt MacPherson (Captain Roger Gaffney), Ralph Tabakin (Dr. Scheiner), Gwendolyn Briley-Strand (Mrs. Watson), Jerome Valantene Gregg (Jerome Franklin), Tanya Lewis (Detective Arata), Mark Rogers (Claude Vetter), E. Dawn Samuel (Lorena Lester), Joy Jones (Evangeline Cray).

STORY: When Pembleton and Bayliss are called to witness the body of a twelve-year-old girl who has been stabbed and sexually assaulted, it brings back horrible memories of the Adena Watson case (Episodes 2: "A Ghost of a Chance" and 5: "Three Men and Adena").

Despite the pressure, Frank insists that he be allowed to pursue this case solo with no partner and no "red ball" designation. Hurt and angry at being distrusted by his partner, Tim also bristles at the suggestion that Adena's killing went unavenged due to his mistakes as a rookie, and is eager to start his own investigation.

HIGHLIGHTS: Videographer Brodie admits to having a crush on Sergeant Kay Howard (first hinted at in Episode 41: "Sniper, Part One"), although she believes it's all just a put-on by her male colleagues.

Bayliss finally puts the ghosts of Adena to rest as well as he ever will, discarding the photograph of the murdered child that has adorned his desk for three years.

In addition to looking backward, the episode also foreshadows future events, in that Lieutenant Giardello scolds Pembleton for letting his increasingly volatile temper get the better of him. Gee warns Frank against bursting a blood vessel, while worrying about the possibility that his detective's hotheaded nature will land him in the hospital. If only Frank had listened...

One of the nation's hottest comics, Chris Rock guest-stars as a child killer in "Requiem for Adena."
Everett Collection

COMMENTARY: The previous episode, "Stakeout," provided a helpful refresher course on past events, which could prove invaluable for the new viewer when confronted with this episode, a sequel to a story broadcast three years earlier. The detectives themselves have to struggle to recall the critical details of Adena Watson's murder.

If the notion of bringing back old stories years later seems daring, NBC now had room to let *Homicide* experiment. Improved ratings gave Fontana and his team more freedom. This situation is paralleled onscreen when Colonel Barnfather and Captain Gaffney tell Gee that because his squad's clearance rate is up, they can afford to indulge the Lieutenant's unorthodox leadership.

Although writer Julie Martin returns to the Watson case, she doesn't let Bayliss close it now, either. The episode reopens old wounds for no better reason than to pick at the emotional scabs. Tim walked out of Episode 5: "Three Men and Adena" haunted by the knowledge that he had never closed the case. This time, he is no closer to any answers.

In fact, the hilarious scene of Frank and Tim trying to interrogate the astonishingly stupid reprobate Carver Dooley plays almost like a demented parody of the elegant and literary interrogation in Episode 5: "Three Men and Adena."

Critic David Bianculli, always a *Homicide* booster, lauded the episode as being "brilliant not only for the many moods and twists it provides, but for giving us another helping of the best ensemble acting on TV."

Entertainment Weekly compared the episode to that week's *NYPD Blue*, which also featured a child killing, "but on *NYPD Blue* it was another open-and-shut case for the frictionless partnership of Simone and Sipowicz." The magazine concluded that it was "further evidence that *Homicide: Life on the Street* has unseated *NYPD Blue* as TV's best cop drama."

NOTES: Chris Rock, stand-up comic and former star of *Saturday Night Live,* turns in an excellent performance as Carver Dooley, combining his finely honed comic timing with the gut-wrenching horror of the crime to create a character both extremely amusing and deeply disturbing.

Rock is considered one of comedy's hottest new stars, and has earned Emmy nominations for his HBO special *Bring the Pain* (1996) and for his political commentary on *Politically Incorrect with Bill Maher* (1996–). He can also be seen in such films as *Beverly Hills Cop II* (1987), *New Jack City* (1991), *Boomerang* (1992), *Panther* (1995), and *Lethal Weapon 4* (1998).

Episode 51: "Full Moon"

[Production Code 410]
Original air date: April 5, 1996.
Written by Eric Overmyer; story by Tom Fontana, Henry Bromell, and Eric Overmyer; directed by Leslie Libman and Larry Williams.

Additional Cast and Guest Stars:

Max Perlich (J. H. Brodie), Ron Brice ("Mr. Evans"), Charisse Brown ("Mrs. Evans"), Timothi-Jane Graham (Ramona), Karen Tsen Lee (night manager), Christopher Tarjan (New Moon owner), the Reverend Horton Heat (preacher), M. Cochise Anderson (Lonny Askew), Christopher Lopez (Walter Gonzalez), Laura Robbins (Jennifer Wells), Donna Sacco (Vicki Acquaviva), Alida Yath (Ophelia Gonzalez), Timothy Hayes Lynch (Greg Muir).

STORY: A shooting at the New Moon Hotel in the outskirts of Baltimore brings Detectives Lewis and Kellerman out on a night lit by a full moon. Their search through the shady denizens of the New Moon turns up little in the way of clues, but plenty of lowlifes with something to hide.

HIGHLIGHTS: Although they never catch their killer, Kellerman and Lewis do take the time to attend the demolition of the Lafayette Courts housing project, which Lewis reveals is where he grew up. After listing his first girlfriends from that part of his life, Meldrick can scarcely bear to watch the building torn down. He ultimately keeps a brick from the demolition as a memento.

This episode features the second nude scene of the season. As in Episode 34: "Fire, Part One," Detective Kellerman tries to retain his professional composure when a lovely lady provocatively strips in front of him.

COMMENTARY: If ever there was a better contrast between old-school *Homicide* and the "new look" *Homicide* than the back-to-back broadcasts of these last two segments, it has yet to surface. Episode 50: "Requiem for Adena" showcases *Homicide*'s stars, Kyle Secor and Andre Braugher, brooding and bickering as always. Fast on its heels, though, is this rambling, digressive episode packed with weirdness and high style, presided over by *Homicide*'s new leads, Clark Johnson and Reed Diamond. In the previous episode Pembleton confronted Bayliss over whether his obsession is to avenge Adena's memory or to soothe his wounded pride. Here, in this episode, when asked if he dreams about famous people, Kellerman admits he dreams about Bugs Bunny.

While Detectives Kellerman and Lewis do have their share of dark emotions to divulge (Mike's divorce, Meldrick's childhood in the projects), they do so with less brooding intensity than their fellow detective pair, and with more twisted humor.

NOTES: The husband-and-wife directing team of Leslie Libman and Larry Williams would also helm part of the season finale of Season Five, Episode 77: "Partners and Other Strangers."

This episode was held back from its original place right after the two-part "Sniper" group (Episodes 41 and 42) because NBC wanted to move the more sensational episodes to the head of the season and leave the weird ones for last.

Episode 52: "Scene of the Crime"

[Production Code 421]
Original air date: April 12, 1996.
Written by Anya Epstein and David Simon; story by Henry Bromell and Tom Fontana and Barry Levinson; directed by Kathy Bates.

Additional Cast and Guest Stars:
Victor L. Williams (Ishmael Al-Hadj), Peter Gerety (Officer Stuart Gharty), Max Perlich (J. H. Brodie), Laurie Kennedy (Felicity Weaver), J. Michael Hunter (Lieutenant Nat Galvin), Joey Scherr (Hamp Mears), Linda Cavell (Mrs. Dunham), Pat Dade (Monica Murphy), Kevin Jiggets (Raheem El-Amin), Clayton LeBoeuf (Colonel George Barnfather), Jaki-Terry (Mrs. Hermos), Gary D'Addario (Lieutenant Jasper).

STORY: For the past year, the Highland Terrace apartment complex has been policed by a private security force run by the Muslims, who, despite their inflammatory and controversial politics, have maintained peace and order in the complex where the cops could not. However, when a murder does occur, Detectives Kellerman and Lewis find that they cannot get any information or assistance from the Terrace's occupants. Meanwhile, while investigating an unrelated case, Detectives Russert and Munch learn that the black community has reason to distrust the police.

HIGHLIGHTS: The tension between perfectionist Russert and slap-dash Munch reaches a peak here, showing just what a mismatched pair they are. The events of the hour provoke unprecedented tension between partners Lewis and Kellerman, as well. Although race has never been an issue in their relationship before (or since), the case at hand gets under each's skin.

Munch is discouraged by his current partner, and longs for his previous partner, the departed Stan Bolander. After calling the Big Man no less than twenty-six times, Munch becomes convinced Bolander will return shortly, only to have his hopes dashed and his feelings crushed when the ex-detective elects not to show up after all.

Ironically, this episode introduces a character who would ultimately be used a sort of Bolander substitute. Peter Gerety plays officer Stuart Gharty, and reprises the role a year later in the two-part Season Five finale. Gharty would join as a regular in Season Six.

COMMENTARY: A troubling, worrisome hour, this episode challenges the very notion of police as heroes. Cowritten by David Simon, the story tackles important but unconventional dramatic ideas such as when police should call for backup, and the politics of leaking stories to the press.

Rather than merely paint the Muslims as all-purpose bad guys, writers David Simon and Anya Epstein take great pains to show the good that this group has done for their community. Under their protection, the residents can truly feel protected, as, without them, the drug dealers had reigned unchallenged by the ineffectual police. The group's manipulation of race for political advantage may anger some of the detectives (like Kellerman), but it is not far removed from the manipulative political games played by the cops themselves (such as Lieutenant Giardello's masterful use of a press leak to put pressure on Colonel Barnfather).

NOTES: Actress Kathy Bates (the Oscar-winning star of the film *Misery*, 1989) adds her contribution here as guest director. The actress had previously directed a segment for PBS' *Great Performances* in 1995. Nevertheless, Bates is better known for her acting talents, having earned a Golden Globe nomination for her role in *Fried Green Tomatoes* (1991) and an Obie Award for her stage work in the off-Broadway show *Frankie and Johnny in the Clair de Lune.* She has also been nominated for a Tony, received the Los Angeles Drama Critics Award, the Outer Circle Critics Award, and the Dramalogue Award for her outstanding work on stage and screen. Not surprisingly, Bates also sports a *St. Elsewhere* credit, which may have been one of the reasons she got the chance to direct a *Homicide* episode. (Producer Tom Fontana has often looked to the rosters of his former series to staff his current one.)

Her facility with actors is obvious from the excellent performances throughout. Yet she also displays a strong visual style as well. The look of this episode is as close to the original bleak look of the series as anything after Wayne Ewing's departure at the end of the first season.

This episode also introduces actor Peter Gerety as Stuart Gharty. The subject of an Internal Affairs probe and the object of Megan Russert's ire, Gharty would later be promoted to Internal Affairs as a detective and subsequently join the Homicide Squad as a peer in the fifth-season finale.

Episode 53: "Map of the Heart"

[Production Code 417]
Original air date: April 26, 1996.
Written by Michael Whaley and James Yoshimura; directed by Clark Johnson.

Additional Cast and Guest Stars:
Terry Kinney (Richard Laumer), Max Perlich (J. H. Brodie), Walt MacPherson (Captain Roger Gaffney), Harlee McBride (Dr. Alyssa Dyer), John Fiske (Buster Simmons), Joe Glenn (Morris Laumer), Liz Noone (Felicity Fenwick), Ralph Tabakin (Dr. Scheiner), Judy Thornton (Judy).

STORY: The discovery of a dead man floating in a swimming pool sets Detectives Pembleton and Bayliss on a complicated trail that will pit them against the shadowy operatives of the National Security Administration.

Their chief suspect is Richard Laumer, a cartographer with the NSA. However, the detectives cannot arrest their prime suspect, as an NSA agent arrives at the precinct to tell them that their investigation must be stopped and even threatens the detectives' lives if they proceed.

HIGHLIGHTS: This is the first time that the Lunch Bandit, an unknown villain responsible for swiping the squad's lunches, is mentioned. For two years the Lunch Bandit has been able to be undetected, but new guy

Mike Kellerman is so bothered by this lawlessness that he takes it as a personal mission to capture and unmask the culprit.

In fact, videographer Brodie will be the one to identify the Lunch Bandit (see Episode 67: "The Documentary"). In this segment, Brodie "practices" being a detective, pacing around in the Box spouting ridiculous TV-cop clichés to himself.

Brodie's scene is a superfluous bit of comic relief, but his role as the squad's videographer becomes significant for this installment's video-related themes. Laumer's incriminating evidence is a videocassette he demands that the detectives watch. Meanwhile, Munch and Kellerman argue about a possible "hot" VCR stolen from the Arson Unit.

COMMENTARY: True to form, James Yoshimura serves up a heady blend of hard-edged drama with plenty of comic relief. It is too bad that the episode focuses on Andre Braugher and Kyle Secor, since conspiracy-buff Richard Belzer would have loved the scenario that reads more like an episode of *The X-Files*. (Belzer would get his chance to appear in the real *X-Files* in 1997, playing his Detective Munch character.) Veiled threats, fake names, shadowy figures at clandestine meetings, and the ever-present sense of being manipulated by an unseen force all contribute to an atmosphere never before tried on *Homicide*.

Even Munch, Kellerman, and Brodie get in on the act, with a surreal, twisted conversation, which they conclude never happened about a nonexistent topic none of them knows anything about.

This is one episode that bears, or even demands, multiple viewings to untangle the complicated plot and duplicitous character motivations.

NOTES: Detective Lewis's absence from the proceedings can be explained by the fact that actor Clark Johnson became the first cast member to direct an episode, taking the reins behind the camera for the first time. He has a great script with which to work, and the scenes at the Baltimore aquarium make a superbly visual set piece.

Episode 54: "The Damage Done"

[Production Code 419]
Original air date: May 3, 1996.
Written by Jorge Zamacona; story by Henry Bromell and Tom Fontana; directed by Jace Alexander.

Additional Cast and Guest Stars:

Erik Todd Dellums (Luther Mahoney), Kevin Thigpen (Drak Fortunado), Ingrid Rogers (Amy Jennings), Sean Akil Wingate (Pendell), Granville Adams (Westby), Saverio Guerra

(Deano Hoover), Arthur Eric Hunter (Mr. Fleming), Lance Lewman (Detective Bob Castleman), Louis B. Murray (Andrade).

STORY: For every detective, there is the case that defies closing. For Bayliss, it was Adena Watson, his first case on the Homicide Squad, while for Mike Kellerman, it is an apparent drug war on Baltimore's streets.

The real culprit is arch drug lord Luther Mahoney, a slippery and arrogant criminal mastermind who has used his drug profits to fund good works for the city. Mahoney may be the villain behind the scenes, but, like the NSA operatives of the previous episode, he has rendered himself untouchable.

HIGHLIGHTS: Meldrick Lewis makes a passing reference to being in love, a comment whose full significance only becomes apparent in the next episode. Mike Kellerman also has a brief romance, with a young schoolteacher named Amy Jennings, a flutter in his heart that never has a chance to blossom.

Away from the inflammatory politics of the Muslims (see Episode 52: "Scene of the Crime"), race has once again settled into the deep background. No one even seems to notice or care that white policeman Kellerman is flirting with a black woman from a drug-embattled neighborhood.

While discussing the allure of the drug culture, Kellerman and Lewis ask one another if they have ever been tempted to steal some of the vast sums of money that they uncover in raids. Kellerman is quick to insist he has never felt the temptation, and would gladly shoot his partner if he ever succumbs. Such sentiments become all the more poignant when, the next year, Mike is accused of taking bribes.

Upset over the drug war, Giardello expresses his anger in bizarre Zen koans that did much to cement his reputation among viewers as a leader who takes the idea of poetic justice fairly literally.

COMMENTARY: This episode rightly could also be called "The Benefit Done," since writer Jorge Zamacona unwittingly provided the show with one of the series' most popular recurring characters. In some ways the episode is a follow-up to Episode 52: "Scene of the Crime," in that it explores the problems of the inner city and the devastating effect of drugs and violence. The opening sequence documents the progress of dope from the back of a truck to the streets (along with yet another onscreen killing!), and shows an even grittier, nastier side of Baltimore than usual.

However, the highlight of the episode is the smarmy supervillain Luther Mahoney, played with memorable unction by Erik Todd Dellums. The character proved so popular that the writers were obliged to bring him back repeatedly. The Mahoney character allowed *Homicide* to develop a more accessible "good guys versus bad guys" story line while also delving deeper into aspects of the real drug culture never before dramatized.

NOTES: In addition to bringing Lewis and Kellerman and Mahoney together for the first time, this episode also provides another of Meldrick's encounters with a pun-named character, this time a Narcotics detective with a name that sounds suspiciously like "hemp."

Another Narcotics detective, Bob Castleman, is introduced, who would later have a more significant role in relationship to Luther Mahoney in Episode 81: "Blood Ties, Part Three."

Episode 55: "The Wedding"

[Production Code 420]
Original air date: May 10, 1996.
Written by Henry Bromell; directed by Alan Taylor.

Additional Cast and Guest Stars:

Max Perlich (J. H. Brodie), Ami Brabson (Mary Pembleton), Karen Williams (Barbara Shivers), "Margaret May" [actually Melissa Leo] (Carrie Howard), Kevin Grantz (Paul Lupkis), Chuck Paris (uniform), Ivan Scott (announcer), Ralph Tabakin (Dr. Scheiner), Russell Wilson (Simon Jackson).

STORY: Detective Lewis surprises his coworkers with a stunning announcement of his marriage, that day, to Barbara Shivers, a woman they did not even know he was seeing. His fellow detectives are puzzled, and almost believe that it's all some gargantuan put-on.

With everyone busy on the arrangements, it falls to Lieutenant Giardello and Sergeant Howard to take the case of radio shock-jock Kevin Lugo, found shot to death in a parking lot. This is Gee's first time out on the street in many years, and before the night is over he will have killed a suspect in a surprise shoot-out.

HIGHLIGHTS: The wedding brings the characters out of their respective shells in some unexpected ways. Kay Howard's sister, Carrie Howard, visits from Florence, Italy, and proves herself an aggressive flirt. Carrie's presence pits Mike Kellerman and Tim Bayliss against one another in a show of competitive machismo of almost cavemanlike proportions.

During the wedding reception, Megan Russert remarks that her daughter Carolyn needs a father figure. Perhaps to provide that father figure, and perhaps to fill a void in her own life left after her husband's death, Russert would leave the squad at the end of the season to follow her new boyfriend to France.

On top of this, Frank Pembleton becomes a father figure himself, when Mary goes into labor during the reception.

Gee finds himself out on the streets facing the kinds of challenges he is always demanding that his detectives overcome. Ultimately he is plagued with guilt for having to shoot and kill a suspect.

COMMENTARY: As the season draws to a close, *Homicide* brings out the big guns: onscreen killings, a wedding, and a birth! Welcome to *"All My Children: Life on the Street."*

Of course, writer and executive producer Henry Bromell twists the situation into something suitably bizarre. Detective Lewis may be getting married, but to a woman never before even mentioned, and the nuptials are brought on so suddenly that the rest of the cast spends the hour debating whether the whole thing is some demented practical joke. In fact, Detective Munch refuses to be convinced even when he actually witnesses the wedding. Gee kills a man, but as a result of another practical joke. The one case of the episode remains unsolved, and most of the cast are made to look stupid and foolish.

Producer Tom Fontana tried to add even more hype to the already bloated episode with this cryptic comment to the press: "Because it's *Homicide*, you don't know whether the baby will live or die." Nothing in the episode itself suggests such a dire and unpleasant outcome.

NOTES: Although credited as "Margaret May," the actress playing Carrie Howard is none other than Melissa Leo herself (a fact admitted by NBC's press releases, but concealed in the onscreen credits). The transformation is astonishing, and demonstrates once again the untapped abilities of this underused performer. Thanks to the already disjointed editing patterns of *Homicide's* style, the fact that Carrie and Kay do not appear onscreen together is only evident on repeated viewings.

Episode 56: "Work Related"

[Production Code 422]
Original air date: May 17, 1996.
Written by Tom Fontana; directed by Jean de Segonzac.

Additional Cast and Guest Stars:

Max Perlich (J. H. Brodie), Ami Brabson (Mary Pembleton), Sean Whitesell (doctor), Jeffrey Perry Czerbinski (Ian McKenzie), Michael Willis (Darin Russom), Stephen Angus (paramedic), Erica Van Wagener (paramedic), Anna Belknap (Julia Pfeiffer), Herb Levinson (Dr. Lausanne), Kristin Rohde (Sergeant Sally Rogers).

STORY: For Detective Meldrick Lewis, his job offers an escape from his recent marriage that has already turned sour. His case is a literal "red ball," with a poor motorist killed instantly when a red bowling ball was dropped off an overpass through his windshield.

Although he has a beautiful newborn daughter, Olivia, at home, Detective Frank Pembleton is still a temperamental workaholic. A double murder at a fast-food joint pushes him too far, leading to a stroke, and, as his family and coworkers anxiously wait, the doctors admit they don't know if he will ever recover.

HIGHLIGHTS: Meldrick's "red ball" case is yet another example of the detective's propensity for living in a pun-filled world. When Meldrick decides not to waste any more effort on the case, he gives a superb example of his skewed priorities and complete disregard for proper procedure.

COMMENTARY: Although some papers inaccurately reported that Pembleton dies in this episode, the effect is really no less traumatic to his many legions of devoted fans.

The season finale for *The X-Files* featured Agent Fox Mulder's mother in a coma, and the in season finale of *Law and Order* prosecutor Claire Kincaid is killed in a car crash. TV viewers had good reason to feel their characters were being taken away one by one. *New York* magazine lamented, "Was it really necessary to hype the ratings of a terrific show by threatening the life of the best actor on series television?"

NOTES: Andre Braugher had grown tired of his role as Frank Pembleton, and worried about the apparent infallibility of the character. His skills as an interrogator had thrilled fans and writers alike, and resulted in episode after episode of Frank badgering confessions out of suspects. Pembleton had become a supercop who could do no wrong.

"Tom, something has got to be done," Braugher told producer Tom Fontana, "I need a change."

Fontana considered, and proposed that Frank be the victim of a stroke. When he returned for the fifth season, he would have to struggle to relearn how to walk, how to talk, how to be a detective.

"This hits me where I live," Braugher beamed.

CHAPTER 7

The Fifth Season: Breathing Space

"Luckily, we at NBC are in an enviable position," NBC Entertainment president Warren Littlefield told the press with no small pride, "Our success allows us to pick some of our favorites and commit to them, allowing time to truly be a success."

After surging back in just three years to being the number one network from third place, NBC could indeed afford *Homicide* even more slack than it had already given the embattled drama. If *Homicide* had survived during NBC's darkest days, then the newly resplendent NBC could make the ultimate show of faith by renewing *Homicide* for not just one full season, but two.

Littlefield ordered a startling forty-four episodes (almost as many as the show had made in the past four years), guaranteeing both a fifth and a sixth season.

With the network pressure relieved, the producers no longer had to pursue sensationalism with as much fervor as they had in 1995–96. Consequently, Season Five displayed more eccentricity, experimentalism, and daring than its predecessor.

Not least among the season's bold initiatives was the gradual and traumatic recovery of Detective Frank Pembleton following his stroke. This subplot showcased actor Andre Braugher's remarkable abilities, but sidelined the show's most famous character at the height of his popularity.

Viewers inundated producer Tom Fontana's office with calls and letters complaining about how frustrating it was to see Pembleton in such a state. Fontana was delighted to hear their complaints, since he had intended to make the audience feel the same disappointment that Pembleton himself would be feeling.

Unfortunately, the producers had expected Frank's recovery to be a ratings-rich television event, with the stroke being a surefire cliffhanger to keep viewers coming back for the new season. The plan backfired, however, and viewers tuned out the program when the star of the show was no longer the dramatic focus. Supervising producer James Yoshimura admitted, "When the numbers came out, we were just mystified."

As the season progressed, Frank lost his infallibility and self-confidence, his partner, and his family. As if putting the show's ostensible star through such an ordeal was not enough, Season Five also all but ruined Detective Mike Kellerman's career. Although he had an unwavering devotion to the ethics of policework, he would be tarnished with accusations of wrongdoing, yanked off the street for the better part of the year, and left in emotional shambles. Videographer Brodie would be evicted from his apartment, and newcomer Dr. Julianna Cox would have to attend therapy sessions to deal with her own father's murder. As icing on the cake, Tim Bayliss would reveal that his trademark sensitivity owes much to his own sexually abused childhood.

With the freedom imposed by the double-season order by NBC, the writers and producers of *Homicide* could venture onto riskier, more mature ground in its plot lines than those of the previous year. Arguably, the fifth season was as edgy and disturbing as anything since the show's 1993 premiere.

Homicide Online

The 1996–97 season also saw *Homicide* come of age on the Internet's World Wide Web. Already the program had garnered a strong and loyal base of "wired fans" who traded their thoughts in online discussion groups (see Appendix G). With the fifth season, NBC chose to get in on the game themselves.

In November 1996, NBC Interactive's vice president Edmond Sanctis announced the birth of *Homicide*'s official Web site at www.nbc.com/homicide. Sanctis promised "an intriguing and in-depth look at the award-winning television series" with "the same provocative, gritty style as the on-air show."

Indeed, the site is a jittery, colorful, eclectic place full of edgy graphics, interviews, and news. While most corporate-produced Web sites of this sort pale in comparison to the better-designed, more entertaining, and technologically more ambitious work done by fans, nbc.com's *Homicide* site is a rare exception and a true standard-bearer.

Second Shift

During *Homicide*'s mid-season six-week hiatus, NBC unveiled a spin-off of the series to help sate the fans' appetites. In a nod to *Homicide*'s many online fans, this spin-off was not to be found anywhere on the TV dial, but exclusively on the Web.

Edmond Sanctis and his staff had long wanted to expand one of NBC's primetime series into an online version, and *Homicide* was the perfect candidate. For one thing, NBC owns the show, which saved costly negotiations with an outside producer.

More importantly, however, Sanctis asked, "Why start from scratch when we have a fan base from which to work?"

Tom Hjelm, producer of the *Homicide* Web site, agrees, "*Homicide* had a pretty loyal following on the Internet already."

On February 14, 1997, *Homicide: Second Shift* was born. The online series covers the exploits of the detectives that come to work when the TV characters go home (the people Pembleton once called "shadows"). The cast of *Homicide: Second Shift* includes Detectives Ray Cutler, Layton Johnson, Tony Bonaventura, and "LZ." No actors played these roles in the traditional sense; they are virtual stars, concocted by Tom Hjelm and his team.

"We have a staff of six people who serve any number of functions," says Hjelm. Ayelet Sela writes the broad story lines, which are fleshed out by the rest of the team. Tom Fontana, producer of *Homicide: Life on the Street*, reads and approves the scripts to verify that the online series maintains the flavor of the TV show. Finally, software programmer Joseph Nekulak composes the interactive elements of the so-called "websodic."

"This is a very exciting first for both media," boasted Warren Littlefield, "We have taken the marriage of television and the Internet to a new level." Tom Rogers, president of NBC Cable and Business Development, added, "The *Homicide: Second Shift* websodic represents a significant step forward for NBC Interactive and NBC Entertainment."

Sanctis explains, "Through interactive design and technology, viewers can get interactively involved in each episode. The user actually becomes a participant by being able to explore the crime scene and uncover the evidence."

"When I first saw it, I was stunned," Fontana told *USA Today*, "I felt like this is the beginning of the thing that's going to put me out of business."

To create each episode, Hjelm and his crew would shoot photos at the Fells Point Recreation Pier set, record the voices of actors, add sound effects, and employ Java applications and embedded audio to make the multimedia project come alive. Each installment would take a user about twenty minutes to navigate.

In a clever move, nbc.com kept fresh episodes of *Second Shift* coming throughout the summer, while the TV series was off the air.

Homicide: Second Shift not only gave fans an extra fix of *Homicide: Life on the Street* on top of the TV experience, but also gave NBC a chance to spy on viewer habits. Since its debut, *Homicide: Second Shift* has developed a base of almost three million users who stay and explore the "websodic." By watching user traffic, nbc.com discovered evidence that more and more viewers are watching the show on TV while exploring the Web site at the same time. This can only mean Americans are increasingly bringing their home video and computers experiences closer together.

Having already achieved considerable success with the *Law and Order* crossover, it didn't take long for Fontana and Hjelm to start scheming crossovers between *Homicide: Life on the Street* and *Homicide: Second Shift*. In June 1997, *Homicide: Second Shift* hosted a guest appearance by Erik Todd Dellums as Luther Mahoney. Although the notorious drug lord had been killed on the TV show (in Episode 75: "Deception"), he appeared in flashbacks in *Homicide: Second Shift*. "Having a talent like Erik take a guest-starring role in *Second Shift* contributes immensely to the stature and level of production value for our new interactive medium," enthused Sanctis.

The following month, Reed Diamond made the crossover as Detective Kellerman. This time Shawn Hardin of NBC Digital Productions did the gushing: "We are thrilled to have an actor of the caliber of Reed Diamond to initiate this next phase of our interactive entertainment programming."

As *Homicide: Life on the Street* geared up for its sixth season, Fontana and Hjelm began talking about a crossover in the other direction, i.e., bringing characters from *Homicide: Second Shift* to the TV show.

Intercast

In addition to the innovative websodic, the folks at nbc.com also tried another experimental connection between the online and onscreen *Homicide's*. www.nbc.com/homicide unveiled Intel's Intercast technology, a way to transform the passive TV viewing experience into a CD-ROM-style multimedia presentation.

A PC outfitted with Intercast would allow the viewer-user to watch *Homicide* on their computer screen, augmented with text and graphics as glorified onscreen footnotes.

Imaginary Forces

The new season also unveiled a brand-new opening title sequence. The original sequence, a grainy collage of black-and-white images of Baltimore scenes, was the work of Baltimore film producer Mark Pellington. The new titles were created by the Los Angeles agency Imaginary Forces, the same graphic artists responsible for the title sequence for the film *Seven* (1995). Like their work on *Seven*, Imaginary Forces served up a jittery patchwork of disturbing pictures and crude type fonts.

Unfortunately for NBC, the expensive new titles had the opposite effect they had intended. Instead of adding a level of style and prestige to the show, viewers objected to the colorful, overproduced look. An online poll on the Web site revealed the cold, hard numbers. Eighty percent of the viewers preferred the older title sequence.

Best of the Best

TV Guide singled out *Homicide* as one of the ten very best shows of the year, Andre Braugher as one of the ten best performers of the year, and Episode 59: "Prison Riot" as one of the top 100 episodes of television *ever*.

The Television Critics Association awarded *Homicide* two prizes during its summer Press Tour in California. In addition to the Outstanding Achievement in a Drama Series award, the TCA cited Andre Braugher for Individual Achievement in a Drama Series.

Despite such accolades, and NBC's significant multi-season commitment, *Homicide* continued to struggle in the ratings. The audience gains made in the fourth season started to level off. Night after night, the Nielsen numbers went to *Homicide's* take-no-chances competitor, *Nash Bridges*.

"I can't believe we're not beating *Bridges*," bemoaned Fontana, "Not to take anything away from it, but come on!"

Hiatus

In the spring, the major networks pulled many established shows off the air for a while to give new programs a try-out. The mid-season replacement is a time-honored network tradition, and one that served *Homicide* very well indeed back in 1994. If *Homicide* left the air for six weeks to let a rookie show get a chance, it was both fair payback time for *Homicide* and a tacit acknowledgment of *Homicide's* new status as an "established" program.

Fans were less than pleased, though, to find their beloved *Homicide* usurped for over a month by the overblown *Crisis Center* (1997). *Crisis Center* turned off so many viewers that it hurt *Homicide's* already shaky ratings when the schedule returned to normal. NBC had preempted *ER* as well, but only to give the already long-running and Emmy-winning *Law and Order* a shot at a wider audience.

NBC's cavalier (and destructive) attitude toward scheduling hindered *Homicide*'s ability to fight back against *Nash Bridges*. During the summer, NBC's Preston Breckman elected not to run *Homicide* reruns but instead to hand the Friday-night slot over to the heavily advertised but lightly watched thriller *Profiler* (1996–). *Homicide* fans were discouraged, and ratings for *Profiler* were abysmal. They were so abysmal, in fact, that NBC reversed their decision mid-summer and returned *Homicide* to its proper home on July 25.

However, the decision came too late, as the damage already was done. Nobody tuned in for the returning *Homicide* either, leaving the show buried between 74th and 83rd place out of 114 (compared to *Nash Bridges* hovering at 48).

NBC had squandered what little audience attention they had.

EMMY SNUBS

Despite the continued critical accolades for *Homicide*, the series was once again snubbed by the Emmys. The fifth season, which featured some of the riskiest and most audacious work since its beginning, received merely token nods for Outstanding Guest Actress in a Drama Series (Anne Meara, in "Hostage, Part Two") and Best Casting. Meanwhile, *NYPD Blue* (1993–) won eleven nominations and *ER* (1994–) won a staggering twenty-two.

Why has one of the most consistently praised drama series in television history been overlooked by the Emmys year after year? Much of the reason is that *Homicide* is shot in Baltimore, far from the heart of the television industry in Los Angeles. Its cast and producers do not socialize with the Emmy voters on the West Coast, and instead spend their time working hard on their art.

Secondly, the Emmys are not really an award for excellence, but an award for popularity. Only when *The X-Files* (1993–) broke through into mainstream success did it start getting nominations. *Homicide*'s middling numbers ensure that it will continue to be an Emmy long shot.

One industry observer noted that Andre Braugher was not nominated this year because of his diminished role following the stroke. The irony is that Braugher had suggested the stroke as a way to push his acting abilities, as the flawless-interrogator role was no longer challenging him. When the Emmy voters no longer saw Pembleton bearing down on suspects in the Box, they lost interest, when in fact he was doing some of the most difficult work of his tenure on the show.

S E A S O N   F I V E

September 1996–May 1997
60-minute episodes
Fridays, 10:00 p.m. EST

Production Team:

Barry Levinson (executive producer), Tom Fontana (executive producer), Jim Finnerty (co-executive producer), Gail Mutrux (consulting producer), Debbie Sarjeant (co-producer), James Yoshimura (supervising producer), Julie Martin (supervising producer), Paul Attanasio (creator), Anya Epstein (story editor), David Simon (story editor), Darryl LeMont Wharton (staff writer), Lee Bigelow (script supervisor), Stephanie Fontana (writer's assistant), Vince Peranio (production designer), Tina Negro (costume designer), Susan Kessel (set decorator), Douglas J. Cuomo (music), Chris Tergesen (music coordinator), Lynn Kowal (main title theme), Louis DiGiaimo (casting director), Pat Moran (Baltimore casting director), Lorenzo Millan (boom), Bruce Litecky (sound mixer), Jean de Segonzac (director of photography), Alex Zakrzewski (additional director of photography), Kathi Ash (location manager), Cindy Mollo (editor), Jay Pires (editor), Jay Rabinowitz (editor), Imaginary Forces (title sequence), Gary D'Addario (technical adviser), Johanna Persons (vice president in charge of production).

Regular Cast:

Richard Belzer (Detective John Munch), Andre Braugher (Detective Frank Pembleton), Reed Diamond (Detective Mike Kellerman), Michelle Forbes (Chief Medical Examiner Julianna Cox), Clark Johnson (Detective Meldrick Lewis), Yaphet Kotto (Lieutenant Al Giardello), Melissa Leo (Detective Kay Howard), Max Perlich (J. H. Brodie), Kyle Secor (Detective Tim Bayliss).

Episode 57: "Hostage, Part One"

[Production Code 501]
Original air date: September 20, 1996.
Written by James Yoshimura; story by Tom Fontana and Julie Martin; directed by Ted Demme.

Additional Cast and Guest Stars:

Ami Brabson (Mary Pembleton), Gary D'Addario (Lieutenant Jasper), Julie Lauren (Officer Schanne), Art Donovan (Uba's neighbor), Clayton LeBoeuf (Colonel George Barnfather), Walt MacPherson (Captain Roger Gaffney), Karen Bralove (Marie Smith), Kate Kiley (Maureen Tarkoff), Herb Levinson (Dr. Lausanne), Monroe Thomas (Michelle Berti), Judy Thornton (Judy).

STORY: Following his stroke, Detective Pembleton returns to the Homicide Unit, but is limited to half days and light duty until he passes the firing-range test. This means that Pembleton is sidelined when the squad faces a "red ball" case of a maniac taking hostages at a middle school. While the police scramble to learn how many children he has hostage, the shooter makes his demands: he wants some beer.

HIGHLIGHTS: Captain Roger Gaffney, oozing with antagonism, accuses Lieutenant Giardello of letting his squad fall apart. In a wry jab at *Homicide*'s direct competition, Gaffney compares the comings and goings of detectives to the TV show *Nash Bridges*.

Megan Russert's departure does have an almost soap-operatic feel. We are told Detective Russert got pregnant and ran off with a French diplomat. In real life, actress Isabella Hofmann got pregnant and ran off with former costar Daniel Baldwin. Russert would appear as a voice only for Episode 65: "Control," and later would return in full form in Episodes 77: "Partners and Other Strangers" and 78: "Strangers and Other Partners."

Meanwhile, Russert's former partner Detective Munch seethes with resentment at Frank Pembleton's return to duty, playing off previously established character developments. In Episode 25: "The City That Bleeds" Munch rankled at Pembleton's cold reaction to the horror of their fellow detectives being shot. With Pembleton now the injured party, Munch calls Mary Pembleton frequently to check up on his colleague, a show of compassion that Frank rebuffs. The tension between them crackles throughout the episode, heightened by Frank's hostility to all attempts to accommodate his diminished state.

COMMENTARY: Technical adviser and occasional guest star Gary D'Addario explained on NBC's *Homicide* Web site that Pembleton's return was partly based on the real case of a Baltimore police officer named Hackley. In a landmark decision by the pension hearing board, the department concluded that if an officer was capable of answering phones and performing a minimal level of administrative work, that was enough for the officer to return to work.

Desperate to qualify on the range and return to his job on the streets rather than simply making coffee, Frank heads to the range to practice. The scene is a highly cinematic one, photographed with panache by Jean de Segonzac. Future episodes would wisely replay this scene in the opening "Previously on *Homicide: Life on the Street*" introductions.

This episode also features a remarkable scene in which Brodie is taping the reactions of the kids at the school to the hostage situation. As one girl watches her classmate's corpse taken away, she assumes the presence of Brodie and his videocamera are proof that the events are not real after all, and that it's just a movie being filmed. The girl's desperate attempts to deny what she has just witnessed can make even the most detached viewer somewhat queasy.

Critics loved the season premiere, with Braugher's too-little, too-late Emmy nomination the central feature of most reviews. Michelle Greppi of the *New York Post* called the premiere "an incredible two-parter that's going to raise the Emmy bar to the highest levels." Matt Roush, always a *Homicide* booster, raved that *Homicide* would be "propelled into a new, raw direction by tonight's poignant, then explosive, performance by Emmy-nominated Andre Braugher." *Entertainment Weekly* called the premiere "crackling," and announced, "*Homicide* is off to a fabulous start." The *Baltimore Sun*'s David Zurawick wrote, "[Braugher] has taken his game, as they say, to another level and it is a level you will not see anywhere else on weekly television, Emmy or no Emmy."

Audiences agreed, and "Hostage" brought NBC an 8.6 Nielsen rating, with some of the series' best ratings ever for the key demographics. Above all, it beat the season premiere of *Nash Bridges*. An estimated 12.3 million people tuned in to see Detective Pembleton recovering from his stroke.

NOTES: Actor Kyle Secor's severe, closely shaved haircut took many viewers by surprise. Secor explained that he was often distracted by having his hair touched up before each take, and he had it cut off so he could concentrate on his performance better. "I bought a bottle of shampoo the other day," the actor told *TV Guide*, "and it'll last me for 187 years, so I saved money on this thing, too."

Episode 58: "Hostage, Part Two"

[Production Code 502]
Original air date: September 27, 1996.
Written by Julie Martin; story by Tom Fontana and James Yoshimura; directed by Jean de Segonzac.

Additional Cast and Guest Stars:
Ami Brabson (Mary Pembleton), Gary D'Addario (Lieutenant Jasper), Anne Meara (Donna DiGrazi), Geoffrey Nauffts (Gerry Uba), Zeljko Ivanek (Assistant State's Attorney Ed Danvers), Clayton LeBoeuf (Colonel George Barnfather), Rhonda Overby (Dawn Daniels), Ralph Tabakin (Dr. Scheiner), Monroe Thomas (Michele Berti), Richard Pilcher (Sergeant Deutch), Sharon Ziman (Naomi).

STORY: The hostage situation reaches its crisis when the Quick Response Team (QRT) storms the school just in time to rescue the children, and the outlaw ends up in the hospital. Only then does the squad realize that the hostage taker is Jerry Uba, a suspect for whom Detective Bayliss has been looking.

Meanwhile, Frank Pembleton stops taking his medicine altogether, hoping that his mind will clear up enough so that he can return to the street.

HIGHLIGHTS: Prosecutor Ed Danvers reveals that he is engaged to Meryl Hanson, a public defender. The news hurts Detective Howard, since she still has feelings for him.

Season Five's comic relief subplot gets underway with the revelation that videographer Brodie has been evicted from his apartment and has taken to sleeping in the squadroom. Over the next few weeks, he will be invited in, and subsequently kicked out of, almost every one of his coworkers' digs. This week, the (un)lucky roommate is John Munch.

Meanwhile, the tension between Munch and Pembleton continues, further aggravated by Frank's mental slips. He calls the coffee a "bagel," forgets his home phone number, and generally seems as helpless and feeble as ever.

COMMENTARY: As "red ball" stories go, the "Hostage" episodes managed to get dramatic punch without compromising too much of the show's integrity. While, once again, the real-life Baltimore (a place where most killings are drug related) has been transformed into a place where lunatics kill six people in a single day, the structure of the basic story seems more natural than usual. The Homicide guys stand around anxiously sipping coffee until midway through Part Two. Only once the crisis is over does their job begin.

NOTES: Anne Meara won an Emmy nomination for her guest role as Mrs. DiGrazi, the schoolteacher taken hostage by Jerry Uba. Meara's role is small (one of the smallest in Season Five) but poignant. She is a dedicated teacher who dearly loves her job. The experience of seeing a madman gun her students down convinces her to retire.

Episode 59: "Prison Riot"

[Production Code 503]
Original air date: October 18, 1996.
Written by Tom Fontana; story by Tom Fontana and Henry Bromell; directed by Kenneth Fink.

Additional Cast and Guest Stars:

Charles S. Dutton (Elijah Sanborn), David Eigenberg (Alex Robey), Dean Winters (Tom Marans), Helen Carey (Maggie Conroy), Heather Simms (Maya Sanborn), John Epps

Charles Dutton guest-stars
in a story based on painful
truth. Photofest

(Trevor Douglas), Chauncey Hill (Kingston Sanborn), Tim McAdams (James Douglas), Mark Rogers (Claude Vetter), Sharon Ziman (Naomi).

STORY: When a riot breaks out at the state penitentiary, the entire Homicide Squad responds to the call, except desk-bound Detective Pembleton.

At the prison, the squad discovers the bodies of Trevor Douglas (one of the vid-kid murderers from Episode 36: "Autofocus") and wife-killer Claude Vetter (from Episode 50: "Requiem for Adena"). One convict, lifer Elijah Sanborn, knows what really happened. Detective Bayliss manipulates the man's family, hoping to coerce him into revealing what he knows.

HIGHLIGHTS: This powerful episode highlights Tim Bayliss. Among other things, it is learned that he was once (briefly) arrested for protesting human-rights abuses in El Salvador, and that he still is disturbed about his dysfunctional relationship with his late father (a situation which will be explained more fully in Episode 68: "Betrayal").

Meanwhile, Pembleton continues to skip his medicine in the hopes of clearing his concentration for the firearms test. Brodie deduces this from Pembleton's behavior and confronts Frank, who has to humbly admit that he has underestimated the deceptively naive-looking young man.

COMMENTARY: Advertised by NBC under the title "Lockdown," the episode opens with a rather ominous warning: "This episode has a level of violence unusual for the series." Although this is partly true (the riot itself and a flashback to a pair of murders), the real violence is the emotional violence that the various characters mete out to one another.

Singled out by *TV Guide* as one of the 100 best episodes of television *ever*, "Prison Riot" is not easily forgotten. Borrowing ideas and dialogue directly from Simon's book, Fontana and Bromell's script revisits many old plot lines by presenting past bad guys now rotting away behind bars. In addition to highlighting former villains Tom Marans, the Douglas cousins, and Claude Vetter, "Prison Riot" also brings back copycat sniper Alex Robey.

Stylishly visual and graced with three superb musical set pieces (thanks to Ken Fink and Chris Tergesen), the hour really belongs to guest star Charles Dutton. Dutton is a character actor of enormous range, whose credits include *Cat's Eye* (1985), *Mississippi Masala* (1991), *Alien 3*(1992), *Rudy* (1993), *Cry, the Beloved Country* (1995), *A Time to Kill* (1996), and *Mimic* (1997). With his presence, Dutton adds a personal touch to the proceedings. In 1968, Dutton stabbed a man in a street fight in Baltimore, and served seven and a half years for it. As *TV Guide* says, "There's hard-earned truth in his acting, and it takes this outstanding series to a new level."

NOTES: For all its masterful touches, the episode does have a few cracks in its facade. Elijah Sanborn is in prison for life after avenging his wife's murder. Yet his revenge-inspired killing fourteen years previously occurred at a time when Maryland did not offer "life without parole." In 1982, a murder conviction could bring either life or death sentences. If Sanborn wasn't on death row, and he was a model prisoner as the story claims, then he would be eligible for parole in about six years. His attitude and actions are based on his conclusion that he will spend the rest of his life in prison, which is a plot mistake few viewers would be likely to catch.

Longtime fans would be more likely to catch the gaffe involving Bayliss's activist past, in which he was once arrested for protesting human-rights abuses in El Salvador. Actor Kyle Secor felt it came out of left field, and approached Tom Fontana with a suggestion of his own that he felt would tie his character together better (see Episode 68: "Betrayal"). That Tim once spent some time behind bars (no matter how briefly) for political protesting is a revelation that doesn't quite fit with Season Three's Episode 15: "Fits Like a Glove." There it was indicated that the only peccadillo in Tim's past was a youthful conviction for misdemeanor gambling back in 1984.

This episode marked the debut of *Homicide's* online Intercast transmission. For the few thousand viewers with Intercast installed on their PC, they could watch tonight's episode in a small window on the computer screen along with supplemental windows providing additional information, such as comments by technical adviser Gary D'Addario, or background details about the plot and characters. However, *Entertainment Weekly* criticized the supplements as unimaginative, noting that "if you're going to watch *Homicide* on a three-inch window on your PC, you're ripe for meatier distractions than these barely interactive cue cards."

Episode 60: "Bad Medicine"

[Production Code 504]
Original air date: October 25, 1996.
Written by David Simon; story by Tom Fontana and Julie Martin; directed by Kenneth Fink.

Additional Cast and Guest Stars:
Erik Todd Dellums (Luther Mahoney), Zeljko Ivanek (Assistant State's Attorney Ed Danvers), Ami Brabson (Mary Pembleton), Toni Lewis (Detective Terri Stivers), Akili Prince (Vernon Troy), Pat Dade (lawyer), Walt MacPherson (Captain Roger Gaffney), Kristin Rohde (Sally Rogers), Barnett Lloyd (Range Sergeant), Cleo Reginald Pizana (Detective Bob Connelly), Richard R. Salamanca (Detective Tom O'Neill), Sharon Ziman (Naomi).

STORY: A string of heroin overdoses puts Lewis and Kellerman once again on the trail of drug lord Luther Mahoney. Kellerman is taken off the case, however, by an FBI probe into accusations that the Arson Unit was taking bribes. While under investigation, Kellerman is assigned to administrative duties, much like Pembleton.

Without a partner, Detective Lewis joins forces with Detective Terri Stivers from the Narcotics Division, but the slippery Mahoney once again avoids apprehension.

HIGHLIGHTS: A major story thread for the season gets under way in this episode as Mike Kellerman is accused of accepting bribes and finds himself under investigation by the FBI (see also Episode 34: "Fire, Part One"). In past episodes, Kellerman has been quite vocal in establishing his high ethical standards. However, *Homicide* never provides independent verification of his innocence, viewers are just asked to take his word for it. Counting against him is the fact that he has upgraded to a new and larger boat (trading in Season Four's *Lady Bug* for the charter-fisherman *Case Closed*), and that he did sell Munch a "hot" VCR taken from the Arson Unit (see Episode 53: "Map of the

Heart"). Even his coworkers have their doubts. This story line would become one of the defining elements of the fifth season, and perfectly illustrates how easily unfounded allegations can destroy a person's reputation.

With his partner sidelined, Lewis pairs with Terri Stivers from Narcotics. Actress Toni Lewis would reprise the character several times throughout the season before joining the cast as a regular in Season Six.

In other plot turmoil, Brodie continues his travels in and out of various character's abodes. He elects to move out of Munch's apartment (prompted by an unnamed something in John's medicine cabinet), and comes to live with Tim. This move provides a rare glimpse of Tim at home. The detective lounges around in a flowing purple robe, and watches *Mighty Mouse* cartoons.

COMMENTARY: Actor Erik Todd Dellums returns for the first of many Luther Mahoney sequels. The character had been invented as a onetime role, but proved to be very popular. Bringing Mahoney back was a natural decision. On the one hand, his cold villainy provided a perfect foil for the rising star of Detective Meldrick Lewis. At the same time, Mahoney's character helped the show tackle the complex issues of the drug trade, adding a depth and a realism that more than compensated for the pulpy "good cop versus bad guy" tone of his stories.

NOTES: Always trying to keep the show close to its journalistic roots, David Simon based his script on a number of real Baltimore deaths in which heroin had been laced with the poisonous Scopolamine.

Episode 61: "M.E., Myself and I"

[Production Code 505]
Original air date: November 1, 1996.
Written by Lyle Weldon and Emily Whitesell; story by Tom Fontana; directed by Michael Fields.

Additional Cast and Guest Stars:

Edward Herrmann (FBI Agent Thomas Pandolfi), Zeljko Ivanek (Assistant State's Attorney Ed Danvers), Ami Brabson (Mary Pembleton), Karen Williams (Barbara Lewis), Beau James (Detective Higby), Ralph Tabakin (Dr. Scheiner), Kevin Beeken (Detective Bob Thompson), Henry R. Ford (Josiah Cox), David Maxwell Hall (Motorcycle Cop), Cleo Reginald Pizana (Detective Bob Connelly), Alexander Webb (Glenn Nellis), Sharon Ziman (Naomi).

STORY: The freewheeling Dr. Julianna Cox returns home to Baltimore to take over as the new chief medical examiner. Her first case throws Cox into the difficult politics of a big-city police department. She discovers that

Detective Higby of Homicide's second shift and one of her own staff members ruled a murder as an overdose so as not to have to investigate it.

HIGHLIGHTS: Having been taken in and kicked out by both Munch and Bayliss, Brodie comes to stay at Detective Lewis's place, and almost singlehandedly derails Meldrick's shaky marriage to Barbara Shivers-Lewis (see also Episode 55: "The Wedding").

COMMENTARY: Introducing Dr. Julianna Cox helps compensate for the loss of a strong female presence that occurred when Isabella Hofman's Detective Russert left the show. Although some fans didn't quite warm to the new character, it cannot be said that she is not a very strong presence. *Entertainment Weekly* wrote, "With the arrival of each new cast member, *Homicide: Life on the Street* just keeps getting cooler and cooler."

In one wonderfully devised scene, Cox reveals to Detective Bayliss that her father has just passed away, and she means literally that her father has *just* passed away. Her sorrow is unfolded slowly throughout the scene, culminating at the point when Bayliss and the audience finally realize whose body she is standing over. The full significance of this event would not be explained until Episode 63: "The Heart of a Saturday Night."

NOTES: Edward Herrmann guest-stars as an FBI agent hell-bent on uncovering every single one of Kellerman's hidden vices. Herrmann is a familiar face from his many roles in such features as *The Paper Chase* (1973), *The Great Gatsby* (1974), *The Great Waldo Pepper* (1975), *Reds* (1981), *Annie* (1982), *The Man with One Red Shoe* (1985), *The Purple Rose of Cairo* (1985), *The Lost Boys* (1987), *Born Yesterday* (1993), *Nixon* (1995), and *A Civil Action* (1998). Herrmann also once played another Herman, starring as Herman Munster in the 1995 television remake *Here Come the Munsters*. However, the role that may have had the most influence on his being cast in *Homicide* was his stint as Father Joseph McCabe on *St. Elsewhere*.

Episode 62: "White Lies"

[Production Code 506]
Original air date: November 8, 1996.
Written by Anya Epstein; story by Tom Fontana and James Yoshimura; directed by Peter Weller.

Additional Cast and Guest Stars:

Scott Bryce (Philip Engle), Rebecca Boyd (Gail Ingram), Clayton LeBoeuf (Colonel George Barnfather), Granville Adams (Westby), Pete Burris (examiner), Stephen Lejnar (Mitch Roland), Jeremiah Mickens (Samuel Colby), Laurie Solow Miller (receptionist).

STORY: A young woman is found dead in her bed, apparently of natural causes. The case pits Detective Munch against Dr. Cox, as the detective suspects the dead woman's husband of lying, while the chief medical examiner rules the death a drug overdose instead of a murder.

Meanwhile, Detective Kellerman finds his reputation ruined by the accusations that he accepted bribes from arson suspect Mitch Roland. He submits to a polygraph test and passes, but so did Roland, which means one of them is lying.

HIGHLIGHTS: Brodie's search for a place to stay takes a new turn when Meldrick Lewis kicks him out and Kay Howard invites him to stay with her. The young videographer still has a crush on the sergeant, but out of respect for her reputation with the men of the squad, he declines her offer.

Brodie is not the only one with unrequited longing. Frank Pembleton, too, yearns for that which he cannot have, at least not yet. He wants to be back on the street working murders, and back in the Box working suspects (goals which he will achieve in just two more episodes).

The allure of working murders has apparently affected Tim Bayliss as well. Back in Episode 49: "Stakeout," Bayliss planned to leave Homicide to move to southern California, then reconsidered and elected to stay until he closed the Lambert case. This week, he has a chance to close that case, which he ruins by confusing the suspect with his out-of-left-field speech about leaving Baltimore for sunny California. It seems most likely that his subconscious mind spoke out, disrupting the interrogation and providing the detective with a face-saving excuse for abandoning his earlier plan.

COMMENTARY: Richard Belzer has never complained about his relatively minor role on *Homicide*, and in fact has repeatedly commented on how proud he is to be a part, no matter how small, of such a quality production. As rare as they are, episodes where he is front and center are always a treat. Although frequently portrayed as a somewhat sloppy detective, John Munch shows an uncommon ferocity here. Ironically, it is misplaced, as he ruthlessly dogs a man to try to get a confession even though the case is not a murder.

NOTES: This week's guest director is actor Peter Weller, known for his roles in *The Adventures of Buckaroo Banzai Across the 8th Dimension* (1984), *Leviathan* (1989), *Road to Ruin* (1991), *Sunset Grill* (1993), *The New Age* (1994), and *Mighty Aphrodite* (1995). In 1994, Weller began adding to his acting credits by directing *Partners*, a made-for-TV movie which he also wrote.

The episode's story borrows somewhat from David Simon's book, which also tells the tale of a man concealing his wife's heroin overdose. After years of original, and increasingly sensational, stories, the fifth season of *Homicide* marks a surprising but welcome return to David Simon's nonfiction source material.

Not only does this episode refocus attention onto the show's journalistic origins, it also features something of a pictorial homage to the old, nuked-out look of the first season. As Pembleton reminisces about his past glories in the Box, we are treated to a flashback sequence of clips from old episodes, all shown in the harsh, decolorized look that producer Barry Levinson abandoned in 1994.

One touch out of synch with the old-school *Homicide* is the scene in which Dr. Cox visits the jailed husband to ask why he confessed. The moment recalls similar postmortems (excuse the pun) by Lieutenant Giardello in Episode 18: "Happy to be Here," and Kay Howard in Episode 10: "Bop Gun."

Like them, Cox is looking for an explanation to put her mind at ease. However, many real police officers who are fans of the show objected to the sight of a medical examiner talking to a suspect. In their zeal to introduce the new cast member to audiences quickly, *Homicide*'s creators were putting her in places where she wouldn't actually be (in the Homicide squadroom, talking to suspects, on the streets with every murder, etc.).

Episode 63:
"The Heart of a Saturday Night"

[Production Code 507]
Original air date: November 15, 1996.
Written by Henry Bromell; directed by Whit Stillman.

Additional Cast and Guest Stars:
Scott Bryce (Philip Engle), Rebecca Boyd (Gail Ingram), Clayton LeBoeuf (Colonel George Barnfather), Granville Adams (Westby), Pete Burris (examiner), Stephen Lejnar (Mitch Roland), Jeremiah Mickens (Samuel Colby), Laurie Solow Miller (receptionist).

STORY: This unconventional episode covers three murders on a single Saturday night (with the investigations revealed in flashback) and the present-day group-therapy sessions of the survivors as they try to come to grips with their loss. Some of the cases are closed, some are not, but for the survivors the pain will never really end.

HIGHLIGHTS: The therapy session includes the families of the three murders committed that fateful Saturday night, plus an additional member, Julianna Cox, working through her father's death. This is the first time *Homicide* reveals the circumstances of his passing, which viewers probably assumed was the result of an illness. In fact, he was the victim of a car accident when an aggressive driver forced him off the road, although he lingered a long time before dying.

Rosanna Arquette guest-stars as a grieving widow in "Heart of a Saturday Night." Everett Collection

COMMENTARY: Barbara Phillips of the *Wall Street Journal* singled out this installment for praise, calling it "a standout episode." Rarely does TV dramatize the permanent consequences of crime and violence, preferring instead to wallow in the sensationalism of other people's pain which propels—supposedly—higher ratings. Phillips indicated that, by switching between flashbacks and current events with agility, and spending as much time on the emotions of the survivors as the routines of the detectives, the episode "demanded full attention." "The folks at *Homicide* were free to take the easy way out," she wrote, "But they declined."

NOTES: In another homage to the show's old look, the present-day therapy sessions are shown in harsh, decolorized images while the flashbacks to the Homicide Squad at work are in full color.

This stylish, arty outing features several noteworthy guests. Rosanna Arquette and Chris Eigeman appear as two of the survivors. The better-known of the two, Arquette's credits include *After Hours* (1985), *Desperately Seeking Susan* (1985), *Silverado* (1985), *Amazon Women on the Moon* (1987), *New York Stories* (1989), *Flight of the Intruder* (1990), *Nowhere to Run* (1993), *Pulp Fiction* (1994), *Search and Destroy* (1995), and *Crash* (1996). Eigeman can be seen in the acclaimed independent films *Metropolitan* (1990) and *Barcelona* (1994), both of which were directed by filmmaker Whit Stillman.

Notably, Stillman is the guest director of this episode, which shares much of its moving emotions and complex thoughtfulness with Stillman's low-budget dramas.

Episode 64: "The True Test"

[Production Code 508]
Original air date: November 22, 1996.
Written by Noel Behn; story by Tom Fontana and Noel Behn; directed by Alan Taylor.

Additional Cast and Guest Stars:

Elijah Wood (McPhee Broadman), Sagan Lewis (Judge Susan Aandahl), Ami Brabson (Mary Pembleton), Christopher Northup (headmaster), Andy Bowser (Derek), Pat Dade (Lawyer), Geoffrey I. Gissett (Kemp Fowler), Ian Buck (Mad Mel), Bonita Cartwright-Thornton (Louise Buchanan), William Spencer Ross (Jordan Buchanan), Jay Spadaro (Officer Salerno), Sharon Ziman (Naomi).

STORY: A racially motivated killing at an exclusive prep school provokes Bayliss, stirring up some class bitterness in the detective. As such he is eager to see the arrogant McPhee Broadman face justice. Complicating matters, however, is the fact that McPhee's mother is the eminent Judge Susan Aandahl.

Meanwhile, Frank Pembleton passes the firearms test and readies himself to take on the first murder case the next day.

HIGHLIGHTS: Detective Mike Kellerman meets Medical Examiner Julianna Cox for the first time in this episode, and they end up drinking

Elijah Wood, the endearing child star of such pictures as Flipper, *plays a cold-hearted killer in "The True Test," the best rated episode of the season.*
Everett Collection

together in the Waterfront Bar by episode's end. Many viewers suspected that Cox would end up in Bayliss's arms, since the two had flirted rather heavily during her first few episodes. Instead, she and Kellerman would drift together for a mutually destructive relationship, each feeding the other's despair (her grief over her father, his anger about the bribery accusations).

COMMENTARY: The title of this episode, "The True Test," refers to Frank's belief that the Box, not the firing-range test he passes, is the real indicator of his ability to return to work. This segment became Season Five's highest-rated episode. NBC aired it again later in the season (between Episodes 74: "Double Blind" and 75: "Deception").

Bayliss's deep-seated hostility toward McPhee Broadman and his preppy school marks the first conscious foreshadowing of Bayliss's upcoming revelation that he suffered childhood sexual abuse. The detective overemphasizes (and maybe even invents) allegations that McPhee sexually abused his victims along with the more prosaic verbal and physical abuse. Bayliss is heartened to see Judge Aandahl continue to support her child no matter how much evidence piles up against him. There had been moments in the past that seemed to suggest Bayliss' childhood trauma, but only now, after actor Kyle Secor had made his recommendation to the writers, was the connection made deliberate.

NOTES: Guest star Elijah Wood previously worked with Barry Levinson on the feature film *Avalon* (1990), in which Wood played the role of Michael Kaye. He can also be seen in 1992's film *Forever Young*, and 1996's remake of the famed TV series *Flipper*.

Episode 65: "Control"

[Production Code 509]
Original air date: December 6, 1996.
Written by Les Carter and Susan Sisko; story by Tom Fontana and Julie Martin; directed by Jean de Segonzac.

Additional Cast and Guest Stars:
Erik Todd Dellums (Luther Mahoney), Mekhi Phifer (Junior Bunk), Michael Gaston (Alex Clifton), Zeljko Ivanek (Assistant State's Attorney Ed Danvers), Toni Lewis (Detective Terri Stivers), Rhonda R. Overby (Dawn Daniels), Ralph Tabakin (Dr. Scheiner), Michael Willis (Darin Russom), Andrew David DeAngelo (Jimmy Sutter), Richard Pilcher (Sergeant Deutch), Seth Silver (inmate), David St. Louis (angry man), Sharon Ziman (Naomi).

*Rising young star Mekhi
Phifer plays Luther Mahoney's
cowardly nephew, Junior
Bunk. Everett Collection*

STORY: Detective Pembleton is back on the street, but his partner Bayliss is the primary detective on the case of a woman and her children found slain in their home.

Meldrick Lewis gets a third chance at Luther Mahoney when he discovers that the drug lord's nephew is willing to testify. However, Mahoney once again manipulates the system to walk away a free man.

HIGHLIGHTS: The romance between Mike Kellerman and Julianna Cox heats up when they spend the night together on Mike's new boat.

COMMENTARY: NBC's previews boasted, "The baddest of the good is back!" Pembleton's return is tentative, though. Still recovering from his stroke, he is forgetful and misspeaks himself. He has to dictate his thoughts into a tape recorder continuously in order to protect himself against his untrustworthy memories. When he strides into the Box for the first time and confidently reassures the suspect there is nothing to worry about, that it's just a room, the moment means so much more to the audience as the realization comes that the reassurance is as much—or more—for his own benefit.

NOTES: In this, the third Luther Mahoney episode, Mahoney's nephew Junior Bunk is played by actor Mekhi Phifer. Spike Lee fans will recognize Phifer from *Clockers* (1995), in which he played the lead character Strike. Previously, Phifer had worked with Andre Braugher in *The Tuskegee Airmen* (1995), and with Richard Belzer in Spike Lee's *Girl 6* (1996). The young actor later appeared in the 1997 feature *Soul Food*. Phifer reprised his role as Junior Bunk Mahoney in the Season Six opener, Episode 79: "Blood Ties, Part One."

Episode 66: "Blood Wedding"

[Production Code 510]
Original air date: December 13, 1996.
Written by Matthew Witten; story by Tom Fontana and James Yoshimura; directed by
Kevin Hooks.

Additional Cast and Guest Stars:

Zeljko Ivanek (Assistant State's Attorney Ed Danvers), Al Freeman Jr. (Deputy
Commissioner James Harris), Helen Carey (Maggie Conroy), R. Emery Bright (Julius J.
Cummins), Ralph Tabakin (Dr. Scheiner), Delaine Yates (Meryl Hansen), Brian Constantini
(Pires), Dan Delafield (Graves), Neal Moran (Goodman), Cleo Reginald Pizana (Bob
Connelly), Judy Thornton (Judy).

STORY: In a grueling turn of events, State's Attorney Ed Danvers'
fiancée, Meryl Hanson, is shot and killed while shopping for a wedding dress.
The case is Frank Pembleton's first as a primary detective since his stroke, and
the distraught Danvers believes Frank isn't up to the task.

HIGHLIGHTS: Although Detective Kellerman and Dr. Cox have spent
the night together, their relationship has yet to develop into anything emotionally satisfying for either of them. This episode marks the start of a severe
downward spiral for Kellerman, as his despair over the bribery probe and his
destructive relationship with Cox takes him in the same direction that Beau
Felton went in Season Three, into the bottle.

COMMENTARY: This is the second of two episodes singled out by the
Wall Street Journal for attention. Critic Barbara Phillips notes that crime has
lasting effects that forever alter the lives of the victims. While most TV crime
shows depict the endless chase of good against bad, *Homicide* stops every once
in a while to linger on the anguish of the victims. Episode 10: "Bop Gun";
Episode 22: "Every Mother's Son"; and Episode 39: "A Doll's Eyes" have all
earned their places in the roster of *Homicide*'s best hours by virtue of this very
emphasis. How many TV shows would dare to put their viewers through such
torment?

Producer Tom Fontana has a tradition of abusing the main characters of
his series, and this week prosecutor Ed Danvers is portrayed as vulnerable,
alone, and devastated after seeing his beloved shot down before his eyes. Just
as Episode 32: "Colors" and the Kellerman-bribe story line put the detectives
on the receiving end of the often callous investigative process, here Danvers
gets to experience firsthand the indifference of the legal system, an indiffer-

ence he himself had helped to foster over the years. "Last Friday's episode," Phillips writes, "used that history to create an episode of rare power."

NOTES: This week's guest director Kevin Hooks, the son of veteran actor Robert Hooks, has credits both as an actor and a director. He played roles in *Strictly Business* (1991), *Innerspace* (1987), *A Hero Ain't Nothin' But a Sandwich* (1978), as well as the television series *The White Shadow* (1978). Hooks also directed the feature films *Black Dog* (1998), *Fled* (1996), *Passenger 57* (1992), and *Strictly Business* (1991), as well as episodes of NBC's *Profiler* (1996–) and HBO's *Tales from the Crypt* (1989–).

Al Freeman Jr. returns to reprise his role as Deputy Commissioner James Harris. In a pointed scene, Harris tells Lieutenant Giardello that he promoted Roger Gaffney to captain largely in order to remind the upstart Giardello that he ought to be more politically pliant. Harris still holds a grudge about the Congressman Wade affair (see Episodes 23: "From Cradle to Grave" and 24: "Partners"). Harris thinks Gee didn't do enough to protect the congressman or his interests. The antagonism between the two men would reach a climax in Episode 76: "Narcissus" and its immediate aftermath.

Episode 67: "The Documentary"

[Production Code 511]
Original air date: December 13, 1996.
Written by Eric Overmyer; story by Tom Fontana, James Yoshimura, and Eric Overmyer; directed by Barbara Kopple.

Additional Cast and Guest Stars:
Melvin Van Peebles (Bennett Jackson), Barry Levinson (himself), Kristin Rohde (Sally Rogers), Zité Bidanie (motorist), La Kishia Davis (Alicia Duncan), Rich Gordon (Stan Rogan), Europe Harmon (Levon Carter), Walt MacPherson (Captain Roger Gaffney).

STORY: On New Year's Eve, the detectives gather around the squad-room TV to watch the documentary on the Homicide Unit that J. H. Brodie has created in his spare time during the last year.

Gee and the others are worried to learn that Brodie has sold the documentary to PBS, the public television network. To counter their criticisms, Brodie defends his work as exhibiting the same pursuit of truth that drives them in their work.

HIGHLIGHTS: Among other revealing details caught on tape, Brodie has videotaped the Lunch Bandit in action and thereby closes the longest-running open case in *Homicide* history. To the surprise of everyone, the Bandit is Gaffney!

In Episode 79: "Blood Ties, Part One," it is revealed that Brodie has won an Emmy for this documentary, *Back Page News: Life and Homicide on the Mean Streets of Baltimore,* and he subsequently moved to Hollywood (explaining his absence from the cast following Max Perlich's departure). This is a particularly arch in-joke, since *Homicide* was again ignored by the Emmy voters despite its continued high stature among TV critics.

Julianna Cox and Mike Kellerman decide to restart their relationship with a more traditional date, rather than hopping into bed for another one-night stand. This is one relationship Brodie has not videotaped, but he does have on tape Lewis and Stivers sharing a drink, Kay Howard in the arms of her still-unidentified boyfriend, and Gee stepping out on the town with not one but two beautiful young ladies at the same time.

COMMENTARY: This episode is arguably the most complex intertwining of reality and fiction yet aired on *Homicide.* Unraveling its many layers of in-jokes and references would take days. Brodie's documentary uses the

Melvin Van Peebles, the man who created "blaxploitation," guest stars in "The Documentary."
Everett Collection

Homicide title theme music, and his editing technique of repeating some shots comes under criticism from the detectives, who think it's a amateurish mistake. The detectives take bathroom breaks during the commercials, and complain that the show doesn't have enough action.

In one sequence, Kellerman and Lewis chase a suspect around a corner into the production team of *Homicide: Life on the Street*, which includes Barry Levinson playing himself! If this isn't twisted enough for the viewers, and they are not baffled enough by the sight of Brodie advising Barry Levinson on how to make *Homicide* more realistic, then it should be remembered that this scene is a fictional adaptation of the real-life incident in October 1996 when security guards chased a shoplifter into *Homicide*'s cast and crew. That poor thief mistakenly assumed the cast were real cops, and surrendered himself (the Washington-Baltimore NBC affiliate ran an interview with the security guard during the post-*Homicide* news broadcast).

The most poetic effect of the blurring of reality and fiction, though, occurs in Brodie's impassioned speech at the climax. The detectives' criticisms and his counterarguments match exactly what David Simon went through in writing and publishing his *Homicide* book. Simon and Brodie both had to justify the impolitic invasions of privacy their works inflicted on detectives and suspects by citing the greater good of documenting the truth about police work.

NOTES: This segment is of course not really directed by Brodie (or by actor Max Perlich, either, for that matter). It is, however, directed by two-time Oscar-winning documentarian Barbara Kopple, whose credits include *Harlan County, U.S.A.* (1976), *Keeping On* (1981), *American Dream* (1990), *Beyond 'JFK': The Question of Conspiracy* (1992), *Fallen Champ: The Untold Story of Mike Tyson* (1993), and *A Century of Women* (1994).

The lonely and morbid Bennett Jackson, whose sordid life is the case covered by Brodie's program, is played by guest star Melvin Van Peebles. In 1971, Van Peebles wrote, directed, and starred in the explosive *Sweet Sweetback's Baadasssss Song*. The film was rated X by a frightened white ratings board for its frank approach to racial issues, but nevertheless managed to make profound waves throughout the film industry, spawning a genre of black action films sometimes referred to as "blaxploitation."

Isabella Hofmann does appear in this episode, briefly, in footage never before shown. However, she did not return to film this cameo for "The Documentary." Instead, Brodie's documentary is comprised of many shots actually taped by the actor while shooting previous episodes.

Episode 68: "Betrayal"

[Production Code 512]
Original air date: January 10, 1997.
Written by Gay Walch; story by Tom Fontana and Julie Martin; directed by Clark Johnson.

Additional Cast and Guest Stars:

LaTanya Richardson (Lynette Thomson), Tommy Hollis (Nelson Henson), Rebecca Boyd (Gail Ingram), Helen Carey (Maggie Conroy), Taborah Johnson (Susan Winslow), Julie Lauren (Officer Anne Schanne), Brian Constantini (Pires), Pat Dade (Monica Murphy), Neal Moran (Goodman), Cleo Reginald Pizana (Detective Bob Connelly), Judy Thornton (Judy).

STORY: Now the time has come for Detective Mike Kellerman to testify before the grand jury regarding allegations that he and other Arson detectives were taking bribes. However, the beleaguered detective finds he has few options in his attempt to clear his name.

Meanwhile, Detective Bayliss is facing some demons of his own, with yet another case involving a dead little girl.

HIGHLIGHTS: Bayliss drops a bombshell in this episode, revealing a painful secret he has kept within himself for years, namely that, as a child, he was sexually abused by his uncle, and his father never believed him or helped him. Although performer Kyle Secor came up with the idea only relatively recently, it fit so naturally with his character that it would seem the writers had been foreshadowing the revelation all along.

After baring his soul in such a deeply personal way, Tim breaks up with Frank. The two would not partner again until almost the end of the season, and even then Bayliss would be frequently absent from the squadroom as he tended to the needs of his now-decrepit uncle in an effort to resolve his anger and hatred.

COMMENTARY: Advertised as "Hidden Rage," this is a story about who tells on whom, and who protects whom. Kellerman is making a delicate mental calculus as he decides whether or not to testify. He does not want to name his colleagues as being dirty cops, but has no choice but to speak up if they accuse him. His code ("Cops don't rat out cops") is very clear to him, but he fears that others cannot recognize those values as deeply as he does.

Tim is equally certain that parents need to protect their children. He is furious that this victimized little girl could have been slowly beaten to death while no one spoke up. He remembers how equally tortured he was when he had turned to his own father for help and got none.

Notably, *NYPD Blue* also featured a similar story line the same season, when Detective Russell, played by Kim Delaney, revealed that she, too, was a victim of childhood sexual abuse.

NOTES: Detective Lewis appears only briefly at the end, once again explained by Clark Johnson's turn behind the camera. Johnson's second directorial outing is an emotional and intense one. Actress LaTanya Richardson, playing the woman who stands up for her boyfriend even when she knows he killed her child, gives a richly nuanced performance. Not to take anything away from Anne Meara (see Episode 58: "Hostage, Part Two"), but if any guest performer deserved an Emmy nod this year, Richardson should have topped the list.

Episode 69: "Have a Conscience"

[Production Code 513]
Original air date: January 17, 1997.
Written by James Yoshimura; directed by Uli Edel.

Additional Cast and Guest Stars:

Erik Todd Dellums (Luther Mahoney), Rebecca Boyd (Gail Ingram), Stephen X. Lee (Ben Roh), Jade Wu (Sun-Rae Roh), Granville Adams (Westby), Walt MacPherson (Captain Roger Gaffney), Judy Thornton (Judy), Michael Angelo, Barry D. Bradford, Verna Lee Day, Barbara Johnson, Walter L. Lindsey, and Rhonda Rene (witnesses).

STORY: Although the grand jury has cleared Mike Kellerman of the bribe-taking charges, the detective finds his life has not, and seemingly cannot, return to normal. Thus, he takes personally his latest case, that of a Korean grocery-store owner who has been executed by Luther Mahoney's drug pushers.

Kellerman's despair turns suicidal and Lewis, terrified of losing yet another partner, intervenes. As their coworkers cheerfully party at the Waterfront Bar, they have a tense standoff.

HIGHLIGHTS: There is an interesting contrast between partners Kellerman-Lewis and Pembleton-Bayliss that unfolds in this episode. In the previous episode Tim Bayliss revealed one of his hidden secrets and it drove a wedge between him and Frank. By this episode, Tim is actively avoiding Frank.

Both Frank and Meldrick were cold and aloof when their respective partners needed more closeness or affirmation. Both Tim and Mike took that distance as a personal offense, a sort of rejection. However, unlike their fellow officers, the grueling emotional rift that opens between Mike Kellerman and Meldrick Lewis during this hour ends up bringing them closer together.

However, future events will throw Lewis and Kellerman even farther apart, beginning with the circumstances of Episode 75: "Deception."

COMMENTARY: One of the most difficult viewing experiences of any TV series, this episode is so intense that most fans disliked it. The various Internet chat rooms and e-mail lists bustled with fan commentary criticizing the episode. Even hard-core fans of one of the most gritty and challenging shows in network history had found that there is some subject matter too traumatic to be entertaining. Adding to the extreme discomfort of the episode, the same week's episode of *ER* featured the suicide of a recurring character, and it was broadcast exactly twenty-four hours earlier. Obviously there is only so much death and pain TV viewers can take.

In retrospect, "Have a Conscience" stands out as a bold episode. Like Episode 5: "Three Men and Adena," it draws its power from nothing more than people talking. The superb dialogue by *Homicide*'s reigning King of Anguish, James Yoshimura, and breathtaking performances by Clark Johnson and Reed Diamond, make this one unforgettable, harrowing hour.

NOTES: Chief Medical Examiner Cox appears on crutches in this episode. In another blurring of the line between fact and fiction, Cox explains that she tripped over her dog. This is in fact what happened to actress Michelle Forbes. Forbes was disappointed that the writers included that embarrassing detail onscreen. "It was a drag," she told the press.

Forbes was also embarrassed to admit that, although she plays a hard-bitten forensic scientist on TV, in real life she is quite squeamish. "I was crying, looking at the X rays, and thought, 'Wow, I'm playing this brassy medical examiner, doing autopsies, and I can't even look at my X rays. It's pathetic.'"

This episode also features another, even more subtle, in-joke. At one point, Detective Pembleton talks about one of his open cases, the Bianculli murder. David Bianculli is a television critic with the *New York Daily News* who has been one of *Homicide*'s most vocal supporters. Despite his loyal trumpeting of the show, writer James Yoshimura has his namesake killed under less than dignified circumstances at a topless bar.

Guest director Uli Edel previously helmed Madonna's erotic thriller *Body of Evidence* (1993) as well as several episodes of the quirky TV series *Twin Peaks* (1990–91).

Episode 70: "Diener"

[Production Code 514]
Original air date: January 31, 1997.
Written by Christopher Kyle; story by Tom Fontana and Julie Martin; directed by Kyle Secor.

Additional Cast and Guest Stars:
Glenn Fitzgerald (Jeff McGinn), Zeljko Ivanek (Assistant State's Attorney Ed Danvers), Ami Brabson (Mary Pembleton), Allan H. Gray (Dontae), Charles Matheny (Matthew Bridgewell), Jay Spadaro (Officer Salerno), Gemmi Teleki (Laura Bridgewell), Judy Thornton (Judy), Michael Willis (Darin Russom).

STORY: The case of a murdered socialite becomes explosive when a critical piece of evidence turns up missing. The victim's diamond ring might implicate the killer, or provide him with a defense. However, the ring has been stolen by someone in the Medical Examiner's Office.

HIGHLIGHTS: Already abandoned by his partner Tim Bayliss, Frank Pembleton doesn't see the warning signs of his wife Mary's discontent. She asks to see a marriage counselor, but he blindly ignores her complaints. Always an obsessive workaholic, Frank has hurt those closest to him by his continued single-mindedness following his stroke.

While Pembleton is reluctant to see a counselor, Mike Kellerman has a more open attitude. The depressed detective tells his partner Meldrick that he will see a therapist, particularly in light of his suicide attempt in the previous episode.

COMMENTARY: When the character was first introduced, Julianna Cox displayed a fiery sense of professionalism. Under her new rule, the Medical Examiner's Office has become more responsive than ever before. One of her first acts was to fire a veteran M.E. for unethical (but nonetheless common) behavior. Tonight's episode puts Cox on the spot, uncovering one of her recent hires as a thief. Her sense of betrayal is powerful, and in some ways is similar to Kellerman's despair.

NOTES: With this episode Kyle Secor joins Clark Johnson among the ranks of *Homicide* stars to direct. Unfortunately, Secor is saddled with a somewhat limp script, and does not get a chance to show his skills to their best advantage.

The title "Diener" is not a joke on producer Barry Levinson's famed breakthrough film *Diner* (1982). It actually refers to the individual who starts an autopsy procedure with the Y-shaped abdominal incision, and finishes by sewing up the body. The name comes from the German word meaning "assistant."

Episode 71: "Wu's On First?"

[Production Code 515]
Original air date: February 7, 1997.
Written by David Simon and Anya Epstein; story by James Yoshimura and Julie Martin; directed by Tim McCann.

Additional Cast and Guest Stars:
Eric Stoltz (Drew Kellerman), Tate Donovan (Greg Kellerman), Joan Chen (Elizabeth Wu), Pat McNamara (Mr. Kellerman), Lance Carter (Editor), Clayton LeBoeuf (Colonel George Barnfather), Tom McCarthy (Bob Parker), Rhonda Overby (Dawn Daniels), Faith Potts (Maureen), Michael Salconi (Alfred), Barry Sigismondi (Saul), Sharon Ziman (Naomi).

STORY: Elizabeth Wu, the new crime-beat reporter for the *Baltimore Sun*, clashes with Detective Pembleton over the recent cop-killing of a Calvert County officer. Lieutenant Giardello admires Wu's ability to play the game, even though she is being manipulated both by Colonel Barnfather and the cop killer himself.

Meanwhile, Detective Kellerman's woes increase thanks to the untimely arrival of his lowlife brothers Drew and Greg.

HIGHLIGHTS: After her recent troubles (see Episode 70: "Diener"), the last thing Cox needs is a group of rowdy bullies trashing her morgue and stealing body parts. That Mike Kellerman agreed to take his brothers there shows just what power they have over him, even after all these years.

COMMENTARY: Like Episode 67: "The Documentary," this episode draws not so much on police work for its story but on the work of reporters. Elizabeth Wu's attitude, approach, and workplace are all remarkably similar to her counterparts in the Homicide Squad. She interviews witnesses, tries to check the veracity of their statements, and struggles to find the truth of the incident. It is not stretching the point to say that Pembleton is antagonistic toward her in part because they are so similar.

NBC announced that Wu would become a recurring character, but she did not appear again in the fifth season.

NOTES: This episode reunites three of the costars of the 1990 feature film *Memphis Belle*. In addition to Reed Diamond, actors Eric Stoltz and Tate Donovan appear as Kellerman's brothers. Ever since *Memphis Belle*, the three have been good friends. "I love them like the brothers I am thankful I never had," Stoltz told *People* magazine. Stoltz also admitted that he and Tate Donovan improvised a lot of their dialogue in an effort to fluster Reed Diamond. "It was mayhem," Stoltz says.

Guest star Joan Chen, as crime reporter Elizabeth Wu, was announced as a recurring character. Everett Collection

Stoltz can also be seen in *Fast Times at Ridgemont High* (1982), *Mask* (1985), *Say Anything* (1989), *Bodies, Rest and Motion* (1993), *Naked in New York* (1993), *Killing Zoe* (1994), *Pulp Fiction* (1994), and *Rob Roy* (1995). Donovan, the high-profile former boyfriend of the star of the TV sitcom *Friends* (1994–), Jennifer Aniston, has starred in *Into Thin Air* (1985), *Clean and Sober* (1988), *Ethan Frome* (1992), *Love Potion #9* (1992), and provided the voice of Disney's *Hercules* (1997).

Guest star Joan Chen appears as reporter Elizabeth Wu. Chen can be seen in *The Last Emperor* (1987), *Night Stalker* (1987), *Twin Peaks* (1990), *Heaven and Earth* (1993), *On Deadly Ground* (1994), *Judge Dredd* (1995), and *Precious Find* (1996).

Episode 72: "Valentine's Day"

[Production Code 516]
Original air date: February 14, 1997.
Written by Tom Fontana; directed by Clark Johnson.

Additional Cast and Guest Stars:
Neil Patrick Harris (Alan Schack), Linda Dano (Dr. Miano), Stephen X. Lee (Ben Roh), Ami Brabson (Mary Pembleton), Karen Williams (Barbara Lewis), William Cote (Officer

Keane), Ray Glanzman (Officer Hannigan), Taunya L. Martin (Inez Prince), Jade Wu (Sun-Rae Roh), Sharon Ziman (Naomi).

STORY: Videographer J. H. Brodie assists Detective Munch on what at first appears to be a suicide. When suspicion turns to Alan Schack, a drug-dealing university student, Schack beats up Brodie who, even while hospitalized, helps develop a trap to get Schack to confess.

Meanwhile, Detectives Kellerman and Bayliss investigate a serial bomber, and discover the killer is the orphaned son of the Korean store owner that Luther Mahoney had had killed (see Episode 69: "Have a Conscience").

HIGHLIGHTS: Mary and Frank Pembleton consult a marriage therapist, but to no avail. By the episode's end, Mary takes their daughter Olivia and leaves her husband.

Chief Medical Examiner Cox also has cause to brood when she is called to the cemetery to check the spelling on her father's tombstone (see also Episode 63: "The Heart of a Saturday Night").

COMMENTARY: In this Brodie-centered episode (see also Episode 67: "The Documentary"), the videographer even gets to play a critical role in the investigation. The experience is so invigorating, it causes him to experience a miraculous sudden recovery. One minute Brodie's hospitalized from a vicious beating, the next he's out and about as if nothing happened.

Time is also compressed in the matter of Korean grocer Roh's case. Less than a month has elapsed since the broadcast of Episode 69: "Have a Conscience," so, assuming the onscreen events occur in roughly the same chronology, there has simply not been enough time to try and acquit Roh's killer.

NOTES: The ads for this episode, renamed "Cruel Innocence" by NBC's hype-mongers, emphasized the guest star, insisting "you've never seen Neil Patrick Harris like this before!" Since Harris had played a villain in *Quantum Leap* (1989–93) after leaving *Doogie Howser, M.D.* (1989–93), that promise is a little overdone. Nevertheless, director Clark Johnson coaxes a fine bad-guy performance out of the young star, even if the overall effect does seem like a repeat of Episode 64: "The True Test."

Meanwhile, *Donnie Brasco* (1997) was opening in theaters, offering a big-screen experience not dissimilar to *Homicide*. In addition to performances by *Homicide* veterans Bruno Kirby, Zeljko Ivanek, and Walt MacPherson, *Donnie Brasco* could also trace its connections to the small screen through its writer (Paul Attanasio), and producers (Barry Levinson, Gail Mutrux, and Louis DiGiaimo).

Episode 73: "Kaddish"

[Production Code 517]
Original air date: February 21, 1997.
Written by Linda McGibney; story by Julie Martin, James Yoshimura, and Ron Goldstein; directed by Jean de Segonzac.

Additional Cast and Guest Stars:
Pamela Payton-Wright (Sister Magdalena Weber), Jean Louisa Kelly (Sarah Langdon), Robert Riggs (George Young), Kristin Rohde (Sally Rogers), Richard Pilcher (Sergeant Mark Deutch), Joe Perrino (Young John Munch), Billie Jackson (Detective Kate McClendon), Neil Lewis (Dreyfus), Kennen Sisco (Young Helen Rosenthal), Nathan Stolpman (Young George), Patrick Trainor (Joe Langdon).

STORY: Detective John Munch faces a very personal case: tracking the killer of his high-school sweetheart, Helen Rosenthal. The experience not only dredges up painful memories of his youth, but also brings him back into touch with his lapsed Jewish faith.

HIGHLIGHTS: The young Johnny Munch spouts off about how in the future, TV will have five hundred channels and everyone's needs will be taken care of by an efficient technocracy. What he says, though, is word for word how the mature John Munch harangues Bolander and Lewis in the precredits sequence of Episode 14: "Nearer My God to Thee."

Speaking of prescience, this episode is something of a trial run of the Munch-Kellerman partnership to come in Season Six.

COMMENTARY: Executive producer Tom Fontana told *TV Guide* that on *Homicide*, "finding God is an ongoing adventure."

It's an adventure normally experienced by tortured Catholic Frank Pembleton. Indeed, Frank revisits his own faith in this episode, with a repeat appearance by Pamela Payton-Wright as Sister Mary Magdelena (see also Episodes 14: "Nearer My God to Thee"; 15: "Fits Like a Glove"; and 16: "Extreme Unction"). But this episode also takes Munch into Pembleton's country, as he struggles to connect spirituality with the cold, hard facts of murder.

Writers Julie Martin and James Yoshimura have learned well from their mentor Tom Fontana. Their story brings anguish to Munch as he learns that the girl he had such an intense unrequited crush on back in high school has been so cruelly treated by fate.

NOTES: During the same television season, *The X-Files* also broadcast an episode titled "Kaddish," the term for a Jewish prayer made to mourn the death of someone close.

Episode 74: "Double Blind"

[Production Code 518]
Original air date: April 11, 1997.
Written by Lee Blessing and Jeanne Blake; story by Tom Fontana and James Yoshimura; directed by Uli Edel.

Additional Cast and Guest Stars:
Lee Tergesen (Officer Chris Thorman), Edie Falco (Eva Thorman), Monica Kenna (Billie Rader), Zeljko Ivanek (Assistant State's Attorney Ed Danvers), Robert Bornath (George Bayliss), Ray Felton (Rinaldi), Larry E. Hull (Charlie Flavin), Maureen Kerrigan (Lucille Rader), Gary Lee Leventhal (Desk Sergeant), Susan M. Lynskey (Bonnie Tiles), Paul Meshejian (Reich), Jay Spadaro (Officer Salerno), Letha V. Walker (Lillian), Michael Williams (Sayles).

STORY: Blinded patrolman Chris Thorman (see Episodes 3: "Son of a Gun"; 4: "A Shot in the Dark"; and 6: "A Dog and Pony Show") is called before a parole board to testify, as Charlie Flavin, the man who shot him in the head, is up for a parole.

Meanwhile, the newly repartnered Frank Pembleton and Tim Bayliss have all but switched roles on the case of a girl who killed her abusive father. This time, it's Frank who wants to look the other way while the usually sensitive Tim shows a ruthless dedication to duty.

HIGHLIGHTS: In yet another nod to the discrepancy between TV cop clichés and *Homicide's* brand of realism, Detective Pembleton tells a witness not to leave town until the matter is settled. As the man stares back in surprise, Frank admits he's only joking as he'd always wanted to say that to *someone*.

Detective Kellerman has a conversation with Dr. Cox that is very far from joking. He admits a dark and personal secret to Julianna. She is horrified when he reveals that he really was suicidal that night on the boat (see Episode 69: "Have a Conscience").

COMMENTARY: After a six-week hiatus for NBC to try out—and to give up on—*Crisis Center* (1997), at last the cantankerous detectives return to their Friday-night home. David Bianculli of the *New York Daily News* writes, "After as many annoying weeks off as the much more popular *ER*, NBC's *Homicide: Life on the Street* returns tonight with a fresh episode—and reclaims instantly its status as the best drama series on television." (*Homicide's* return to the airwaves was still a little tentative, the following week saw a repeat of Episode 64: "The True Test" rather than a new episode).

This episode, like last season's Episode 50: "Requiem for Adena," has the audacity to revisit characters and story threads four years old now, as well as ideas picked up in mid-sentence from episodes that few of *Homicide*'s current audience had ever even seen. The story is difficult, too, with situations defying easy answers.

NOTES: The popular Washington–Baltimore–area R&B band the Nighthawks appear as themselves in the opening sequence.

Episode 75: "Deception"

[Production Code 519]
Original air date: April 25, 1997.
Written by Debbie Sarjeant; story by Tom Fontana, Julie Martin, and James Yoshimura; directed by Peter Medak.

Additional Cast and Guest Stars:

Erik Todd Dellums (Luther Mahoney), Lewis Black (Lazlo "Punchy" DeLeon), Toni Lewis (Detective Terri Stivers), Rebecca Boyd (Gail Ingram), John Louis Fischer (Special Agent Borders), Clayton LeBoeuf (Colonel George Barnfather), Christopher Mann (Brookdale), Robert Bornath (George Bayliss), James Brown-Orleans (Nathan), Robert Carlson (Denys), Deborah Hazlett (Fallon), Brian Hemmingsen (Pugliese), Malcolm Smith (DEA Agent), Ralph Tabakin (Dr. Scheiner), Sharon Ziman (Naomi).

STORY: After years of frustration in their pursuit of drug lord Luther Mahoney, Detectives Lewis, Kellerman, and Stivers find a way to catch Mahoney, as Mahoney's latest heroin shipment inadvertently has fallen into the cops' hands. They substitute baking soda for the smack and all hell breaks loose as Mahoney struggles to maintain control of his empire. However, the sting operation spins into disaster, and Lewis and Mahoney find themselves in a very tense showdown.

HIGHLIGHTS: Although the focus of the hour is the final confrontation with Luther Mahoney, writer Debbie Sarjeant (*Homicide*'s long-standing supervising producer) also serves up some welcome comic relief with Detective John Munch. His Zen-like non-case (the investigation of the murder of a man who is not dead) strangely parallels an episode of TV's famed detective series *Columbo* (1971–93). Both stories involve a killer duping a detective into digging up a parking lot in search of a body only to then bury the body when the lot is repaved.

COMMENTARY: *Homicide* kicks off the May sweeps with a heavily advertised return of arch nemesis Mahoney, for his fifth and final appearance.

Entertainment Weekly noted that the episode "was not the season finale, but surely its climax."

Viewers tuning in to see the outcome of the Lewis-Mahoney standoff probably never expected to see *Homicide*'s favorite villain drop dead. Although the episode features onscreen gun violence and even a car chase, it's pure *Homicide* through and through. The death of Mahoney would linger in the consciences of the detectives well into the next season.

This exceptionally tense episode does feature one error worth noting: the undercover DEA officer playing the Nigerian courier says that Lagos is the capital of Nigeria. However, Abuja is the current capital, not Lagos.

NOTES: *Homicide* coproducer Debbie Sarjeant pens her first script for the show, turning in a memorable and groundbreaking episode.

NBC boasted in press releases that *Homicide* was still showing good growth in its audience base of advertiser-friendly demographics, and that the series was besting *Nash Bridges* by nine percent among adults eighteen to forty-nine, and by as much as forty-seven percent in upscale demographics.

Episode 76: "Narcissus"

[Production Code 520]
Original air date: May 2, 1997.
Written by Yaphet Kotto; directed by Jean de Segonzac.

Additional Cast and Guest Stars:

Zeljko Ivanek (Assistant State's Attorney Ed Danvers), Toni Lewis (Detective Terri Stivers), Roger Robinson (Burundi Robinson), Regi Davis (Malawi Joseph), Marc Freeman Hamm (Benin Crown), Gary D'Addario (Lieutenant Jasper), Clayton LeBoeuf (Colonel George Barnfather), Walt MacPherson (Captain Roger Gaffney), Rhonda Overby (Dawn Daniels), Richard Pilcher (Sergeant Mark Deutch), Jeffrey C. Westby (Officer Schenker).

STORY: What at first glance seems like an open-and-shut case soon pits the Homicide detectives against their own department when they start to unravel a sinister connection between Deputy Commissioner James Harris and the militant African Revival Movement.

HIGHLIGHTS: Colonel Barnfather appears at his most human in this episode, a man in conflict with politics and duty on the one hand, and his own conscience on the other. While in past episodes he has maneuvered things for his own political advantage, here he is seen drawing a line in the sand, beyond which he will not go. Like Giardello, he is repulsed by the lengths to which Commissioner Harris will go to protect himself (theft, blackmail, betrayal, and even authorizing the QRT to kill his former partner, Burundi Robinson).

COMMENTARY: Yaphet Kotto once grumbled that producer Tom Fontana wasn't letting his character grow as much as the others. In this powerful episode, Kotto takes matters into his own hands, somewhat literally. While his costars jockeyed for opportunities behind the camera, Kotto elected to make his contributions on paper, as the screenwriter of "Narcissus." Naturally enough, Kotto puts the spotlight on his own role.

More importantly, though, Kotto's script illuminates tricky racial issues the series often skirted. Andre Braugher once remarked that *Homicide* needed to address racial discord more directly. Like Kotto, in this episode he gets his wish.

Deputy Commissioner Harris is the main player in the tale, although Al Freeman Jr. did not return for this episode and Harris never appears onscreen. What matters is the way Harris can manipulate people from behind the scenes, orchestrating a tragedy to protect his own career. If his actions seemed mercenary in Episodes 23: "From Cradle to Grave" and 24: "Partners," then his behavior tonight is downright frightening.

Although Detective Kellerman makes no more than a cameo appearance in the episode (just long enough to show us that he, Lewis, and Stivers are still coming to grips with killing Mahoney in last week's episode), there is an interesting contrast set up between his recent experiences and Harris's dirty dealings. Kellerman was unjustly accused of taking bribes, and the mere suggestion has dogged him and compromised his career. Harris, though, stole drugs from evidence control, sold them back to the dealer he busted, pocketed the money, and has had a stellar career for the following twenty-five years. With his power and position, he can, and does, authorize the cold-blooded murder of his former partner in order to keep him silent.

This situation is more than just the old adage of absolute power corrupting absolutely, this is corruption that itself leads to power.

The showstopper, though, is the final scene. Gee can rage all he wants, but in the end the average American watching at home could care less about a bunch of black people killing each other. A middle-class couple is depicted watching dispassionately at home as the horror unfolds on the TV screen. They change channels, utterly uninterested.

NOTES: Actor-writer Yaphet Kotto says that the story came to him during a five-hour-long meditation.

Episode 77: "Partners and Other Strangers"

[Production Code 521]
Original air date: May 9, 1997.
Written by Anya Epstein, James Yoshimura, and Darryl LeMont Wharton; directed by
Leslie Libman and Larry Williams.

Additional Cast and Guest Stars:

Jon Seda (Detective Paul Falsone), Peter Gerety (Detective Stuart Gharty), Toni Lewis
(Detective Terri Stivers), Harlee McBride (Dr. Alyssa Dyer), Clayton LeBoeuf (Colonel
George Barnfather), Walt MacPherson (Captain Roger Gaffney), Robert Bonarth (George
Bayliss), Robert Carlson (Officer Denys), Aaron Hern (Aaron Moss), Judy Thornton
(Judy), Scott Winters (Eddie Dugan).

STORY: The discovery of former Homicide detective Beau Felton's
body, the apparent victim of a shotgun suicide, sends the department reeling.
Auto Squad detective Paul Falsone believes that Felton, on being ousted from
the force in disgrace, joined forces with an auto-theft ring, and later killed himself from guilt over selling out.

However, Dr. Cox's autopsy reveals Felton was murdered. Internal
Investigations soon admits that Felton had never resigned in disgrace. Actually,
he was an IID undercover operative in the auto-theft group.

HIGHLIGHTS: Former detective Megan Russert returns from Paris to
assist with the investigation. Medical Examiner Alyssa Dyer makes a return
appearance, as well. (She was last seen in Episode 53: "Map of the Heart.")

The most important returning character, however, is Stuart Gharty, last
seen in Episode 52: "Scene of the Crime." When he and Russert last saw each
other, she had him brought up on charges for not responding to a 911 call.
Since then, he has become a detective in the Internal Investigations Unit, and
was responsible for sending Beau Felton into a den of trouble much more dangerous than what he himself had avoided.

In addition to returning characters, this episode also introduces a new one
in the form of Detective Paul Falsone of the Auto Squad.

COMMENTARY: USA Today's Matt Roush enthused, "Homicide…
ends one of its finest seasons with a tough, unsentimental two-parter that confronts the weathered ensemble with the harsh realities of the job . . . . Cheery,
it isn't. Jittery, palm-sweatily memorable? You bet."

Michelle Greppi of the New York Post was more arch: "Homicide finale:
headless body in flawless show."

As season finales go, however, this two-parter is almost tailor-made to
alienate casual viewers. Last season's soapy tricks of weddings and strokes were

much more accessible than this complex blend of story lines that even a hard-core fan would need a flowchart to figure out.

To fully appreciate what this hour has to offer, writers Anya Epstein, James Yoshimura, and Darryl LeMont Wharton expect the viewers to have fresh in their minds Episodes 11: "See No Evil"; 19: "Crosetti"; 20: "The Last of the Watermen"; 25: "The City That Bleeds"; 31: "Nothing Personal"; 41: "Sniper Part One"; 52: "Scene of the Crime"; 68: "Betrayal"; 69: "Have a Conscience"; 72: "Valentine's Day"; 75: "Deception" ; and 76: "Narcissus". In addition, it wouldn't hurt to be conversant with Episode 3: "Son of a Gun," as well.

Furthermore, of the sixteen major characters that have been regulars over the history of this show, twelve of them appear in this episode, and a thirteenth (Beau Felton) is of pivotal importance. In other words, only three regulars that would ever be seen on *Homicide* are absent from this episode.

NOTES: Dr. Cox describes Beau Felton's cadaver as a cross between TV-PG and TV-M. She is referring to a new television ratings system that was adopted in the United States during *Homicide's* fifth season. Under pressure to regulate the amount of violent and sexual content to which children are exposed by watching TV, broadcasters and cablecasters adopted a system of ratings modeled on movie ratings that would identify shows by content. These symbols appear in the upper portion of the screen at the start of each program. Thanks to its mature subject matter, *Homicide: Life on the Street* was most commonly rated TV-14, indicating children under fourteen should not view the series unsupervised.

Episode 78: "Strangers and Other Partners"

[Production Code 522]
Original air date: May 16, 1997.
Written by David Simon, James Yoshimura, and Tom Fontana; directed by Kenneth Fink.

Additional Cast and Guest Stars:
Jon Seda (Detective Paul Falsone), Peter Gerety (Detective Stuart Gharty), Ami Brabson (Mary Pembleton), Jay Spadaro (Officer Salerno), Scott Winters (Eddie Dugan), Maryland governor Parris Glendening (as himself), Baltimore mayor Kurt L. Schmoke (as himself)

STORY: The Homicide, Auto, and Internal Investigations divisions work together on the Felton case, trying to determine if Felton was exposed, or if his disguise remained intact to the end. At stake is the chance to discover whether or not the Auto Squad has a dirty cop.

As the slain detective is being honored, Lieutenant Giardello learns of a new departmental policy. From now on, detectives will be rotated through the various divisions on a three-month basis, meaning that Homicide will no longer be the elite of the department, and come the fall they may all be gone.

HIGHLIGHTS: Mary (now six months pregnant with their second child) at last returns to her husband Frank Pembleton. In turn, Frank vows that he will no longer let his job interfere with his family, even if that means he must leave Homicide.

While Frank and Mary reunite, Mike Kellerman and Julianna Cox begin to separate. Kellerman is realizing that their alcohol-washed relationship is doing neither of them any good, and he has to take control of his life before he follows Beau Felton down the path to self-destruction and death.

COMMENTARY: *Entertainment* Weekly noted that *Homicide* had just sold its reruns to the Lifetime cable network, whose motto is "Television for Women." With the season finale sporting the largest female cast yet for the series (Isabella Hofmann, Michelle Forbes, and Melissa Leo), the magazine wrote, "Which doesn't mean this is Television for Women. As the one of the best dramas in prime-time history, *Homicide* is Television for Everyone."

However, the finale sidelines Detectives Howard and Russert while the men (Pembleton, Gharty, and Falsone, backed by Munch and Bayliss) complete the investigation. Gee forcibly removes Howard and Russert from the case and has them, instead, arrange Beau's funeral. Let the boys chase the bad guys while the girls worry about clothes.

As a send-off episode for Leo and Hofmann, "Partners and Other Strangers" does give the actresses a chance to shine, even if it isolates them from the main plot. Giardello removed them out of fear that the two women, having been close to Felton in life, would be too emotional to handle the matter properly.

His decision results in an unfortunate double standard, as Gee let Crosetti pursue Chris Thorman's shooter (see Episode 3: "Son of a Gun"), and, later, let Lewis investigate Crosetti's death (see Episode 19: "Crosetti"). Just because such a double standard on Gee's part is depicted, does not mean that the writers endorse that attitude. However, it's worth noting that neither actress would be back for the sixth season.

For once, the cast changes would be arranged in advance, thanks to the plot device of the shift rotations. As cliffhangers go, this was a rather oblique way to end the season. *Homicide*'s finale shared some aspects in common with the finales of *The X-Files*, with its apparent shotgun suicide of a main character, and *NYPD Blue* with one detective being made to look bad in order to be used as an undercover operative and another detective possibly becoming involved in killing a bad guy. However, *Homicide* concluded these more dramatic story lines before the fadeout, and chose instead as its cliffhanger a change in the police department's administrative policies(!).

The policy in question was a real one, recently instituted in Baltimore and reported in *Baltimore* magazine by David Simon. Thomas Frazier took the job of police commissioner in 1994. One of his first steps was to institute a much-maligned four-year limit on assignments to specialized units.

Frazier had noticed that the city's best cops drifted up the ranks to units like Homicide. He figured that by rotating officers through departments, there would be greater sharing of knowledge and skills. However, it also meant that detectives would have little time to develop specialized skills before moving on to a post with different demands. David Simon reported that the quality of drug investigations plummeted as inexperienced detectives took over. Meanwhile, many top Homicide detectives retired rather than leave the elite squad of the police.

NOTES: Baltimore mayor Kurt Schmoke makes his third cameo on *Homicide*, this time with true-to-life Maryland governor Parris Glendening. "The *Homicide* television series is one in which we, as Marylanders, can take great pride," said Glendening to the press, "It combines a stellar cast, an outstanding creative team and a skilled technical workforce that richly deserves the many awards it has received, and the outstanding reputation it has accumulated since it first aired in 1992. I was very pleased and flattered to have a role in this excellent program."

CHAPTER 8

The Sixth Season: Last Call...Maybe

"I'm very concerned about it," admitted producer Tom Fontana. "I mean, I think NBC wants to renew *Homicide* for another year past this year, but I'm not sure we can get the numbers up to where NBC wants them to be for renewal."

"If we don't [beat *Nash Bridges*]," explained writer-producer Anya Epstein, "NBC is going to cancel us."

As *Homicide* began its sixth year, it entered yet another struggle for survival, yet one more battle with the ratings. Each episode cost some $1.3 million, vastly more than a newsmagazine show would cost. As newsmagazines go, ABC's *20/20* had the Friday-night slot locked up. NBC Entertainment president Warren Littlefield admitted, "We're comfortable that we can't beat *20/20* in the time period, but we want to be the highest-rated drama, and that's achievable."

In other words, if *Homicide* couldn't beat *Nash Bridges* in the ratings, and NBC was going to lose money anyway, they would be better off losing less money by replacing *Homicide* with a much less expensive 10:00 P.M. version of its newsmagazine *Dateline*.

"We love the show and we want it to continue," said Littlefield, "but we have to be competitive."

Season Five may have been intelligent, provocative, challenging, and mature, but it was not competitive. The season ranked in 69th out of 155 shows.

The Yellow Brick Road

If *Homicide* seemed not long for this world, the producers could be forgiven for starting to think of the future. Barry Levinson and Tom Fontana formed a partnership called, unsurprisingly, Levinson/Fontana Productions. Although

Fontana quipped that his job with the new company was to be "The Guy Who Isn't Levinson," in fact the first production for the partnership was largely Fontana's baby.

Levinson/Fontana Productions was contacted by HBO, which was hoping for an original drama series to run in conjunction with their documentary series about crime, *America Undercover* (1996–). "We were looking for a singular voice," explains Chris Albrecht, president of HBO Original Programming. Naturally he thought of the creators of *Homicide: Life on the Street*.

Levinson and Fontana were coincidentally already developing an idea for a show set inside a prison.

On July 12, 1997, HBO aired the first of an eight-episode miniseries called *Oz*, Levinson/Fontana's gritty drama about the new, state-of-the-art Oswald state prison facility, derisively called "Oz" and "The Emerald City" by its hardened denizens.

Just as Fontana had tapped the *St. Elsewhere* staff for *Homicide*'s crew, this time he turned to *Homicide* veterans to staff the new show. *Oz*'s cast included Terry Kinney (NSA mapmaker Richard Laumer from Episode 53: "Map of the Heart"), Jon Seda (Detective Paul Falsone), Lee Tergesen (blinded patrolman Chris Thorman), Edie Falco (Eva Thorman), Sean Whitesell (Dr. Devilbliss), and Dean Winters (Tom Marans from Episodes 31: "Nothing Personal"; 38: "Hate Crimes"; and 59: "Prison Riot"). The crew for the new show included cinematographer Jean de Segonzac and directors Alan Taylor, Nick Gomez, Darnell Martin, and Leslie Libman and Larry Williams.

Other cast members participating were Rita Moreno, Ernie Hudson, and B.D. Wong. Moreno noted that they were being paid very little for the job, "but you do it because you don't have the opportunity, particularly in TV, to work with such a high-quality writer."

Fontana wrote every one of the eight scripts himself (by hand), and complained the experience gave him severe writer's cramp. But it was worth it, as Fontana came away from the project glowing with praise for HBO.

When Fontana had accepted the 1997 "Q" Award on behalf of *Homicide*, from Viewers for Quality Television, the producer thanked NBC for being the only network that would put his difficult, unconventional programs on the air. HBO, however, changed that. The cable channel wanted to compete with the networks on dramatic series, but knew that the networks had a virtual monopoly on that kind of entertainment. What HBO could do to compete, though, was to offer talented producers an environment of greater creative freedom than the networks.

Fontana continually fumed about NBC's meddlesome refinements, but found HBO surprisingly laid-back. Not only did he have less interference from network executives on *Oz*, but he also relished the greater permissiveness of cable to deal with mature ideas more frankly than family TV could allow. When he returned to NBC to begin work on Season Six of *Homicide*, Fontana left behind a great deal of freedom to face a network all but hostile to his ideas. HBO happily renewed *Oz* for a full season of twenty-two episodes, while NBC readied to put *Homicide* out of its misery.

Partly discouraged by the impending threats of cancellation, and partly worn down by years of battling NBC, Fontana found himself growing tired of *Homicide*. "I'm not bored," Fontana said, "but a writer needs to plow new fields." He would spend more time during this season in his native Manhattan, leaving it to Julie Martin and James Yoshimura to keep *Homicide* on track.

Television for Women

In April 1996, *Homicide* began a syndicated run of repeats on the Lifetime Cable Network.

Promoted as "Television for Women" and one of the per episode top-rated cable networks, Lifetime paid the handsome sum of $425,000 to buy the reruns of *Homicide*. At about the same time, FX (the cable arm of the Fox Network) paid $400,000 for repeats of *NYPD Blue*.

The deal not only gave *Homicide's* producers a healthy influx of cash and a nice piece of publicity, but also promised to bring in new viewers during a critical time in the show's history. Traditionally, syndicated reruns on cable increased audiences for the original episodes of those programs. *Murder, She Wrote* (1984–96), *Wings* (1990–96), and *Sisters* (1991–) all had experienced audience booms thanks to cable reruns. If *Homicide* needed anything, it needed more viewers.

However, NBC chose not to run any repeats of *Homicide* during the summer break between Seasons Five and Six. When their decision to run *Profiler* (1997–) during *Homicide's* Friday-night slot resulted in some of the worst ratings NBC had ever seen for that slot, the network hastily returned *Homicide* to its home in late July. However, audiences already had drifted away, and *Homicide's* late, unheralded return was seen by only a pitiful 5.8 million viewers.

As Season Six started, with all eyes focused tightly on the ratings, Nielsen reported some very discouraging numbers. The first few episodes of the season achieved ratings that were almost half of what the show used to get. Episode

81: "Blood Ties, Part Three" received a 6.4 rating, compared to *Nash Bridges'* 8.1 for the same week.

Recognizing the handwriting on the wall, Tom Fontana and Barry Levinson signed an exclusive network-television development deal with Rysher Entertainment, the producer of *Nash Bridges*.

All Change

In addition to turmoil behind the scenes, Season Six would also involve some of the most severe disruptions throughout the cast in the series' history. The fifth-season two-part finale, "Partners and Other Strangers"/"Strangers and Other Partners" left the fate of the detectives up in the air with the cliffhanger announcement that they would be rotated through other departments on a three-month basis. The idea was more than just a clever plot device, however, since it accurately reflected a rather boneheaded notion really implemented in Baltimore's police force.

The two-part season finale also introduced newcomers Paul Falsone (Jon Seda) and Stuart Gharty (Peter Gerety), but it was not until after the episodes aired that NBC decided not to renew the contracts for Melissa Leo and Max Perlich. Therefore, neither character would have the opportunity to film an official good-bye scene. When the series returned for Season Six, they would simply be gone.

Perlich's departure could easily be blamed on the actor's bad behavior. Shooting loaded weapons at neighbors outside one's home does tend to have its consequences. However Leo's firing was more controversial. The actress had been featured in the tabloids for her battle with John Heard (see Melissa Leo's biography), but, unlike Perlich's headline-grabbing actions, Leo was the victim in this case. Surely NBC was not ousting the popular actress solely because of the cruelty of her ex-lover?

However, NBC had never been particularly keen on Leo. They consistently complained to Fontana that she ought to wear more makeup and dress in a more feminine way. Her legal troubles may have merely provided a convenient smokescreen for NBC to kick out a strong woman with whom they had never really felt comfortable.

After Leo wrote an impassioned press release bemoaning her treatment, Fontana suddenly took the blame for the decision, claiming he had grown tired of writing for her. Perhaps this is true, and perhaps Fontana was merely covering for those who wrote his paychecks and had the future of his show in their hands. It is worth noting that in February at the *Homicide* seminar at

Baltimore's Museum of Television and Radio, Fontana told attendees very specifically that no cast members would depart at the end of the season.

In any event, as Season Six began, the writers would have to write out both Kay Howard and Brodie while bringing in a total of *four* new detectives. In addition to Gerety and Seda, *Homicide* also hired the virtually unknown Callie Thorne, and gave a regular role to Season Five's supporting player, Toni Lewis. In all, it would be the biggest cast shakeup yet.

By the end of the season, the cast would be further disrupted with the departure of the show's most beloved actor of all. "It's necessary for my growth as an actor," explained Andre Braugher of his shocking decision. The actor felt he had nowhere left to go with his role as Pembleton, and a still-promising career elsewhere ahead of him. Braugher's wife, Ami Brabson, had just given birth to their second son, Isaiah, and they decided to leave Baltimore to move back to New Jersey. Braugher insisted that he would stick around for one last year, but if *Homicide* made it to Season Seven, it would do so without him.

Of course, that was the question! *Homicide* had always been an ensemble cast, but Braugher's role had been the most popular. Even with the knowledge that Braugher was leaving, the producers continued to write Season Six scripts with Pembleton and Bayliss as the leads. Producer James Yoshimura explained that the ratings were always better when Frank was the focus. Could the series survive without him?

Fontana pointed to Dick Wolf's success with *Law and Order* as proof that no cast member is irreplaceable. However, *Law and Order's* approach had always favored plot over character, the opposite of *Homicide's* focus.

The Prodigal Son

Fontana and Wolf had plenty of chances to compare notes on the matter when they engineered yet another crossover between *Homicide* and *Law and Order.* "We had such a good time with it the first time, we said, 'Why not try again?'"

At first, Fontana and Wolf had hoped to push their luck with an even more ambitious stunt: a crossover that would have blended *Homicide* with *Law and Order* as well as *ER.* The logistical challenge of filming in two cities had been a tremendous hurdle back in 1996, and yet Fontana and Wolf were excited by the challenge of adding Chicago and Los Angeles as well. (*ER* is mostly filmed on a Hollywood soundstage, with some exteriors shot on location in Chicago.)

The insurmountable hurdle, though, was not the logistical one, but the reluctance on the part of *ER's* creators at Warner Brothers. Already reeling from the challenge of staging a live broadcast for their season premiere, and continually burdened by the feature-film career of star George Clooney, *ER*'s makers decided the difficulty of the crossover outweighed the questionable benefits of fusing with such a low-rated drama.

If *ER*'s decision seemed a little vain, the politics were not lost on Fontana. As the producer became fond of saying, the three drama shows were like a family: "If *ER* is NBC's golden child—with the good grades, great at sports—and *Law and Order* is the stable oldest child, then we're the juvenile delinquent whom Mom and Dad love and support despite our misbehavior."

As Season Six began its rocky road, with the future of *Homicide* seriously in doubt, whether NBC really loved its prodigal son was a good question. Despite the ultimatum to raise its ratings or be canceled, NBC ran no promotional TV spots for the series premiere (which aired several weeks after the other NBC series had had their highly touted premieres). Perhaps this would be the beginning of the end.

Back from the Brink

The ratings of the new season failed to surpass those of *Nash Bridges* except during the *Law and Order* crossover. With all signs pointing toward imminent cancellation, fans began bracing themselves for the loss of one of TV's greatest dramas. However, in the early days of 1998, NBC Entertainment president Warren Littlefield stunned even the makers of *Homicide* by announcing the show's renewal for a seventh season, despite its failure to pass the ultimatum.

"Surprised? This has all happened so fast, I don't know what I am," producer Tom Fontana told the *Baltimore Sun*, "All I can say is that we're thrilled NBC decided that we'll be back."

The about-face had more than a little to do with sudden changes in NBC's dominance of prime-time television. In a matter of only weeks, NBC lost its highly profitable professional football contract to both CBS and ABC, and then reeled from Jerry Seinfeld's decision to retire his top-rated sitcom, *Seinfeld*, at the end of the 1997–98 season. To retain *ER*, NBC ended up agreeing to pay Warner Bros. a record-setting $13 million per episode. As the dust settled, NBC realized how much they really had lost. *Homicide* was not a big hit, but it was a known quantity revered by critics and loyally watched by an audience of precisely the right demographics desired by advertisers. Canceling it and taking a risk with a replacement would have been a foolish move for a network struggling not to lose any more of its former prestige and position.

Tom Fontana humorously offered to Littlefield that *Homicide* could take the Thursday, 9:00 P.M. slot opening up in the wake of *Seinfeld*'s departure, and his show could form a block of dramatic television with *ER*. Littlefield said no. Fontana then joked that he would have the detectives on his show wear football helmets to help make up for the loss of the NFL.

The fact that Fontana could joke about *Homicide's* renewal was a relief to all fans of quality TV. The best damn show on television had once again been spared.

S E A S O N   S I X

October 1997–May 1998
60-minute episodes
Fridays 10:00 P.M. EST

Production Team:

Barry Levinson (executive producer), Tom Fontana (executive producer), Paul Attanasio (creator), Jim Finnerty (co-executive Producer), Gail Mutrux (consulting producer), Eric Overmyer (consulting producer), James Yoshimura (supervising producer), Julie Martin (supervising producer), Anya Epstein (producer), David Simon (producer), Darryl LeMont Wharton (staff writer), Stephanie Fontana (writer's assistant), Vince Peranio (production designer), Susan Kessel (set decorator), Tina Nigro (costume designer), Douglas J. Cuomo (music), Chris Tergesen (music supervisor), Lynn Kowal (title theme), Louis DiGiaimo (casting), Pat Moran (Baltimore casting), Lorenzo Millan (boom), Bruce Litecky (sound mixer), Alex Zakrzewski (director of photography), Kathi Ash (location manager), Ned Bastille (editor), Cindy Mollo (editor), Jay Rabinowitz (editor), Imaginary Forces (title sequence), Gary D'Addario (technical adviser), Jim McGee (executive in charge of production).

Regular Cast:

Richard Belzer (Detective John Munch), Andre Braugher (Detective Frank Pembleton), Reed Diamond (Detective Mike Kellerman), Michelle Forbes (Chief Medical Examiner Julianna Cox), Peter Gerety (Detective Stuart Gharty), Clark Johnson (Detective Meldrick Lewis), Yaphet Kotto (Lieutenant Al Giardello), Jon Seda (Detective Paul Falsone), Kyle Secor (Detective Tim Bayliss), Callie Thorne (Detective Laura Ballard).

Episode 79: "Blood Ties, Part One"

[Production Code 601]
Original air date: October 17, 1997.
Written by Anya Epstein; story by Tom Fontana and Julie Martin; directed by Alan Taylor.

Additional Cast and Guest Stars:

James Earl Jones (Felix Wilson), Lynne Thigpen (Regina Wilson), Jeffery Wright (Hal Wilson), Ellen Bethea (Thea Wilson), Toni Lewis (Detective Terri Stivers), Hazelle Goodman (Georgia Rae Mahoney), Mekhi Phifer (Junior Bunk), Robert Chew (Wilke Collins), Richard Pilcher (Sergeant Mark Deutch), Gary D'Addario (Lieutenant Jasper), Clayton LeBoeuf (Colonel George Barnfather), Walt MacPherson (Captain Roger Gaffney).

STORY: When Detectives Pembleton and Bayliss return to Homicide they meet three newcomers: Detectives Falsone and Gharty (with whom they had worked in Episode 78: "Strangers and Other Partners"), and Detective Laura Ballard, recently arrived from Seattle.

Pembleton and the rest of the squad investigate a murder in a hotel bathroom outside a black-tie event honoring Baltimore philanthropist Felix Wilson. Meanwhile, newly partnered Falsone and Lewis discover that Georgia Rae Mahoney is trying to exact revenge on the detectives responsible for the death of her brother, Luther.

HIGHLIGHTS: Like the top-heavy Episode 34: "Fire, Part One" from Season Four, "Blood Ties, Part One" has too much story to tell in too little time.

First, there are the cast changes: Detective Kay Howard is gone (rotated into the Fugitive Unit), as is videographer Brodie (off to Hollywood after winning an Emmy, no less, for his documentary). While Pembleton and Bayliss spent the summer in the Robbery Unit, Kellerman is returning to Homicide from Auto, and Lewis has been in Missing Persons. Former Auto Squad detective Paul Falsone and former Internal Affairs detective Stuart Gharty have been rotated into Homicide (conveniently so, since both men got a taste of the job in last year's finale). Terri Stivers is no longer with the Drug Squad, but with Robbery instead. Last, but not least, Detective Laura Ballard is a recent arrival, joining the Homicide Unit from her hometown Seattle's police department.

While Pembleton and Bayliss are still partners, theirs is the only alliance to survive into this "new age." Gharty and Ballard are a team, Kellerman is now paired with Munch, and Lewis is partners with newcomer Falsone.

Then, there are old plot threads to tie up (or abandon). Cox and Kellerman are no longer an item, and issues like Pembleton's stroke and Bayliss's sexual abuse are all but forgotten.

This premiere episode of the season also has some new story lines to unveil. The central plot, concerning the killing of Fabulous Felix Wilson's domestic, will cover three episodes. More importantly, this episode reopens

James Earl Jones gives the struggling Homicide *a boost in its sixth season with a three-episode-long guest turn.* Everett Collection

old wounds regarding Luther Mahoney's shooting, and provokes newcomer Falsone to start investigating whether Kellerman, Lewis, and Stivers are guilty of any wrongdoing.

This is a particularly troubling subplot. Falsone, who will be made increasingly sympathetic to viewers as the season progresses, is pitted against three detectives about whom the audience has come to care. Kellerman has already been through one investigation, and in many ways that was what pushed him over the edge regarding Mahoney in the first place. Stivers and Lewis lied to protect their friend and colleague, and are now being dragged back into the mess they hoped to avoid.

COMMENTARY: With so much exposition to process, the episode scarcely has any time left for storytelling of any depth. So, instead, screenwriter Anya Epstein substitutes flashy action. A sniper shooting at cops from a motorcycle, using 50mm rounds! A helicopter chase! Luther Mahoney's evil sister! This episode almost mandates the use of exclamation points to describe it.

The critics weighed in with virtual exclamation points of their own. "Except for one moment in tonight's opener," writes David Bianculli, "I was on the edge of my seat . . . . At that moment, a surprise shooting shocked me right onto my feet." Caryn James of the *New York Times* praised the episode as "all the sophisticated writing, terrific acting and intensity that mark it as one of the finest dramas around." The *Hollywood Reporter* wrote, "Production elements are as excellent as ever and the characters, including the new regulars, are as rich as ever. The playing under director Alan Taylor is as strong as ever. And the series is as superior as ever. Case closed." *Entertainment Weekly* gave an "A–" grade to what it called a "corker" of a season premiere, concluding, "For what more could you ask?"

Alan Sepinwall of the *Star-Ledger*, though, noted that the episode seemed awash in sensationalism. "Where'd all these shoot-outs and chase scenes come from?" Sepinwall asks, noting that executive producer Tom Fontana takes all blame (and credit) for such changes in style. "I don't want us to have a style every week that we feel we have to conform to," Fontana is quoted as saying, "The Luther Mahoney story has always been a very big, operatic story, and we felt it could support helicopters and all that stuff."

NOTES: Although Detective Laura Ballard has not been with the Homicide Unit for long, she has had the chance to work enough cases to be commended by the top brass for her skills. Viewers who pay close attention to the case board will see that among the cases she has worked are "Stringfield" and "Doherty." These aren't just randomly selected fictional names for victims, these are obscure in-jokes for hard-core *Homicide* junkies. During the previous summer, fans conversing on the online alt.tv.homicide newsgroup revealed rumors that Melissa Leo was to be replaced by Shannon Doherty or Sherry Stringfield. In fact, executive producer Tom Fontana was the source of this disinformation, leaking false news to fans in a perverse attempt to keep fans guessing.

Some fans did not take kindly to Fontana's manipulations, and started denouncing him. In turn, Fontana included the names on the board under Ballard's, as if thumbing his nose at the handful of viewers who would even get the joke.

The real highlight of the episode is the wonderful guest role for acclaimed actor James Earl Jones. Throughout the three-part "Blood Ties" story, Jones plays Felix Wilson, a fictional character loosely based on Famous Amos. Jones's deep, mellifluous voice has graced such characters as Mufasa in *The Lion King* (1994) and Darth Vader in the *Star Wars* films (1977, 1980, 1983). Other films in which he can be seen include *The Great White Hope* (1970), *The Man* (1972), *A Piece of the Action* (1977), *King Lear* (1977), *Blood Tide* (1982), *Soul Man* (1986), *Matewan* (1987), *Coming to America* (1988), *Field of Dreams* (1989), *The Hunt for Red October* (1990), *Patriot Games* (1992),

Sommersby (1993), *A Clear and Present Danger* (1994), *Cry, the Beloved Country* (1995), *A Family Thing* (1996), and *Looking for Richard* (1996).

Joining Jones for the "Blood Ties" trilogy is actress Lynne Thigpen, best known to TV viewers for her work on *Where in the World is Carmen Sandiego?* (1993–) Thigpen has also appeared in such movies as *Tootsie* (1982), *Lean on Me* (1989), *Bob Roberts* (1992), *The Paper* (1994), and *Naked in New York* (1994).

Also guest-starring in this week's episode is Mekhi Phifer, reprising his role as Junior Bunk, Luther Mahoney's nephew (see Episode 65: "Control").

Episode 80: "Blood Ties, Part Two"

[Production Code 602]
Original air date: October 24, 1997.
Written by David Simon; story by Tom Fontana and James Yoshimura; directed by Nick Gomez.

Additional Cast and Guest Stars:

James Earl Jones (Felix Wilson), Lynne Thigpen (Regina Wilson), Jeffery Wright (Hal Wilson), Ellen Bethea (Thea Wilson), Toni Lewis (Detective Terri Stivers), Armando Benitez (himself), Scott Erickson (himself), Jay Spadaro (Officer Salerno), Brian Tarantia (Scott Russell), Farid Arefzaden (boy with beer), Norman Aronovic (Bob Jesburger), Rusty Clauss (Madame Bouchard), Collins Harris (boy with basketball), Bob Moore (Fred Shuster), Mets Suber (Samuel Bissainthe), Alan Wendl and Christopher Walker (fans).

STORY: Although standard procedure for a murder investigation would be to examine those closest to the victim first, both Lieutenant Giardello (friends with Mrs. Wilson) and Detective Pembleton (awed by Felix Wilson's contributions to the black community) resist even the suggestion that he or any member of his family could be implicated in the murder of their domestic servant.

Meanwhile, Detectives Munch and Kellerman investigate a killing at Camden Yards during a Baltimore Orioles ball game.

HIGHLIGHTS: After the bombast of the season premiere, it's refreshing to see *Homicide* settle into some of its older ways. The Camden Yards tale is richly comic, and depicts Detectives Munch and Kellerman well.

Just in the previous episode, Junior Bunk Mahoney shot Kellerman in the arm with .50-caliber ammunition, yet Kellerman now seems not to have been injured much at all. The gory spurt from his arm that happened in that episode would seem to have suggested that he was much more severely injured than he now appears.

COMMENTARY: This is a particularly controversial episode that provoked the ire of many *Homicide* fans, who objected to the characterization of Frank Pembleton. The online magazine *Salon*, a longtime *Homicide* booster, may have put it best in a review on October 28: "The first two episodes of *Homicide* this season were a disappointment at best and, at worst, they were just plain wrong.... Who was this Frank Pembleton we saw last week, not being hungry, not being aggressive, not being thorough?... What's going on?"

Frank Pembleton, as portrayed by Andre Braugher, always has distinguished himself as a zealous and unyielding investigator, one who believes all murders must be avenged and all killers brought to justice. How can he, then, in this episode, move to protect Felix Wilson, refusing even to consider the possibility of Wilson's involvement, without compromising that trademark integrity?

In the story's defense, *Homicide* has earned its critical acclaim in part because its characters are so realistically drawn. Other TV shows content themselves with simplistic motivations and predictable character reactions. On *Homicide*, the cast plays everyday people, which is to say that they are not always so easily pegged.

Additionally, it is perhaps too superficial a reading of Pembleton's past actions to say he has no regard for the race of the victim or the accused. In Episode 1: "Gone for Goode," he objected to the idea of being partnered with a white detective. In this present episode, Pembleton reacts angrily to what he perceives as a racist slur by Detective Gharty, but his reaction is not nearly as violent as his response to slurs by Roger Gaffney in Episode 15: "Fits Like a Glove."

There are indeed a number of investigations from past episodes that can be used as examples of Pembleton's relentless pursuit of all killers. On closer examination, though, Pembleton's actions may seem less cut and dried. In Episodes 11: "See No Evil" and 12: "Black and Blue," Pembleton's investigation of Lieutenant Tyron alienated most of the police department. Tyron was, notably, a white cop accused of shooting an unarmed black suspect. In Episode 32: "Colors," Pembleton shows no mercy in his investigation of Bayliss's cousin. Again, it was a case of a white man killing an unarmed member of a minority. In Episode 44: "I've Got a Secret," a case of a white woman doctor accused of contributing to the death of a black-skinned criminal again provoked Pembleton's self-righteousness.

Some of Frank's most impassioned investigations have been of racists. Gordon Pratt (Episode 27: "End Game") and Alexander Rousch (Episode 46: "For God and Country") severely rattled Pembleton's characteristic cool demeanor, and Frank showed little interest in unmasking the police officer who killed Gordon Pratt in revenge.

Some viewers, like those at *Salon*, concluded that past actions depicted Frank as the kind of detective who would be unmoved by Felix Wilson's race or social stature and would handle the case as if it were any other. However, the same examples could be used to suggest that Frank is very conscious of race and his reluctance to implicate Wilson is not so unusual.

As an alternative explanation for Pembleton's behavior, Verne Gay of *Newsday* wrote, "Consider that last season, both Giardello and Pembleton had deep misgivings about their careers and lives.... Then, they come under the charm of Wilson, a black man of accomplishment, wealth and success. Everything they believe they are not.... So, do they overlook Wilson because of his race? Or because of his accomplishments? The latter. It's a subtle difference, but a big one, and in such differences, brilliant drama is born."

It is worth remembering that, just last year in Episode 68: "Betrayal," Pembleton had actively interfered with an interrogation because he did not want to see a young girl convicted for standing up to her abusive father. Perhaps, in the aftermath of his stroke and his recognition of the fragility of his own family life and health, the detective had lost, or, at least, reconsidered, his previous sense of self-righteous zealotry.

In short, perhaps Pembleton's actions in this episode are not quite so uncharacteristic after all.

NOTES: *Homicide*'s producers had long wanted to stage a murder at Baltimore's best-known attraction, Camden Yards. Since the owners of the Orioles had no intention of associating Baltimore's top tourist spot with crime, the closest *Homicide* had yet come was in Episode 10: "Bop Gun," in which a tourist was slain near Oriole Park.

Producers David Simon and James Yoshimura told *Sports Illustrated* that it was a stroke of "pure, unencumbered genius" to have both killer and victim be rude, obnoxious Yankee fans who brought their violence with them all the way from Long Island. The Maryland Stadium Authority agreed to the idea, and happily lent out Orioles pitchers Armando Benitez and Scott Erickson for walk-on roles.

For some reason, NBC's *Homicide* Web site claimed that the Oriole players who appeared in this episode were Roberto Alomar and Lou Angeles.

In the end, though, the baseball references were unfortunately obsolete. When *Homicide* filmed the episode during the summer, Simon and Yoshimura anticipated that the Orioles would be in contention for the pennant race. However, the Orioles were eliminated by the Cleveland Indians, rendering the episode a little out of date.

Episode 81: "Blood Ties, Part Three"

[Production Code 603]
Original air date: October 31, 1997.
Written by David Simon and Anya Epstein; story by Tom Fontana, Julie Martin, and James Yoshimura; directed by Mark Pellington.

Additional Cast and Guest Stars:
James Earl Jones (Felix Wilson), Lynne Thigpen (Regina Wilson), Jeffery Wright (Hal Wilson), Ellen Bethea (Thea Wilson), Toni Lewis (Detective Terri Stivers), Zeljko Ivanek (Assistant State's Attorney Ed Danvers), Clayton LeBoeuf (Colonel George Barnfather), Ami Brabson (Mary Pembleton), Marc John Jeffries (Jack Collins), William Cote (Keane), Lance Lewman (Detective Bob Castleman), Dina Napoli (TV reporter).

STORY: Recent revelations have cast suspicion on the Wilsons, much to the dismay of Pembleton and Giardello. Now there is no alternative but to pursue the wealthy family as they would any suspects. However, the lack of physical evidence makes it difficult to proceed. Detective Pembleton has an off-the-record conversation with Felix and Hal Wilson, hoping to finally put his mind at ease about who killed their Haitian housekeeper Malia Brierre, and why.

HIGHLIGHTS: When Wilke Collins—the drug dealer who fingered Junior Bunk for shooting at Lewis, Kellerman, and Stivers in Episode 79: "Blood Ties, Part One"—turns up dead, Detective Falsone continues his quest to discover the truth behind the killing of Luther Mahoney (see Episode 75: "Deception"). Under his prodding, Medical Examiner Cox begins to wonder if her brief affair with Detective Kellerman clouded her judgment during Mahoney's autopsy, and if she had unwittingly contributed to a lie.

COMMENTARY: The conclusion to "Blood Ties" is a showpiece of acting, highlighting Andre Braugher and guest star James Earl Jones to great effect. The essence of the drama is a rather unlikely plot device whose only function is to get Pembleton and the Wilsons in a room together, talking. In the end, this is a better piece of drama than of realistic writing.

"Blood Ties, Part Three" parallels Episode 64: "The True Test" (last season's highest-rated installment). Both stories involve the privileged son of a member of Baltimore's elite, lashing out in violence because, for all his material comforts, he feels something missing in his family relationships. In both stories, the parent assists the police in uncovering the child's misdeeds, but then the parental instincts return and they rush to protect their child from the consequences of their crimes.

Viewers who were disconcerted by Pembleton's behavior in the last two episodes will be comforted to see him return to "normal," but only those viewers who were not so puzzled will really understand why he has such a change of heart.

The controversy exists because of the notion that the otherwise relentless Detective Pembleton is apparently throwing an investigation, whatever the possible reasons may be, race- or class-consciousness. It should be noted that Giardello's similar behavior is not in question, as his fierce loyalty is a well-established character trait. In the past he has been willing to go to great lengths to guard his allies. However, Pembleton is another matter.

The controversy disappears, however, when the full context of his past actions are considered. Pembleton is not the one-note supercop many fans would like him to be. Instead, he is a human being, with a complex set of motivations, one of which is vanity. Pembleton takes great pride in his instincts, and enjoys taking credit when his instincts close a case. His antagonism toward working with a partner, and his dislike of working full-squad "red ball" cases, is because he hates to share the spotlight!

As an investigator, Pembleton uses his instincts to determine a course of action, which he pursues single-mindedly until it either closes the case or runs dry and forces him to change tactics. He hates to pursue more than one theory at a time, because he wants to demonstrate how infallible his instincts are.

For example, in Episode 66: "Blood Wedding," Pembleton and Bayliss disagree whether Ed Danvers' fiancée was killed by a novice or an experienced armed robber. Pembleton denounces any attempt to follow Bayliss' theory of the case, and, ultimately, Frank's instincts prove correct. In Episode 28: "Law and Disorder," Pembelton works a case with Lewis, and insists that they canvas the ghetto first. Lewis argues that Pembleton is being racist to assume the killer was from the poor side of the tracks, but Pembleton believes it to be the most likely answer. When their investigation turns up nothing, Pembleton switches gears and begins hunting for a white, middle-class suspect with the same vigor.

This same behavior pattern reveals itself in this present episode. Pembleton honestly is convinced that the Wilsons are innocent, and he resists attempts to question them because he "knows" his instincts are right. He is wrong, however, and admits it when the evidence against the Wilsons starts to grow. Ultimately, Frank has so much respect for Felix Wilson that the detective allows his emotions to influence his instincts. This is not racist behavior on Frank's part, merely a very human error that all of us are prone to make.

NOTES: The guest director, Mark Pellington, is a Baltimore-based film-maker whose previous contribution to the series was the original black-and-white title sequence that aired from 1993–96.

NBC's ill-advised TV ad spots for this episode, aired immediately after "Part Two," revealed the identity of the killer. How such a marketing decision was intended to *increase* viewership of a murder mystery is a question for the ages!

Episode 82: "Birthday"

[Production Code 604]
Original air date: November 7, 1997.
Written by Anya Epstein and David Simon; story by Julie Martin; directed by Alison McLean.

Additional Cast and Guest Stars:
Toni Lewis (Detective Terri Stivers), Alison Folland (Grace Rivera), Hazelle Goodman (Georgia Rae Mahoney), Helen Carey (Maggie Conroy), Ami Brabson (Mary Pembleton), Granville Adams (Officer Westby), Christopher James Fischer (Matt Northup), Sean Whitesell (Dr. Eli Devilbliss), Susan Allenbach (Dr. Porter), Stephen Angus (Alex Carew), Rick Holloway (Ted Ganz), Billie Jackson (Lieutenant Kate McClendon), Katrina Owens (Angela Tripp), Charles Pendleton (Manny Korman), Holly Twyford (Ivy Kiriakis), H. Michael Walls (Anders Corolli).

STORY: Detectives Paul Falsone and Meldrick Lewis join forces with Detective Terri Stivers (now rotated into the Sex Crimes Unit) to investigate a series of brutal rapes.

HIGHLIGHTS: Mary Pembleton goes into labor, but experiences severe medical complications.

COMMENTARY: The increased exposure of Detective Falsone from the previous episode, this one, and the *Law and Order* crossover episodes to come, led some viewers to proclaim that *Homicide* was turning into "The Paul Falsone Show." Indeed, Jon Seda's character gets a disproportionate amount of airtime across these three weeks, especially for such a new addition to the cast. However, with *TV Guide* hailing Seda as an important star, the decision makes marketing sense.

Despite the apparent focus of the episode on Falsone and his one-man mission against the evils of the world, the real heart and soul of this episode is in its subplot. Detective Mike Kellerman continues to experience the fallout from his shooting of drug lord Luther Mahoney (see Episode 75: "Deception").

Columnist Leonard Pitts of the *Miami Herald* was deeply impressed. He notes how Americans were growing increasingly suspicious of the justice system, their growing dissatisfaction reflected in popular entertainment. Hollywood and TV readily provide a secret wish-fulfillment of vigilante cops and action heroes who take down the bad guys with brute force, and no defense lawyers are needed.

Pitts writes, "Week after week, *Homicide* picks at the [Mahoney] shooting like a wound, tearing away bits of scab, making us think when we'd rather not. It's only television, but television has done a valuable thing here. It has crafted a morality play that illuminates dark corners of doubt, tallies the price of compromise, forces some needed wondering."

NOTES: Billie Jackson, as Sex Crimes lieutenant Kate McClendon, previously appeared in Episode 73: "Kaddish." In the intervening episodes, her character had been promoted from detective to shift commander.

Episode 83 "Baby It's You, Part One" (*Law and Order* Episode 163):

Original air date: November 12, 1997.
NOTE: This episode is a part of the *Law and Order* TV series, as the first part of a two-episode joint production with *Homicide*.
Written by Jorge Zamacona; directed by Ed Sherin.

Regular Cast:
Jerry Orbach (Detective Lennie Briscoe), Benjamin Bratt (Detective Reynaldo Curtis), S. Epatha Merkerson (Lieutenant Anita Van Buren), Sam Waterston (Assistant District Attorney Jack McCoy), Carey Lowell (Assistant District Attorney Jamie Ross), Steven Hill (District Attorney Adam Schiff).

Additional Cast and Guest Stars:
Maureen Anderman (Gail Janaway), Dan Hedaya (Leslie Drake), Tom Tammi (Dr. Steven Janaway), Zeljko Ivanek (Assistant State's Attorney Ed Danvers), Dan Frazer (Judge Barry McLellan), Richard Council (John Law), J. K. Simmons (Dr. Emil Skoda), Richard Belzer (Detective John Munch), Yaphet Kotto (Lieutenant Al Giardello), Jon Seda (Detective Paul Falsone), Taro Alexander (Paul Delacourte), Sam Valle (Johnnie Ramirez), Leslie Hendrix (Medical Examiner Rogers), John Fiore (Detective Profaci), Pamela Nyberg (Jeri Stein), Anne Bonvegna (Cassie Nobels), Maribel Gonzalez (Lucia

Cottone), Isabel Segovia (Mrs. Ana Ramirez), Anne Frith (Sadie Appleyard), Ajay Kothari (Virgil Pipino), Melanie Vesey (Michelle), Richard Litt (Gronbeck), Gia Galeano (Gia), Billy Gillespie (Assistant Medical Examiner), Mick O'Rourke (cameraman), Johnny Moreno (Detective), Bob Wilson, Nanvy Nichols, Dana Smith Croll, and Ray Virta (reporters).

STORY: The death of a fourteen-year-old supermodel prompts a criminal investigation by Detectives Briscoe and Curtis. When the trail leads to Baltimore, they enlist the aid of Detectives Munch and Falsone in gathering evidence. As the media attention around the case increases, the district attorneys begin to suspect the girl's own father may have raped her to death.

HIGHLIGHTS: In recombining *Law and Order* with *Homicide*, the producers of both shows put into practice some lessons learned from the first go-around. Producer Tom Fontana decided he liked especially the chemistry between Detectives Briscoe and Munch (played by Jerry Orbach and Richard Belzer), so they became something of an "odd couple" pair for this two-part tale.

"Belzer and I have so much fun together," jokes Orbach, "Maybe we'll do a sitcom called *Briscoe and Munch*, kind of like, you know, two retired cops that become private detectives."

COMMENTARY: The first *Law and Order–Homicide* crossover (see Episodes 45: "Charm City" and 46: "For God and Country") brought in some of the best ratings in the history of either show. Only *Homicide*'s Episode 10: "Bop Gun," with mega–guest star Robin Williams and the sanctified Thursday night-time slot did better. Naturally, a sequel was demanded.

In fact, NBC Entertainment president Warren Littlefield pressured both shows to get the crossover underway as soon as possible. Producers Tom Fontana of *Homicide* and Dick Wolf of *Law and Order* waited two years, hoping to avoid the logistical challenges that caused them so many headaches the first time. For a moment, they tried to increase the logistical burden by attempting to include *ER* in the mix. That *ER* politely declined the offer is perhaps a godsend, as this second crossover is a much more coherent whole than the one from 1996.

Last time, Universal Television insisted that the *Law and Order* episode be self-contained for syndication purposes. For "Baby, It's You," Wolf got Universal to agree that the story really could be a two-part tale told across both shows. In other words, to understand the whole, viewers have to watch both programs.

The cast of *Law and Order* appreciated the change of pace that working with *Homicide* provided. "[*Homicide*] is a little more kinetic, a little more frantic if you will," says actor Benjamin Bratt.

"It's almost like joining an improv group," added Orbach.

Homicide star Clark Johnson, who was all but left out of the crossover festivities, was less enthusiastic. "They're trying to make it out like it's cutting-edge, like it's groundbreaking," quipped Johnson to Baltimore's NBC affiliate Channel Four, "I happen to know that *Petticoat Junction* and *Green Acres* did it years ago."

NOTES: Although both shows had undergone some cast changes since the previous crossover, the behind-the-scenes personnel returned to reprise their duties. Writer Jorge Zamacona again penned scripts for both the *Law and Order* and *Homicide* segments, while Ed Sherin (*Law and Order's* director) called the shots.

At least one returning face caused *Homicide* fans a little distress. While *Homicide's* casting director Pat Moran maintains a policy that no actor may appear on the show in more than one role, *Law and Order* has no such dictum. In fact, *Law and Order* is renowned for reusing actors in many different roles. Back in 1996, J. K. Simmons appeared on the *Homicide* half of the crossover tale as the sinister Alexander Rousch (see Episode 46: "For God and Country"). Since then, Simmons joined *Law and Order* in a recurring role, as psychiatrist Emil Skoda. Attentive viewers recognized Simmons' face in this episode, although now playing another character, causing some unfortunate cognitive dissonance.

Ironically, the previous psychiatrist character had been played by Carolyn McCormick, who had appeared on *Homicide* as the wife of sniper William Mariner (see Episode 41: "Sniper, Part One"). In fact, a large number of *Homicide* actors (including Melissa Leo, Reed Diamond, Zeljko Ivanek, and Walt MacPherson) have appeared on *Law and Order* as other characters.

Episode 84: "Baby It's You, Part Two"

[Production Code 605]
Original air date: November 14, 1997.
NOTE: This episode of *Homicide* is the second part of the two-episode joint production with the series *Law and Order*, which began with Episode 83: "Baby It's You, Part One." Written by Jorge Zamacona; directed by Ed Sherin.

Additional Cast and Guest Stars:

Maureen Anderman (Gail Janaway), Dan Hedaya (Leslie Drake), Zeljko Ivanek (Assistant State's Attorney Ed Danvers), Sagan Lewis (Judge Susan Aandahl), Tom Tammi (Dr. Steven Janaway), Benjamin Bratt (Detective Reynaldo Curtis), Cary Lowell (Assistant

District Attorney Jamie Ross), Jerry Orbach (Detective Lennie Briscoe), Sam Waterston (Assistant District Attorney Jack McCoy), Thomas M. Brooks (law clerk), Angie Levrone (Monica Mason), Rachel Layne Sacrey (Brittany Janaway), Sam Valle (Johnnie Ramirez), Sharon Ziman (Naomi).

STORY: New York prosecutor Jack McCoy teams with Baltimore's Ed Danvers to prosecute the father of the dead supermodel. As the trial proceeds, new evidence comes to light that changes the direction of the case altogether.

HIGHLIGHTS: *Law and Order*'s prosecutor Jack McCoy is the kind of lawyer Frank Pembleton might be: relentless, zealous, righteous. In his determination to punish the guilty, McCoy has sometimes been accused of abusing his prosecutorial discretion. He certainly has shown a proclivity toward weaving elaborate or contrived theories of crimes in order to charge suspects that might otherwise slip through his fingers.

By way of contrast, *Homicide*'s Ed Danvers is sort of an anti-McCoy. Levelheaded and professional, Danvers is more concerned with winning than with punishing. His is the more realistic, if less dramatic, character. When presented with shaky evidence, Danvers will not risk a jury trial, but would rather accept a plea agreement. Danvers is certainly not prone to convoluted theories devised solely to get into a courtroom. He would rather avoid the risks of a trial whenever possible.

Seeing these two characters working together, with their natural differences brought out by the collaboration, is a true highlight of this crossover special.

COMMENTARY: Part of *Homicide*'s appeal is the flexibility of its format. Some of its most memorable episodes have been those that break the usual formula. Episode 10: "Bop Gun"; Episode 33: "The Gas Man"; Episode 49: "Stakeout"; and Episode 67: "The Documentary" are all striking changes of pace. In preserving the continuity of the *Law and Order* crossover, writer Jorge Zamacona has the trial (usually the second half of a *Law and Order* episode) take place on *Homicide*. This not only gives some welcome screentime to Zeljko Ivanek as prosecutor Ed Danvers, but lets *Homicide* explore some new territory, as well.

However, in the final analysis, it's director Ed Sherin's masterful ability in maintaining *Homicide*'s style that keeps the episode from losing its flavor altogether. The cast of *Law and Order* are prominent, and the story stays true to that show's dictum to take stories "ripped from the headlines." In this case, the story is, in essence, an adaptation of the JonBenet Ramsey murder case, and, to the extent *Homicide* cast members appear, they are supporting player Zeljko Ivanek and newcomer Jon Seda.

*Sam Waterston's name
was misspelled as
"Waterson" during the
opening credits of "Baby
It's You, Part Two."*
Everett Collection

Whether the crossover muted *Homicide*'s voice or not, it worked its ratings magic. While *Homicide*'s sixth season had seen the lowest ratings ever for the series, "Baby It's You" earned an impressive 11.4 rating for the *Law and Order* half, and a very respectable 10.3 for the *Homicide* half.

NOTES: Richard Belzer made a little television history by becoming the first actor to play the same character on three different shows in the same week. In addition to his appearance on both installments of "Baby It's You," Belzer also played Detective John Munch in the *X-Files* episode "Unusual Suspects" shown on the Fox Network on Sunday, November 16, 1997. Producer Vince Gilligan of *The X-Files* proposed the crossover as part of a flashback story set in Baltimore in 1989, and asked *Homicide* producer Tom Fontana if they could borrow an actor or two.

The two shows were no stranger to each other. Zeljko Ivanek (*Homicide*'s prosecutor) had played an impressive villain on *The X-Files*, and former *Homicide* producer Jorge Zamacona left Fontana's employ to assist *X-Files* creator Chris Carter on his new series, *Millenium* (1996–). Richard Belzer had long been a fan of *The X-Files*, and harbored a love of conspiracy lore in his personal life as well. So, he was thrilled at the notion of appearing on *The X-Files*.

Tom Fontana was unsure how NBC would react to the suggestion. The crossover with *Law and Order* gave NBC a promotional coup, but a stunt designed to give a rival network some promotional leverage would be quite another matter. To Fontana's surprise, NBC Entertainment president Warren Littlefield thought the idea was "a goof," and happily let Belzer appear as Detective Munch on the Fox show.

Fontana noted, "It's like an all-Belzer week on television."

Belzer's guest spot on *The X-Files* even outstripped his previous *Law and Order*/*Homicide* crossover in the ratings. According to Nielsen, "Unusual Suspects" achieved a 13.0 rating, with 12.6 million people tuning in.

Episode 85: "Saigon Rose"

[Production Code 606]
Original air date: November 21, 1997.
Written by Eric Overmyer; story by Tom Fontana and James Yoshimura; directed by Nick Gomez.

Additional Cast and Guest Stars:

Camille McCurty Ali (Officer Toinette Perry), Vanessa Brown (Lucy Nguyen), John Tran (Tom Nguyen), Dion Graham (Curtis Lambright), Ellen McElduff (Billie Lou), Bonnie Webster (Sergeant Siobhan Burns), Helen Carey (Maggie Conroy), Russ Carter (Officer Jones), Lisa Newman-Williams (Jane Jones), David Elias (Dr. Eisenberg), Susan Rollman (nurse), Ellie Wang (Mrs. Nguyen).

STORY: When the Nguyen family is massacred at their Vietnamese restaurant in a well-planned robbery, only their two surviving children, Tom and Nancy, can identify the killer. Detectives Pembleton and Lewis, though, are pained to learn that the Nguyens were killed by a beat cop from their neighborhood. In fact, the cop even had moonlighted for the Nguyens as a security guard.

HIGHLIGHTS: Georgia Rae Mahoney is released from jail, with charges against her dropped. Realizing that she intends to blackmail him, Detective Kellerman finally confesses the whole story to Dr. Julianna Cox, (See also Episodes 75: "Deception"; 79: "Blood Ties, Part One"; and 80: "Blood Ties, Part Two.")

COMMENTARY: Although NBC's promotional ads bizarrely implied that the dirty cop who robbed and killed the owners of the Saigon Rose restaurant was in fact Detective Kellerman, this episode is surprisingly free of sensationalism.

Trading bombast for reflection, the story is a work of quiet horror. There is little to the mystery, as the killer is identified before the first commercial break, and there are no twists to the plot. Instead, writer Eric Overmyer lets the story gradually unfold layers of truth, exposing the ugliness of one human soul.

The ugliness becomes even more horrific when it becomes clear that writer Eric Overmyer based his script on a real-life incident that occurred in New Orleans.

NOTES: Baltimore high-school students John Tran and Vanessa Brown got their big break as Tommy and Nancy Nguyen respectively. Although Brown had some acting experience beforehand, Tran had merely driven his sister to the *Homicide* audition and wound up landing a part for himself.

The shellfish allergy that brings Detective Laura Ballard to the hospital and near death was inspired by actress Callie Thorne's own food allergies. Once the writers learned that the frail Thorne could not eat a large number of very ordinary foods, they decided to rib her about it in the script.

Episode 86: "The Subway"

[Production Code 607]
Original air date: December 5, 1997.
Written by James Yoshimura; directed by Gary Fleder.

Additional Cast and Guest Stars:
Vincent D'Onofrio (John Lange), Bruce MacVittie (Larry Biedron), Wendee Pratt (Joy Tolson), Kristen Rohde (Sergeant Sally Rogers), Lisa Matthews (band member), Tom Teti (transit supervisor), O'Bryant Kenner (commuter), Laura Macdonald (jogger), Charles Wellington Young (conductor), Shari Elliker (woman), John Lumin and Russell Andrews (emergency medical technicians).

STORY: Detective Pembleton spends a harrowing hour in the subway with a dying man trapped between the train and the platform. Meanwhile, Detective Bayliss tries to determine if the man was pushed or whether he fell in by accident, while Detectives Lewis and Falsone search for the victim's girlfriend.

HIGHLIGHTS: It is very rare for *Homicide* to feature a living victim, as it does in this story. The man trapped between the subway and the platform lingers just long enough to make Pembleton feel some very intense grief. Usually, the detectives greet a cold corpse, and only encounter the stings of anguish and emotion in the families of the deceased. Nonetheless, in Episode 38: "Hate Crimes," Pembleton arrived in time to hear the dead man breathe his last words, and in Episode 39: "A Doll's Eyes," the victim was left brain-dead but still breathing throughout the episode.

However, the sixth season increased this human-anguish factor as it wore down the squad's detectives. For example, just a few weeks earlier, Falsone interviewed a victim who eventually died at the conclusion of Episode 82: "Birthday."

COMMENTARY: Writer James Yoshimura proves that he has not lost his touch, with yet another truly grueling screenplay. In a interesting experiment, the drama unfolds in real-time, chronicling the last hour of one man's life.

Entertainment Weekly graded the episode "A+," praising Vincent D'Onofrio's "explosive guest turn," and announcing that "The Subway" is "as gripping an hour of television as you're ever likely to see."

Tom Shales wrote in the *Washington Post* that "the full impact of tonight's episode is considerable. You may tremble." Shales concludes that, "this installment of *Homicide* is a tour de force for D'Onofrio and Braugher."

NOTES: Guest star Vincent D'Onofrio first drew critical attention for his performance in *Full Metal Jacket* (1987). Since then, the versatile character actor has played director Orson Welles in *Ed Wood* (1994) and a alien-possessed farmer in *Men In Black* (1997).

Joining D'Onofrio as guests are a few members of Baltimore's rock scene, appearing in walk-on roles. Lisa Matthews, lead singer of the local band Love Riot, appears as a witness, and recorded the song "Killing Time" exclusively for *Homicide*. Baltimore radio station WHFS's disk jockey Shari Elliker also makes a cameo appearance as a witness in the subway.

The guest director for this harrowing installment is Gary Fleder, whose previous credits include directing the thrillers *Things to Do in Denver When You're Dead* (1995) and *Kiss the Girls* (1997).

Episode 87: "All Is Bright"

[Production Code 608]
Original air date: December 12, 1997.
Written by Rafael Alvarez; story by James Yoshimura and Julie Martin; directed by Matt Reeves.

Additional Cast and Guest Stars:

Carol Kane (Gwen Munch), Peter Maas (himself), Kathryn Erbe (Rita Hale), Ellen McElduff (Billie Lou), Rahalen Nassri (Elizabeth), Joey Perillo (Bernard Munch), Jay

Spadaro (Officer Salerno), Rosemary Polen (Margaret Longley), Rhona Raher-Olefsky (Cordelia), Deena Lynn Rubinson (Alisa), Erika Lynn Rupli (Audrey), Rhea Seehorn (Jenny).

STORY: As the Christmas holiday approaches, Detectives Ballard and Gharty investigate the death of a sexually promiscuous man who was infected with AIDS. The partners find themselves at odds over how vigorously to pursue the case, once they learn that the crime was an act of revenge by a former girlfriend whom the man had infected.

Meanwhile, John Munch is reunited with his ex-wife Gwen when she asks his help to plan her mother's funeral.

HIGHLIGHTS: Detective Bayliss finally reveals his crush on Dr. Cox, buying her a Christmas gift and planting a kiss on her lips at the squad's party at the Waterfront Bar.

COMMENTARY: Rather than calling this a "holiday season," it more likely should be called the "season of the walking dead." Perhaps as a metaphor for the producers' awareness that *Homicide* was a dead letter in NBC's eyes, the stories have been frequently populated by characters who have been "murdered" but are not dead just yet. This episode has Rita Hale join the ranks of John Lange of Episode 86: "The Subway" and Grace Rivera of Episode 82: "Birthday" as one of the doomed. The twist here is that Rita Hale has avenged herself on her killer, murdering the man who gave her AIDS (in a story that shares some similarities to the classic 1949 film noir D.O.A.).

The script also addresses the same themes of justice and punishment that have been a hallmark of the season. In Episodes 79–81: "Blood Ties, Parts One–Three," Ballard and Gharty criticized Pembleton for showing Felix Wilson preferential treatment. Now, Ballard is prepared to overlook Rita Hale's crime, and Gharty's attitude may be professional detachment or it may be prejudice.

The tensions between Detectives Falsone and Kellerman about the Mahoney shooting also provide a contrast. Whether Kellerman's actions in Episode 75: "Deception" were morally or legally justified has become a raging debate among viewers by this point, and there are no easy answers.

This episode asks the audience to decide what they think concerning the question of whether some crimes should go unpunished, if some acts of vigilantism are acceptable or not, and to what extent sympathy with the accused effects our desire to see justice done.

This is pretty heavy stuff for a Christmas episode! Other shows serve up treacly images of their casts singing carols and lighting trees; *Homicide* blares the angry sound of Suzanne Vega's song "Blood Makes Noise" and fades out on a scene of Ballard being tested for AIDS. NBC rightfully promoted this episode with an ironic promise of "A *Homicide* for the holidays."

NOTES: Although the thoughtful part of the hour concerns the Ballard-Gharty plot (which is the first time viewers have really seen these characters in action all season, although newcomer Paul Falsone has been highlighted in almost every episode), the fun part concerns the subplot with Munch and his ex-wife. This part of the story features some noteworthy guest stars, not least of which is Carol Kane as Gwen Munch. Kane is best known to TV viewers for her role as Simka on the sitcom *Taxi* from 1981–83, but she has also played in such feature films as *Dog Day Afternoon* (1975), *Annie Hall* (1977), *The Muppet Movie* (1979), *The Princess Bride* (1987), *Scrooged* (1988), and *Trees Lounge* (1996).

Returning in his role as Bernard Munch is character actor Joey Perillo, and Peter Maas (the award-winning, best-selling author of such books as *Serpico* and *Underboss*) appears as himself in a bitterly funny cameo.

Episode 88: "Closet Cases"

[production code 609]
Original air date January 2, 1998.
Written by Christopher Kyle; story by James Yoshimura and Julie Martin; directed by Leslie Libman and Larry Williams.

Additional Cast and Guest Stars:

Peter Gallagher (Chris Rawls), Toni Lewis (Detective Terri Stivers), Hazelle Goodman (Georgia Rae Mahoney), Brian Van Holt (Peter Fields), Monica Trombetta (Janine), Joe Grifasi (Lieutenant Walter Neal), Bobby Brown (Terry), Michael Chance (Jake), Paul Chidariu (Derek), Richard Dallam (Tony), William Cote (Officer Keane), Jon Orofino (Officer Hoskins), Beau James (Detective Higby), Kirk Pemberthy (Sam Farrell), Judy Thornton (Judy), Sharon Ziman (Naomi).

STORY: When a gay man is found murdered in the dumpster behind a gay nightspot, Detectives Pembleton and Bayliss suspect a hate crime.

Meanwhile, Detectives Kellerman, Lewis, and Stivers agree to stand up to Georgia Rae Mahoney. Kellerman meets with her, and says that they refuse to be blackmailed. She admits she was bluffing about the existence of a videotape, but still believes he killed her brother wantonly (see also Episodes 75: "Deception" and 82: "Birthday").

HIGHLIGHTS: After spending the last three weeks sleeping with Julianna Cox, Tim Bayliss is upset to find himself dumped by the mercurial M.E. Cox just wanted a fling for the holidays, and as the New Year begins she's ready to get back to work. Stung by her coldness, Bayliss starts examining his own history of failed relationships, his comfort level around other men, and begins to explore his bisexual side. In particular due to the circumstances of his present investigation, Tim discovers that his own attitudes toward homosexuality have changed over the years (see also Episode 38: "Hate Crimes"). In the spirit of exploring his own sexuality, Bayliss accepts a dinner-date invitation from Chris Rawls, the owner of the club where the body was found.

COMMENTARY: To ring in the New Year, *Homicide* aired its most controversial episode ever. Actor Kyle Secor had suggested to producer Tom Fontana that, as a natural outgrowth of last year's revelation that Bayliss had been sexually abused as a child (see Episode 68: "Betrayal"), Bayliss might discover a sexual attraction to men.

"The possibility of a gay relationship is something that's been percolating with this character for a long time," Secor told the *Los Angeles Daily News*. Fontana agreed, especially since some viewer mail had already asked if Bayliss might be gay.

In Episode 13: "A Many Splendored Thing," Bayliss is extremely discomforted by the S & M sexuality of a recent murder victim, but secretly went out to strip clubs clad in black leather to explore what Pembleton called "his dark side." In Episode 17: "A Model Citizen," Bayliss found himself having sex in a coffin with the morbidly sexual Emma Zoole. In Episode 38: "Hate Crimes," the detective seemed almost overcompensating in his homophobia. To Secor, Fontana, and the writers, they were taking the character in a surprising, but not unprecedented, direction.

As word of the story line leaked out, though, it provoked powerful reactions in many fans, some of whom revealed their own homophobic prejudices, while some wondered if the story line was merely a stunt designed to generate ratings. However, NBC did not promote the new developments in any way (the promotional ads for "Closet Cases" focused instead on the Kellerman-Mahoney subplot). Secor admitted that NBC's censors gave them a hard time in preparing the episode, and that the network was skittish about the whole thing.

To Secor and the writers, this was a chance to break new ground. "I don't know a lot about the workings of people who are actually bisexual, and many people don't," said Secor, "that's rarely discussed on TV." The actor also pointed out that this was a chance "to explore the bigotry and prejudice that goes on inside and outside the squadroom."

288 Homicide: Life on the Street

As for the content of the episode itself, Bayliss merely agrees to go out to dinner with a gay man. The date itself is not shown, and when it is discussed in the next episode, Bayliss says he did not sleep with Rawls. Compared to the graphic nature of the heterosexual romances depicted on rival *NYPD Blue*, this was pretty tame stuff. But the issue of homosexuality is such an intensely divisive one, that no matter how interesting the new ground being broken by the creators of *Homicide* was, and no matter how tastefully they broke that ground, the result bitterly divided the program's audience.

NOTES: In an odd, seemingly irrelevant moment of this challenging episode, Lieutenant Giardello has an argument with another Homicide shift commander about the use of a laptop computer. The scene is an in-joke that features the first crossover from *Homicide*'s online version *Homicide: Second Shift* to the TV version. Previously, characters such as Detective Kellerman and Luther Mahoney had appeared in the Web-based serial, but this time actor Joe Grifasi appears as the serial's Lieutenant Walter Neal. The scene is directly rated to the then-current online story, "doa.exe."

Episode 89: "Sins of the Father"

[Production Code 610]
Original air date January 9, 1998.
Written by Darryl LeMont Wharton; story by James Yoshimura and Julie Martin; directed by Marry Harron.

Additional Cast and Guest Stars:
Stephanie Roth (Pamela Ridenour), Laurence Mason (Dennis Rigby), George Diggs (William Rigby), Leeanna Saunders (Mazie Rigby), Granville Adams (Officer Westby), Calen Camero Johnson (corner kid), James L. Bland (homeless man), Ginny Brown Graham (Dorothy Nichols), Susan Huey (Jenny Torgerson), Charles J. Musumeci (Robert Morris), Tara Nicholson (waitress), Shelley Stokes (neighbor), George Watson (Tricky), Judy Thornton (Judy).

STORY: A rich white man is found lynched in a ghetto of Baltimore, with no apparent motive or suspect. History unveils the most important clues when Detectives Lewis and Falsone learn that the victim's ancestor was a notorious Civil War bounty hunter who captured freed blacks and sold them back into slavery, and that the crime scene itself was once a part of a route used by blacks to escape slavery.

HIGHLIGHTS: Following Tim's date with Chris Rawls, the rumor is spreading through the station house that Bayliss is possibly gay. Detective Gharty, never a tactful or open-minded fellow, taunts Pembleton with the rumors. Although Frank is confused by these recent developments, and not altogether sure of his own feelings about them, he's a loyal partner and the way he stands up to the small-minded Gharty is priceless. Frank points out, almost in threatening terms, that he's noticed Bayliss has a thing for Gharty's partner, Detective Laura Ballard.

COMMENTARY: Bayliss's attraction to fellow detective Laura Ballard seems greater in the episode as it was transmitted than the actors had intended when the episode was filmed. Actor Kyle Secor told the *Boston Herald* that "a key moment got lost on the editing floor." As the two detectives wandered through an art museum at the end of the show, Bayliss originally kept his eyes on an adjacent gay couple.

That this idea was omitted from the final cut reveals some of the ambivalence that the producers were feeling about having opened up a can of worms in Episode 88: "Closet Cases." Secor was eager to pursue the bisexuality of his character (no doubt aware that such a move might finally win him some of the publicity and attention so far lavished on his costar Andre Braugher). Braugher was less fascinated with the new developments, saying that "it hasn't grown to be as significant as its publicity." Neither actor had any idea how the notion would be fleshed out in future episodes, since the cast of *Homicide* is given scripts only one week before each episode is filmed. The writers found themselves unsure how to proceed, and so they decided to push Bayliss into the background for a few weeks and concentrate on other subplots and characters.

As if the controversy over Bayliss's sex life was not enough, *Homicide* quickly turned its attention to another divisive issue: slavery. The lingering aftereffects of this atrocity, abolished generations ago, continue to poison American society and show no signs of abating.

In this episode, the young man Dennis Rigby finds himself in an underclass of both race and economics. He is black, with all the societal hurdles that imposes, and from a poor family. His family's poverty is in no small way a consequence of slavery, since slavery prevented his ancestors from earning or collecting wealth. His great-great-great-grandfather was a free man, and owner of his own farm, who was captured and sold into slavery.

Many black families have been a part of this nation for hundreds of years, yet their contributions were devoted to expanding the wealth and position of white families. Now, even though slavery itself is long gone, those white families continue to prosper and benefit from those immoral gains of the past, while those black families still struggle to catch up to where they should have been in the first place.

When Rigby sees that Martin Ridenour, the descendant of his great-great-great-grandfather's kidnapper Patty Ridenour, is a rich and successful man (for whom the Civil War is a source of family pride, and whose success is partly built upon the injustices committed against people like the Rigbys), he becomes enthralled with the idea of revenge. But as Detective Lewis points out in a terrific interrogation scene in the Box, Rigby's violent retribution has only made him now the villain. He has not settled the score at all, he has perpetuated it.

The episode also features a parallel subplot in which Pembleton and Bayliss debate whether or not to charge an elderly woman with murder, and ultimately decide to let her go free. As in Episodes 79: "Blood Ties" and 87: "All Is Bright," as well as the lingering subplot of Kellerman's killing of Luther Mahoney, this story line deals with which violent acts are decreed to be crimes deserving of punishment. There are some violent acts that are frequently, and/or deliberately, overlooked by law enforcement groups. Rigby's violent actions are clearly wrong, but the audience is made to feel some sympathy with his motivations, as well as some recognition that the bounty hunter Patty Ridenour committed much worse crimes but was never called upon to account or pay for them. The wounds of slavery can be every bit as recent and raw to some people as the more direct connections between such life-threatening situations as the AIDS plot line of Episode 87: "All Is Bright."

NOTES: The author of the teleplay is Darryl LeMont Wharton, one of a small number of African-American dramatic writers working in the film and television industry. After graduating from Ithaca College in 1990, Wharton contacted the Maryland Film Commission and landed a job on the production of David Mamet's award-winning motion picture *Homicide* (1991). Thereafter, Wharton joined the crew of the (completely unrelated) TV series *Homicide* as a production assistant, and also appeared in Episode 18: "Happy to Be Here."

In 1994, Wharton presented series producer Tom Fontana with a script he had written, but Fontana did not read it for several years. When the producer finally got around to reviewing Wharton's submission, the erstwhile production assistant was promoted to staff writer.

While serving on the staff of *Homicide*, Wharton has also pursued his personal projects as well. With funding from the Maryland State Arts Council and leftover 16mm film stock from *Homicide*'s crew, Wharton has written, produced, directed, and acted in a short film called *Detention* (1997).

Episode 90: "Shaggy Dog, City Goat"

[Production Code 611]
Original air date January 16, 1998.
Written by Eric Overmyer; directed by Kyle Secor.

Additional Cast and Guest Stars:

Steve Allen (Mr. Cochran), Jayne Meadows (Mrs. Cochran), Toni Lewis (Detective Terri Stivers), Hazelle Goodman (Georgia Rae Mahoney), Ellen McElduff (Billie Lou Hatfield), Katherine Kelly (Donna McCord), Jack Frost (Dr. Jack Frost), Bob Lau (process server), Josh Pais and David Harscheid (medical examiners), Doug Roberts (Donald Tochterhagen).

STORY: At a meeting, Medical Examiner Julianna Cox tells her medical colleagues about a recent case in which a man jumped off a seven-story building in order to commit suicide, but was fatally shot in the chest by a shotgun blast fired through the building's windows while he fell past!

Meanwhile, Detectives Ballard and Gharty investigate the slaying of a drug dealer renowned for selling bogus drugs, which leads them into the hills of Appalachia.

HIGHLIGHTS: Georgia Rae Mahoney exacts her revenge with a multi-million dollar lawsuit naming Detectives Kellerman, Lewis, and Stivers in the wrongful death of her brother Luther. Provoked by the suit, Lewis confronts Mahoney and winds up hitting her in the mouth, and getting himself summarily suspended from the police force as a result.

COMMENTARY: The sight of Meldrick Lewis walking quietly out the squadroom door after being suspended left many fans distraught. Unfounded rumors of actor Clark Johnson's quitting had circulated among the *Homicide* Internet community, and the fadeout scene had all the hallmarks of a goodbye. Producer Tom Fontana spoke out about the rumors, calling them "bullshit," and adding that Lewis would be absent for a while from the show but he was most definitely going to return.

In fact, just about everybody was set to return. In a surprise announcement that floored even the producers of *Homicide*, NBC announced that the show had been renewed for a seventh season, with all cast members, except Andre Braugher, Ami Brabson, and Michelle Forbes, signed for the seventh season. With the exception of the *Law and Order* crossover episodes, though, *Homicide* had failed to beat *Nash Bridges* in the ratings, which NBC had earlier set as a do-or-die ultimatum. By the first few weeks of 1998, though, NBC's world had changed.

Jerry Seinfeld had recently announced that he would not continue his hit sitcom *Seinfeld* (1990–98) past the present season, preferring instead to let it end while still at a creative peak. In the wake of that devastating development, NBC found themselves in a bruising contract negotiation with Warner Brothers, the producers of *ER*. To keep *ER* in their schedule, NBC agreed to pay $13 million per episode (ten times what they spent per episode of *Homicide*). To further complicate matters, one of NBC's top choices to succeed *Seinfeld* in the Thursday night slot, *Mad About You* (1992–   ) was threatening to jump ship to a different network. Finally, to top all these discouraging matters, NBC lost its highly profitable professional football contract to both CBS and ABC.

Thus, NBC had seen their unrivaled dominance of prime-time television shaken in a matter of only weeks. Warren Littlefield, the President of NBC Entertainment, realized that *Homicide* was a highly acclaimed program with a low budget and good advertiser-friendly demographics despite middling ratings, and decided that in such a time of transition, "Why would we want to say good-bye to a show that is this good?"

NOTES: A fellow medical examiner, at the annual meeting of the National Association of Medical Examiners where Maryland's Chief Medical Examiner Julianna Cox is to be honored, declares that Dr. Cox's story is so outrageous it could be an "urban myth." In fact, the story has circulated as an urban legend for a long time, and is a favorite hypothetical question used in criminal law classes. According to *Homicide* fan and archivist Dennis Kytasaari, a former president of the American Academy of Forensic Sciences, Don Harper Mills, told the legend at a 1987 gathering for the enjoyment of his fellow medical examiners.

Also to be noted is a fine performance by renowned comedian and talk-show host Steve Allen and his wife, comedienne Jayne Meadows, as the elderly, squabbling couple inadvertently involved in the shooting that prompts Dr. Cox's story.

Episode 91: "Something Sacred"

[Production Codes 612 and 613]
Original air date January 30, 1998.
NOTE: This episode is a two-part segment run as a two-hour episode.
Written by Anya Epstein (Part One) and David Simon (Part Two); directed by Uli Edel.

Additional Cast and Guest Stars:
Zeljko Ivanek (Assistant State's Attorney Ed Danvers), Toni Lewis (Detective Terri Stivers), Clayton LeBoeuf (Colonel George Barnfather), Leslie Silva (Sister Dyanne

The Sixth Season: Last Call...Maybe 293

Attwood), Ellen McElduff (Billie Lou Hatfield), Monica Trombetta (Janine), Victor Anthony (Pedro Velez), Michael Anthony Pena (Luis Carranza), Avery Kidd Waddell (Rock Rock), Jay Spadaro (Officer Salerno), Sharon Ziman (Naomi), Melvin L. Cauthen (commuter), Earl F. Hilliard Jr. (Officer Parker), John Opladen (Father Walcott), Jonathan Orcutt (Stephen Zaymore), Joe Orofino (Officer Hoskins), Steven Pope (dealer), Doug Roberts (Donald Tochterhagen), Timothy Scanlin (thug), Rozwill Young (Swami Ajay Prabhunanda).

STORY: The vicious slaying of two prominent Catholic priests ignites a "red ball" case for the squad, with the prime suspects being two Guatemalan refugees that the Church maintains are innocent. Detectives Ballard and Gharty, with the assistance of Detectives Pembleton and Stivers, have to investigate accusations that one of the victims had been sexually abusing altar boys, but find, to their surprise, the answer to their murder mystery on a west Baltimore drug corner and in the person of a drug-dealing teenager named Rock Rock.

HIGHLIGHTS: Detective Terri Stivers joins the squad in this episode, having just been rotated into the Homicide Unit from the Sex Crimes Unit.

Following his suspension, Meldrick Lewis disappears, prompting rumors that he may have killed himself, been killed by Georgia Rae Mahoney, or possibly skipped town altogether. In fact, he is conducting a secret and illegal investigation into the Mahoney organization, all the while resenting the trouble his former partner, Kellerman, has caused for him. Kellerman, realizing that Lewis is studiously avoiding him, becomes drunk, and savagely beats a bystander for the simple crime of looking too much like the late Luther Mahoney.

COMMENTARY: After preempting *Homicide* for some figure-skating coverage the previous week, NBC decided to make amends by splicing both parts of this two-part story together to make a two-hour movie, which aired at 9:00 P.M. on Friday, January 30, 1998. The *Hollywood Reporter* declared that the special episode "testifies to the show's brilliance." Its quality notwithstanding, the scheduling move provided ample testimony to NBC's marketing brilliance, since it doubled *Homicide*'s available audience for the evening. No sooner had the "movie" completed than the network began hinting that future two-hour specials might be possibilities.

However, the combining of what had been intended as two separate episodes into one did wreak small havoc with the dramatic effectiveness of some of the script. The mysterious disappearance of Meldrick Lewis loses much of its punch, since he surfaces again in the bottom half of the segment. From the audience's perspective, he has been missing for only an hour, rather than a week. Similarly, the first half of the segment involves the absence of a number of detectives, with Bayliss away on vacation and Falsone at a custody hearing with his ex-wife. Like Meldrick's "gone today here tomorrow" stunt, the two-hour format blunts, to a small degree, this sense of disruption in the regular routine of the squadroom.

By and large, though, the movie format helps the drama. This present episode has much in common with the white-glove murders from Season Three (see Episodes 14: "Nearer My God to Thee"; 15: "Fits Like a Glove"; and 16: "Extreme Unction"). In this case, Detective Stu Gharty essays the role previously played by Frank Pembleton, that of the Catholic detective whose faith is tested by the case at hand. If God's own servants can be cut down with such cruelty, what does that say for the existence of a benevolent and all-powerful God? Or, to paraphrase Gharty's assessment, what sense is there in his attending Mass faithfully each week and looking to the priests for salvation, when he can do so little to protect them from the mundane evils of the physical world?

The similarities, however, end in the nature of the evil depicted. The third season's case involved a highly unlikely villain: a cross-country female serial killer who left a distinctive calling card at the scene of each crime and may or may not have suffered from a multiple-personality syndrome. In contrast, this present episode depicts a much more realistic and plausible story of teenaged street thugs who kill simply for money. However, this decision to avoid sensationalism also deprives it of the high-pitched drama of the white-glove case. By presenting the two episodes in a two-hour format, the slower pace and smaller scale of the story seem less of a drawback, and the overall effect is more of a grand epic, full of small character details. This is indeed a dignified *Homicide* movie, and hopefully a harbinger of more "movies" to come.

NOTES: Although a high number of *Homicide*'s tales have been adapted from true stories (many of them specifically from Baltimore crimes reported by journalist-turned-producer David Simon), this double-length episode marks the first time NBC promoted this factual basis. Actor Yaphet Kotto told the local news, "I don't think you can do television today without having a reality-based issue, a reality-based story, or reality-based characters."

The event in question occurred in Buffalo, New York (producer Tom Fontana's hometown), in 1987. Two priests were murdered, and the police originally suspected a pair of Central American teens. However, the episode also draws considerable influence from David Simon's experiences on a Baltimore street corner, described in his latest book, *The Corner* (1997, New

York: Broadway Books). Simon scripted the second half of the story and has fleshed out the factual aspects of the Buffalo case. He has added his own psychological insight into the drug-slinging teenager, Rock Rock, and the method that Pembleton and Ballard use to break through to Rock Rock by showing him the Chesapeake Bay, one small part of the vast world beyond his west Baltimore ghetto that he has never had the opportunity to see.

READER'S NOTE: The remainder of Season Six (1997–98) of *Homicide: Life on the Street* aired too late for inclusion in this book.

Appendix A

EPISODE CHECKLIST

This episode checklist is presented in the order intended by the series' producers. The numbers in parentheses refer to the actual entries as determined by the actual show dates in the episode guide. This list only covers episodes of *Homicide: Life on the Street*, and does not list the two episodes of *Law and Order* that appear in the preceding episode guide.

SEASON ONE

1. "Gone for Goode" (Episode 1)
2. "A Ghost of a Chance" (Episode 2)
3. "The Night of the Dead Living" (Episode 9)
4. "Son of a Gun" (Episode 3)
5. "A Shot in the Dark" (Episode 4)
6. "Three Men and Adena" (Episode 5)
7. "A Dog and Pony Show" (Episode 6)
8. "And the Rockets' Dead Glare" (Episode 7)
9. "Smoke Gets in Your Eyes" (Episode 8)

SEASON TWO

10. "See No Evil" (Episode 11)
11. "Black and Blue" (Episode 12)
12. "A Many Splendored Thing" (Episode 13)
13. "Bop Gun" (Episode 10)

SEASON THREE

14. "Nearer My God to Thee" (Episode 14)
15. "Fits Like a Glove" (Episode 15)
16. "Extreme Unction" (Episode 16)
17. "Crosetti" (Episode 19)
18. "The Last of the Watermen" (Episode 20)
19. "A Model Citizen" (Episode 17)
20. "Happy to Be Here" (Episode 18)
21. "All Through the House" (Episode 21)
22. "Nothing Personal" (Episode 31)
23. "Every Mother's Son" (Episode 22)
24. "From Cradle to Grave" (Episode 23)
25. "Partners" (Episode 24)
26. "The City That Bleeds" (Episode 25)
27. "Dead End" (Episode 26)
28. "End Game" (Episode 27)
29. "Law and Disorder" (Episode 28)
30. "The Old and the Dead" (Episode 29)
31. "In Search of Crimes Past" (Episode 30)
32. "Colors" (Episode 32)
33. "The Gas Man" (Episode 33)

SEASON FOUR

34. "Fire, Part One" (Episode 34)
35. "Fire, Part Two" (Episode 35)
36. "Autofocus" (Episode 36)
37. "A Doll's Eyes" (Episode 39)
38. "Heartbeat" (Episode 40)
39. "Hate Crimes" (Episode 38)
40. "Thrill of the Kill" (Episode 37)
41. "Sniper, Part One" (Episode 41)
42. "Sniper, Part Two" (Episode 42)
43. "Full Moon" (Episode 51)
44. "For God and Country" (Episode 46) [*Please note that this is the second part of a story begun on* Law and Order, *which is Episode 45 in the episode guide.*]
45. "The Hat" (Episode 43)
46. "I've Got a Secret" (Episode 44)

47. "Justice, Part One" (Episode 47)
48. "Justice, Part Two" (Episode 48)
49. "Stakeout" (Episode 49)
50. "Requiem for Adena" (Episode 50)
51. "Map of the Heart" (Episode 53)
52. "Scene of the Crime" (Episode 52)
53. "The Damage Done" (Episode 54)
54. "The Wedding" (Episode 55)
55. "Work Related" (Episode 56)

SEASON FIVE

56. "Hostage, Part One" (Episode 57)
57. "Hostage, Part Two" (Episode 58)
58. "Prison Riot" (Episode 59)
59. "Bad Medicine" (Episode 60)
60. "M.E., Myself and I" (Episode 61)
61. "White Lies" (Episode 62)
62. "The Heart of a Saturday Night" (Episode 63)
63. "The True Test" (Episode 64)
64. "Control" (Episode 65)
65. "Blood Wedding" (Episode 66)
66. "The Documentary" (Episode 67)
67. "Betrayal" (Episode 68)
68. "Have a Conscience" (Episode 69)
69. "Diener" (Episode 70)
70. "Wu's on First?" (Episode 71)
71. "Valentine's Day" (Episode 72)
72. "Kaddish" (Episode 73)
73. "Double Blind" (Episode 74)
74. "Deception" (Episode 75)
75. "Narcissus" (Episode 76)
76. "Partners and Other Strangers" (Episode 77)
77. "Strangers and Other Partners" (Episode 78)

SEASON SIX

78. "Blood Ties, Part One" (Episode 79)
79. "Blood Ties, Part Two" (Episode 80)

80. "Blood Ties, Part Three" (Episode 81)
81. "Birthday" (Episode 82)
82. "Baby, It's You, Part Two" (Episode 84) [*Please note that this is the second part of a story begun on* Law and Order, *which is Episode 83 in the episode guide.*]
83. "Saigon Rose" (Episode 85)
84. "The Subway" (Episode 86)
85. "All Is Bright" (Episode 87)
86. "Closet Cases" (Episode 88)
87. "Sins of the Father" (Episode 89)
88. "Shaggy Dog, City Goat" (Episode 90)
89. "Something Sacred, Part One" (Episode 91)
90. "Something Sacred, Part Two" (Episode 91)

READER'S NOTE: The remainder of Season Six (1997–98) of *Homicide: Life on the Street* aired too late for inclusion in this book.

Appendix B

GET THE MUSIC BACK

As he awaits what will be his final interrogation in the investigation of Adena Watson's murder, "the araber" Risley Tucker waits patiently and quietly in the squad's coffee room. Atop the fridge sits an old TV and a plastic Godzilla figurine. His face an emotionless mask, the araber watches a music video of the band Lush. The light and airy music reflects none of the somber mood of both Tucker and his interrogators.

During its first season, *Homicide* rarely used music to underscore the drama. Jeff Rona's ethereal background music (replaced by Douglas J. Cuomo's rhythmic instrumentals in subsequent seasons) and Lynn F. Kowal's almost thunderous title theme gave a distinctive flavor to the series, but most of the drama played out with only the dialogue of the characters to establish a rhythm.

In Episode 6: "A Dog and Pony Show," Lieutenant Giardello decries how the music of his neighborhood, once a beautiful blend of ethnicities, has been supplanted with the "same dull beating sound: bam, bam, BAM!" In the book *Homicide*, journalist David Simon described how the cruel rhythms of the urban soundscape provided something of a soundtrack to the summer's killing spree. But it would not be until the show's second season that the producers recognized how they could use music as a metaphor for the violent actions and emotions of the stories.

In 1994, executive producer Tom Fontana hired thirty-five-year old recording engineer Chris Tergesen to assist with Episode 12: "Black and Blue." Fontana wanted to close the episode with a montage that would tie together the various subplots using a Handel passacaglia being played by Detective Stan Bolander and his new girlfriend, a cellist named Linda.

Tergesen did more that just that. He pointed out to Fontana that *Homicide* often included "long segments of the show where dialogue wasn't the signature and the imagery moved very fast." Tergesen suggested that *Homicide* was screaming out for a soundtrack.

Although Tergesen worked on Episode 12: "Black and Blue" first, NBC's decision to run Episode 10: "Bop Gun" out of sequence unveiled the new musical approach at full throttle right away. With songs like Seal's "Killer" and Buddy Guy's "Feels Like Rain" played at full volume, *Homicide* suddenly seemed more urgent, and more cool.

By the third season, Tergesen's deft interweaving of music and pictures had become such an established trademark that writers and directors began requesting particular songs in the scripts. Given the relatively similar musical tastes of the show's production team, though, Tergesen found the requests leaning heavily toward the world of alternative rock. Tergesen and the producers had to pay careful attention to keeping the musical range wide.

After airing the fifth season's Episode 67: "The Documentary," thirty-five NBC affiliates found their switchboards swamped with calls from viewers desperate to know who performed the featured track "Boom, Boom, Boom." (The answer is the Iguanas.) Meanwhile, fans chatting on the Internet's alt.tv.homicide started clamoring for a soundtrack album, or at least for NBC to identify the songs during the closing credits.

In response, NBC established a page at their very impressive *Homicide* Web site (www.nbc.com/homicide) called "Rhythm of the Street." At this site, viewers not only can look up the names of songs and their performers, but they also can click on the album-cover icons to order CDs directly.

Bands like Morphine found that exposure on *Homicide* could lead to bigger album sales. "I was impressed with how loud it was–they really cranked it," Morphine's Mark Sandman told the *Dallas Morning News*, "That was pretty satisfying. I didn't realize how many people watched the show." For artists that did not get much radio time, a *Homicide* appearance could make a big difference.

Sometimes, *Homicide* could give a special boost to a local band as well. The Nighthawks, a Baltimore band with a strong hometown following and a twenty-five-year-long career of performing with rock's greatest stars, appeared in a fifth season episode. Baltimore bar band Love Riot played in several installments, writing one song, "Killing Time," exclusively for Episode 86: "The Subway," and recording it live on *Homicide*'s set. Lisa Matthews, lead singer of Love Riot, even appears as a witness in "The Subway."

SEASON ONE

Episode 3: "Son of a Gun"
Miles Davis—"All Blues"

Episode 8 "Smoke Gets in Your Eyes"
Elvis Presley—"Love Me Tender" (performed by Ned Beatty)

SEASON TWO

Episode 10: "Bop Gun"
Buddy Guy—"Feels Like Rain"
Seal—"Killer"
Public Enemy—"Get Off My Back"
Eric B. and Rakim—"Chinese Arithmetic"
Sonny Boy Williamson—"Don't Start Me to Talkin'"

Episode 12: "Black and Blue"
Just Like Jane—"Slow Fire"

Episode 13: "A Many Splendored Thing"
Donna Summer—"Bad Girls"
Scarlet Bride—"Hideaway" and "Out of Time"
Soul Asylum—"Whoa"

SEASON THREE

Episode 14: "Nearer My God to Thee"
Abbey Lincoln—"When I'm Called Home"
Steve McCormick—"Too Hot"
Skoota—"A Winner"

Episode 17: "A Model Citizen"
Nine Inch Nails—"Hurt"
Philip Keveren—"Introspection"

Episode 18: "Happy to Be Here"
Monkeyspank—"So What"
Jack Walrath and Larry Willis—"Green Eyes" and "Blues in F"
Steve McCormick—"Sweet Mama River"

Episode 19: "Crosetti"
John Lee Hooker—"I Cover the Waterfront"
Louis Armstrong and Earl Hines—"Weather Bird Rag"
Chris Carter—"Ain't Got No Home"
Paula Lockheart—"Howlin' at the Moon"
Philip Keveren—"Prelude for Lisa"

Episode 20: "The Last of the Watermen"
Counting Crows—"Raining in Baltimore"
Gregg Swann—"Bored to Tears"
Sky Kings—"We Got It Goin' On"

Episode 21: "All Through the House"
Nat King Cole—"Joy to the World"
Steve Almaas—"Lonely Boy"
The Pretenders—"Have Yourself a Merry Little Christmas"

Episode 22: "Every Mother's Son"
Belly—"Full Moon, Empty Heart"

Episode 23: "From Cradle to Grave"
The Pretenders—"Stand by You"
Jens Fisher—"Twin Souls"
Liquor Bike—"Swallow Me"
Monkeyspank—"Hero"

Episode 24: "Partners"
Aerosmith—"Shut Up and Dance"

Episode 25: "The City That Bleeds"
Peter Gabriel—"No Self-Control"

Episode 26: "Dead End"
Rusted Root—"Drum Trip"
Lisa Germano—"The Darkest Night of All"

Episode 27: "End Game"
Morphine—"Cure for Pain"

Episode 28: "Law and Disorder"
Tori Amos—"Crucify"
Latitude—"Dancing Cloud"

Episode 29: "The Old and the Dead"
Lou Reed—"Busload of Faith"

Episode 30: "In Search of Crimes Past"
Bus Stop—"Next to You"
Nikki—"That's Why"

Episode 31: "Nothing Personal"
Candlebox—"Change"
Ben Sher—"Handprints"
Franklin Kiermyer—"Peace on Earth"

Episode 32: "Colors"
The Kinks—"A Well-Respected Man"

Episode 33: "The Gas Man"
The Spinners—"Working My Way Back to You"
Blondie—"Heart of Glass" and "Call Me"
Chic—"I Want Your Love"
Gloria Gaynor—"I Will Survive"
Electric Light Orchestra—"Sweet Talkin' Woman"
Earth Wind and Fire—"Boogie Wonderland"
The Bee Gees—"Tragedy"

SEASON FOUR

Episode 34: "Fire, Part One"
Jimi Hendrix—"All Along the Watchtower"
Portishead—"It Could Be So Sweet"

Episode 35: "Fire, Part Two"
Matthew Sweet—"Walk Out"
Live—"I Alone"
Estrojet—"Magnet"

Episode 36: "Autofocus"
Morphine—"Buena"
Tony Bennett—"I Thought about You"

Episode 37: "Thrill of the Kill"
Garbage—"A Stroke of Luck"

Episode 38: "Hate Crimes"
Barenaked Ladies—"What a Good Boy"

Episode 40: "Heartbeat"
Leonard Cohen—"Suzanne"
Gregg Swann and Beggar's Choice—"Bored to Tears"

Episode 41: "Sniper, Part One"
Joan Osborne—"One of Us"

Episode 42: "Sniper, Part Two"
Annie Lennox—"Whiter Shade of Pale"
Dada—"Feel Me Don't You"

Episode 43: "The Hat"
Dame Joan Sutherland, Luciano Pavarotti, Richard Bonynge, National
    Philharmonic Orchestra—"Ahno Credea Mirati Si Presto Espino" from
    Vincenzo Bellini's opera *La Sonnambula*
Leontyne Price, Jon Vickers, Rita Gorr, Robert Merrill, Sir Georg Solti, Rome
    Opera Orchestra—"Ritorna Vincitor" from Guiseppi Verdi's opera, *Aida*

Episode 44: "I've Got a Secret"
Mike Dugan—"No Talking"

Episode 46: "For God and Country"
Edwin Hawkins Singers—"I'm Going Through"
Bill Perry Blues Band—"Fade to Blue"

Episode 48: "Justice, Part Two"
Hothouse Flowers—"Stand Beside Me"

Episode 50: "Requiem for Adena"
PJ Harvey—"Working for the Man"

Episode 51: "Full Moon"
The Reverend Horton Heat—"In Your Wildest Dreams"
Bill Perry Blues Band—"Down"

Episode 52: "Scene of the Crime"
Jef Lee Johnson—"Jungle"

Episode 53: "Map of the Heart"
Newton Wayland—"Coral Reef Rapsody"
Dire Straits—"Your Last Trick"

Episode 54: "The Damage Done"
Dawn Penn—"You Don't Love Me (No, No, No)"
Garbage—"Vow"

Episode 55: "The Wedding"
Lazy Boy—"Club Urchin," "Latin Quarter," "The Mole," and "Junction City"

SEASON FIVE:

Episode 57: "Hostage, Part One"
Cowboy Junkies—"This Street, That Man, This Life"

Episode 58: "Hostage, Part Two"
Neville Brothers—"Fearless"

Episode 59: "Prison Riot"
Collective Soul—"Bleed"
Joan Armatrading—"Down to Zero" and "Sometimes I Don't Wanna Go
    Home"

Episode 60: "Bad Medicine"
Tom Waits—"Till the Money Runs Out" and "Cold, Cold Ground"

Episode 61: "M.E., Myself, and I"
Los Lobos—"Georgia Shop"
Jimmy Scott—"There's No Disappointment in Heaven"

Episode 62: "White Lies"
The Subdudes—"Tell Me What's Wrong"
Garbage—"Only Happy When It Rains"

Episode 63: "The Heart of a Saturday Night"
The Eels—"Not Ready Yet"

Episode 65: "Control"
James Brown—"Night Train"

Episode 66: "Blood Wedding"
Torn and Frayed—"Reason"

Episode 67: "The Documentary"
The Iguanas—"Boom Boom Boom"

Episode 68: "Betrayal"
Love Riot—"Never Change"

Episode 69: "Have a Conscience"
Laurence Nugent—"Longing for Peace"
Roomful of Blues—"Duke's Blues"

Episode 70: "Diener"
The Eels—"Guest List"
Big Walter Horton—"Trouble in Mind"
William Clarke—"A Good Girl Is Hard to Find"

Episode 73: "Kaddish"
Little Anthony—"Shimmy, Shimmy, KoKo Bop"
The Shirelles—"Dedicated to the One I Love"

Episode 74: "Double Blind"
The Nighthawks—"Inaugural Freeze"
Miles Davis—"Concierto de Aranjuez" (after the Guitar
Concerto of that name by Joaquin Rodrigo)

Episode 75: "Deception"
Faith No More—"Evidence"

Episode 77: "Partners and Other Strangers"
Love Riot—"Never Change"

Episode 78: "Strangers and Other Partners"
Soul Coughing—"Super Bon Bon"
Civil Tones—"Trepidation" and "Only Onions"

SEASON SIX

Episode 79: "Blood Ties, Part One"
Jason Stevens Quartet—"Say What"
Terrell—"Black and White Blues"
Run On—"Bring Her Blues"
INXS—"Elegantly Wasted"

Episode 81: "Blood Ties, Part Three"
Lauren Hoffman—"Strange Man"

Episode 82: "Birthday"
Big Head Todd and the Monsters—"Circle"
Kristen Barry—"God in the Box"

Episode 84: "Baby, It's You, Part Two"
Meredith Brooks—"What Would Happen"
Blind Faith—"Can't Find My Way Home"

Episode 85: "Saigon Rose"
Charley Miller—"Lullaby Peace Dreams"
The Subdudes—"All the Time in the World"

Episode 86: "The Subway"
Love Riot—"Killing Time"

Episode 87: "All Is Bright"
Suzanne Vega—"Blood Makes Noise"

Episode 88: "Closet Cases"
Patti Labelle—"New Attitude"

Episode 89: "Sins of the Father"
Nina Simone Group—"Sinnerman"

Episode 90: "Shaggy Dog, City Goat"
John Campbell—"Couldn't Do Nothin'"

Episode 91: "Something Sacred"
Public Enemy—"Lost at Birth"
John Mooney—"Wish I Were in Heaven Sitting Down"
Mississippi Fred McDowell—"Jesus on the Main Line"
Blind Willy McTell—"You Got to Dire"

READER'S NOTE: The remainder of Season Six (1997–98) of *Homicide: Life on the Street* aired too late for inclusion in this book.

Appendix C

GLOSSARY

Aquarium, the: A glassed-in corridor in the Homicide Unit where suspects, witnesses, and families of victims wait.

araber: A nomadic vegetable peddler. One araber, named Risley Tucker, was the prime suspect in the Adena Watson case.

Baltimore, Maryland: The twelfth-largest city in the United States, and the location where *Homicide* takes place. Nicknamed "Charm City," and also "The City That Reads" (which inspired the title for Episode 25: "The City That Bleeds"). Pronounced by locals as "Bawlmer."

Baltimore Sun, The: The principal newspaper for Baltimore, for which journalist David Simon has covered the crime beat for many years. Fictional character Elizabeth Wu (introduced in Episode 71: "Wu's on First?") is a crime beat reporter for the *Sun*.

Board, the: The central feature of the Homicide Unit is a dry-erase board that lists all the detectives on shift. Underneath each detective's name are listed the cases assigned to them, identified by the name of the victim and a number indicating the chronology of the murders. Names listed in red signify open cases, names in black are closed cases. Occasionally, a blue name will signify a case reopened from a previous year. At the end of each shift, the Board is flipped to reveal the names of the detectives on the other shift. A simple glance at the color scheme of the Board reveals which detectives have the best clearance rate for cases.

Box, the: The most famous aspect of the Homicide Unit is a simple brick-walled room with one door, a window, and a one-way mirror. This is the place where detectives interview suspects and try to elicit confessions. From behind the mirror, other detectives can watch the interrogation take place.

Charm City: Nickname for Baltimore, Maryland.

dunker: Slang for an easy case.

Eromitlab: "Baltimore" spelled backwards, and the solution to the game of hangman that inspired fictional character William Mariner to shoot bystanders from rooftops in Episode 41: "Sniper, Part One."

Fells Point: A subdivision of Baltimore by the harbor where most of *Homicide's* principal photography takes place.

Gold Star bags: Fictional drug lord Luther Mahoney marked his particular brand of heroin with a pair of gold stars (stickers, like those that would honor a student in elementary school) on the plastic baggie.

Lunch Bandit, the: Considered the longest-running open case in Homicide history, the case of the "Lunch Bandit" confounded the unit for years. Someone was stealing lunches from the squadroom fridge, and although Detective Mike Kellerman set his sights on catching the culprit, ultimately it took videographer J. H. Brodie to do so.

Primary, the: On TV, as in the real-life Baltimore police, Homicide Detectives work in pairs. When a call comes in, the detective to answer the phone is automatically the primary investigator on the case, and that detective's partner is usually the secondary.

Quick Response Team (QRT): Detective Tim Bayliss joined the Homicide Unit from the QRT, which is sort of like the Baltimore SWAT team. The QRT is trained to respond to extremely tense crisis situations. The QRT Lieutenant, Jasper, is portrayed by Gary D'Addario, the real-life Baltimore Homicide Lieutenant on whom the character of Al Giardello was based.

"red ball": A high profile case that has such political and/or public relations importance that it is placed at the highest priority for the squad. The primary detective receives the full support of the department for extra detectives and resources, but will also be under tight scrutiny and pressure from the media and the bosses to close the case quickly.

Waterfront Bar, the: The Waterfront is a real bar in Fells Point that became such a common hangout for members of *Homicide's* staff that it became a feature of the series. Detectives Lewis, Munch, and Bayliss go into partnership with one another to buy the bar during the 1994–95 season.

Appendix D

THE *HOMICIDE* SEMINAR AT THE MUSEUM OF TELEVISION AND RADIO

The *Homicide* Seminar at the Museum of Television and Radio was held on February 10, 1997, in New York City. The Museum's president, Robert Batscha, moderated a panel composed of cast members Richard Belzer and Kyle Secor with producer Tom Fontana and writers Julie Martin, James Yoshimura, and David Simon.

After a series of clips of scenes from the TV series, the panelists answered questions from the audience, ranging from Detective Bayliss's childhood abuse to the role of music on the NBC show.

Appendix E

HOLLYWOOD ON THE HARBOR

In February 1997, Baltimore's Admiral Fell Inn began sponsoring weekend walking tours of Charm City that highlighted locations used in movies and television shows filmed locally. Naturally enough, most of the noteworthy sites hail from *Homicide: Life on the Street*. The two-hour tour includes lunch at the Waterfront Hotel (the bar fictionally owned by Detectives Bayliss, Munch, and Lewis) and features stops at St. Stanislaus Church (where serial killer Annabella Wilgis dumped the white-gloved bodies of her victims), the pier (where Detective Crosetti killed himself), and the Recreation Pier building that doubles as the police HQ on TV. The tour also covers locations used in the films *Avalon* (1990), *Sleepless in Seattle* (1993), and the made-for-television film *Washington Square* (1997).

Tickets can be ordered by calling Concierge Plus at (410) 547-0479.

Appendix F

THE BOOKS

Homicide: A Year on the Killing Streets by David Simon
1991, New York: Houghton Mifflin Books (ISBN 0-449-90808-9)

Essential reading for any self-respecting *Homicide* fan, David Simon's book chronicles his experiences and observations after spending a year with the Homicide Unit of the Baltimore Police Department. Readers familiar with past episodes, especially those of the first two seasons, will likely experience a kind of déjà vu reading Simon's journalistic accounts of the real events that inspired them. On the one hand, the stories will seem familiar, but on the other hand, the names and characters are different.

The Corner: A Year in the Life of an Inner-City Neighborhood by David Simon and Ed Burns
1997, New York: Broadway Books (ISBN 0-7679-0030-8)

Following his success with *Homicide*, Simon spent a year with the other side, too, hanging out with the drug dealers and users of a Baltimore open-air drug market for a year. Simon cowrote *The Corner* with Ed Burns, a former Baltimore Homicide Detective who had partnered with the Detective on whom Frank Pembleton was based.

Homicide: Life on the Street—The Novel by Jerome Preisler
1996, New York: Boulevard Books (ISBN 1-57297-227-0)

Intended as the first in a series of tie-in novels, Preisler's book is something of a disappointing start. Although Preisler has caught Detective Munch's speech patterns perfectly, he has missed the essence of the show. Unlike the TV version, the novel is a fairly typical whodunnit, in which Detectives Pembleton and Munch have to figure out the complicated motives of their suspects to uncover the truth. On the show, as in real homicide work, motives are often irrelevant to closing the case.

Preisler's book also suffers from some unfortunate continuity errors, resulting from changes in the show that occurred after he wrote the manuscript. The novel takes place after Olivia Pembleton's birth, but has no reference at all to Frank's debilitating stroke or to the sudden departure from the squad of Detective Megan Russert.

Appendix G

HOMICIDE RESOURCES

There are two principal outlets for fans to discuss *Homicide: Life on the Street* on the Internet. The newsgroup **alt.tv.homicide** has been very active in breaking news about the series. As an introduction to the group, interested parties should read the FAQ (Frequently Asked Questions) at **http://bird.tapon-line.com/~lemp/Homicide/homicide.faq**.

For those who prefer e-mail, Sandi Lemon administers a *Homicide* e-mail list that is available both as individual postings and in digest form. Lemon also organizes semiregular chats on America OnLine for interested fans. To subscribe to the e-mail list, send the message "subscribe homicide [your first and last name]" to **listserv@listserv.aol.com**.

Homicide: Life on the Street

World Wide Web pages

READERS NOTE: This list covers Web sites that were active at the time this book was written. There were a few fan-maintained sites that disappeared from the web about the time that NBC's official site really got up and going. It is possible that some of these addresses may have changed or been taken off-line since compiled.

http://members.aol.com/hlots98/hgloss.htm Fan John Bobby's *Homicide* glossary is cross-referenced by episode title.

http://members.aol.com/jimking/index.html A rather unique fan site maintained by Jim King, who has painstakingly recreated the case board from the Homicide Unit, tracking the names of all the cases listed under the detectives' names over the series' history.

http://members.tripod.com/~DaveLocke/links Dave Locke's page is a very useful and frequently updated collection of links related to *Homicide*, to various web pages and to a wide selection of articles about the series.

http://members.visi.net/~paulette/HLOTS/index.html, This site is maintained by Amanda Paulette, includes photos from the series and links to other *Homicide* sites.

http://www.cullasaja.com/Homicide "Homicide Online" is a fan-maintained site that includes an extensive FAQ.

http://www.geocities.com/Hollywood/4693/homindex.html This fan-produced site, maintained by Dou-Yan Yang, includes an exclusive interview with *Homicide* writer-producer James Yoshimura.

http://www.geocities.com/Hollywood/9086/homicide.html Fan Katie Conley's site includes pictures, sound files, links, and a collection of *Homicide* articles.

http://www.gl.umbc.edu/~jlempk1/homicide.html The longest-running fan-produced *Homicide* site on the Web, this site was declared one of the "Top five percent of the Web" by Point Communications in 1996.

http://www.lifetimetv.com/thetube/homicide/homicide.html The official site maintained by Lifetime Cable Television, which runs *Homicide* reruns, has content that in many ways resembles NBC's, but is much less developed.

http://www.nbc.com/homicide The official site is maintained by NBC. This is where to go to find video clips, press releases, biographies of the cast, episode guides, and the interactive spin-off drama *Homicide: Second Shift*.

http://www.xnet.com/djk/HomicideLifeontheStreet_2.shtml An extremely detailed episode guide maintained by a fan, Dennis Kytasaari, this site displays a level of research that puts most fan-produced sites to shame.

Addresses:

Tom Fontana, Executive Producer
Homicide: Life on the Street
Baltimore Pictures
1701 Thames Street
Baltimore, MD 21231-3417

Barry Levinson, Executive Producer
Homicide: Life on the Street
Baltimore Pictures
1701 Thames Street
Baltimore, MD 21231-3417

Lifetime Cable Television
World Wide Plaza
309 West 49th Street
New York, NY 10019-7316
(212) 424-7000

Warren Littlefield, Entertainment President
NBC—National Broadcasting Co., Inc.
3000 West Alameda Avenue
Burbank, CA 91523-0002
(818) 840-4444

Robert C. Wright, President and CEO
NBC—National Broadcasting Co., Inc.
30 Rockefeller Plaza—Room 5279
New York, NY 10112-0002
(212) 664-4444

Appendix H

HOW TO BE AN EXTRA

"Extras" are non-speaking roles that provide atmosphere and realism to scenes. If an extra is given a line of dialogue, then they are considered a "day player" and must join the Screen Actors' Guild before being allowed to appear in any future scenes.

Homicide: Life on the Street pays extras forty dollars for an eight-hour day. Since shooting may well take eight to ten hours a day, any additional time is paid hourly at time and a half. Extras are expected to report to the set early and must remain until their scenes have been completed.

Viewers interested in becoming extras on *Homicide: Life on the Street* should send a photograph along with their name, age, and telephone number to the following address:

Attention: Casting
Northern Entertainment
1701 Thames Street
Baltimore, MD 21231-3417

Bibliography

Articles

Adalian, Josef. "*Homicide* premiere: New faces, old places," *New York Post*, 17 October 1997.

_____. "Oh, Kay! *Homicide* actress is bumped off," *New York Post*, 13 June 1997.

"Andre Braugher wants to get off the street," Associated Press, 12 September 1996.

"As Melissa Leo's world turns," *USA Today*, 21 March 1997.

"Bad blood," *People*, 9 December 1996.

Baldwin, Kristen. "The hot rock," *Entertainment Weekly*, 19 September 1997.

Bark, Ed. "*Homicide* awaits verdict," *Dallas Morning News*, 4 May 1995.

Bash, Alan. "*Homicide* spins off interactive Web serial," *USA Today*, 11 February 1997.

_____. "Investigating new challenges," *USA Today*, 17 July 1996.

_____. "Name game a shot in the arm for *Homicide*," *USA Today*, 1 December 1995.

Beale, Lewis. "The *Diner* man commits *Homicide*," 31 January 1993.

Bianculli, David. "As always, changing *Homicide* right on target," *New York Daily News*, 20 September 1996.

_____. "Baltimore blues: The first great show of 1993," *New York Daily News*, 29 January 1993.

_____. "*Homicide*: Absolute killer of a drama," *New York Daily News*, 14 October 1994.

_____. "*Homicide* once more into the box..." *New York Daily News*, 17 October 1997.

_____. "*Homicide* plays renewal roulette," *New York Daily News*, 23 February 1995.

_____. "Important clue to *Homicide* mystery," *New York Daily News*, 11 November 1994.

_____. "Must-seethe TV: *Homicide* reopens cops' old wounds," *New York Daily News*, 11 April 1997.

_____. "Quality (*Homicide*) vs. quantity (*ER*)," *New York Daily News*, 28 October 1994.

_____. "*St. Elsewhere* alive in *Homicide*," *New York Daily News*, 2 February 1995.

_____. "Stunning *Homicide* on target, as always," *New York Daily News*, 28 March 1996.

_____. "Superb *Homicide* hits street running," *New York Daily News*, 19 October 1995.

Blain, Glenn. "*Homicide* at Memorial Stadium," *USA Today*, 11 October 1992.

Buchalter, Gail. "He won't take a role that's demeaning," *Parade* magazine, 4 May 1997.

Butterfield, Alan and Larry Haley. "More skinny on Ned Beatty—he's shed his wife, too!" *National Enquirer*, 22 June 1997.

Carlson, Peter. "The American way of murder," *Washington Post* magazine, 19 June 1994.

Carman, John. "An NBC battle for coveted Thursday spot," *San Francisco Chronicle*, 11 January 1994.

_____. "Will NBC kill off *Homicide*?" *San Francisco Chronicle*, 5 May 1995.

Carmody, John. "The TV column," *Washington Post*, 16 June 1997.

Carter, Bill. "Pure Baltimore, right down to the steamed crabs," *New York Times*, 24 January 1993.

_____. "Robin Williams, seriously speaking," *New York Times*, 6 January 1994.

Castro, Peter. "Richard Belzer," *People*, 29 March 1993.

"Cheers and jeers," *TV Guide*, 15 November 1997.

"Choice reruns," *Entertainment Weekly*, 18 April 1997.

Colby, Allison. "*Homicide: Life on the Street*," *Village Voice*, 31 December 1996.

Collins, Monica. "Let *Homicide* live," *Boston Herald*, 4 May 1995.

Collins, Monica, Andy Edelstein, Mark Lasswell, and Ed Weiner. "TV's Top 10 Performers," *TV Guide*, 10 January 1997.

Cossack, Roger, and Greta Van Susteren. "Can real police officers take the same liberties as tough TV cops?" *USA Weekend*, 18-20 April 1997.

"A crossover episode with *Homicide*," *TV Guide*, 12 November 1997.

Cunningham, Kim. "Fratricide on *Homicide?*" *People* (online edition), February 1997.

Davies, Jonathan. "*Homicide* has two casualties," *Hollywood Reporter*, 16 June 1997.

"Death of a marriage for *Homicide* star," *The Globe*, 18 March 1997.

DuBois, Stephanie. "The videoland view," *Los Angeles Daily News*, 14 October 1997.

Edelstein, Andy. "*Law and Order* déjà vu," *Newsday*, 13 September 1990.

Elias, Justine. "From the people of *Homicide*," *New York Times*, 6 July 1997.

Enderst, James. "NBC's *Homicide* probably can't live up to all the hype," *Hartford Courant*, 29 January 1993.

Engstrom, John. "Long way home," *Chicago Tribune*, 27 April 1995.

Farber, Stephen. Untitled article, *New York Times*, 18 April 1982.

Farkash, Michael. "*Law and Order, Homicide: Life on the Street*," *Hollywood Reporter*, 17 November 1997.

"Fire power," *Entertainment Weekly*, undated 1996.

Flaherty, Mike. "Death becomes him," *Entertainment Weekly*, 16 February 1996.

Flint, Joe. "NBC gnashes teeth over Eye's Bridges," *Variety*, 22 April 1996.

Fretts, Bruce. "Copping an attitude," *Entertainment Weekly*, 28 January 1994.

_____. "*Homicide* honcho Tom Fontana gets away with murder in *Oz*, his explicit new HBO prison drama," *Entertainment Weekly*, 11 July 1997.

_____. "Remote patrol," *Entertainment Weekly*, 16 May 1997.

_____. "Take our awards for it," *Entertainment Weekly*, 6 June 1997.

_____. "The cat in the hats," *Entertainment Weekly*, 10 January 1997.

_____. "The dead beat," *Entertainment Weekly*, 5 February 1993.

_____. "The week," *Entertainment Weekly*, 27 January 1995.

_____. "The week," *Entertainment Weekly*, 15 February 1995.

_____. "The week," *Entertainment Weekly*, 14 April 1995.

_____. "The week," *Entertainment Weekly*, 20 October 1995.

_____. "The week," *Entertainment Weekly*, 3 November 1995.

_____. "The week," *Entertainment Weekly*, 9 February 1996.

_____. "The week," *Entertainment Weekly*, 5 April 1996.

_____. "The week," *Entertainment Weekly*, 12 April 1996.

_____. "The week," *Entertainment Weekly*, 26 April 1996.

_____. "The week," *Entertainment Weekly*, 6 November 1996.

_____. "The week," *Entertainment Weekly*, 15 November 1996.

_____. "The week," *Entertainment Weekly*, 5 September 1997.

_____. "Zeljko Ivanek," *Entertainment Weekly*, 13 June 1997.

Gable, Donna. "Home for *Homicide*," *USA Today*, 29 January 1993.

Gay, Verne. "Death-defying *Homicide*," *Newsday*, 16 October 1997.

_____. "NBC sets *Homicide* adrift on Friday," *Newsday*, 13 October 1994.

Gerhart, Ann, and Annie Groer. "For *Homicide*'s Dellums, strife on the street," *Washington Post*, 4 February 1997.

_____. "*Homicide* star testifies," *Washington Post*, 20 March 1997.

_____. "Kotto's long-time-no-see lady love," *Washington Post*, 10 March 1997.

_____. "Kotto's love arrives at last," *Washington Post*, 30 May 1997.

_____. "Michael Willis' woolly ride to *Men In Black*," *Washington Post*, 21 July 1997.

"God and television," *TV Guide*, 29 March 1997.

Goff, John. "*Homicide: Life on the Street*: Gone for Goode," *Variety*, 27 January 1993.

Goldberg, Robert. "A TV cop show like *Blues* but better," *Wall Street Journal*, 1 February 1993.

_____. "Larson's swan song; Levinson's reprieve," *Wall Street Journal*, October 1994.

Goodman, Tim. "Both *Homicide* and *NYPD Blue* undergoing changes," *San Francisco Chronicle*, 21 July 1997.

_____. "Show's music has its own rabid fans," *Contra Costa Times*, 30 January 1997.

Gray, Ellen. "A bunch of Munch," *Philadelphia Daily News*, 12 November 1997.

_____. "New season uncertainty provides some of the drama," *Philadelphia Daily News*, 20 August 1997.

Greppi, Michelle. "Cop show is arresting," *New York Post*, 6 January 1994.

_____. "Emmy's kneejerk nominations," *New York Post*, 25 July 1997.

_____. "413 Hope Street," *New York Post*, 1997.

_____. "*Homicide* awaits its fate," *New York Post*, 11 February 1994.

_____. "*Homicide* fights for life," *New York Post*, 6 January 1994.

_____. "*Homicide* finale: Headless body in flawless show," *New York Post*, 9 May 1997.

_____. "*Homicide* makes case for Emmy," *New York Post*, 24 October 1997.

Grove, Lloyd. "The bulletproof comedian," *Washington Post*, February 1997.

Hinckley, David. "*Homicide* could be a killer," *Daily News*, January 1993.

Holloway, Diane. "*Homicide* kills off its riveting season," *Austin-American Statesman*, 5 May 1995.

_____. "*Homicide* returns, despite NBC's criminal treatment," *Austin-American Statesman*, 14 October 1994.

"*Homicide* actor charged with gun violations," Associated Press, 19 December 1996.

"*Homicide* actor takes offense at verbal assault," Associated Press, 1 February 1997.

"*Homicide* hunk reveals wild plot to woo wife," *The Star*, 15 February 1994.

"*Homicide: Life on the Street*," *Entertainment Weekly*, 12 September 1997.

"*Homicide* star suspected of marriage plot," *Philadelphia Daily News*, 11 March 1997.

"*Homicide*: There's new life on this street," *TV Guide*, 2 March 1996.

Hull, Dana. "In Baltimore, a show to die for," *Washington Post*, 25 April 1997.

"It's murder out there," *Entertainment Weekly*, 8 August 1997.

James, Caryn. "*Law and Order* meets *Homicide*," *New York Times*, 7 February 1996.

_____. "Rogues in cahoots with the FBI," *New York Times*, 17 October 1997.

Jarvis, Jeff. "*Homicide*," *TV Guide*, 6 February 1993.

_____. "The very hot *Homicide* … Donohoe … and Hamlin," *TV Guide*, 30 January 1993.

Johnson, Sharon. "You know the face of Jon Polito," *Harrisburg Patriot*, 7 August 1995.

Johnson, Steve. "Real teamwork: NBC finally scores in its game of mix and match," *Chicago Tribune*, 7 February 1996.

Jubera, Drew. "TV's real black drama," *Atlanta Journal and Constitution*, 9 April 1995.

Kaltenbach, Chris. *Homicide* article from *Sunspot* (the online edition of *Baltimore Sun*), 1997.

King, Susan. "*Homicide* actor is perfectly Frank," *New York Post*, 28 August 1995.

———. "When race isn't a factor," *Los Angeles Times*, 27 August 1995.

Kitman, Marvin. "*Homicide*, another shot," *Newsday*, January 1994.

———. "Too good to last," *Newsday*, 31 January 1993.

Kolinski, Michael. "A killer of a drama—*Homicide: Life on the Street*," *Television Today*, Summer 1995.

Koltnow, Barry. "Horrecide" *Chicago Tribune*, 23 January 1994.

Lambert, Pam, and Sarah Skolnik. "She's all right, Jack," *People*, 4 December 1995.

Lempka, Jason. "Hollywood on the harbor," press release, 1997.

Leonard, John. "City of angels," *New York*, 17 October 1994.

———. "Robin 'hood," *New York*, 10 January 1994.

———. "Swept away," *New York*, 10 June 1996.

———. "Wild about Barry," *New York*, 1 February 1993.

Letofsky, Irv. "*Homicide: Life on the Street*," *Hollywood Reporter*, 17 October 1997.

Lorando, Mark. "Will *Homicide* live or die?" *Times-Picayune*, 13 January 1994.

Luscombe, Belinda. "Public service TV," *Time*, 21 October 1996.

Marchese, John. "Andre Braugher," *US*, April 1996.

McDaniel, Mike. "Diamond not in the rough," *Houston Chronicle*, 16 November 1995.

McDonald, Stef. "Short cuts," *TV Guide* (online edition), 25 October 1996.

McMillen, Liz. "*Homicide*'s last shooting," *Washington Post*, 30 April 1995.

Meisler, Andy. "*Homicide* is back, in a cloud of tension," *New York Times*, 12 October 1994.

Mendoza, N. F. "Isabella Hofmann finds herself rising fast in the *Homicide* ranks," *Los Angeles Times*, 26 February 1995.

———. "Who's afraid of Richard Belzer" *Los Angeles Times*, 1 October 1995.

Merryman, Kathleen. "A softer side to *Homicide*," *News Tribune*, 19 September 1996.

"Mid-season winners and losers," *Entertainment Weekly*, 13 December 1996.

Millman, Joyce. "Blue glow," *Salon*, 28 October 1997.

_____. "Freaky Friday," *San Francisco Examiner*, 9 April 1995.

_____. "The last show standing," *Salon*, 7 May 1997.

Millner, Denene. "Life off the street," *Daily News*, 14 April 1996.

Mills, Nancy. "Other side of the badge," *Boston Herald*, 22 December 1995.

_____. "Red hot right now," *Cosmopolitan*, February 1994.

Mink, Eric. "Back on the crime beat," *Daily News*, 16 October 1994.

_____. "The big guns line up again for *Homicide*," *Daily News*, 5 January 1994.

_____. "*Homicide* continues to hit the bulls-eye," *Daily News*, 27 April 1995.

_____. "The *Homicide* cops are all over television's case," *Daily News*, 21 October 1994.

_____. "*Homicide* facing the final lineup," *Daily News*, 27 January 1994.

_____. "*Law* and *Homicide* make a dream team," *Daily News*, 7 February 1997.

Mitchell, Sean. "Beatty on board," *Los Angeles Times*, 22 December 1996.

Morrison, Mark. "*Homicide*, starring Ned Beatty," *US*, March 1993.

"Most recent addition to *Homicide* always wanted to be an officer," *Austin American-Statesman*, 9 September 1995.

"Netrave," *The Net*, July 1997.

"New faces on old shows," *Entertainment Weekly* Online, 1996.

O'Connor, John. "Daring to be different on TV, a medium where safety thrives," *New York Times*, 1 April 1993.

_____. "Four weeks probation for police drama," *New York Times*, 6 January 1994.

_____. "From darkly powerful to kinky, and back," *New York Times*, 4 May 1995.

_____. "*Homicide* survives, but in what condition?" *New York Times*, 10 November 1994.

_____. "New NBC crime drama from a long tradition," *New York Times*, 29 January 1993.

_____. "When fiction is more real than 'reality,'" *New York Times*, 7 February 1993.

Odintz, Andrea, and Rich Sands. "That's a wrap! The season's spiciest finales," *TV Guide*, 13 April 1996.

Okamoto, David. "Music becomes *Homicide* costar," *Dallas Morning News*, 5 January 1996.

"100 greatest episodes of all time," *TV Guide*, 4 July 1997.

Pacheco, Patrick. "Huggable he's not," *Los Angeles Times*, 14 July 1996.

Pergament, Patrick. "NBC banks on glitz, not substance," *Buffalo News*, 11 January 1994.

Phillips, Barbara. "Life after death," *Wall Street Journal*, 16 December 1996.

Pitts, Leonard. "Our motto: 'Justice for some,'" *Miami Herald*, 13 November 1997.

Podhertz, John. "*Homicide* a direct hit," *New York Post*, 13 October 1994.

"Prime-time TV rankings," *Los Angeles Times*, 6 August 1997.

"Print it!" Associated Press, 9 October 1996.

"Probation for John Heard," Associated Press, 26 May 1997.

"Quality is often nipped in the bud," *USA Today*, 4 May 1993.

Rabinowitz, Dorothy. "Teen and Torie killers," *Wall Street Journal*, 10 January 1994.

Robins, J. Max. "NBC docs won't appear with NBC cops," *TV Guide*, 9 September 1997.

Rohan, Virginia. "It's not the same old squad," *The Record*, 17 October 1997.

Rohrer, Trish. "Escape from *Oz*," *New York Magazine*, 14 July 1997.

Rosenberg, Howard. "Arresting cop shows are rare, except this year," *Los Angeles Times*, 21 October 1994.

_____. "Crime and punishment never looked so good," *Los Angeles Times*, 3 November 1995.

_____. "*Homicide* deserves its latest reprieve," *New York Times*, 6 January 1994.

Roush, Matt. "A prime partnership," *USA Today*, 7 February 1996.

_____. "Back on the streets," *USA Today*, 6 January 1994.

_____. "Dead-on, disturbing *Homicide*," *USA Today*, 27 January 1995.

_____. "Emotions run deep in wrenching *Homicide*," *USA Today*, 9 May 1997.

_____. "*Homicide* ends season with a bang," *USA Today*, 5 May 1995.

_____. "*Homicide* finale keeps excellence intact," *USA Today*, 31 March 1993.

_____. "*Homicide* shifts off the street, into bed," *USA Today*, 11 November 1994.

_____. "*Homicide* still shoots holes in the competition," *USA Today*, 14 October 1994.

_____. "*Homicide* to follow its odd, arresting beat," *USA Today*, 17 July 1995.

_____. "Levinson's *Homicide* TV noir for the '90s," *USA Today*, 24 January 1993.

_____. "Superb *Homicide* still makes perfect case for itself," *USA Today*, 6 January 1994.

Rudolph, Ileane. "Breaking through," *TV Guide*, 13 April 1996.

Schwed, Mark. "Kill or be killed," *TV Guide*, 30 January 1993.

Sepinwall, Alan. "End of an exile," *Newark Star-Ledger*, 17 October 1997.

_____. "There are a million stories in the naked city, but not too many involving women, apparently," *Newark Star-Ledger*, 10 June 1997.

_____. "Were Richard Belzer and John Munch separated at birth?" *Newark-Star-Ledger*, 21 February 1997.

Shales, Tom. "*Homicide*: A heart-stopping subway stop," *Washington Post*, 5 December 1997.

_____. "*Homicide*: Back with a bang," *Washington Post*, 14 October 1994.

_____. "*Homicide*: High-caliber return," *Washington Post*, 6 January 1994.

_____. "*Homicide*: NBC's next victim?" *Washington Post*, 27 April 1993.

Sharkey, Betsy. "A comfortable collision," *Mediaweek*, 13 November 1995.

_____. "*Homicide*'s second life," *Mediaweek*, 9 June 1997.

Shister, Gail. "Hell hath no fury like a *Homicide* Cop in arrested development," *Salt Lake Tribune*, 12 January 1994.

_____. "*Homicide* swan song for Braugher," Knight-Ridder Tribune News Service, 25 July 1997.

_____. "Jon Polito's acting career is just killing him," Knight-Ridder / Tribune News Service, 25 May 1994.

Siegel, Ed. "*Homicide*: The season's finest hour," *Boston Globe*, 6 January 1994.

Simon, David. "The chief concern," *Baltimore* magazine, July 1996.

Slewinski, Christy. "Beatty hands in his shield; *Homicide* now down two cops," *Daily News*, 20 June 1995.

_____. "*Homicide*: Quality in search of ratings," *New York Daily News*, 21 October 1994.

_____. "Kyle Secor secures his spot in series squad room," *New York Daily News*, 7 February 1996.

_____. "Reed Diamond finally one of the good guys," *Chicago Tribune*, 7 December 1995.

Snierson, Dan. "Odd coupling," *Entertainment Weekly*, October 1997.

Spake, Amanda. "*Homicide*'s commanding presence," *Salon*, 12 October 1995.

_____. "The man behind TV's best-written show," *Salon*, 12 October 1995.

Starr Seibel, Deborah. "*Homicide*," *TV Guide*, 29 April 1995.

Strauss, Bob. "Double *Homicide*," *Entertainment Weekly Online*, 1996.

"The 40 most fascinating people on TV," *People*, 2 September 1996.

Tomashoff, Craig. "Picks and Pans," *People*, 7 November 1994.

Toscano, Michael. "Killing time in Baltimore," *Entertainment@Home*, June 1997.

Troy, Patricia. "Sixty-Minute men and women," *Written By*, September 1997.

Tucker, Ken. "Back on the beat," *Entertainment Weekly*, 24 December 1993.

_____. "Baltimore bullets," *Entertainment Weekly*, 5 May 1995.

_____. "Cops and ribbers," *Entertainment Weekly*, 5 May 1995.

_____. "One good cop show," *Entertainment Weekly*, 29 January 1993.

_____. "The week," *Entertainment Weekly*, 26 March 1993.

_____. "The week," *Entertainment Weekly*, 17 May 1996.

_____. "The week," *Entertainment Weekly*, 20 September 1996.

_____. "The week," *Entertainment Weekly*, 13 October 1997.

_____. "Turning up the heat," *Entertainment Weekly*, 16 February 1996.

_____. "TV winners and losers," *Entertainment Weekly*, May 1997.

Tush, Bill. "*Law and Order, Homicide* to team up again," *CNN Online*, 12 November 1997.

"TV mailbag," *Houston Chronicle*, 17 November 1996.

"TV's top 20 sexy stars," *TV Guide*, 28 November 1997.

Tyrer, Thomas. "Low ratings, high praise: *Homicide* fights for its life," *Electronic Media*, 10 May 1993.

"Up front—Clark Johnson," *People*, 1 September 1997.

Walter, Tom. "NBC throws *Homicide* a lifesaver," *Commercial Appeal*, 11 January 1994.

Wambaugh, Joseph. "*Homicide*: The best show you're not watching," *TV Guide*, 28 December 1996.

Weinraub, Bernard. "Director says studio stole details in book for use in TV series," *New York Times*, 3 June 1992.

Weinstein, Steve. "Acclaimed *Homicide* hoping to stay alive," *Los Angeles Times*, 14 October 1994.

Weiss, Max. "Copland," *Baltimore* magazine, October 1997.

"We'll see you back at the station house," *Newsweek*, 27 October 1997.

Werts, Diane. "*Homicide*: Unsung hero serves up the real deal," *Newsday*, 19 October 1995.

Williams, Scott. "Despite fears, *Homicide* is painless," *Daily News*, 1997.

_____. "The new new guy and the old new guy of *Homicide*," Associated Press, 22 December 1995.

Williams, Stephanie. "Life on the set," *TV Guide*, 28 December 1996.

_____. "The best show you're not watching," *TV Guide*, 28 December 1996.

Winslow, Harriet. "Barry Levinson's *Homicide*; an inside look at NBC's Baltimore police series," *Washington Post*, 31 January 1993.

_____. "Life on TV's mean streets," *Washington Post*, January 1994.

"Yaphet Kotto awarded badge," Associated Press, 17 February 1997.

"Yaphet Kotto reveals in royal lineage in forthcoming autobiography, *The Royalty*," *Jet*, 7 November 1997.

Zoglin, Richard. "Baltimore bullets," *Time*, 1 February 1993.

Zurawick, David. "Baltimore may lose *Homicide*," *Baltimore Sun*, 10 February 1994.

_____. "Black-and-white TV," *Baltimore Sun*, 30 January 1996.

_____. "Gutsy *NYPD Blue* cops 26 Emmy nominations," *Baltimore Sun*, 22 July 1994.

_____. "*Homicide* and the pace that kills," *Los Angeles Times*, 30 November 1992.

_____. "*Homicide, Law and Order* in another fun get-together," *Baltimore Sun*, 12 November 1997.

_____. "*Homicide* lives on NBC as network orders 22 episodes," *Baltimore Sun*, 16 May 1995.

_____. "*Homicide* renewed, but location iffy," *Baltimore Sun*, 16 February 1994.

_____. "Killer time slot hurts *Homicide*," *Chicago Sun-Times*, 3 March 1993.

_____. "Look out, *Nash Bridges*," *Baltimore Sun*, 21 July 1997.

_____. "Low ratings may kill *Homicide*," *Los Angeles Times*, 8 July 1997.

_____. "NBC hopes sexy lieutenant will bring heat to *Homicide*," *Baltimore Sun*, 14 October 1994.

NBC Press Releases:

"Academy Award–winning actress Kathy Bates will direct episode of NBC's critically acclaimed *Homicide*," 15 February 1996.

"Award-winning drama *Homicide: Life on the Street* returns to the airwaves," 21 July 1997.

"Barry Levinson to direct season finale episode of NBC-TV's *Homicide: Life on the Street*," 26 January 1995.

"Critics renew praise for NBC's *Homicide: Life on the Street*," 19 October 1994.

"Emmy Award–winning drama series *Homicide: Life on the Street* returns to NBC January 6, with Robin Williams in first episode," 30 November 1993.

"Fans rejoice as *Homicide: Life on the Street* returns," 9 April 1997.

"*Homicide* episodes to be repeated before September 20 season premiere," 4 September 1996.

"*Homicide: Life on the Street* actor crosses over to nbc.com in *Homicide: Second Shift*," 23 June 1997.

"*Homicide: Life on the Street* honored at Catholics In Media Awards ceremony," 3 November 1997.

"Honors abound for NBC stars and shows in recent awards programs," 15 March 1993.

"Isabella Hofmann returns for two-part season finale of NBC's *Homicide: Life on the Street* to air May 9," 7 May 1997.

"James Earl Jones guest-stars in three-part season premiere episode of NBC's *Homicide: Life on the Street*," 6 October 1997.

"Jay Leno guest-stars on NBC's *Homicide: Life on the Street*," 4 January 1996.

"*Law and Order / Homicide: Life on the Street* crossover episodes Wednesday, November 12, and Friday, November 14," 21 October 1997.

"nbc.com creates Internet history," 11 February 1997.

"nbc.com launches *Homicide: Life on the Street* Web site," 25 November 1996.

"NBC News and NBC Entertainment honored with prestigious 1993 Peabody Awards," 31 March 31 1994.

"NBC picks up acclaimed drama *Homicide: Life on the Street*," 3 November 1994.

"NBC renews award-winning series *Homicide*: Life on the Street," 13 May 1994.

"NBC's critically acclaimed drama *Homicide: Life on the Street* continues ratings momentum, hitting season high on February 10," 16 February 1995.

"New season production begins on *Homicide: Life on the Street*, NBC's critically acclaimed, award-winning drama series," 28 July 1994.

"Premiere of NBC drama series *Homicide: Life on the Street* draws high numbers, helps drive another Thursday win," 7 January 1994.

"Reed Diamond of *Homicide: Life on the Street* meets counterparts in *Homicide: Second Shift* on nbc.com," 21 July 1997.

"Reed Diamond to join the cast of NBC's *Homicide: Life on the Street*," 10 June 1995.

"Series star Clark Johnson directs episode of *Homicide* April 26," 23 April 1996.

"Series star Yaphet Kotto scribes *Homicide* episode to air May 2," 30 April 1997.

"Suspect in cop shootings apprehended in this week's episode of NBC's acclaimed drama *Homicide: Life on the Street*," 9 February 1995.

"Television critics honor NBC with three 1997 Television Critics Association Awards," 21 July 1997.

"Tim Russert guest-stars on NBC's *Homicide: Life on the Street*," 2 March 1995.

"TV critics agree, *Homicide* is best drama on television: case closed," 25 September 1996.

Books

Simon, David. *Homicide: A Year on the Killing Streets*, Boston: Houghton Mifflin Company, 1991.

Interviews

Black, Tony. Interviewed by David Kalat, November 1996.

Braugher, Andre. Interviewed by NBC CyberChat (http://www.nbc. com/homicide), 16 May 1996.

Fontana, Tom. Interviewed by Marinex Multimedia Corp. (http://www. pathfinder.com), 1995.

Klvana, Katherine. Interviewed by David Kalat, November 1997.

Kotto, Yaphet. Interviewed by NBC CyberChat http://www.nbc.com/homicide, 2 May 1997.

Suniewick, Russ. Interviewed by David Kalat, April 1996.

Willis, Michael. Interviewed by David Kalat, June 1997.

Yoshimura, James. Interviewed by Dou-Yan Yang, (http://student-www.uchicago.edu/users/dyang1/homicide), February 1997.

Online Sources

http://www.imdb.com

http://www.interlog.com/~kotto/royalty.html

http://www.nbc.com/homicide

http://www.pathfinder.com

Miscellaneous

Attanasio, Paul. Original teleplay for "Gone for Goode."

Campbell, Arch. NBC Channel 4, news broadcasts on 12 November 1997, 14 November 1997, 21 November 1997.

Levinson, Barry, and Tom Fontana. Memo, issued 24 September 1992.

Index

T

Tabakin, Ralph, 85, 88, 110, 115, 119, 136, 145, 150, 154, 158, 164, 166-67, 171, 184, 197, 201-202, 207, 212, 215, 227, 232, 238, 240, 253

Taylor, Alan, 117, 119, 186, 215, 237, 262, 267, 270

Tergesen, Chris, 131, 133, 145, 225, 230, 267, 301-302

Tergesen, Lee, 84, 112-13, 115, 117, 122, 151, 252, 262

Thigpen, Lynne, 67, 268, 271, 274

Thorne, Callie, 82-83, 265, 267, 283

Tomlin, Lily, 23-24, 195-97, *196*

Toys, 91, 104

V

Van Patten, Tim, 93, 168-69

Van Peebles, Melvin, 25, 241-43, *242*

Verdon, Gwen, 67, 112-13

Very Brady Sequel, A, 26

W

Waltemeyer, Donald, 57

Ward, Mary, 85, 145, 147-48, 159, 161

Waterfront Bar, The, 146-49, 155, 159, 168, 206, 238, 245, 312, 315

Waters, John, 24, 84, 88, 105, 120-22, 142, 164-65

Waterston, Sam, 199-201, 277, 280-81

Wayans, Damon, 95

Weller, Peter, 25, 188-89, 233-34

Wharton, Darryl LeMont, 24, 150-51, 225, 256-57, 267, 288, 290

Whitesell, Sean, 115, 120, 158, 190-91, 216, 262, 276

Williams, Drexel, 106, 127

Williams, Karen, 85, 215, 232, 249

Williams, Robin, 23-24, 128-29, 132-33, 139, 278

Willis, Michael, 85, 89, 119-20, 148-49, 202, 216, 238, 247

Wolf, Dick, 130, 175-76, 178, 265-66, 278

Wood, Elijah, 25, 237-38

Worden, Donald, 29, 34, 135, 157

X

X-Files, The, 26, 64, 94, 140, 213, 217, 224, 251, 258, 281-82

Y

Yates, Peggy, 84-85, 156, 158-59, 167, 170, 193

Yoshimura, James, 24, 96-98, 113-14, 117, 120, 131, 135-36, 141, 145, 148, 151, 155, 159, 161-62, 164, 168, 183, 188, 190-91, 212-13, 220, 225, 227, 233, 240-41, 245-46, 248, 252-53, 256-57, 263, 265, 267, 271, 273-74, 282-84, 286, 288, 313

Z

Zakrzewski, Alex, 145, 225, 267

Zamacona, Jorge, 24, 115-16, 119, 141, 145, 149, 156, 159, 161, 166, 183, 187, 198, 201, 213-14, 277, 279, 280-81

About the Author

DAVID KALAT is the author of A *Critical History and Filmography of Toho's Godzilla Series* (McFarland and Co., 1997), a study of the forty-year history of Japan's most famous film exports.

Mr. Kalat is also the founder of All Day Entertainment, a producer of Digital Video Discs (DVDs), releasing classic and obscure motion pictures in high-quality collector's editions exclusively on this new home video format.

As a member of the Washington-Baltimore film production community where *Homicide: Life on the Street* is shot, Kalat has had many contacts with the television series. He previously worked at the motion-picture lab where *Homicide* processed each episode's film, and was involved in the very first season's production. As operations manager of D.C. Post, one of the region's most esteemed film and video postproduction houses, Kalat worked closely with Emmy-winning editor Tony Black, who edited *Homicide's* pilot installment.

Mr. Kalat taught screenwriting at the John Waldron Arts Center in Bloomington, Indiana, and was on the Board of Directors for the Bloomington Playwrights Project, one of Indiana's most acclaimed theater companies. Kalat also sports credentials as a freelance cinematographer and animator, and has directed several award-winning short films. His most recent film premiered at Washington, D.C.'s famed Biograph Theater.

He was born in Philadelphia on April 7, 1970, and grew up in the Raleigh-Durham area of North Carolina. He earned his bachelor of arts at the University of Michigan in 1988, graduating with highest honors from the Film and Video Studies program. He lives in Alexandria, Virginia, with his wife Julie and daughter Ann.